# VOX MYSTICA
## ESSAYS ON MEDIEVAL MYSTICISM

This volume celebrates the distinguished career of Valerie Lagorio, whose scholarship has been enormously influential in the study of medieval mysticism. As befits its honoree, this collection seeks to make a major contribution in the field of mystical studies, bringing together the diversity of topics and approaches which Professor Lagorio herself both pioneered and encouraged. These include mystical discourse in Middle English secular poetry, the use of patristic models by the English mystics, and essays on English and Continental women's mysticism. There are also articles devoted to individual authors, such as Julian of Norwich, Richard Rolle, Teresa of Avila, and Mechthild of Magdeburg, and individual texts covering, among others, *The Cloud of Unknowing*, *The Sister-Books*, Bridget of Sweden's *Revelations*, and the letters of Mechthild of Hackeborne. A number of essays illuminate the complicated textual history of particular works; others examine the influence of earlier theological authorities on later mystical works, or view phenomena in medieval mysticism in the light of recent developments in literary theory, gender, comparatist, and cultural studies, while remaining sympathetic to the historical and social context. Lastly, the volume also contains an edition and a translation of previously unpublished mystical texts.

# VOX MYSTICA

## ESSAYS ON MEDIEVAL MYSTICISM

### IN HONOR OF
### PROFESSOR VALERIE M. LAGORIO

*Edited by*
ANNE CLARK BARTLETT

*with*

THOMAS H. BESTUL, JANET GOEBEL
*and* WILLIAM F. POLLARD

D. S. BREWER

BV
5075
.V68
1995

First published 1995
D. S. Brewer, Cambridge


ISBN  0 85991 439 9




D. S. Brewer is an imprint of Boydell & Brewer Ltd
PO Box 9, Woodbridge, Suffolk IP12 3DF, UK
and of Boydell & Brewer Inc.
PO Box 41026, Rochester, NY 14604–4126, USA


British Library Cataloguing-in-Publication Data
Vox Mystica:Essays on Medieval Mysticism
in Honor of Professor Valerie M. Lagorio
I. Bartlett, Anne Clark
248.220902
ISBN 0–85991–439–9

Library of Congress Cataloging-in-Publication Data
Vox mystica : essays on medieval mysticism in honor of Professor
Valerie M. Lagorio / edited by Anne Clark Bartlett . . . [et al.]
    p.    cm.
Includes bibliographical references.
ISBN 0–85991–439–9 (hbk. : alk. paper)
    1. Mysticism – History – Middle Ages, 600–1500.  I. Lagorio,
Valerie Marie, 1925–  .  II.  Bartlett, Anne Clark, 1960–  .
BV5075.V68  1995
248.2'2'0902–dc20                                         94–45700

The paper used in this publication meets the minimum requirements
of American National Standard for Information Sciences –
Permanence of Paper for Printed Library Materials, ANSI Z39.48–1984

Printed in Great Britain by
St Edmundsbury Press Ltd, Bury St Edmunds, Suffolk

# CONTENTS

# FOREWORD
## SOME PERSONAL REFLECTIONS

A few years ago, I was delighted to discover that plans were underway for a festschrift for Valerie M. Lagorio devoted to medieval mysticism. Subsequently, I was very gratified to contribute an essay – expanded from my dissertation research done under her direction – to a volume that promised to unite so many distinguished contributors for such a worthy purpose. Now, due to circumstances beyond the original organizers' control, I find myself serving as chief editor of the festschrift. I am profoundly honored to be able to pay tribute to Valerie Lagorio in this way.

Let me share briefly two anecdotes that illustrate what working with Valerie has meant to me. The first involves the delivery of my first conference paper, at the 1989 International Congress on Medieval Studies, at Western Michigan University in Kalamazoo, Michigan. I was scheduled to give this presentation on Friday afternoon at 1:30. All that morning I'd worked myself into a frenzy – reading the paper aloud over and over, trying to memorize every possible point of emphasis, and struggling to avoid every potential stutter or mispronunciation. About 1:15 I headed shakily for the meeting room, with a white-knuckled grip on my briefcase. I was perspiring profusely in my uncharacteristically demure, flowered-print dress, which I had bought expressly for this session as a type of camouflage. My hope was that this attire would make me look fragile and defenseless, and that no one would ask me any difficult questions. (As it happened, this strategy did not work.)

Despite my careful preparations, the delivery of my first conference paper began as an utter disaster. When I walked into the room reserved for my session, I expected to find the presider and the other panelists shuffling their papers and preparing to begin. But the room was packed to overflowing with an uncomfortable audience (the temperature inside was at least 100 degrees) and the speaker's table was empty. So I sat down at the table alone, feeling extremely conspicuous, and completely terrified. And I waited. The minutes ticked by: 1:23 passed, and then 1:25, and 1:29. Finally, at 1:30, a harried-looking woman rushed in, apologized, and informed me that she would be the substitute presider, since the scheduled presider had fallen ill. She also mentioned that one of the other two panelists had canceled out, and that she didn't know where or even who the other panelist was. Given these factors, she said, I could feel free to expand my remarks if I wanted to. Of course, by this time, in my terror, I couldn't have departed from my text if my life depended on it. So I thanked her, grimly, and we decided to wait for a few more minutes.

Then, at approximately 1:35, I heard a flurry of activity behind me and in breezed Valerie. With a cool rustle of silk and perfume, she swooped up behind me and, sizing up the situation immediately, gave me an extravagant hug and said, in a stage whisper that carried across the room: "You'll be marvelous," and then she took a seat, with great aplomb, in the back row. It was a miracle.

The crowd relaxed. Out of the corner of my eye, I could see my undergraduate mentors (who had come to hear my first conference paper) smile and nudge each other. At last, the other panelist (now apparently able to muster up her own courage) came up to the table from the audience, and the session began.

This conspicuous support for her students, and for new scholars in general, is one of the aspects of Valerie's academic persona that I most admire. Her schedule at Kalamazoo was no doubt packed with appointments and meetings. She was under no obligation to attend my session – in fact, I had no idea she was planning to come. She wasn't required to give me a public show of endorsement, especially before she'd heard my paper! But she did, and I'll never forget it.

The second anecdote illustrates the dynamism of the scholarly relationship that developed between Valerie and me. I did an independent study with Valerie during the Summer of 1990 on Middle English devotional writing, which she very kindly held at her home. Naturally, I had gone into this study with concerns that I wanted to pursue: namely, women's literacy, medieval misogyny, and the representation of gender in these devotional texts. And consequently, I prepared for our sessions by taking notes on the passages in the texts that I'd read which I felt illustrated some crucial aspect of these issues. But these were not necessarily the things that Valerie wanted me to concentrate on, and before long, she made that abundantly clear. She would listen patiently to my commentary on say, the ostracism of Margery Kempe, and then she'd ask me about, for example, the function of a particular set of images in a complete work, or the structural relationship of one section of a text to the whole book. And so out tutorials would continue. For weeks, we continued our impassioned discussions around her dinette table. Sometimes neither of us managed to finish a complete sentence for hours.

I remember one sticky August afternoon with particular clarity. Perhaps it was a moment of passage. We were engaged in an impassioned *disputatio* on the *Ancrene Riwle* and the questions, interpretations, and points of conflict bounced back and forth between us like ping pong balls. Then suddenly both of us stopped talking and looked at one another; Valerie wiped her brow and we began to laugh. We looked at her cats, who were lying in lazy curls on the carpet, ignoring us. Valerie got up, poured us each a glass of sherry and we sat there at her table, sipping and chatting like old friends. Valerie had argued with me precisely because she wanted me to understand thoroughly the language, the conventions, the traditions of the texts themselves, before I began to problematize them, or assess them in their social and cultural contexts. And now I appreciate her insistent focus on these questions.

But I didn't necessarily understand that then, and Valerie patiently gave me the room I needed to figure things out for myself. My hope is those of us who know Valerie will carry on the traditions of solid scholarship, generous mentorship, and gracious good humor that she so unfailingly practised. Valerie Lagorio is truly a "speculum scholasticorum," an example for us all.

*Anne Clark Bartlett*

# INTRODUCTION
## METHODS, PRACTICES, COMMUNITIES, TEXTS

As all who know her will readily agree, paying tribute to the multifaceted scholarship of Valerie Lagorio is a daunting task. It is impossible to overestimate the distinctive contribution of Valerie Lagorio to the study of medieval mysticism. Just a few of the items included in her enormously influential body of scholarship are studies of the motif of Christ as Mother in English and Continental medieval mystical discourse, comprehensive surveys of the medieval female mystics, the latter no doubt inspiring numerous articles, conference papers, and dissertations. With Sister Ritamary Bradley, Valerie Lagorio compiled the indispensable *The Fourteenth-Century English Mystics: a Comprehensive Annotated Bibliography*. Her most recent accomplishment is her collaboration (with Michael G. Sargent and Ritamary Bradley) on the compendious "English Mystical Writings," included in the ninth volume of the *A Manual of the Writings in Middle English, 1050–1500* (New Haven, Conn.: The Connecticut Academy of Arts and Sciences, 1993), a dazzling survey of primary and secondary sources for the study of medieval English mystical writers and texts. And, of course, Valerie Lagorio is probably best-known as founder and editor of *The Fourteenth-Century English Mystics Newsletter*, which later became *Mystics Quarterly*.

But Valerie Lagorio's contributions to the field of mystical studies cannot be measured solely in terms of her scholarly productivity, no matter how vast. She has nurtured and enriched the study of mysticism in many other valuable ways. Valerie Lagorio has made an indelible mark on this field through her capable organization of conferences and symposia, her inspiring teaching and generous mentoring of new scholars, and through her magnetic public presence: her charm, her ready wit, and her remarkable energy and style. She represents a true and enduring exemplar for scholars of the medieval mystical tradition.

As befits its honoree, this collection of essays brings together the diversity of topics in mystical studies that Valerie Lagorio both modelled and encouraged. The collection likewise includes the wide variety of approaches to mystical texts which she helped to develop and perpetuate.

*Vox Mystica* begins with some methodological reflections. With its broad theoretical, historical, and theological applications, Rosemary Drage Hale's contribution, " 'Taste and See, For God Is Sweet': Sensory Perception and Memory in Medieval Christian Mystical Experience," provides a fitting starting point for this collection. Hale examines the relationship between the "outer" physical senses of

*Introduction*

taste, touch, sight, smell, and hearing with the "mystical sensorium" that replicates these faculties in the soul. This approach to mystical texts by (for example) Margaretha Ebner and Meister Eckhart provides a provocative lens through which to view the vexing mind/body dualism that troubles both medieval and modern authors.

Following this analysis is John Hirsh's "Religious Attitudes and Mystical Language in Medieval Literary Texts: An Essay in Methodology." In this essay, Hirsh reads passages from *Sir Gawain and the Green Knight*, *Havelok the Dane*, and *Lay le Freine*, in order to show how inextricably the language of the mystical and the mundane are intertwined in medieval discourse. And in the context of post-modern debates about the "situatedness" of criticism, Hirsh credits Valerie Lagorio with boldly and self-reflectively showing through her scholarship "that religious attitudes are amenable to academic discourse."

Alexandra Barratt takes up another important methodological problem, the history of the reception and recirculation of mystical texts and the ideological biases that such processes inevitably involve. Barratt examines the history of what she terms "readings and misreadings" of Julian of Norwich's revelations. Her contribution, "How Many Children Had Julian of Norwich? Editions, Translations, and Versions of Her Revelations" shows how the theological, social, and aesthetic assumptions of scholars have helped create an amazingly diverse array of Julians. Barratt's essay documents representations of the fourteenth-century English anchoress that range from "Julian the proto-Protestant" to Julian the Georgian Gentlewoman."

Frank Tobin's methodological reflection calls upon scholars to examine the writings of medieval visionaries in their broadest intellectual and historical contexts. His essay, "Medieval Thought on Visions and Its Resonance in Mechthild von Magdeburg's *Flowing Light of the Godhead*," views the text in question as part of a visionary tradition that begins with the biblical prophets and extends through the Middle Ages and beyond. Tobin's argument suggests that women visionaries must be seen as vital members of this mystic continuum, rather then as isolated prophetic voices. Mechthild von Magdeburg's work alone illustrates the extent to which the writing of female mystics was shaped by the work of other notable visionary authors, both female and male, ancient and medieval.

The second part of this collection builds on these methodological reflections by examining a variety of mystical discourses in practice. Toward this end, Ritamary Bradley provides a beautifully comprehensive analysis of the life and piety of Beatrice of Nazareth. Bradley's essay, "Beatrice of Nazareth (ca. 1200–1268), A Search for her True Spirituality," examines Beatrice's *Vita* (composed by an anonymous monk), as well as Beatrice's own mystical text, *The Seven Experiences of Loving*. Her comparison of the two works reveals both the distinctiveness of Beatrice's prophetic voice and her strategic incorporation of conventional aspects of medieval mysticism.

Robert Boenig's study likewise compares the views of two distinctive authors on a single topic. His contribution, "Saint Augustine's *jubilus* and Richard Rolle's *canor*," examines the complex relationship between these two doctrines of mystical music. Beonig's painstaking analysis shows that for both of these authors *musica mystica* possesses deeply ambiguous meanings and functions. Music can be holy as well as carnal. It can express the highest devotion, but can also seduce the senses.

Edwin L. Connor examines the potential influence of a twelfth-century spiritual practice on a late-fourteenth-century mystical text. His " 'Goostly Freend in God': Aelred's *De spiritualis amicitia* as a source for *The Cloud of Unknowing*" documents the surprising pervasiveness of affective spirituality in the *Cloud*, long considered the most apophatic of English devotional texts. Connor argues persuasively that this affective orientation reveals itself most clearly in the Cloud-author's reflections on the value of friendship, probably borrowed from Aelred of Rievaulx's celebrated treatise on fraternal love.

Beverly Boyd's "Chaucer's Moments in the 'Kneeling World' " also finds affective mystical expression in some unexpected places, in the *Canterbury Tales* and some of Chaucer's short lyrics. Boyd examines the mystical implications of the Marian devotion exhibited in "The Prioress's Tale" and "The Second Nun's Tale," as well as the free-standing lyric "An ABC."

Elizabeth Armstrong's "Womanly Men and Manly Women in Thomas à Kempis and Saint Teresa of Avila" takes up the relationship between established gender roles and the mystical experience that by definition seeks to transcend such intellectual categories. Comparing Teresa of Avila's *Way of Perfection* and Thomas à Kempis's *On the Imitation of Christ*, Armstrong maintains that both authors develop a spiritual ideal in which the alleged flaws of one sex can be corrected by the careful cultivation of the assumed strengths of the other sex: "as Thomas counsels men to be quiet and obedient, Teresa counsels women to a 'holy daring.' "

Mary E. Giles' "Holy Theatre/Ecstatic Theatre" explores perhaps the most flamboyant expression of mystical inspiration considered here. Giles explores the relationship between theatre and religion, focusing on the public mystical "performaces" of Sor Mária of Santo Domingo. During her ecstasies, Sor Mária offered counsel, answered theological queries, and enacted events from the Gospels. This essay argues compellingly that the *Via negativa* of Sor Mária's mystical theatre foreshadows the dramatic conventions of such modern playwrights as Antonin Artaud, Peter Brook, Jacques Copeau, and Jerzy Grotowski.

The third section of this volume deals with the formation of communities where mysticism flourished. Anne Clark Bartlett's essay, " 'A Reasonable Affection': Gender and Spritiual Friendship in Middle English Devotional Literature" uncovers a discourse of what she terms "familiarity" in mystical and devotional texts, which challenges conventional scholarly views regarding the enforcement of strict sexual segregation between medieval women and men. Evidence within the texts, as well as records that survive independently, suggest that contact between female and male religious was not as unusual or as inherently scandalous as traditional scholarship has often assumed.

Also examining the close working relations between pious women and men, Ann Hutchison documents the spiritual activities of early recusant communities in

"Three Recusant Sisters." Hutchison analyzes biographies and letters from such women as Mary Champney, Anne Stapleton, and Elizabeth Sander. These materials illustrate the dangers faced by Catholics during the early recusant period and offer a fascinating glimpse into their devotional practices and even convent life.

Gertrud Jaron Lewis examines yet another form of communal mystical practice. Her "Music and Dancing in the Book of Sisters" challenges the remarkably persistent notion that medieval nuns lived austere, silent, and humorless lives. Lewis documents the frequent references in fourteenth-century convents to joyous music and singing. *The Book of Sisters* offers an especially clear demonstration that the nuns' love for music shaped their everyday devotions as well as their visionary writing. The musical fervor of Adelheid Geishörnlin illustrates the effect that music could have on these nuns: "after an exhilarating spiritual experience, [she] was so filled with 'superabundant joy and sweetness' that she spontaneously jumped up and started whirling around the altar like a spinning top."

The final section of this collection concerns mystical texts as material artifacts. Margot King offers a translation of some letters from Mechthild of Hackborn, taken from *The Book of Special Grace*. These letters, "To a Laywoman in the World," "Good Consolation to the Same Woman," "A Letter to the Same Woman: An Excellent and Good Teaching," and "To the Same woman: A Useful Admonition" are dedicated specifically to Valerie Lagorio. In addition to testifying to the deep friendship between Margot and Valerie, they eloquently illustrate the intimate friendships possible between pious women in the Middle Ages, a topic that deserves much further consideration.

Next, Stephen E. Hayes contributes a critical edition of a previously unedited mystical text. *Of Three Workings of Man's Soul*, a Middle English prose meditation on the Annunciation. Previously dismissed by scholars as second-rate mysticism, this work deserves close attention because it is one of the vast number of medieval devotional texts available to the newly-expanded English audiences of the late fourteenth century. This work also models types of what we might loosely term "popular mysticism" practised by these groups of readers. The social, cultural, and political implications of this shift in the production and circulation of medieval religious discourse should not be underestimated.

Finally, James Hogg's "Saint Birgitta's *Revelationes* Reduced to a Book of Pious Instruction" offers a different perspective on the same cultural phenomenon. This essay shows in great detail what can happen to a mystical text as it becomes translated, edited, and reshaped for a new audience. Hogg argues that a compiler's effort to make Saint Birgitta's revelations accessible and appropriate for its wider readership resulted in significant omissions and additions to the original version. These changes correspond to the compiler's assumptions about the intellectual deficiencies of an anticipated audience, expectations regarding readers' sensibilites, and responses to the specific social and political circumstances relevant to the work's new historical context.

We offer these essays as a tribute to the tremendous impact of Valerie Lagorio on the study of medieval mysticism.

# METHODS

# "TASTE AND SEE, FOR GOD IS SWEET"
## SENSORY PERCEPTION AND MEMORY IN MEDIEVAL CHRISTIAN MYSTICAL EXPERIENCE

### ROSEMARY DRAGE HALE

> To articulate the past historically does not mean to recognize it the way it really was. It means to seize hold of a memory . . .
> WALTER BENJAMIN

> Religious experience can be indescribable in that . . . every experience in some sense eludes description: as it were, the ocean of nuances in actual life is infinite or at least indefinitely explorable, and we can always find new things and subtleties to add. NINIAN SMART

STANDING NEAR the *fin-de-millennium*, we read medieval mystical texts across a vast expanse of time attempting to understand them amidst the ruins of a post-Cartesian, post-Hegelian, post-Foucauldian, post-modern edifice. My own quest for greater understanding is constructed upon an observation, perhaps naively obvious. Medieval mystical texts are borne of remembered religious experience, recollections of union with or nearness to God filtered through memory and embodied with an array of associated sensory imagery. The experiences they narrate are not only lodged in personal histories of private lives, but embedded in historical time as well. We cannot help but to view them as "Other."

Two inter-related strands of thought frame this essay and are intimately braided with medieval notions of memory and the recollection of personal experience. The first concerns that which might be called the mystical sensorium, the sensory system of the soul, and the second embraces the notion of the corporeal body as it is fixed to the image of the soul. The soul is seen by the medieval mystic to possess its own sensuous body inextricable from the body proper and transformed by it. What made up the body for the medieval mystic – body parts and five senses – can be viewed as "duplicated" in an interior existence, that of the soul. Metaphors for the body and sensory images are fused within the mystic's soul. The mouth, the tongue, the throat, limbs, womb, breasts, hands, feet, eyes, ears, hair – the per-fected body of the soul – are all manifestly present in intimate moments with the divine godhead. In her analysis of sensory perception and memory in the scholastic work of Richard Fournival, Elizabeth Sears notes that the organic nature of the

3

human body was submitted to an analysis such that "parts of the human body, including the sense organs, were found to be so constituted that they could not be more perfectly adapted to the faculties of the human soul."[1]

A case in point: Margaretha Ebner, a fourteenth-century Dominican nun from the convent Maria Mödingen wrote a spiritual autobiography which enables us centuries away to sense not just the importance of the body to the medieval mystic, but the significance of the sensory experience as well. On one occasion she remembers a carved wooden figure of the Christ-child,[2] which, one day, as she held it in her arms, she saw come to life . . . and she heard the Christ-child ask to be nursed.

> The Lord compelled me with great sweetness, longing and desire to nurse Him in His infancy. He said to me: "If you do not nurse me I will take myself away from you at the moment you love me the most." So I took the image out of the cradle and laid it on my bare breast with great longing and sweetness and felt then the strongest possible grace in the presence of the Lord . . . My longing and desire was in nursing him, so that through His pure humanity I might be purified and set afire by Him with His burning love, and His divine essence together with all loving souls who lived in truth. . . . Since then, whenever I sit to say my Paternoster, I am powerfully compelled by a resolute love to press him to my breast. This gives me the greatest grace and sweetness, such that I can think of nothing other than Him. A certain desire and longing is very strong and mighty in me. During the day I received our Lord in an interior manner with a very strong Christian love, full of God's presence, which I openly received directly into my soul. And I knew, on account of the love which had compelled my soul, that I had in me the living power of God, His holy blood and flesh. I allowed Him during the day to bring love and compassion alive in me. The desire which I had for the images was changed there into the Holy Sacrament for me . . . One night as I lay sleeping and matins was called, I was constrained by the usual vow of silence and thought myself unable to get up. Then my most beloved Lord spoke to me: "Stand up and come to me in the choir." . . . Then the great desire came over me for the

---

A portion of this paper was presented at the 29th International Congress on Medieval Studies in Kalamazoo, Michigan, 1994 at a session sponsored by *Mystics Quarterly*. It is a work-in progress still in its early stages of development. With heartfelt gratitude to Valerie Lagorio for her mentorship over the past many years I am happy to offer it for her *Festschrift*.

1 See Elizabeth Sears, "Sensory Perception and its Metaphors in the Time of Richard Fournival" in *Medicine and the Five Senses* edited W. F. Bynum and Roy Porter. (Cambridge: Cambridge University Press, 1993): p. 19.

2 The wooden effigy of the Christ-child present in Margaetha's account now located on the altar of the chapel at Maria Mödingen is still regarded by members of the local community, both cloistered and lay, to be a miraculous image. Recent votive images declaring gratitude to the Christ-child effigy for curing illnesses of children are displayed on the chapel wall.

Baby of our Lord and I took the image and pressed it to my bare breast with all my power and might and I felt a human touch from His mouth on my bare breast.[3]

Central to Margaretha's first person account is the description of the interior nature of the grace she *feels*, a grace which is grounded in the exterior touch of the human mouth of the child on her breast. It would be a mistake to call her narration a visionary experience. She does *see* the effigy; she also *hears* it become the Holy Child, but, most importantly, it is the sensation of the human *touch* which carries for her the primary essence of her personal knowledge of the Incarnation.

The sense of touch as a gateway to greater and deeper contact with God is acknowledged in early Christianity by the patristic writers, particularly Origen, and discussed by medieval scholastics such as Aquinas.[4] In a Thomistic analysis knowledge occurs within a physical matrix and the primary function of the sensible world is to provide analogies that can be used by the rational mind, or even by the mystic's soul, to image spiritual truths.[5] From the bodily sensorium, Thomas explicitly gave primary to the sense of touch stating that "touch is the foundation of all other senses."[6]

In his recent work on mystical union Nelson Pike offers a provocative discussion of the tactile sense. He notes that "the verb 'to touch' is not a perception verb as is, for example, 'to hear' or 'to see.' Things having no sense faculties at all can touch things – as for, example, the bottom of the boat *touches* the shallow reef in the middle of the lake. The perception verb that goes with the sense of touch is 'to feel'."[7] Such ambiguity between the tactile perception of touching or being touched and the evocative verb "to feel" lies at the heart of the profound

---

3 *Nun han ich ain bilde der kinthait unsers herren in ainer wiegen. so ich denne von minem herren so creftiklichen gezwungen wirde mit so grosser suesseket und mit lust und begirden und auch von siner guetigen bet and daz mir auch von minem herren zuo gesprochen wirt: "saugest du mich nit, so wil ich dir mich underziehen, so du mich aller gernost hast", so nim ich daz bilde uzze der wiegen und leg ez an min blozzes herze mit grossem lust und suessiket und enphinde denne der aller creftigosten genade mit der gegenwertkeit gotz daz ich da nach wunderun, wie unser liebiu frowe die emssigen gegenwertket gocz ie erliden meht . . . aber min begirde und min lust ist in dem saugen, daz ich uz siner lutern menchet gerainiget werde und mit siner inbrunstiger minne uz im enzundet werde und ich mit siner gegenwertket und mit siner suezzen genade durchgossen werde, daz ich da mit gezogen werde in daz war niezzen sines gotlichen wesens mit allen minneden selen, die in der warhet gelebt hant . . . wirt mir der lust, den ich han zuo den bilden, da verwandelt in daz hailig sacrament. [in dem enpfande ich ainer menschlichen berüerde sines mundez an minem blossen haerzen]* Strauch, p. 87.
4 See Karl Rahner's "La début d'une doctrine des cinq sens spirituels chez Origène" in *Revue d'ascétique et de mystique* 13 (1932): pp. 115–145.
5 See Margaret Miles' *Fullness of Life: Historical Foundations for a New Asceticism* (Philadelphia: Westminster Press, 1986): p. 125.
6 *Tactus est fundamentum omnium sensuum.* Aquinas, Commentary, II *de Anima*, lect. 19. N.B. Meister Eckhart uses the same words in his Commentary on Genesis, no. 156.
7 Nelson Pike, *Mystic Union: An Essay in the Phenomenology of Mysticism* (Ithaca: Cornell University Press, 1992): p. 45.

importance that the fourteenth-century Flemish mystic, Jan Ruusbroec, attached to the sense of touch.[8] In several passages from *The Sparkling Stone* he unites the sense of touch with that of taste, intimating the structural homologies of active and passive, inward and outward: "When we feel that God touches us within, we can taste his fruit and his food, because his touch is his food."[9] For Ruusbroec, an interior touch and its consequent taste of sweetness accompanies a knowing that is expressed by the verb "to feel" (*ghevoelen*). The process of perception driven by desire occurs within the soul.

> And therefore, when we feel that he with all these riches would be ours and dwell with us forever, then all the powers of the soul open themselves, especially the power of desire and all the rivers of the grace of God flow forth. The more we taste of them, the more we long to taste and the more we long to taste, the more deeply we are in contact with his touch; the more deeply we are open to his touch, the more deeply his sweetness flows in and around us; the more it flows in and around us, then we feel that we know that God's sweetness is incomprehensible and bottomless. And hence the Prophet says: "Taste and see, for God is sweet" (Ps. 34.9) . . . Thus God's bride in the Song of Songs also says, "I sat under the shadow of him whom I desired, and his fruit is sweet to my taste."[10]

The braided unity of *touch* and *taste* and *sight* make sense in terms of the interior spirituality of the Christian mystics. In the physical world, tactile touching occurs outside the body; taste, like the sense of smell, must occur within the body. Whether it is sensed materially from the physical environment or immaterially in the state of ecstasy, taste emanates from inside the mouth. For the Christian mystics there is an element of inverted mimesis present in the process. In the Johannine sense the Logos was made Flesh and then eaten through reception of the Eucharist. The mystical experience reflects a theological inversion – tastes the sweetness of the divine flesh within, converts to word through written recollection the experience of

---

[8] For a brief discussion of the sense of touch in Ruysbroeck see James Wiseman's introduction to *John Ruusbroec: The Spiritual Espousals and Other Works* (New York: Paulist Press, 1983): p. 14–15.

[9] *Als wij des ghevoelen, dat ons god van binnen gherijnt, soe smaken wij sijnder vrocht ende sijnder spijsen, want sijn gherijnen dat es sihn spisen. Van den blinckenden steen*, edited by Lod Moereels (Amersterdam: Lannoo, 1976): p. 94.

[10] *Ende hier-omme als wij dan dat ghevoelen, dat hi met al deser rijcheit onse wilt sij, ende altoes met ons wonen wilt, hier-jeghen ontpluken alle die crachte onser zielen, ende sonderlinghe onse ghierighe ghelost. Want alle die riveren der ghenaden gods, die vloeyen; ende soe wijs meer ghesmaken soe ons meer vloeyen; lust te smakene; ende soe ons meer ghelust te smakenne, soe wi dieper crighen in sihn gherinen; ende soe wij diepere crighen in dat gerinen god, soe ons die vloede sijnre soeticheit meer doervloeyen ende overvloeyt sijn, soe wij bat ghevoelen ende bekinnen dat die soeticheit gods ombegriplijc es ende soner gront. Ende hir-om spreect die prophete alsus: "Smaect ende siet, want god es soete." . . . Ende dit tuycht ons die bruyt gods inden catiken ende spreect aldus, "Ic hebbe gheseten onder des-gheens scaduee dien ic begherde, ende sine vrocht es soete mijnder kelen."* Moereels, p. 90.

6

divine union. Adam and Eve sought to savor the sweet fruit of knowledge and suffered exile from Paradise. The mystics seek to savor the sweet fruit of divine knowledge with the reward of divine union.

The medieval mystics renunciated the world and most particularly the world of the body – through flagellation, fasting, silence, ritual mortifications. The concept "no pain, no gain" that sports enthusiasts in our secular society have taken on as a tee-shirt motto – for proof that the beautiful body results only when one puts the body through certain mortifications – had its own application for the medieval mystic. Holiness – the state of grace that they sought, the perfecting of the soul – could only result from arduous discipline of the body. The body was denied sensual pleasures of all sorts. But the appetites sensed by the body were experienced – fully satisfied – by the soul with perfect joy. If the mystic fasted, the soul could enjoy tasting all the more. If the mystic thirsted, the soul could reel from intoxicating wine. If the mystic were silent, the soul could converse at length with God. Worldly desires denied to the body became heavenly delight for the soul. The language of hunger and desire come together so that affection and love are the food which satisfies the soul. Through renunciation, all joys and pleasures which could be experienced sensually by the body were marked then as sacred, set apart, savored by the spiritual senses.

A paradoxical interaction between the act of world renunciation and the rich experience of the mystical sensorium is especially marked in the work of Meister Eckhart.

> Note that anyone who wants to hear God speak must become deaf and inattentive to others. This is what Augustine said in Book IV of the Confessions: "Do not be empty, my soul. Let your heart's ear be deaf to the tumult of your emptiness." And in Book IX of the Confessions: "What is like your Word? . . . If the tumult of the flesh is silent in one and if the sense images and the soul is silent and if imaginary revelations, all tongues, all signs, and whatever is impermanent is silent . . . then he himself may speak through himself so that we may hear his Word" . . . Therefore let yourself be deaf in order to hear: "He made the deaf hear." (Mk. 7)[11]

Eckhart's asceticism differs from that of Heinrich Seuse and Johannes Tauler and from that of the cloistered women whom these three Dominican preachers guided spiritually. While the others suggest that the five senses, when directed toward God, provide the connection for direct perception of the divine, Eckhart argues

---

[11] *Sed notandum quod volens audire deum loquentem oportet obsurdescere aliis audiendis et intendendis. Et hos est quod Augustinus dicit IV Confessionum 9c "noli esse vana, anima, mea: obsurdescere – vel obsurdesce in aure cordis a tumultu vanitatis tuae." Et 1.IX Confessionum: "quid es mile verbo tuo? . . . Cui sileat tumultus carnis Phantasie et ipsa sibi anima sileat . . . sileant imaginariae revelationes, omnis lingua, omne signum et quidquid transeundo fit . . . et loquator ipse solus . . . per se ipsum, ut audiamus verbum eius . . . Obsurdesce igitur, ut audias, Marc. 7: "surdos fecit audire."* Lateinischen Werke 1, edited Josef Koch (Stuttgart: Kolhammer, 1964): pp. 618–619.

that the intellect may, through perfect detachment from all created images in the world, perceive God in a direct unmediated sense. His notions of distance and detachment from the world (*gelâzzenheit* and *abegeschiedenhiet*) give "a more metaphysical flavor" to his asceticism.[12]

> Now someone might say: Did Christ have immovable detachment, even when he said, "My soul is sorrowful unto death." (Mt. 26:38), and did Mary as she stood under the cross and lamented? How can this co-exist with immovable detachment? Here you must know that the masters say there exist two sides to every human: One is called the outer self, which is one's sensuality, with the five senses serving him, and yet the outer person works through the power of the soul. The other side of the human is called the inner person, which is one's interiority. Now you should know that the spiritual person, who loves God does not use his outer person for the power of the soul, except when the five senses need it and his inwardness turns from the five senses, except for when the five senses are a guide and a leader for him.[13]

Asceticism itself became the source for intimate knowledge of the divine for Eckhart. After purifying the "vision" from world-created or -related images, he can say that "the eye in which I see God is the same eye in which God sees me; my eye and God's eye are one eye and one sight and one knowing and one loving."[14] There is a palpable difference in a very brief comment Mechthild von Magdeburg wrote while attempting to explain both the source of her inspiration and her necessity for recording her experiences. "I cannot write," she says, "rather I see it with the eyes of my soul and hear with the ears of my eternal spirit and feel in the members of my body the power of the holy spirit."[15]

---

[12] See Frank Tobin, *Meister Eckhart: Thought and Language* (Philadelphia: University of Pennsylvania Press, 1986): p. 119.

[13] *Nu möhte ein mensche sprechen: hate Kristus ouch unbewegeliche abegescheidenheit, do er sprach: 'min sele ist betrüebet biz in den tot und Maria, do si stuont under dem kriuze, und saget man doch vil von ir klage, – wie mac diz allz bestand mit unbewegelicher abgeschiedenheit? Hie solt du wizzen, daz die meister sprechent daz an einem ieclichen menschen zweier hande menschen sint: der eine heizet der uzer mensche, daz ist diu sinnelicheit; dem menschen dieent die fünf sinne und würket doch der uzer mensche von kraft der sele. Der ander mensche heizet der inner mensche, daz ist des menschen innerkeit. Nu solt du wizzen, daz ein geistlicher mensche, der got minnet, gebruchet der sele krefte in dem uzern menschen niht vürbaz, wan als die fünf sinne ze not bedürfen; und diy inwendicheit enkeret sich niht ze den fünf sinnen, wan als verre als si ein wiser und win leiter ist der fünf sinne.* Quint, Deutsche Werke 5, pp. 419–420.

[14] *Daz ouge, da inne ich got sihe, daz ist daz selbe ouge, da inne mich got sihet: min ouge und gotes ouge daz ist ein ouge und ein gesiht und ein bekennen und ein minnen.* Quint, Deutsche Werke 1, p. 201.

[15] *Ich enkan noch mag nit schriben, ich sehe es mit den ovgen miner sele and hoere es mit den oren mines ewigen geistes und bevinde in allen liden minnes lichamen, die kraft des heiligen geistes.* (IV, 13) Mechthild von Magdeburg, *Das fließende Licht der Gottheit* edited by Hans Neumann, p. 127.

8

The Bride in the Song of Songs is, for Mechthild as for other medieval mystics, the soul. Her writing is modeled on the court poetry of the thirteenth century and this is apparent in her delineation of the five senses as kingdoms of the Bride. She says, "The Bride had five kingdoms. The first is the Eyes, which are inhabited by tears and adorned with power. The second is Thought, which is inhabited by conflict and adorned with advice. The third is Speech, which is inhabited by necessity and adorned with loyalty. The fourth is Hearing, which is inhabited by the word of God and adorned with consolation. The fifth is Touch, which is inhabited by force and adorned with pure practice."[16] While elsewhere in her text she refers to the sense of smell, particularly of fragrances – the soul smells of balsam, for example – in this case, the sense of smell does not rule a kingdom in her soul. Mechthild's purpose in identifying these particular five kingdoms, a personified sensorium, is to arrange these senses in relation to the body's inclination to sin. Sin, which she personifies as the guardian of the kingdoms, is "clothed in discipline and crowned with patience." The sense faculties she sets up to rule the feudal kingdoms are all under the protection of Sin and remain loyal to the soul. For Mechthild, sight, hearing, speech, thought, and touch were sources of body-oriented sin, whereas the sense of smell stood outside this category and was not associated with the origin of sin.

Placing texts by these mystics, Mechthild von Magdeburg and Meister Eckhart (or even those by Margaretha Ebner), side-by-side brings to light a particularly troublesome question, namely the issue of gender. Recent work in the study of gender and religion has made it clear that all religious experience is gendered – that there is no neuter *homo religiosus*.[17] Certainly this is the case with regard to Christian mysticism – the divinity with which both the male and the female mystic seek unity is male. And in the case of medieval Christian mysticism, both the male and the female mystic regarded the soul – *anima* – as female in more than the grammatical sense. (Most use the masculine pronoun to refer to the body.) In the main, the bridal metaphors are dependent upon a heterosexual relationship between the soul and the Godhead.

Granting then that the essence of the unitive experience is bound to gender, can we say that the experience is somehow tied to questions of socio-biology? Are the gender distinctions present in medieval mystical experience rooted in biological processes? Is the ultimate explanation to be found in human biology? I think not. Instead, it is far more likely that men's and women's bodies are modeled by social

---

16 *Du brut hat fünf kungrich. Das erste sint die ogen, die sint gebuwen mit den trehnen und gezieret mit getwange. Das ander sint die gedenke, die sint gebuwen mit dem strite and gezieret mit dem rate. Das dritte ist das sprechen, das ist gebuwen mit der nut und ist gezieret mit der truwe. Das vierde ist das horen, das ist gebuwen mit dem gottes worte und ist gezieret mit dem troste. Das fünfte ist die berüde, die ist gebuwen mit der gewalt und ist gezieret mit der reinen gewohnheit.* (I.46) Neumann, p. 34.

17 See *Gender and Religion: On the Complexity of Symbols* edited by C. W. Bynum, S. Harrell, and Paula Richman (Beacon: Boston, 1986).

expectations of gender difference. The biologist Ruth Hubbard has noted: "Sex differences are socially constructed not only in the sense that society defines sex-appropriate behaviors to which each of us learns to conform, but also in the sense that those behaviors affect our biology – bones, muscles, sense organs, nerves, brains, circulation, everything. We cannot sort out our biology from our social being because they are inextricable and transform each other."[18]

However, it is far more complicated than this. David Howes, largely responsible for current interest in the anthropology of the senses, relates gender hierarchy in the West to the dominance of the visual paradigm in the aesthetic canon.[19] He claims it "explains why men in Western society generally devalue and avoid touch while women 'prefer touch.'[20] The opposition between the sexes is, therefore, partly expressed and partly constituted by an opposition between the senses."[21] There is extensive variability in terms of the value ratio placed on individual sense faculties over and above others in the medieval mystical sensorium, but both women and men heighten the value of sight and both men and women give primacy to the sense of touch as we have seen in Jan Ruusbroec and Margaretha Ebner.

There is, however, a provocative gender difference in the manner and process of spiritual embodiment in medieval mystical texts suggesting the birth of the Son in the soul. Women mystics recall the feeling of movement in the womb, describe mystical pregnancies and miraculous lactation. As we can sense from Margaretha's description, the experience of the divine and the memory of that experience are mapped on to the physical body. The sensory metaphors they use to narrate the experience come from culturally determined notions of what constituted the maternal in bodily terms. The male mystics also draw upon these culturally fixed values and metaphors. The critical difference lies in the fact that while a woman mystic physically embodies the experience, the male mystic first ingests the Eucharistic host and then recalls the discourse between the divine and his "female" soul.[22]

[18] See Ruth Hubbard, 'Constructing Sex Difference," *New Literary History* 19: 1 (Autumn 1987): 131.

[19] See especially "Controlling Textuality: A Call for a Return to the Senses" in *Anthropologica* 32 (1990): 55–73; "Beyond Textualism and Hermeneutics in Cultural and Religious Studies" in *Journal of Religion and Culture* 4 (1990): 1–8; and "Sense and Non-Sense in Contemporary Ethno/Graphic Practice and Theory" in *Culture* XI (1991): 65–76.

[20] He quotes "prefer touch" from Luce Irigaray's "The Sex Which is not One" in E. Marks and I. de Courtivron, eds., *New French Feminisms* (Amherst: University of Massachusetts Press, 1980): p. 101.

[21] David Howes, "Sensorial Anthropology" in *The Varieties of Sensory Experience* (Toronto: University of Toronto Press, 1991): p. 189.

[22] A clear example of this is narrated in "Das Gnaden-Leben des Friedrich Sunder, Klosterkaplan zu Engelthal" in *Viten- und Offenbarungen in Frauenklöstern des Mittelalters*, edited by Sigfried Ringler (Munich: Artemis, (1980): p. 415. See my discussion of it along with a translated text in "*Imitatio Mariae*: Motherhood Motifs in Devotional Memoirs" in *Mystics Quarterly* 16 (1990): pp. 193–203.

But again, it is not so simple. For the medieval mystic, just as biology and culture are inextricable and transform each other, so also are body and soul moored to one another and they too exercise a transformative effect on one another. The body is not merely a metaphor for the soul's sensuous body; nor are the soul and body merely "structural homologies of one another." Rather, they are constituted of similar substances which they share and exchange. The narratives written by the medieval mystics, both male and female, make clear that they felt their souls to be endowed with spiritual senses, faculties just as immediate as the bodily senses. Just as the medieval scholastics regarded experience as an imprint onto the memory, as a signet ring imprints the wax; likewise medieval mystics recognized that there is an imprint of the body onto the soul and a consequent transformation of the body. Clearly, the gender of that body is a significant issue, albeit one that is mired in the hermeneutic quicksand of ethnocentric methodologies and a tangle and ahistorical interpretations.

There is a long tradition in the history of Christianity in which *gnosis* exists in harmony with a "carnal knowing." For Tertullian, the body was the thinking place of the soul. "The body is washed so that soul may be cleansed, the body is anointed so that the soul may be consecrated, the body is signed with the cross so that the soul may be fortified, the body feeds on the body and blood of Christ so that soul may be fattened on God."[23] Such ideas were a living legacy for the medieval mystic. Mechthild says, "I am utterly astonished and ponder with my human senses that my soul is so wonderful."[24] Margaretha's experience of miraculous lactation clearly demonstrates her notion of the instrumentality of the human body in the mystical moment. As do many of the medieval mystics, she reveals an intense concern with the interaction of the physical and spiritual sensoria. On several occasions she describes the sweet taste of the Eucharist, the increased perception of a spiritual hearing over a physical hearing, the feeling of divine grace as it flows throughout her body and her limbs. And in one dialogue the voice of God tells her, "I am no robber of the senses; I am the illuminator of the senses."[25]

We can never fully know what the body meant to the medieval person, nor the soul. A compendium of natural disasters, famines, and fires, along with the Black Death which took an estimated one quarter of the population of Europe would certainly have had an impact on attitudes toward the body and the soul. Whatever the cultural notions about body and soul, the unmistakable element of individual creative memory, whether poetic as in Mechthild von Magdeburg or autohagiographical as in Margaretha Ebner, played a major role in their attempts to articulate the experience of *unio mystica*. It was *in* and *with* their souls, in the sensorium of their souls, that they sensed themselves thinking, feeling, hearing, tasting an intimacy with God. Their recollections of a unitive experience were, therefore,

---

23 Tertullian. *De resurrectione carnis* 8.
24 *Ich bin sere wunderlich und mich wundert in minen menschlichen sinnen, das min sele als wunderlich ist.* (VI 26) Neumann, p. 234.
25 *Ich bin niht ain berober der sinne, ich bin ain erliuhter der sinne.* Strauch, p. 28.

grounded on the ordinary sense faculties of the body. The sensorium was not the only physical representation affixed to the soul; the soul actually had a body of its own and was the sum of its parts. Mechthild says, "Lord I shall go hungrily and thirstily, in pursuit and with desire, until that playful hour when chosen words flow from your mouth which will be heard by no one but the soul alone who removes herself from the earth and lends her ears to your mouth."[26] In a dialogue between her beloved and her soul, the beloved says, "Love, now begin and let me hear how you can sing" and the soul answers, "Alas, my well-beloved, I am hoarse in the throat of my chastity, but the sugar of your sweet mildness has made my throat to sound again so that I can sing. Therefore your blood and mine are one and undivided; your garment and mine is one and immaculate; your mouth and mine is one bliss."

The medieval mystics not only regard the living soul as a mirror of the body, but the body as raw material for contemplation. Adelheit von Frauenberg, from the Dominican convent Töss, meditated on the care she might offer to an image of the Christ-child. She recalled being filled with the desire to sacrifice her body for its needs, wishing her skin to be used for a diaper, her veins for swaddling, her marrow for nourishment, her blood for a bath and her bones as fuel for a warming fire. She was rewarded by Mary for demonstrating such compassion for the Holy Infant with a drop of the milk he had suckled.[27]

Such descriptions are recorded as hagiographical accounts in the lives of the religious virtuosi either from a first person point of view or reported second-hand. They all involve the memory, but not all spiritual texts use the memory in the same manner. Seuse, for example, in reference to his own contemplative experience of dialogue with the divine, makes an explicit disclaimer at the opening of *The Little Book of Eternal Wisdom* saying that,

> This did not take place in the manner of bodily conversations or with answers perceptible through the senses. It happened only in meditation, in the light of sacred scripture whose answers can never deceive. Thus the answers are taken either from the mouth of Eternal Wisdom – responses it spoke itself in the gospels – or from the most exalted teachers. They embrace either the same

---

[26] *Herre, so Beite ich dennemit hunger und mit durste, mit jagen und mit luste unz an die spilenden stunden das us dinem gotlichen munde vliessen die erwelten wort die von nieman gehort mer von der sele allein, die sich von der werden enkleidet und leit iir ore fur dinen munt.* (II. 6) Neumann, p. 45.

[27] *Sunderlich do hat sy alwegent min und andacht zu unsers herren kinthait und erbott sich unser frowen dik andaechtekeit, das sy ir moeschte zu hilf sin kumen, irem ainigem lieb. Sy begert mit hertzlicher minender begird das aller ir lib gemartet wurd dem suessen kindli ze dienst; sy begert das ir ir hut wurd abgezogen unsern herren zu ainer windlen, ir adren ze feemly im zu ainem roekli, und begert das ir marg gebulgret wurd im zu ainem mueslin, und begert das ir blut vergossen wurd im zu ainem baedli, und ir gebain verbrennet wurd im zu ainem fur, und begert das ir flaisch alles verschwanet wurd fur alle sunder und gewan denn ainem hertlichen jamer, das ir an troepfli wer worden wond der milch, so unser frowen enpfiel, do sy unsern herren sogt. Das Leben der Schwestern zu Töss,* edited by Ferdinand Vetter (Berlin: Weidmannshe, 1906): p. 52.

words or the same meaning, or such truth as is in agreement with the sense of sacred scripture. The visions that follow did not occur in a bodily manner, they are all allegorical.[28]

For whatever reasons Seuse felt an acute need to make such an assertion, it is rare in medieval mystical texts. Mystics are more often likely to identify that the experience did take place, and frequently state that it cannot be articulated in human language. Mechthild does just that when she responds to the criticism for her long account of hearing John the Baptist sing the mass. She says that "one cannot grasp divine gifts with human senses," and the "The mass which John the Baptist sang for the poor maid [herself] was not physical; it was rather so spiritual that the soul alone saw, understood, and enjoyed it. But the body did not benefit from it, except to grasp the nobility of the soul with its human senses. Therefore the words had to sound human."[29]

The elusive conversion of religious experience to utterance through the aid of memory is expressed by the mystic as ineffability or inexpressibility. Angela de Foligno, an Italian contemporary of Mechthild von Magdeburg, frequently interrupted her dictations to her scribe to lament that nothing of what she had said was comparable to what she really heard, saw, tasted, and felt – that she is only dictating the 'likeness' of her experience. The ineffability topoi punctuate mystical literature in all religious traditions. The resources of language are deemed inadequate to convey, recover, remember what happened to the mystics when they attained union with the divine. The picture or sign theory of language identifies the basic function of language as that of creating or evoking images in the mind of the receiver which correspond to those of the sender, a theory which falls squarely into the visually-biased preference of our own culturally determined sensorium. Nevertheless, linguistic expression cannot be made to resemble the referent – outside of onomatopoeia and hieroglyphics – in the same way that performances and photographs do. Language is deficient in its referential capacity to express the numinous or the transcendent. In the face of the ineffable, language labors under

---

[28] *und daz geschah nit mit einem liplichen kosenne noh mit bildricher entwurt, es geschah allein mit betrahtunge in dem licht der heiligen schrift, der entwurt bi nuti getriegen mag, also daz die entwurt genomen sint eintweder von der Ewigen Wisheit munde, diesi selber sprach an dem evangelio, oder aber von dien hohsten leren; und begrifent eintweder du selben wort oder den selben sin oder aber sogtan warheit du nah dem sinne der heiligen scrift geright ist, usser der mund du Eiwif Wisheit hat geredet. Die gesihte, die hie nach stent, die geschahen och nut in liplicher wise, su sint allein ein usgeleitu bischaft.* Deutsche Schriften edited by Karl Bihlmeyer (Stuttgart: Minerva, 1907): p. 197.

[29] *Man mag gotliche gaba mit menschlichen sinnen nit begrifen . . . Das Johannes Baptistat der armen dirnen messe sang, das was nit vleischlich, es was geistlich, das die sele alleine beschowete, bekante und gebruchte; aber derlicham hatte not da von, denne er von der sele edelkeit in sinen menschlichen sinnen mohte begriffen; darumb mussent du wort menschlichen luten.* (VI. 36) Neumann, p. 244.

crushing limitations. Dante stated too that "the vision was greater than his speech could show, that it failed at such a sight."[30]

I began with the assumption that for the mystic, as for all of us, language and the world are co-extensive – language is disclosure. It allows for the appearance of meaning out of concealment, a theologically-packed notion. Any recognition of meaning or experience is an event of language. The mystic lives daily life in an experiential world, a world where language is still in effect. Therefore, language is the basic tool, albeit ineffective. Interpreting the meaning of an experience or expressing one's response to it are linguistic operations which require description. All descriptions of a personal experience encounter to some degree or other the limitations of language and require the application of creative memory in alliance with the sensorium. After all, just how does an orange taste?

Walter Ong argues that our sensory perceptions are abundant and overwhelming – that it is impossible to attend to them all. Culture teaches us to specialize. For the modern West the emphasis is decidedly visual, hence we "see" the mystics as "visionaries," perhaps a greater misnomer than the term "mystic" itself. "Sight," says Ong, "reveals only surfaces. It can never get to an interior, but must always treat it somehow as an exterior. If understanding is conceived of by analogy with sight alone rather than by analogy with hearing and smell and taste and touch, understanding is *ipso facto* condemned to dealing with surfaces which have a beyond it can never attain to."[31] More optimistically he claims that "the sensorium is a fascinating focus for cultural studies. Given sufficient knowledge of the sensorium exploited within a specific culture, one could probably define the culture as a whole in virtually all its aspects."[32] We miss something of the sensory dynamic of the world or culture of medieval mystics if we persist in interpreting their experiences solely as "visions." We can only approach the study of medieval mysticism and its cultural domain through the visual medium of the mystics' texts, their recollections of religious experience, but perhaps we can begin to do more than translate the words if we take a "hermeneutical turn" – instead of reading the texts, we could be learning to sense them.[33]

---

[30] *Da quinci innanzi il mio veder fu maggio che 'l parlar mostra, ch'a tal vista cede.* Dante, Par. XXXIII 55–56.

[31] Walter Ong, *The Presence of the Word* (New Haven: Yale University Press, 1967): p. 74.

[32] Walter Ong, "The Shifting Sensorium" in *The Varieties of Sensory Experience* edited by David Howes (Toronto: University of Toronto Press, 1991): 28.

[33] The notion of such a "hermeneutical turn" is best articulated by David Howes in "Beyond Textualism and Hermeneutics in Culture and Religious Studies" in *Journal of Religion and Culture* 4 (2) 1990: 1–8; "Sense and Nonsense in Contemporary Ethno-Graphic Practice and Theory" in *Culture* XI (1–2) 1990: 65–76; and in the volume he edited, *The Varieties of Sensory Experience* (Toronto: University of Toronto Press: 1991).

# RELIGIOUS ATTITUDES AND MYSTICAL LANGUAGE IN MEDIEVAL LITERARY TEXTS
## AN ESSAY IN METHODOLOGY

*Sir Gawain and the Green Knight,*
*Havelok, Lay le Freine*

JOHN C. HIRSH

I

AMONG THE SEVERAL contributions which Valerie Lagorio has made to medieval studies, this one stands out: her conviction that religious attitudes are amenable to academic discourse. Even now, this relatively uncomplicated premise is far from being universally accepted, and in the past, even the recent past, it has been regarded as decidedly unnecessary. Indeed, it has sometimes seemed a matter of irritation to some medievalists that there is an aspect of the Christian devotional tradition which esteems humility more than letters, and Morton Bloomfield no doubt spoke for many when he remarked of Julian of Norwich that "at present her mystical experience is somewhat overrated."[1]

Yet it must be admitted that this somewhat tiresome disinclination to engage religious attitudes has sometimes had reason behind it. It cannot be said that such investigations were always innocent of partisan considerations which now seem quite removed from the putatively disinterested procedures of modern scholarship, though equally what has presented itself as scholarly objectivity has sometimes set its face against any concern for religious attitudes at all.[2] But as scholarship has

---

[1] *Speculum* 55 (1980), 548, in a review of Edmund Colledge, O.S.A. and James Walsh, S.J., eds., *A Book of Showings to the Anchoress Julian of Norwich*, Studies and Texts 35 (Toronto: Pontifical Institute of Medieval Studies, 1978). One difficulty with this edition is the extent and nature of its annotation, and the impression it leaves that Julian's spirituality is largely the product of literary sources. But a less learned spirituality is not necessarily inferior, and Bloomfield's objection seems focused more on the mystic than on the edition.

[2] For an interesting example see David Knowles, *Cardinal Gasquet as an Historian*, originally published as the Creighton Lecture (London: Athlone Press, 1957), reprinted in *The Historian and Character and Other Essays* (Cambridge: Cambridge University Press, 1963),

itself become more engaged, admitting new questions of gender, race and class into discourse, a certain broadening of critical attitude has become apparent.[3] The result has been that certain hitherto marginalized topics have been accorded a new degree of respect, and the range of discourse surrounding them has considerably broadened.

In the course of these developments interest in religious texts, unpublished ones in particular, has increased, and with it a welcome inclination to take seriously texts hitherto regarded as "minor," though the manuscripts in which such texts are preserved are often approached for their codicological interest, rather than for any intrinsic interest the works they contain may reveal. Perhaps as a result, there has been a tendency to treat certain concepts categorically, even ones like "mysticism," which continue to mean different things to different scholars.[4]

But the fixing of a definition can have a complicated effect on any attempt to discern the actual significance of a given religious phenomenon. Many medieval authors, for example, have represented the intersection of divine and human worlds with a sense of disparity, but not always of disquiet. Thus although the realization of supernatural presence can cause even fictional characters to reform goals, attitudes and objectives, it equally can confirm them in a course already chosen, and I propose here that the treatment of behavior and motivation in the face of supernatural religious phenomona in certain literary texts bears a relationship to the more direct encounters of the mystic. From one point of view, after all, mysticism represents only one aspect of a religious attitude within which the relationship between a devout person and a transcendent absolute becomes manifest. And although poet and mystic both agree that God may respond directly to prayer, or even speak uninvited, both equally understand that mysticism does not

pp. 240–263. There are of course other examples: G. G. Coulton's position is still very important, since his attitudes have had particularly wide circulation, and sometimes even now impair the temper and extent of the discourse among those working in the area. On Knowles' own attitudes see Dom Adrian Morey, *David Knowles, A Memoir* (London: Darton, Longman & Todd, 1979), responded to in Christopher Brook, Roger Lovatt, David Luscombe and Aelred Sillem, *David Knowles Remembered* (Cambridge: Cambridge University Press, 1991), see particularly Sillem, pp. 27–46.

3  The bibliography is now far too extensive to list here, but see for example two recent anthologies of medieval feminist criticism both published by the University of Georgia Press: *Women and Power in the Middle Ages*, eds. Mary Erler and Maryanne Kowaleski (1988), and especially *Medieval Women and the Sources of Medieval History*, ed. Joel T. Rosenthal (1990), both of which contain relevant methodological contributions. More traditional studies have also shown a greater interest in gender: two volumes edited by John A. Nichols and Lillian Thomas Shank deserve special mention, *Medieval Religious Women*, Volume I *Distant Echoes*, and Volume II *Peace Weavers*, nos. 71 and 72 of the Cistercian Studies Series (Kalamazoo, MI: Cistercian Publications Inc., 1984 and 1987).

4  Or even different things to the same scholar. Late in life Hope Emily Allen revised many of her attitudes and opinions, though her language remained (in many cases) the same. See my *Hope Emily Allen, Medieval Scholarship and Feminism* (Norman, Oklahoma: Pilgrim Books, 1988), pp. 146–152.

undermine more traditional forms of spirituality, rather it supports them, and indeed from one point of view constitutes their foundation.[5] The connections between mysticism, spirituality and literature are thus complex, but they are real and lasting, and they find expression in a complex of attiudes towards religion present in the period.

Concern with the supernatural was more general in literary texts of the period than it is sometimes understood to have been, and several late medieval works give good evidence of contemporary attitudes. But the evidence they offer is complicated by their narrative setting and by their literary form. Imagery, for example, often plays a crucial role, conveying meaning less by argument than by wonder, a trait poet and mystic both share. Likewise, a concern with gender can have a religious as well as a narrative effect, and further define the circumstances within which the supernatural is represented.

But for the poet, narrative circumstance is hardly less important than the supernatural presence itself, and can sometimes limit the depth to which the poet or translator is able to explore its significance. In spite of these (and other) difficulties, however, the appearances of religious attitudes in literary works are important, both because of the resonances they reveal in texts directed towards a lay audience, and because of the openings they offer for understanding the religious attitudes of the period.

II

There is a scene in *Sir Gawain and the Green Knight* in which the protagonist, riding in prayer through the cold countryside, between forest and swamp, beseeches Christ and his mother "of sum herber" (755) so that he might attend at Christmas mass and matins the following morning; he prays, crosses himself several times and proceeds on his way.

In *Havelok* there is another scene where its protagonist, a child and under the power of his enemies, lies bound hand and foot, awaiting the time when he will be drowned in the sea. But when the wife of his would-be murderer and future protector arises at midnight to blow up the fire, she sees a light so bright that, about the boy at least, it seems to be day already. It is as if a "sunne-bem" (593) were being emitted from Havelok's mouth, making the room so bright that it

---

5  Eastern religions in particular often allow for the continuing influence of mystical experience. See Frits Staal, *Exploring Mysticism, A Methodological Essay* (Berkeley, Los Angeles and London: University of California Press, 1975), pp. 92–101, though for Staal mysticism "need not necessarily be regarded as a part of religion" (p. 4; cf. 190–99). Compare Andrew Louth, *The Origins of the Christian Mystical Tradition, From Plato to Denys* (Oxford: Clarendon Press, 1981), especially "The Monastic Contribution," pp. 98–131, and John Bowker, *The Sense of God, Sociological, Anthropological and Psychological Approaches to the Origin of the Sense of God* (Oxford: Clarendon Press, 1973), *passim*.

seems as though wax candles were burning in it. "Ris up, Grim," she calls out to her husband, "and loke wat it menes!" (598).

Finally, there is a scene in the Middle English *Lay le Freine* in which the maid-midwife sets out in the cold, clear night to abandon the yet unnamed child who will shortly be baptized as "Frein" (235). Passing through heath, field and wood under a bright cold moon, she pauses exhausted when, from the cocks crowing and the dogs barking, she sees that she is near a settlement. Finding houses and a church (but neither street nor town) she understands she is near a house of religion, a convent as it transpires. She goes to the church door, where she finds growing a well-branched ash tree, within whose trunk she places the child "for cold," wrapped in a robe. She then blesses it, and "[w]iþ þat it gan to dawe light" (180). The woman turns, and makes her way home again.[6]

Each of these scenes is a preparation for more important events to come: Gawain's encounter at the castle, Havelok's voyages, Frein's discovery and subsequent adventures. If, as I am going to argue, each of these scenes in some sense displays the presence of the supernatural, each also indicates that it is often at the margins of experience that the supernatural presents itself. Each scene is also intimately associated with certain aspects of nature: all three are associated with the cold, and two with the winter and night. What is interesting about the cold in these scenes, however, is the way in which it suggests its opposite, and the way the associated appearance of light further identifies the authorial attitude which informs the event in question. The order to which the passages speak is not social, but neither is it impersonal. All three come at crucial moments of a passage, at a time when there is no turning back, yet when what is to come is not at all clear, and when the next event may well determine the course of things. In such moments events take on a life of their own, and seem to direct not only the protagonist but also the audience to consider the significance of what is to unfold, and to do so against an imagistic background which reveals much.

In *Gawain*, the bare branches and cold birds of the deep forest seem to find an echo in the midnight bedroom (*cleue* 558, 597) in which Havelok lies, and those in turn in the cold night in which Freine is abandoned. But in each case the image does not exist in isolation, and the cold is set against the phenomena which, whether known to the protagonist or not, is about to occur: the refuge for which Gawain prays appears; the light from Havelok's mouth transforms Grim's task; Frein is discovered and protected. In the last two cases, though significantly not in Gawain's, the events are linked to an associated image, that of light. In the case of Havelok, that light is described as being like a sunbeam, but then, in an important

---

6 I cite *Sir Gawain and the Green Knight*, edd. J. R. R. Tolkien and E. V. Gordon, 2nd ed. by Norman Davis (Oxford: Oxford University Press, 1967 rpt. 1972); *Havelok*, ed. G. V. Smithers (Oxford: Clarendon Press, 1987), and *Lai le Freine*, ed. Margaret Wattie, *Smith College Studies in Modern Languages* 10:2 (Northampton, Massachusetts and Paris: Smith College and Librairie E. Champion, 1928), except that I have preferred to write *lay* for *lai* following the practice of the Middle English scribe in lines 22 and 24.

extension, like that of wax candles (*cerges* 594, cf. 2126), suggesting a religious, even a liturgical association, and in any case disarming a simply magical one. There is a humorous echo of this image later in the romance when the boy Havelok is hired as kitchen help, to swill dishes and fetch water, when he also volunteers that he can kindle a fire and make it burn bright (915–16). Later, when Havelok's bride finds herself lamenting her marriage and the light appears again, it is described as fair and bright, and is said to burn like a blaze of fire (1254); subsequently, and at another crucial moment, it returns once again (2122–23), this time preserving not his life but his crown.

The same association of light and heat which stand against cold appears in the *Lay le Freine*, where however the link is made even more explicit. After her prayer, the maid places the child in the tree trunk "for cold" (177), wrapped in the important "pel" (178), where she blesses it "with al hir might" (179). "Wiþ þat" the poem somewhat ambiguously continues, "it gan to dawe liȝt" (180). The birds pipe up, not for cold this time, farmers go their way and the maid heads home, just before the porter from the abbey appears to spot the pel and make his discovery, thanking "Iesu Cristes sond" (198) as he does so. Against the cold stands the subsequent protection of another woman, the porter's daughter, who warms the child and "ȝaf it souke opon hir barm, / & seþþen laid it to slepe warm" (207–08). The association of day and light with protection from the cold carries with it an assurance of divine protection which, as I have argued elsewhere,[7] was one of the chief new concerns of the Middle English translator, who realized providential and religious themes not present in his courtly source.

Neither of these associations of heat and light against cold are present with Gawain at his key moment, and their absence suggests that the poet regards the condition in which he finds himself as conditional and ambiguous, in spite of the apparently miraculous appearance of the castle. His prayer, like the maid's, may anticipate events which are about to unfold and invite the consideration that they are connected, but the crucial moment quickly becomes ambiguous, as, once inside the castle, the wine climbs to Gawain's head, and an old woman passes before his eyes.

But the scene before Gawain reaches the castle is interesting too because it has its mirror in the even more problematic scene at the beginning of the fourth fit, when Gawain awakens on a dark and cold morning to hear the cock crow and see a light burning in his room. This scene has only a chill echo of the supernatural in it, and the sense of expectation it contains is conditioned by the green girdle, and by the short ride Gawain soon must take. His earlier prayers had offered him no safe "herber" (755, cf. 812). He had still to rely upon his "trawþe" and his wits, and the result was always in doubt.[8] This scene, though equally contingent, has no such

---

7  See my "Providential Concern in the 'Lay le Freine'," *Notes and Queries*, n.s. 16 (1969), 85–86.
8  On Gawain's "trawþe" see now Ross G. Arthur, *Medieval Sign Theory and Sir Gawain and the Green Knight* (Toronto: University of Toronto Press, 1987), pp. 90–94 for an interesting

uncertainty. The die has been cast, and it remains only to see what if anything Gawain's new protector, the green girdle, will do. Night changes to day, but the cold remains, and except for the brief respite which the mass brings, there seems to be nothing supernatural in the air, no hint of divine presence – again, the light and the cock crow apart – in the course he has chosen.

In the history of *Gawain* criticism, the main focus has been on the knight himself, on his putative "sin" in accepting the gift and not returning it, and on the moral complexities for the individual his actions reveal. But another aspect of the romance is at once more and less personal. The entry of the divine contextualizes these events, and suggests a different way of understanding what transpires. It is no longer Morgan le Fay who determines the course of things, but a providential and supernatural engagement which manifests itself not only at one key moment, but also in the course of the action, and which allows Gawain the freedom to determine his own course of action, while reducing the manipulative powers of even the most apparently powerful actors to a game. From this point of view it is not simply his bad choice which Gawain regrets, but his momentary blindness to the ideal world in which his deepest values, both sacred and secular, reside. He understands at the end of his quest that he no longer has anything to fear at the Green Chapel, and in the end the unknowing court will restore the balance and welcome him back into the human community which it is his fate to share. The religious attitudes in the romance finally define its context in less individual, and so less modern terms, than the brilliant if paradigmatic narrative has suggested, and in so doing it has placed Gawain's actions in the context of Christian salvational history, and restored hope to its ending.

In what I have said so far I have made certain assumptions about imagery it would be well for me to make explicit. I have been concerned with how images work together, and by implied association, to inform a given, and particularly a transitional, scene. Even when one powerful image, like that of the cold, dominates a scene, it will sometimes trigger a series of associated images which serve to define its implication and effect. This complex pattern, I believe, can sometimes be accounted for by reference to a larger cultural setting, and in this case I believe a religious association, to which it responds. The linking of heat and light with prayer has associations which will be apparent, for example, to any student of English mysticism,[9] though to these have been added one other imagistic pattern, that of passage or voyage. This particular *topos* is of course so familiar that its effect

reading of it as "contingent". But it exists too in a series of less personal associations which help to define its propositional character. John A. Burrow's influential reading in *A Reading of Sir Gawain and the Green Knight* (London, Henley and Boston: Routledge & Kegan Paul, 1967, rpt. 1977) focuses on the concept of sin, of which the green belt becomes "a reminder" (151). But the religious attitudes I have been addressing suggest a somewhat more important role for the supernatural order within which the action is cast.

[9] See Wolfgang Riehle, *The Middle English Mystics*, trans. Bernard Standring (London,

is sometimes lost, but in each of the cases I have been examining it is contextualized in such a way as to bring it vividly into being.[10] The hero's journey is either begun (Havelok), interrupted (Gawain) or ended (Freine) by the manifestation, so that it is as if, for a moment, all of the possibilities of life are renewed, and its goals and meaning are present to the reader.

In her penetrating study of Romanesque church facades in Aquitaine, Linda Seidel alludes to "a new vocabulary of images" (13) which emerges from a complex pattern of influences "political, liturgical, militaristic and poetic" (16), to transform the figurative art of the period.[11] Her approach differs from more traditional treatments, illuminating in their way, like Ilene Forsyth's of the Romanesque *sedes sapientiae* in France, which document a series of statues without contextualizing them, and thus without addressing the complex cultural problems which figural images can reveal.[12] But in treating the attitudes which images in literary texts both inscribe and reflect it is important to remain attentive to context. Figural sculpture, whether on or within a church, places the human actions within a larger setting, and so causes them to partake of resonances which appear in literary texts as well. But in literary texts the role of imagery in encoding meaning is, if anything, even more powerful. Narrative, meaning and attitude are all involved in the passages I have been examining, and seem, like the sculptures in Aquitaine, to be in some sense a new development, a response to the larger religious influences of the period, a movement which involved individual encounters of an even more direct kind.

But there is one other aspect of these passages which I should like to indicate. In each case the conjunction of light and heat with cold is further conditioned by an association with women. It is Grim's wife who calls her husband's attention to the supernatural phenomena taking place in their room; Gawain, alone and friendless, prays to our Lord and also to Mary, whom he calls upon as "myldest moder so dere" (754), a description which stands in direct contrast to his own present condition; the association of women in the *Lay le Freine* is pervasive: mother, maid,

Boston and Henley: Routledge & Kegan Paul, 1981), especially chapter VI "Metaphors for Speaking about God in English Mysticism," pp. 76–88.

10 On the *topos* see Gerhart B. Ladner, "*Homo Viator*: Medieval Ideas on Alianation and Order," *Speculum* 42 (1967), 233–259, best read against the same author's "Medieval and Modern Understanding of Symbolism: A Comparison," *ibid.* 54 (1979), 223–256.

11 Linda Seidel, *Songs of Glory, The Romanesque Facades of Aquitaine* (Chicago and London: The University of Chicago Press, 1981, rpt. 1987). Localized traditional examinations do not engage such questions, see for example Arthur Gardner, *Medieval Sculpture in France* (Cambridge: Cambridge University Press, 1931), pp. 129–148 on sculpture in Romanesque Aquitaine, or Marcel Aubert, *La sculpture française au moyen-âge* (Paris: Flammarion, 1947) pp. 127–134.

12 Ilene H. Forsyth, *The Throne of Wisdom, Wood Sculptures of the Madonna in Romanesque France* (Princeton, NJ: Princeton University Press, 1972); a recent general history tries to strike a balance: see Georges Duby, Xavier Barral i Altet and Sophie Guillot de Suduiraut, *Sculpture, the Great Art of the Middle Ages from the Fifth Century to the Fifteenth Century* (New York: Skira/Rizzoli, 1990), in particular "Sculpture and New Devotions," pp. 181–191.

daughter and girl all conspire, each in her way, to create the scene in question, but I should note that in this case the prayer the maid offers is to Christ, though he is called upon to act for the love of Mary, his mother, an appropriate appeal given the nature of the events, and reminiscent of Gawain's prayer, which concludes with a "pater and aue and crede" (758).

Thus the presence of women at once deepens the significance of the event and provides an appropriate witness to the sacred moment. Gender functions here to focus, to recall from abstract association the images I have indicated, and to locate them in the lives of the men and women concerned. Gender does not simply restate the terms for sacredness which the texts inscribe, but it is deeply involved with the very terms through which that definition is attempted, and perhaps more importantly with the ways in which those terms function in the visible world.[13]

Against the larger pattern I have been concerned with, the explicit association of women with the supernatural is important, though in each case what is being appealed to is less doctrine than spirituality. I understand that the conditions in *Havelok* are different in theological terms from those which obtain in *Gawain* and in the *Lay le Freine*, but imagistically I propose that they are not dissimilar, and that the effect in each case is to establish a sense of the supernatural which springs from a meeting of narrative event, cultural association and the individual inclination – perhaps the faith – of the Middle English author. The narrative requirement was of course what indicated the presence of women in these passages, but in each case the requirement triggered a series of other associations which find deeper resonances outside of the romance tradition, and which inscribe meaning in significant ways. The process in which they take part informs the more compelling issues these texts evoke, issues which engage questions less of theme than of authorial attitude and finally of belief. One of these issues too concerns the depth of the religious attitudes which the texts present, another, the nature of their religiousness, and the extent to which it encodes both religious attitudes and some aspects of visionary spirituality.

### III

Yet even within this interplay, what is it possible to say about the connections, not readily apparent but unmistakably present, between these manifestations and the more powerful ones of which the mystics give evidence? In the medieval period as now revealed religion had many voices, and any encounter with the supernatural was likely to provoke more than one interpretation. But it is still to the mystics that

---

13 See Caroline Walker Bynum, " '. . . And Women His Humanity': Female Imagery in the Religious Writing of the Later Middle Ages," in *Gender and Religion: On the Complexity of Symbols*, eds. Caroline Walker Bynum, Stevan Harrell and Paula Richman (Boston: Beacon Press, 1986), pp. 257–288, and also Bynum's *Holy Feast and Holy Fast: The Religious Significance of Food to Medieval Women* (Berkeley Los Angeles and London: University of California Press, 1986), chapter 10 "Women's Symbols," pp. 277–296.

we must look to ascertain what the parameters of encounter were, how a sense of divine presence was received, and what attitudes subsequently developed. The presence which appeared – not always to those concerned, but finally to the audience – often came suddenly and usually changed things. Sometimes a sense of reassurance accompanied it, as the one involved contended with adversity, and the reader at least became able to perceive the nature of the assistance now available. But the encounter had too the effect of placing action in a broader context, at once deepening and rendering newly intelligible the behavior and motivation of those concerned.

It is these qualities rather than any more definite ones, which are at the heart of the matter. Because we are here dealing with a finally human responsiveness rather than with a particular representation of it, it will not do simply to catalogue the images associated with the manifestation of the supernatural as a way of inspecting the event, or ascertaining when, in fact, a manifestation has occurred. Thus although certain images recur in the texts I have been examining, I cannot say too strongly that it is the context of these images, as much as the images themselves, which encodes meaning. Heat and light, even when cited in a religious passage, do not universally point to a divine presence, nor even to any less specific sense of the supernatural. It is not difficult to find such images as these in a Christian context outside the tradition of Western mysticism upon which, I believe, medieval English texts like the ones I have been examining often depend. Images of light and heat figure, for example, in Origen, where they represent Platonic rather than mystical attitudes,[14] but that is why context is as important as it is, and why it is in the problematic area of human responsiveness that meaning resides. What events lead up to the particular moment? How is the moment itself represented, but also, and not less important, what is its aftermath and effect? How does it tell on those involved, or on the reader? What does the poet's attitude toward the event seem to be? The answers to these questions, I submit, do not admit of a common denominator, but in their aggregate, particularly when questions of literary form are also engaged, they reveal much.

In another place I have argued that late medieval England produced a number of religious practices which formed a kind of border area between mysticism and other kinds of devotion.[15] What emerges in these texts is related, for they too reveal a sense of presence rather than of encounter. There is no overwhelming awareness

---

14 See John Dillon, "Looking on the Light: Some Remarks on the Imagery of Light in the First Chapter of the *Peri Archon*," in *Origin of Alexandria, His World and His Legacy*, eds. Charles Kannengiesser and William L. Petersen, Christianity and Judaism in Antiquity, vol. 1 (Notre Dame, Indiana: University of Notre Dame Press, 1988), pp. 215–230, and compare Riehl, *supra* n. 9, chapter VIII "The Experience of God as a Spiritual Sense Perception," pp. 104–128, for a treatment of the frequent use of sensual terms in English mysticism, a practice "which indeed goes back to Origin" (p. 104).

15 See my *The Revelations of Margery Kempe, Paramystical Practices in Late Medieval England* Medieval and Renaissance Authors, vol. 10 (Leiden and New York: E.J. Brill, 1989), pp. 19, 90–91.

of discovery, no sense at all of union. The supernatural appears, makes itself known or at least felt, and events proceed again. But the presence unmistakably informs the action into which it has intruded. Whether it comes in response to a petition, or simply at a moment of danger, it changes the course of things, and protects some at least of those concerned from harm.

Thus, access to the divine is a complicated matter. As Gawain and Freine's maid both recall, in one way – through prayer – everyone has it, though the form and character of a sought-for response need not conform to human expectations, even when it encompasses them. Thus there is often an element of the unknown in such manifestations, an x in the equation, so that such moments often seem related not so much to the moment of mystical encounter as to its aftermath.[16] The event itself, however important, rushes by, but the entry of the supernatural into human affairs has its effect, and takes its toll. Human agency is neither superseded nor commanded, but it is engaged, and it does not fail to alter course, sometimes in the interests of others. Often the moment has too an organizing effect, appearing to be both a part of a continuing influence, and yet influential itself in providing for future action. However suddenly, however unexpectedly these manifestations occur, they do so in the context of an encounter, and become the single most important link in a chain which seemed to indicate a very different conclusion.

I noted at the beginning of this study that it has been an accomplishment of this volume's honoree to show that religious attitudes are amenable to academic discourse, and I have suggested that these attitudes sometimes become intelligible when poetic topics, and approaches sometimes dismissed as being of limited importance, are used to examine literary forms and narrative moments which inscribe meaning. What emerges in this kind of examination, I believe, is not a simple affirmation of either traditional beliefs or devout practices, but rather an integration of those assumptions which reader and protagonist share, particularly those which, at important moments, record the ways in which the sacred and the secular interact. Of the three texts I have been concerned with, it is of course *Sir Gawain and the Green Knight* which realizes these concerns most fully, and which offers, in its fusion of imagery and narrative, a redefinition of the ways in which meaning emerges in secular and devout, courtly and religious, discourse. Gawain's prayer in the wilderness hangs over the events which follow: the cold and the dark prepare for the light and the fire to come. The linking of religious attitudes and imagery

---

[16] I am thinking here of the fourth of the still valuable criteria for determining religious experience which Joachim Wach has identified, that "it issue in action. It involves an imperative; it is the most powerful source of motivation and action." *The Comparative Study of Religions*, Lectures on the History of Religions Sponsored by the American Council of Learned Societies, new series, no. 4 (New York and London: Columbia University Press, 1958, rpt. 1961), p. 36. See also chapter 4, "The Expression of Religious Experience in Action," pp. 97–120. I have discussed one possible application of Wach's criteria in "The Experience of God: A New Classification of Certain Late Medieval Affective Texts," *Chaucer Review* 11 (1976), 11–21.

associated with mystical encounter has a complex effect in a text like this one, which formulates significance less in theological than in heuristic patterns, and which examines both courtly experience and religious implication in light of their mutual interaction. But in the end attitudes and images together attest to a larger context within which the characters move, and from which they take their bearings. The context serves to complete, rather than to diminish, the individual persons who take part, but equally it strips them, as Gawain learns to his cost, of the assurance that their fortunes lie entirely in their own hands, a truth they had long understood, but seldom acknowledged. As the mystics knew, the encounters of passage are only a shadow and an echo of those to come.

Imagistic and religious patters associated with mystical encounter thus have a complex effect when they appear in literary texts. In their organization and positioning, but also in their associations, they encode both meaning and significance, and in doing so they reveal important dimensions both to the texts in which they appear and to the minds which created them. Thus their recognition both reveals an often unrecognized source of energy and power, and helps the student to speak with some confidence about the often unsuspected interplay of image, attitude, gender, symbol and meaning.

# HOW MANY CHILDREN HAD JULIAN OF NORWICH?
## EDITIONS, TRANSLATIONS AND VERSIONS
## OF HER REVELATIONS

### ALEXANDRA BARRATT

THE VIABILITY OF such concepts as "authorial intention", "the original text", "critical edition" and, above all, "scholarly editorial objectivity" is not what it was, and a study of the textual progeny of the revelations of Julian of Norwich – editions, versions, translations and selections – does little to rehabilitate them. Rather it tends to support the view that a history of reading is indeed a history of misreading or, more positively, that texts can have an organic life of their own that allows them to reproduce and evolve quite independently of their author. Julian's texts have had a more robustly continuous life than those of any other Middle English mystic. Their history – in manuscript and print, in editions more or less approximating Middle English and in translations more or less approaching Modern English – is virtually unbroken since the fifteenth century. But on this perilous journey, many and strange are the clutches into which she and her textual progeny have fallen.

The earliest version of the revelations is the unique copy of the Short Text in BL MS Additional 37790. This was made sometime after 1435 from an exemplar dated 1413, as we know from its opening, which refers to Julian as still alive in that year.[1] The Carthusian monks, who also preserved the unique manuscript copy of *The Book of Margery Kempe*, must be credited with its preservation. The only other pre-Reformation Julian manuscript, dated around 1500, is now Westminster Treasury MS 4 in the Westminster Archdiocesan Archives; it contains selections from the Long Text combined with selections from Walter Hilton.[2] But the only complete manuscripts of the Long Text are post-Reformation, and this fact poses particular problems for the establishment of the text. The seventeenth-century Paris Manuscript (Bibliothèque Nationale fonds anglais MS 40) is already to a certain extent a "modernization", as it has substituted then-current words for those

---

[1] See further *Julian of Norwich's Revelations of Divine Love: The Shorter Version ed. from B.L. Add. 37790* by Frances Beer, Middle English Texts 8 (Heidelberg, 1978), pp. 9–10.
[2] See further *A Book of Showings to the Anchoress Julian of Norwich: Part One: Introduction and the Short Text* edited by Edmund Colledge O.S.A. and James Walsh S.J., Pontifical Institute of Medieval Studies Studies and Texts 36 (Toronto, 1978), pp. 9–10.

that were already obsolete. Opinions as to its exact date vary, [3] but there is no doubt that it is Benedictine and probably belonged to the monastery of exiled English Benedictine nuns in Paris.

There is more consensus about the date of the Sloane Manuscript (BL MS Sloane 2499), the only other independent witness to the Long Text, though not about its textual value. Dated as around 1650, it is written in a hand that resembles that of a Paris Benedictine nun who died in 1671.[4] Marion Glasscoe argues that this manuscript was intended as "a faithful copy of an earlier version", and is not alone in holding that it largely preserves the distinctively Middle English features of the original language. It is, therefore, more of an "edition" and less of a "translation" than the Paris Manuscript.

In 1670 the first printed edition of either Julian text appeared, edited, probably from the Paris Manuscript, by the English Benedictine monk Serenus de Cressy. (Cressy acted briefly as chaplain to the English Benedictine nuns at Paris.) In his address *To the Reader* for the first time someone responsible for transmitting a Julian text left a record of his "editorial" policy:

> I conceived it would have been a prejudice to the agreeable simplicity of the *Stile*, to have changed the Dress of it into our *Modern Language*, as some advised. Yet certain more out of fashion, *Words* or *Phrases*, I thought meet to explain in the Margine.[5]

Most of these marginal glosses are accurate enough, though some, e.g. "mind" for *feeling*, "earnest" for *wilful*, "friendly" for *homelie*, "confessarius" for *domesman*, have an air of guesswork. Cressy had in fact hit upon the very method followed by so many subsequent "modernizers" of Julian's texts: he glosses or (sometime) replaces obviously obsolete individual words and otherwise simply modernizes the spelling of words that appear to be still current. Unfortunately many Middle English words that survive into Modern English have changed their meanings radically and significantly. These "false friends", to use C. S. Lewis's phrase, include such common but structurally essential words as *can*, *wold* (i.e. "would"), *shal* and *may*, and other more technical words vital to Julian's thought such as (notoriously) *substance* and *sensualite*.

Once there is a printed edition of a text as well as manuscript witnesses, the history of reading and misreading becomes more complex. The Upholland Manuscript, written by various English Benedictine Cambrai nuns in the mid- to late-seventeenth century, contains selections from the Long Text, but these were probably copied from Cressy's printed edition rather than from an earlier

---

3 Colledge and Walsh date it as mid-seventeenth century (*ed. cit.* p. 7), while Marion Glasscoe thinks it late-sixteenth or early-seventeenth century: see her "Visions and Revisions: A Further Look at the Manuscripts of Julian of Norwich", *Studies in Bibliography* 42 (1989), 105.
4 Colledge and Walsh, p. 8.
5 *XVI Revelations of Divine Love*, published by S. Cressy (1670), sig. A3[r].

manuscript. In the next century another manuscript version (now BL Sloane 3705) was made. This was a modernized copy of the Sloane Manuscript which had been collated with either the Paris Manuscript or Cressy's edition and included some of their readings.

Until the nineteenth century, then, Julian's Long Text circulated only among English Catholics, and her Short Text was not known at all. Only two copies of Cressy's printed edition are listed in the *Short Title Catalogue*, although in fact more survive in the possession of various Benedictine houses in England and the United States. Colledge and Walsh credit Julian's survival to Father Augustine Baker, but perhaps the nuns of Paris and Cambrai, who provided the manual labour at least to copy the manuscripts, deserve some acknowledgment too.

In the nineteenth century the Long Text began to reach a wider public. George Hargreave Parker, an Anglican priest, reissued Cressy's edition in 1843, writing in his introduction:

> The work is printed verbatim and literatim from the edition of 1670, except in one or two instances where a typographical error was obvious.[6]

This is not quite true. Parker also modernized, or rather regularized to nineteenth-century usage, Cressy's use of capital letters, and removed Cressy's glosses from the margins, gathering them together at the end of the text to form a "glossary of obsolete words and phrases", as he describes it. But he mainly reproduced Cressy's punctuation and paragraphing and tried to give a typographic equivalent of the original ornamentation. He also kept at least two glaring errors in the text itself. In Chapter 7, in the passage that describes the drops of blood flowing down Christ's face, Cressy had printed, "And for the roundness, they were like to the Seal of her Ring." He was followed uncritically by Parker. Both the Paris and Sloane Manuscripts, of course, have the correct though perhaps more unexpected phrase "scale of heryng". Similarly, in Chapter 10 Parker followed Cressy in printing, "One time my understanding was litle down into the sea-ground", where the Paris Manuscript reads "One tyme my vnderstandyng was lett down in to the sea-grounde" and Sloane reads *led* for *lett*. Parker, unlike some later editors, had apparently no gift, or desire, for conjectural emendation.

The main interest of Parker's edition, however, is its motivation. Why should a Victorian Anglican clergyman go to the trouble of reprinting a rather rare Recusant edition of an obscure medieval text? Apparently he saw Julian as an Anglican born before her time: in his introduction he writes that her text

> confirms our belief that even during the worst corruptions of the Romish Church there was a generation within its pale who . . . formed a part of that vital bond which connected the Apostolic Church with the revival of primitive Christianity at the time of the Reformation. It is very interesting to

---

6  Leicester, 1843, p. ii.

trace the strugglings of the writer's mind against pre-conceived and errone-
ous opinions.[7]

Otherwise, Julian gains only cautious and qualified approval:

> The spiritually-minded reader will meet with some few statements in the
> course of the following pages, with which he will not be able to acquiesce; but
> in the main he will meet with much amply to repay a careful perusal.

In contrast to the enthusiasm lavished on Julian in the twentieth century, his
overall assessment of her is somewhat refreshing: "The matter is peculiar; the style
quaint; and the language obscure."[8]

Not much information is available about Parker. He was vicar of a parish in
Bethnal Green, in the slums of London. His other publications were an edition of a
treatise by John Eaton (1575–1641), strongly Protestant in its theology, and a
pamphlet, *Letters on the Great Revolution of 1848*, in which he argued that the
liberal revolutions that occurred throughout Europe in that year were master-
minded by the Pope as a plot to bring all of the continent under his sway. The only
cohesive factor to all three publications, then, seems to be a strong anti-
Catholicism.

Some fifty years later, in 1877, the first printed edition based on the Sloane
Manuscript rather than (directly or indirectly) on the Paris Manuscript appeared.
Henry Collins, an Anglican convert to Roman Catholicism, edited it as *Revelations
of Divine Love*. Twenty years earlier he had published *Difficulties of A Convert from
The Anglican to the Catholic Church*, in which he had appealed to his newly-
acquired co-religionists to treat potential converts with slightly more tact: "kind
and gentle dealings with Anglicans is the only prevailing way of softening their
prejudices, explicating their difficulties, and otherwise preparing a road for complete reunion". One can easily see the appeal of Julian's text to someone with such
anachronistically eirenic ecumenical attitudes.

Collins was a serious and reputable scholar. His edition of Julian was merely one
of numerous spiritual classics that he edited and translated over the years. But his
edition of the Sloane Manuscript is not all that he claimed. Although he called his
publication an "edition", it is really a "modernization": as he explained:

> The antique spelling has been laid aside as unintelligible to all but the learned,
> and some few words have been translated to render the sense intelligible. A list
> of such words appears at the end of this preface. With all this the ordinary
> reader will find sufficient difficulty in mastering the meaning of many
> passages.[9]

---

[7]  *Ed. cit.*, p. vii.
[8]  *Ibid.*, pp. vii–viii.
[9]  *Revelations of Divine Love, shewed to a devout Anchoress, by name, Mother Julian of Norwich*,
     with a preface by Henry Collins (London, 1877), p. xiv.

Futhermore, although he did appreciate that "[t]he MS on which the present edition is formed, differs from that followed by Cressy, both in the division of chapters, and in various readings",[10] he judged none of these differences very important and in fact he relied far more on Cressy's printed edition than he was willing to admit. My own comparison of a sample of the text did not produce a single indisputable instance where he had followed the Sloane Manuscript reading rather than Cressy's on occasions on which they diverged.

Collins did however print the chapter-headings found in the Sloane Manuscript and mainly followed the Sloane rather than Cressy chapter-divisions. Strangely, although he printed the opening of the final passage (thought to be a scribal addition) peculiar to the Sloane Manuscript, beginning "Thus endith the revelation of love", his text stops with the sentence "I pray almighty God that this book come not but to the hands of them that will be his faithful lovers, and to those that will submit them to the faith of Holy Church", although the manuscript itself continues for another half-page. Ironically, the passage omitted includes the sentence, "And beware that thou take not on thing after thy affection and liking and leve another, for that is the condition of an heretique", but it is hard to account for this omission other than by sheer carelessness.

Probably Collins genuinely believed that the differences between the Sloane Manuscript and the Cressy edition were insignificant. He spotted something as obvious as the chapter-headings and incorporated them into his version but he was no doubt working fast (by modern editorial standards) and, impatient with the relative illegibility of the Sloane Manuscript, relied heavily on Cressy. Nor should we criticize him too harshly for this. English was only just beginning to establish itself as a serious academic discipline and there was as yet no "canon" of Middle English prose texts that had to be treated with accuracy and respect. The interest in Julian came, not from academics, but from more and more devout Catholics (Anglican and Roman) who were intrigued or inspired by what Julian had to say – or rather, by what they were led to think she had said.

In 1901 Grace Warrack's version, *Revelations of Divine Love*, appeared. This went through many editions over the next fifty or sixty years, a reprint of the thirteenth appearing as recently as 1958. Warrack knew of the Paris Manuscript as well as Cressy's printed edition but preferred to base her version (her own word) on the Sloane Manuscript. She does not seem to have regarded this as more than a matter of convenience, however, for she wrote of Cressy's edition, "It agrees with the Manuscript now in Paris, but the readings that differ from the Sloane Manuscript are very few and are quite unimportant."[11]

Her statement of her editorial practice is comprehensive, honest and informative:

---

10 *Ibid.*
11 13th ed., repr. 1958, p. xiii.

For the following version, the editor having transcribed the Sloane MS., divided its continuous lines into paragraphs, supplied to many words capital letters, and while following as far as possible the significance of the commas and occasional full stops of the original, endeavoured to make the meaning clearer by a more varied punctuation. As the book is designed for general use, modern spelling has been adopted, and most words entirely obsolete in speech have been rendered in modern English, though a few that seemed of special significance or charm have been retained. . .[12]

She is aware of the potential hazards this policy entails, however, and in Chapter 58, for instance, although she keeps "Substance" for ME *substance*, substitutes an invented term, "Sense-part", for *sensualite* and does not merely "modernize" it to "sensuality". Her "rule of never omitting a word from the Manuscript, and of enclosing within square brackets the very words added" sometimes makes for awkward reading but at least avoids the destruction of evidence. In practical terms her version was a great success and enjoyed a steady sale; unfortunately it still lives on in a way that Warrack herself would surely have deplored, being used by some recent popular versions as a substitute for the Sloane Manuscript itself.

In 1902 a rather different version of Julian appeared. The Jesuit priest George Tyrrell reprinted – yet again – Cressy's 1670 edition, stating in a final note:

That edition has been followed faithfully, except in a few cases where obvious misprints, or the spelling, seemed likely to lead to confusion for the reader.[13]

(He also altered Cressy's punctuation "wherever it seemed needful".) Tyrrell, unlike Parker, did suggest some emendations which he put in square brackets rather than incorporating into the text: in Chapter 7 he prints "the seal [scale] of herring", and in Chapter 10 "my understanding was litle [?led] down into the sea-ground", both changes that suggest he had consulted the Sloane Manuscript, the existence of which he knew.

But the real interest of this edition is not textual. Tyrrell (1861–1909) was a leading figure in the Catholic Modernist movement. Anglo-Irish by birth, he was brought up as an evangelical Anglican but became a Roman Catholic at the age of 18. He joined the Society of Jesus and was ordained priest in 1891. Intellectually brilliant, he became renowned as a spiritual director, retreat conductor and writer, and was a friend of Baron Von Hügel, author of *The Mystical Element of Religion*. But in 1899 he published an article, entitled "A Perverted Doctrine", on the doctrine of eternal suffering which incurred the displeasure of the Jesuit censors at Rome. According to his friend and biographer Maud Petre, this article was inspired by his reading of Julian. From 1900 he was effectively exiled to a remote parish in Yorkshire until dismissed by the Jesuits in 1906. In the following year he was

---

[12] *Ibid.*, pp. xiii–xiv.
[13] *XVI Revelations of Divine Love shewed to Mother Juliana of Norwich 1373* with a preface by George Tyrrell S.J. (London, 2nd imp., 1920).

excommunicated and two years later he died, unreconciled to the Church, and was buried in an Anglican cemetery.

Tyrrell's introduction to the Cressy reprint hints at his own position in 1901. He saw himself reflected in a Julian tormented by those very aspects of Catholic teaching on damnation that caused him distress. Of her treatment of the problem of predestination he wrote:

> It is curious and instructive to see how, in many ways, Mother Juliana's spirit of Catholic-hearted love was cramped in its efforts at self-expression by certain current theological conceptions of the time, whose subsequent Calvinistic developments caused them, even in their more tolerable forms, to be eventually abandoned by the Church.[14]

While Parker had seen Julian as a proto-Protestant and Collins as an early ecumenist, Tyrrell saw her as a fellow Catholic Modernist.

Tyrrell's version was eventually reprinted but not until 1920, by which time Warrack's more successful version had reached its seventh edition. Meanwhile back at the British Museum there had been an exciting new development: the Short Text, which had been seen and described by Francis Blomefield in the eighteenth century, had been rediscovered when in 1909 the Museum purchased the Amherst Manuscript (now BL MS Add. 37790). Two years later a version of it was published by Dundas Harford, whose policy was described as follows:

> The Editor has tried to give the original wording, wherever it would not be positively misleading to the modern reader. He has modernised the spelling. For the punctuation, and the division into paragraphs, he is alone responsible, as there are few stops, and no breaks, in the MS.[15]

Harford also invented chapter headings and a title, *Comfortable Words to Christ's Lovers*, which survived the first two editions but was eventually replaced by *The Shewings of the Lady Julian*.

Harford (1858–1953) was an Anglican priest and Vicar of St Stephen's, Norwich, between 1901 and 1908. Possibly the Norwich connection was the reason he was chosen to edit the newly-found text. He was the first to argue that the Short Text was Julian's original account of her experiences, which she expanded fifteen years later into the Long Text. This hypothesis has been generally accepted and only recently challenged by Nicholas Watson.[16]

It was in the early twentieth century, too, that the dismemberment of Julian, and her reconstitution in the more palatable form of extracts and selections, began – or rather, continued and gathered strength, as both the Westminster and Upholland

---

[14] *Ibid.*, pp. xiv–xv.

[15] *Comfortable Words for Christ's Lovers*, transcribed and edited by Dundas Harford (London, 1911) p. 13.

[16] See his "The Composition of Julian of Norwich's *Revelation of Love*', *Speculum* 68 (1993), 637–683.

manuscripts had long ago ignored the stern warnings of the Sloane scribe against incomplete transmission. In 1908 an anonymous collection, *All Shall Be Well*, was issued. This claimed to extract from Warrack's version

> those few pearls of spiritual thought, hoping that some who are hindered by the lack of time or opportunity or by difficulty of style and language, from giving this wonderful book the study it deserves, may find in them helpful subjects for meditation and prayer.[17]

The compiler also carried a torch for the restoration of the solitary life in the Church of England, murmuring wistfully

> Have we no place in our twentieth century for such as Julian? Are there none whose souls are athirst for God, who are unsuited for a life in Community, unfitted for the ceaseless round of active life which seems unavoidable in our large English sisterhoods, who yet would gladly answer the call to a life of seclusion, devoted to prayer and meditation?[18]

A few years later appeared *The Shewing of a Vision*, extracts from Warrack's version again, compiled by an Anglican sister with a preface by George Congreve S.S.J.E. The tone may be adequately judged by this sample from the preface to the "priceless little book" by "this beautiful character":

> In every page one meets charming tokens of English education and character, traces of love of home, of religion that made her childhood and youth happy, traces of poetic insight, of humour, of happy laughter. . . .[19]

This marks the one and only appearance of Julian as the Georgian Country Gentlewoman.

Julian was becoming a household (or at least parish and convent) name. Yet there was still no edition of any of the manuscript versions that adhered to modern standards of textual scholarship, even though the Early English Text Society had published its first volume in 1864, the Oxford English Dictionary was appearing regularly in fascicle, and diligent Victorian scholars had already edited many Middle English treatises. At the same time there were no real translations either, just those strange hybrids, "modernized versions".

Perhaps because of the success of Warrack's version, only one other version of a complete text, Long or Short, was published between 1902 and 1958: in 1927 the Benedictine Dom Roger Hudleston brought out in a Roman Catholic devotional series a version based on the Sloane Manuscript. This might seem superfluous, but Warrack's publisher had no religious affiliation and perhaps it was felt that Catholic

---

[17] *All Shall Be Well: Selections from the Writings of the Lady Julian of Norwich A.D. 1373* (London, 1908), pp. iii–iv.
[18] *Ibid.*, p. ix.
[19] *The Shewing of a Vision* being extracts from "Revelations of Divine Love" shewed to a devout anchoress by name Mother Julian of Norwich (London, 1915), pp. viii–ix.

ownership rights over Julian needed reasserting. Hudleston also claimed that his version was closer than his predecessors' to the Sloane Manuscript itself:

> While adopting modern spelling throughout, the actual wording of the text has been kept considerably closer to that of the MS than in the editions of Miss Warrack or Father Collins, although really obsolete words have been abandoned in favour of the nearest modern equivalent.[20]

But his support for Sloane was not unqualified: his version is subtitled "edited from the MSS" (possibly because he cites some passages from the Short Text in his notes) and he merely ventured the opinion that Sloane was "perhaps nearer to the original text" than the Paris Manuscript.

In 1958 Sister Anna Maria Reynolds, who had worked on the Short and Long Texts for University of Liverpool dissertations, published a "partially modernized" version of the Short Text.[21] She seems to have been the first person to stress the rhetorical aspect of Julian's prose, describing her as "the first English woman of letters", a term somewhat inappropriate to the early fifteenth century as it suggests someone whose primary interest lies in professional writing. Possibly Christine de Pisan can be regarded as a "woman of letters", but surely not the anchoress Julian, who made no attempt to circulate her writings as far as we know or use them to seek patronage. In some ways this characterization of Julian has in the event had (quite unintended) consequences more harmful than others that are merely ludicrous.

In 1955 the Westminster Manuscript had been identified as containing extracts from the Long Text but again, instead of a scholarly edition of the Middle English, a modernized version was published in 1961. (The neglect of this manuscript, the earliest witness to the Long Text, is extraordinary.) Entitled *Of The Knowledge of Ourselves and of God*, it was edited by James Walsh (like Tyrrell, a Jesuit priest) and Eric, later Edmund, Colledge (like Cressy and Collins, an Anglican convert to Roman Catholicism) and published by the Anglo-Catholic firm Mowbrays complete with *nihil obstat* and *imprimatur*, to make assurance doubly sure. It was "completely modernized in punctuation and spelling, vocabulary and idiom" and emended with reference to earlier "editions" where the editors considered it necessary,[22] so it was a long way from the original manuscript.

In the same year Walsh published a version of the Long Text, in the same series as Hudleston's. For this he used transcripts of the Sloane and Paris Manuscripts made by Sister Reynolds. He outlined his editorial policy as follows:

> I have adopted Paris as the basis of my version, though I have never scrupled to substitute a reading from Sloane whenever this seemed superior, either

---

[20] *Revelations of Divine Love* edited from the MSS. by Dom Roger Hudleston O.S.B. (London, 1927, 2nd ed. 1952), p. viii.

[21] *A Shewing of God's Love* (London, 1958, repr. 1974).

[22] P. xviii.

linguistically or textually. My choice of readings has been governed largely by what appear to me to be the principles of Julian's spiritual theology. In point of fact, I began my version in the settled conviction that there is nothing unorthodox, nothing contrary to Catholic theology, in the *Revelations*.[23]

No doubt as a Jesuit Walsh was understandably reacting against the use to which Tyrrell had tried to put Julian. Nonetheless, this combination of textual eclecticism with theological rigidity is hardly in the best interests of the text, though one is at least grateful for the editorial candour that makes his policy so clear.

In 1966, at a time when there was a strong counter-culture interest in mysticism of all sorts, Penguin published in its Penguin Classics series the first real translation of Julian into Modern English, as opposed to piecemeal modernizations. The translator, Clifton Wolters, was an Anglican priest who had spent most of his working life in Newcastle, in the (then) industrial North-East of England. This is perhaps reflected in the salutary remarks he makes in his introduction:

> Very rarely do works improve by being translated. Julian is more obscure than is generally recognized. Perhaps this is due to the sort of gold-panning treatment she is subjected to by those on the look out for nuggets. Golden sentences there are in plenty, but in the process of isolating them a lot of very rich minerals are sieved away. It is more profitable to treat her as a coalmine and work the seams. The yield is greater and more rewarding.[24]

The resulting translation is very free, more of a paraphrase, and not always successful, notoriously so in the case of one of Julian's "nuggets". It renders the famous line, that in the Sloane Manuscript reads "al shall be wele and al shall be wele and al maner of thyng shal be wele" as "it is all going to be all right; it is all going to be all right; everything is going to be all right". This is at least a genuine attempt to render Julian into Modern English: the "modernizers" who simply keep "all shall be well" misrepresent her, for Middle English *shal* is not accurately represented by Modern English *shall*. But unfortunately Wolters has not gained accuracy by sacrificing elegance, for *shal* does not primarily indicate futurity but rather obligation or necessity. A more accurate translation (though with no claim to elegance) would be "all things must, inevitably, come to good".

Wolters based his translation on the Sloane Manuscript, "generally accepted as the most reliable of the extant versions". But it was not for another ten years that a scholarly edition of that manuscript appeared. The credit for that goes to Marion Glasscoe who in 1976 published her edition with the title *A Revelation of Love*.[25] The next year Frances Beer published an edition of the Short Text in the Heidelberg Middle English Texts series, while simultaneously Colledge and Walsh

---

[23] *The Revelations of Divine Love of Julian of Norwich*, trans. by J. Walsh S.J. (London, 1961), p. vi.
[24] *Julian of Norwich: Revelations of Divine Love* translated into Modern English and with an introduction by Clifton Wolters (London, 1966), p. 20.
[25] Exeter 1976.

published their monumental edition of both the Long and Short Texts, claiming it as the "first critical presentation of the texts of the *Revelations*".[26] For the Long Text they used as their base manuscript not Sloane but Paris. At the same time the editors published a translation of their edition, announcing, "Although numerous beginnings have been made on critical texts . . . the task was only successfully completed this year when the present writers issued their edition" and asserting that all previous translations (including Walsh's own) were now superseded. This assurance was premature. Their edition though respected and widely used has not become the "received version" and that there is some dissatisfaction with it is evidenced by the number of individual and collective projects under way to edit, or re-edit, Julian. This is mainly because their privileging of the Paris Manuscript has not met with general approval, nor has their reason, that is, its (presumed) preservation of Julian's (presumed) rhetorical skill – in some ways a legacy of Sister Reynold's emphasis on Julian as a "woman of letters".

But dissatisfaction runs deeper than this: the whole idea of a "definitive" and "critical" edition has been problematized. Constructing a stemma and using it to reconstruct an archetype as close as possible to the author's "original", closer than any of the presumably flawed and corrupted surviving witnesses, are no longer (and have not been for some time) unchallenged editorial methods. And there were always texts for which they were inappropriate. In the case of Julian's Long Text the only two independent witnesses, the Sloane and Paris Manuscripts, were both written down at least two hundred years after the presumed composition of *A Revelation of Love*. They sometimes disagree significantly. Some of these divergencies may even be due to revision by the author herself for all we know. Nor does the only copy of the Short Text consistently support either manuscript when comparison is possible. A definitive and convincing reconstruction of the "original version" of the Long Text is pretty much of an impossibility; any attempt to produce one will be permeated by subjective editorial judgment. And if ever a text has been at the mercy of editors, their prejudices, quirks, and hidden agendas, it is Julian's.[27] What would be far more useful than further attempts at "critical editions" would be proper editions of the various witnesses. We have an edition of the Short Text, though it perhaps pays too much attention to the Long Text. We also have Glasscoe's edition of the Sloane Manuscript whose unpretentious presentation belies its importance, but it comes with little in the way of glossary or explanatory notes. We still need editions of the Paris Manuscript itself rather than of Paris sometimes conflated with Sloane, and there is no edition at all of the Westminister Manuscript. A reprint, preferably in facsimile, of Cressy's edition of 1670 would also be desirable, for apart from its textual value it throws light on late-seventeenth century English Catholicism and its attitude towards medieval texts. An edition of Sloane 3705, a witness that has no intrinsic textual value, would serve a similar purpose for the eighteenth century: "bad texts" do have certain virtues.

26 *Ed. cit.*, p. 196.
27 See further Glasscoe, *art. cit.*

And what of the translations? It should be obvious that they cannot be made until the Middle English texts have been properly edited, and that they can then be translations, not of "Julian's *Revelations*" but only of a particular version. But the existing translations, and even the various selections, do preserve much valuable information about the reception of the Julian texts and the many ways in which they have been found useful by different readerships at different times. One would not wish to disparage what so many have found there over the last five hundred years, even if readers have mainly found what they wanted to find.

It is not been possible to discuss in detail the problems of translating the Julian texts into Modern English. Briefly, Modern English is not simply Middle English with different spelling and certain obsolete words replaced. Too much else is significantly different, though this is not always immediately obvious. Moreover it is no longer possible to bank on the general awareness or passive knowledge of archaic forms of English which prevailed, at least among the devout, twenty or thirty years ago when the Authorized and Douai versions of the Bible were still widely read, and the Book of Common Prayer in use. One would think it obvious that "modernized" versions are no longer viable, but unfortunately they continue to appear. A recent attempt, which had best remain unidentified, is readable enough but its editors are quite confused about the history of their text, wrongly claiming that the Paris Manuscript is the earliest, and that it contains the Short Text! The version is, unforgivably, based not on the Sloane Manuscript itself, but on Warrack's version of Sloane. A recent selection also bases itself on "Grace Warwick" (*sic*).

Instead of "modernizations", then, we need editions of the Middle English with glosses, annotations and comprehensive glossaries to enable serious students to study Julian's texts in the original. Alternatively, editions with facing-page plain prose translations into Modern English that were not afraid to diverge quite markedly, at least superficially, from the Middle English in order to render the linguistic nuances of the originals might be acceptable. Such books hardly sound like potential best-sellers. But Julian is not really a "popular" author, for all her current popularity. She certainly was not in the past, as the social history of her texts makes clear. Far more stands between modern readers and Julian that just the obsolescence of her own, or her scribes', language. She is often obscure and difficult and must be approached with all the resources of scholarship as well as with good intentions, for we still know too little about her and her texts. (It is interesting that some recent studies of her theology are perfectly happy to base themselves on existing translations rather than the Middle English originals, a method that would be unthinkable in dealing with biblical or patristic texts.) Even the knowledge that is available, for instance about Middle English vocabulary and semantics, has not been fully exploited in the past to elucidate her meaning.

Furthermore, textual scholars have a duty to emphasize that our concept of "Julian of Norwich" can be no more than that of a group of texts of obscure and uncertain history, a view that should modify her current near-canonization. For instance, some Anglican dioceses now celebrate a Feast of St Julian on 8 May, quite an achievement for a shadowy figure of whom we know practically nothing except that she wrote at least two accounts of a series of visions – accounts that may or may not be accurately preserved in the various manuscripts, almost all written long after her death, the exact meaning of which we often do not understand. Such veneration places "Julian" in a very select group of authors of canonized texts, of which only four others spring to mind: Matthew, Mark, Luke and John. We need to ask ourselves whether such an apotheosis really does "Julian", and her readers, a service.

# MEDIEVAL THOUGHT ON VISIONS AND ITS RESONANCE IN MECHTHILD VON MAGDEBURG'S *FLOWING LIGHT OF THE GODHEAD*

## FRANK TOBIN

THOSE OF US WHO explore the world of the medieval mystics are made to suffer cruel indignities. If, for example, we are looking for something in our field in a bookstore, we are directed to the section dealing with witchcraft and the occult. Our fate at the hands of our academic colleagues is often just as dismal, especially if our work on mysticism takes us into the dubious area of visions and visionaries. Not all mystics were visionaries, of course, but very many of them were. When, therefore, in response to a colleague's polite question about one's current research, one launches enthusiastically into a description of the visionary/mystic who has captured one's interest, it does not take long for an indulgent smile to appear on the colleague's face, and one knows that within this cordially nodding head there lies a mind pondering the frivolities and abuses to which academic freedom can lead.[1] If we are unwilling to reduce visions to the categories of psychic disorder, as many did early in this century, we run the risk of being put into one of these categories ourselves, or at least of becoming a campus joke.[2]

Medieval visionaries are admittedly unusual people, but it is unfair and "unscientific" to approach them with the assumption that they can best or only be approached through modern psychology. If we wish to study them with the sympathy and understanding they deserve, we must see them against the background of their intellectual, religious, and cultural environment. And one important feature of this environment is how receptive it was to the occurrence of visions. Certainly the ready acceptance of visions on the part of medieval religious thinkers and the culture they influenced contributed heavily to their occurrence and characteristics. With the exception of a few writers who differ in respect to details rather than in

---

[1] About the only sympathetic listener I have found among local colleagues is an anthropologist who studies strange psychic phenomena among the members of a primitive tribe in New Guinea.

[2] An example of an early and unfortunate encounter between medieval mysticism and psychology is: Oskar Pfister, "Hysterie und Mystik bei Margaretha Ebner," *Zentralblatt für Psychoanalyse* 1 (1911), 468–485.

principle, the medieval attitude towards and understanding of visions was determined by one person – Augustine. Book Twelve of his treatise *On the Literal
Meaning of Genesis*, was, for all practical purposes, the final word on the matter.[3]

It is important to realize at the outset that, for Augustine and for the medieval
world he so deeply influenced, visions were a fact of life. No one seems to have
doubted that agencies outside the human mind other than the usual objects of
sense experience could cause images and thought in the human soul. Visions, in
this sense, and visionary dreams were thought to be more than just rare occur-
rences. Roman thought and culture, but even more to the point, the Bible, that
ultimate supernatural authority for Augustine, a book he knew with astonishing
intimacy and whose mysteries repeatedly provided him with a point of departure in
his search for truth, are filled with visions and dreams caused by supernatural
agencies. Both the Hebrew and Christian parts parts of the Bible recount so many
instances of such experiences that the pious medieval reader could readily conclude
that visions were not that extraordinary a means by which God and spirits – both
good and evil – communicated with mortals.[4] The continuing reports of visions in
post-biblical times and into the Middle Ages shows that visions were widely
perceived not just as occurring in connection with central events in the history of
salvation but were also not infrequently a factor to be met with in the lives and
struggles of Christians, saintly or otherwise.[5] In a word, the existence of visions was
never at issue. For Augustine, then, and for his medieval successors, the question
was not *if* but *how* they were possible.

It is interesting to note that modern editors of anthologies of Augustine's works
often include excerpts of Book 12 of *de Gen. ad lit*, in their presentation of the
essentials of his thought. They do so because it is a crucial document for understanding his theory of knowledge. However, they surgically remove all mention of
visions.[6] They do so most likely to save his reputation, fearing that to admit that
Augustine was so terribly concerned with visions might well compromise him and
the whole body of his thought in modern eyes. For the Bishop of Hippo, however,
the presentation of his theory of cognition has a clearly subordinate function here.
His principal task is to explain how visions are possible; and this is, in his view,

---

3   For the sake of convenience and availability to the reader, references to Augustine's *De genesi
    ad litteram* are from Migne, *Patrologia Latina*, vol. 34. For an improved text and translation
    of Book 12, as well as some excellent commentary, see the less readily available dissertation
    of John H. Taylor, S.J., *De genesi ad litteram, XII* (St Louis University dissertation, 1948).
4   For visions in the Bible, see, for example: J. Lindblom, *Die literarische Gattung der prophetis-
    chen Literatur. Eine literargeschichtliche Untersuchung zum Alten Testament* (Uppsala Univer-
    sitets Arsskrift, 1924; Theologi 1); and H. Rust, *Die Visionen des Neuen Testaments*
    (Pfullingen, 1922).
5   Very significant in the study of medieval visions is the work of Peter Dinzelbacher, espe-
    cially *Vision und Visionsliteratur im Mittelalter* (Stuttgart: Hiersemann, 1981).
6   Two editors who take this approach are: Vernon J. Bourke, *The Essential Augustine* (Indian-
    apolis: Hackett, 1964 and 1974) and John A. Mourant, *Introduction to the Philosophy of
    Saint Augustine* (University Park, Pennsylvania: Pennsylvania State University Press, 1964).

mainly a question of describing the human cognitive faculties and the various ways in which visions may be received by them.

Augustine begins his investigation by examining what would become for the Middle Ages, in part certainly through his raising it to central importance, the most important biblical account of visionary experience; namely, Paul's account of his being "caught up . . . whether still in the body or out of the body" he could not say, " – right into the third heaven . . . caught up into paradise" where he "heard things which must not and cannot be put into human language" (2 Cor. 12:2–4). These verses raise three questions for Augustine. First, are the third heaven and paradise the same thing? Second, why, if Paul is certain about the vision itself, can he be uncertain about whether it happened in or out of the body? Finally, what kind of vision did Paul experience? To the first question – one that by means of the term *paradise* links this supplemental topic tangentially to the main topic of literally interpreting Genesis – Augustine replies that on the basis of the text alone, without examining other scriptural texts or using keen rational insight, there is insufficient evidence to reach a conclusion. He also admits that he is unable to resolve satisfactorily the question of the soul's relationship to the body during Paul's ecstasy. He then proceeds to his chief concern: explaining the different kinds of visions and their relative value.

He begins by stating that the highest form of vision is one in which the object is seen "in itself" (*proprie*) and not in an image or through the body. To explain this he distinguishes three kinds of vision which he terms corporeal, spiritual, and intellectual, and he offers the following example. When we read that we are to love our neighbor, our eyes see the physical words (*corporalis visio* or *per oculos*), our spirit conjures up the image of neighbor, even though he is absent (*visio spiritualis* or *per spiritum hominis*), and we grasp the idea of *love* which has no images similar to it (*visio intellectualis* or *per contuitum mentis*). These three levels of activity are operative in a normal act of cognition and they also provide the basis for understanding visions. *Visio corporalis* is limited to sensation or that which is completely material in an act of knowing or seeing, and without the other kinds of *visio* it does not result in knowledge. *Visio intellectualis* is the only kind of *visio* that is true knowledge because it is the only *visio* that is completely immaterial and thus attains ideas that can be universally predicated. When something is seen *proprie*, or without images, that is, without *visio spiritualis*, and when this occurs *non per corpus*, that is, without any connection to sensation, this is the highest form of vision (Cap. 6, n. 15; PL 34, 458–459).

Most troublesome for Augustine, and thus most in need of clarification, is *visio spiritualis*, that particularly human element in cognition which he sees as being neither completely material nor purely immaterial. After listing several ways he finds *spiritualis* used in scripture, he settles on his interpretation of Paul's use of the word in 1 Corinthians (14: 2–16) to clarify the concept. Spiritual is that which is not a body but is a something (*quidquid enim corpus non est et tamen aliquid est*). This something is similar to a body. It is, namely, the image of an absent material object (*imago absentis corporis*) which cannot be reduced to the act by which it is perceived (*nec ille ipse obtutus quo cernitur*. Cap. 7, n. 16; PL 34, 459). When, therefore, Paul distinguishes in this passage between *mens* and *spiritus*, Augustine takes *spiritus* to signify that step in the process of cognition in which the images of things are in the soul but have not yet been grasped and turned into knowledge by the *mens* (Cap. 8, n. 19; PL 34, 460–461).

It is worth noting that this part of Augustine's explanation of human cognition creates a "place" in the human soul darkly mysterious, where images exist but are not consciously comprehended by the light of intellect. As we shall see, it is not just the human agent who can gain access to this storeroom of images. Spirits, both good and evil, may also enter. This "place" in the soul for images gains further in significance through the modest role Augustine attributes to sense data in his theory of cognition and the corresponding independence of the soul from sense data in its activities. Because the soul is nobler than the body, the body is not to be thought of as acting upon the spirit. Rather, it is the spirit that produces the image in itself, and this image is nobler than the material object it represents (Cap. 16, nn. 32–33; PL 34, 466–467). Thus the soul is conceived of as possessing a rich and sometimes mysterious life of its own apart from its ties to sensation. It is readily apparent that this doctrine provides a fertile basis for explaining various aspects of mystical experience.

If, then, images of absent physical objects are so central to the soul's activities, where do they come from? Augustine posits three sources for the spiritual images of absent physical objects: things we have experienced and stored in the memory (Carthage), things we have not experienced but know to exist (Alexandria), and things that do not exist but which we (*fingentes*) make up. Normally, Augustine continues, we have no problem distinguishing these images from actual objects present to our senses. However, three factors can cause us to confuse objects with their images: immoderately intense focusing of our thought (*nimia cogitationis intentione*), some illness such as delirium caused by fever, or the intervention of a good or evil spirit (Cap. 12, n. 25; PL 34, 463).

It is in this context that Augustine offers his description of ecstasy. In the state of ecstasy the attention of the spirit/soul (*intentio animae*) is altogether turned away and cut off from the senses and its gaze utterly directed either to images (*visio spiritualis*) or to things so immaterial that they cannot be rendered in images (*visio intellectualis*). In ecstasy one is completely oblivious to one's physical surroundings. Here the soul is more separated from the body than while dreaming, but less so than in death (Cap. 12, n. 25; PL 34, 464).

Can one know with certainty whether spiritual visions are natural or supernatural in origin? After describing several cases of visions experienced in connection with illness and fever about which he confesses his inability to provide clarification, Augustine replies that one cannot always establish the cause of such a vision. Just as the senses can be fooled, as when an oar partly under water seems broken, so too can one be deceived in a spiritual vision into thinking images are physical objects. And without divine aid it is possible to confuse an ecstatically experienced spiritual vision with the experience of a dreamer or a disturbed person (*phreneticus*). The reason such confusion is possible is that in all three situations there is no essential difference in *what* is experienced. Despite possible differences as to origin, the *natura visorum* of a dreamer, a disturbed person (*phreneticus*) – although the images these two experience may also be caused by a spirit – and a person in ecstasy is the same. There is no difference in the kind of images they all experience (Cap. 21, 44; PL 34, 472).

One may summarize Augustine's view of the kinds of vision and how they are related thus: Corporeal vision cannot happen without spiritual vision because without spiritual images nothing happens in the soul. Spiritual vision can occur without corporeal vision because not all spiritual images come from the senses but can have other causes, both natural and supernatural. Spiritual vision needs intellectual vision in order to be judged by the mind. Intellectual vision, however, may occur without spiritual vision and is the highest kind of vision. Intellectual vision(s) alone cannot deceive. In them there is no possibility of confusion or doubt because we are seeing not *per aenigmata* but *per speciem* (Cap. 26, n. 53; PL 34, 476). What we see in intellectual vision, e.g., the virtues and vices, has no similarity to images, though our comprehension is indeed qualified by our limited capacity to know. In ecstasy, however, the soul is freed from carnality and confronts the intellectual object more intensely, not spatially but rather in its own manner (*modo quodam suo*). The light which enables the soul to see intellectually is God himself.[7]

Is there a difference, Augustine inquires, between Paul's state of rapture in which he experiernce an intellectual vision and the condition of the blessed in heaven? He replies affirmatively. Besides the permanence of the state of beatitude the blessed shall enjoy as opposed to the temporality of Paul's experience, there will be a certain completeness and order in heaven which was lacking in Paul's rapture. He experienced some confusion, at least about where it took place and whether his spirit was in or out of the body. In heaven all kinds of vision will occur perfectly ordered and fully experienced without confusion by our full natures, that is, when the soul is reunited with its glorified body (Cap. 36, n. 69; PL 34, 484). In his treatment of visions, Augustine frequently uses examples from the Bible to support his views. Joseph and Daniel emerge as the classic interpreters of dreams, Joseph for his services at the court of the pharaoh (Gn. 41) and Daniel for his interpretations of Nebuchadnezzar's nocturnal visitations (Dn. 4 and 5) as well as for his explanation of the handwriting on the wall at Belshazzar's feast (Dn. 5).[8] Other visionary experiences of the prophets that Augustine refers to in his book are Ezekiel's transportation in spirit to the valley filled with dry bones (Ezk. 37) and Isaiah's vision of the Lord on his throne with the six-winged seraphs and the burning coal

---

[7] Cap. 31, n. 59; PL 34, 479–480. What the necessity of divine illumination for human knowledge in Augustine's thought implies for his theory of knowledge is disputed. See Frederick Copleston, S.J., *A History of PHilosophy*, vol. 2: *Augustine to Scotus* (New York: Image/Doubleday, 1985), pp. 64–67.

[8] Augustine makes the point that the interpreter of dreams is much more the prophet than the one experiencing the dream (Cap. 9, n. 20; PL 34, 461).

(Is. 6). Among New Testament figures, Paul, because of his famed rapture, is, of course, central. However, Peter's vision of the disc covered with all kinds of animals and birds (Ac. 10) and John's Revelations furnish Augustine with additional documentation. While not referring to the serious physical consequences of the visions experienced by Daniel – extreme weakness, distortions in body and mind, and periods of unconsciouness (Dn. 7: 28, 8: 27, and 10: 7–9), Augustine does mention similar effects on persons not otherwise identified, who, while having visions of infernal torments, are snatched away from their corporeal senses and lie lifeless (*mortuis similes jacuerunt.* Cap. 32, n. 60; PL 34, 480–481). Thus this frequent effect of a vision on the visionary was well established by Augustine's time, and by calling attention to it here he reinforces it as part of the visionary tradition.

Finally, there is the question of Augustine's interpretation of Moses' visions of God. If Paul's vision retains pre-eminence among the visions of the New Testament by being clearly an example of that highest form of vision – intellectual vision, can one claim parity for the giver of the Old Law? Moses desired to see God not as on the mountain or in the tabernacle, but rather as he is (*in ea substantia, qua Deus est*), not as he might appear to human senses or in spiritual forms similar to physical forms, but as he is (*per speciem suam*), or face to face, to the extent possible by a creature endowed with reason and intellect. Despite passages which muddy the waters for him, Augustine finds enough scriptural evidence to decide that Moses did indeed see God's own being and he thus ranks him together with Paul as the foremost among visionaries (Cap. 27, n. 55; PL 34, 477–478).

A glance through the works of subsequent Western Christian writers shows that Augustine's approach to visions and the conclusions he reached went largely unchallenged and unchanged into the High Middle Ages. Even when an author departs from the Western Father regarding details, the mind set is still clearly Augustinian. Thus, for example, Hugh of St Victor accepts the distinction of *visio* into *corporalis, imaginaria vel spiritualis,* and *intellectualis* and offers this as one possible interpretation of the three heavens. He strikes out on his own only in attempting to distinguish levels of truth contained in dreams and, in a different context, in using the concepts of matter and form to clarify the traditional triple distinction.[9] Richard of St Victor distinguishes four kinds of vision instead of the traditional three by dividing corporeal vision into two kinds: normal use of the sense of sight (the lower form) and this vision when something is shown to it to which great mystical meaning is attached, as in the case of Moses seeing the burning bush (Ex. 3: 1–6).[10] In general, however, Richard seems only marginally interested in visions, concentrating instead on contemplation devoid of the unusual. Bernard of Clairvaux's writings speak much of ecstasy, but it is an ecstasy of love and union rather than one of enlightenment or vision. Indeed, he stresses that any unusual divine enlightenment in this life must be greatly modified for us to

---

9  *In Epistolam II ad Corinthios*; PL 175, 551–553 and *Miscellanae*, Liber 3, Tit. 22; PL 177, 646–647.

10  *In Apocalypsim libri septem*, Liber 1, Ch. 1; PL 196, 686.

receive it, though he does believe that images can arise in us through the agency of good or evil spirits.[11] As in so many other matters, Peter Lombard's position on visions mirrors closely the thought of Augustine, whose very words he frequently borrows in defining the three kinds of vision, in giving them their relative value, in discussing whether Paul was in or out of the body, and in giving Moses' direct vision of God parity with Paul's.[12]

Finally, Thomas Aquinas, who treats visions as a subcategory under prophecy, considers aspects of both prophecy and visions not dealt with by Augustine and distinguishes further the interplay between the three kinds of vision. However, in his discussion of visions we find all the major features of Augustine's thought. Nowhere does he disagree with his illustrious predecessor but rather uses him as his most frequent authority.[13] Two additional points raised by Thomas are of interest if we are to relate traditional points of view on visions and visionaries to Mechthild's writings. First, though Thomas agrees that Moses was the greatest of the prophets – partially because of his having seen God in his substance, he asserts that John the Baptist is to be considered even greater because he belongs to the New Testament, whose ministers more brightly behold the Lord.[14] Second, Thomas poses the question whether the grace of speech, wisdom, and knowledge of which Paul speaks (1 Cor. 12:8) may belong to women as well as men. He answers affirmatively but, mindful of Paul's prohibition against women having authority in the church, he restricts their use of such gifts to private instruction.[15]

Before proceeding to consider the presence of Augustinian thought and tradition regarding visions in the writings of the thirteenth-century visionary and mystic Mechthild von Magdeburg, we should consider what seem to be the most important implications of the Bishop of Hippo's thought for visions, visionaries, and how they were viewed in the Middle Ages. Besides passing on to future generations a strong belief in the existence of supernaturally caused visions and their relative frequency, at least in biblical times, and creating by the examples he used a "canon" of visionaries led by Paul and Moses, but containing several other Old and New Testament figures as well, Augustine formed medieval attitudes in two important ways. First, he defined the kinds of visions possible – corporeal, spiritual, and intellectual – and established their relative value. Second, he reduced to a minimum the differences between visions and normal cognitive experience. He did so, first of all, by capturing them both in a single word – *visio*. *Visio* is everyday cognitive seeing which is knowing in the true and full sense, as in the example of our comprehending the imageless concept *love* when reading that we should love our neighbor; but it is *visions* as well. There is no essential difference in these *acts* of

---

[11] *Sermo 41 in Cantica*, n. 3; PL 183, 985–986.
[12] *In Epistolam II ad Corinthios*; PL 192, 79–83.
[13] *Summa Theologica* 2a 2ae, Q. 171–175.
[14] *Summa Theologica* 2a 2ae, Q. 174, a. 4. Cf. 2 Cor. 3:18 for the allusion.
[15] *Summa Theologica* 2a 2ae, q. 177, a. 2. For Paul's prohibition, see 1 Cor. 14:34 and 1 Tim 2:12.

seeing. They are all *visio*. Second, there is no essential difference in *what* is seen. The objects of *visio*, the *natura visorum*, are also the same, whether one is experiencing cognition through the normal functioning of the senses and the mind, or whether one is dreaming, delirious with fever, or under the spell of a supernatural agency. The sole difference between these kinds of experience lies in what causes them. Certainly medieval visionaries were viewed by their contemporaries as unusual people, but by minimizing the differences between *vision* and *visions* and by confessing that one cannot always distinguish spiritual visions of supernatural origin from normal dreams or the effects of sickness, Augustine contributed much to narrowing the distance between visionaries and the spirituality of less favored believers.

## MECHTHILD VON MAGDEBURG

As we turn our attention to Mechthild, our goal cannot be to demonstrate a direct link between the *Doctor gratiae* and this thirteenth-century beguine and later nun. Despite her obvious artistic and intelletual gifts Mechthild's writings are not grounded in a formal theological education. Here and there one can find, perhaps, evidence that she knew this or that theological tract, just as in her exploitation of genres, conventions, and images, she betrays great familiarity with courtly literature.[16] It seems most likely, however, that most of her knowledge of theology derived from the pastoral efforts – sermons, instruction, the confessional, the liturgy, and the like – of members of the clergy, certainly Dominicans among them, with whom she had frequent contact. The point to be made, therefore, is that the visions that Mechthild's writings include are best understood not as unfiltered expressions of raw personal encounters with the supernatural. Rather, they are experiences – and this fateful term is best taken in the widest possible sense – deeply embedded in a visionary tradition; and Augustinian thought is the dominant component in this tradition. As we shall point out, Mechthild was not at her best in making theological distinctions. We cannot expect to find the carefully articulated thoughts of Augustine mirrored in her writings in any detail. Unmistakably present in her writings, however, is an awareness of the tradition of the prophetic vision, and she consciously identifies with this tradition by viewing herself as part of it and by using the conventions and traditions of thought which became attached to it.

Among the moderate number of biblical figures and saints that Mechthild invokes or mentions in the course of her book, the three most important for her,

---

[16] For Mechthild's dependence on theological traditions, see, for example, Margot Schmidt, "Elemente der Schau bei Mechthild von Magdeburg und Mechthild von Hackeborn. Zur Bedeutung der geistlichen Sinne," *Frauenmystik im Mittelalter*, ed. Peter Dinzelbacher and Dieter R. Bauer (Ostfildern b. Stuttgart, 1985), pp. 123–151.

when it is a question of visions or prophecy, are figures prominent in the Augustinian tradition: Paul, Moses, and Daniel. Five prophets, she tells us, illumine her book: Moses, David, Solomon, Jeremiah, and Daniel.[17] The affinity she feels for Daniel is based on the marvelous wisdom bestowed on him by God's grace while surrounded by enemies (DFL III, 20; N 100, 22–25). She draws upon Daniel again to respond to the question she puts in the mouth of "meister Heinrich." Where did the words she writes come from? Words, incidentally, which she considers woefully inadequate for describing "eternal truth." In responding she implies that the source of Daniel's wisdom is her source as well (DFL V, 12; N 166).

Also serving to corroborate her claims of special grace is Moses, who saw nothing but God (*do er niht wan got ansach.* DFL V, 12; N 166) Thus his prominence seems to rest for Mechthild in part on his having seen God and not something less. She chooses him as a force illumining her book, among other reasons, for the *minnereden* (loving conversations) that he had with God on the lofty mountain (*uf dem hohen berge.* DFL VI 20, 3–10; N 99). More frequent still are references to Paul and his mystical raptures which shall be treated in some detail below.

Striking, indeed, is the pre-eminent position that she accords John the Baptist, to whom she refers more frequently than any other saint except Mary. In her grand vision of heaven, he, along with all spiritual virgins, assumes the place vacated by Lucifer which is above the Seraphim (DFL III, 1; N 75). He is mentioned after Mary and before all other saints in a hierarchy of the virtuous we are asked to emulate (DFL III, 1; N 75) and appears along with her as the only other named saint on the most beautiful arch of the crown Christ is to wear in heaven (DFL VII, 1; N 254–255). One of Mechthild's most vivid visions centers on a mass she, as a poor waif (*arme dirne*), attends at which the Baptist is celebrant (DFL II, 4; N 41–44). When someone objects that as a layperson John could not celebrate mass, she lashes out fiercely that popes, bishops, and priests cannot preach the word as well as he if they do not have like spiritual faith (DFL VI, 36; N 245). The Baptist's lofty stature in her thinking might well be explained through her contact with and obvious admiration for Dominicans whose theological training would contain much of the Angelic Doctor's thought. We have noted how Thomas discusses John the Baptist's greatness vis-a-vis Moses as part of his treatment of visions and prophecy. Mechthild, too, stresses how John alone recognized the divinity in God's son (DFL VI, 36; N 245). Thus his greatness for her stems in great part from his spiritual vision and prophetic gifts.

When she touches upon the subject of visions, however, it is Paul and language assumed from him that we find Mechthild most frequently employing. In rapture

---

[17] References to Mechthild's work are taken from Mechthild von Magdeburg, *Das fließende Licht der Gottheit* (DFL) ed. Hans Neuman (N), Bd. 1, completed by Gisela Vollmann-Profe (Munich and Zurich: Artemis, 1990). Here: DFL III, 20 (Book III, chapter 20); N 100 (Neumann's edition, page 100).

she identifies with him and his ecstatic experience: "Paul, I have been wondrously transported with you (*Paule, ich bin wunderlich uf gezuket mit dir.* DFL II, 24; N 59). As important as Paul's rapture is for her as exemplary for herself and her experiences, greater still is the influence of his language, which might well be considered a co-determinant of her own. Because Paul's rapture, with Augustine's assistance, became the definitive visionary experience for medieval Christianity, Paul's language in describing it became the traditional means of describing all visions and lent a certain legitimacy to visionaries who adopted it. Mechthild was not slow to recognize and exploit this fact, and echoes of 2 Corinthians 12 can be frequently heard when she describes her raptures. Thus, for example, her body, too, loses all strength under the impact of God's greeting, as the soul separates from the body and becomes conscious only of its divinely invigorated self, leaving the body as in a sweet sleep.[18] Again with Paul's words clearly in mind, she describes her vision of Sister Hiltegunt as occurring in such a manner that she did not know whether heaven came to her or she to heaven (DFL II, 20; N 53). As we have seen, the soul's obliviousness of its physical surroundings, as mentioned by Paul, became a central issue for Augustine. When responding to the question how God receives her in her transports, she again answers with Paul: "The human eye has never seen it; the human ear has never heard it; the human mouth could never utter it."[19]

We have noted that Paul's description of the soul's relative independence from the body during transports is confirmed and intensified in the Book of Daniel and in Augustine's references to ecstatics who lie lifeless. In her vision of hell, the foul odor and unearthly heat Mechthild encounters produce similar effects. She can neither sit nor walk, and is bereft of her senses for three days, like one "whom thunder has struck" (DFL III, 21; N 102). By mentioning these effects of the vision on her, she again places herself squarely in the mainstream of the orthodox visionary tradition.

When we shift our attention from Mechthild's use of important figures and conventions to the concepts central to this tradition, the waters seem, at first glance, muddy indeed, and the fault lies not entirely with us. While *Das fließende Licht der Gottheit* bears witness to a literarily gifted author, conceptual clarity is not a hallmark of her work. For example, in the spirited defence of her vision of John the Baptist, when she responds to the charge that John, as a lay person, could not have celebrated mass, she stresses the impotence of "fleshly" eyes and ears to comprehend divine and spiritual truth (DFL II, 4; N 41–44). Certainly the point is well taken. However, how this refutes the objection that John, the lay person,

---

[18] "Der ware gottes gruos, . . . der hat so grosse kraft, das er dem lichamen benimet alle sin macht. . . . So scheidet dú sele von dem lichamen mit aller ir maht, wisheite, liebin und gerunge, sunder das minste teil irs lebendes belibet mit dem lichamen als in eime suessen schlaffe" (DFL I, 2; N 7).

[19] "Wie ich denne enpfangen werde, das gesach nie menschen oge, das gehort nie menschen ore, es mohte nie menschen munt gesprechen." DFL VII, 25; N 275. The reference is to 1 Cor. 2:9 with contamination from 2 Cor. 12:4.

could not celebrate mass remains a mystery. Likewise, in Chapter 3 of Book IV, which catches our attention most of all because of her depiction of a vision of a marvelous stone which declares itself to be Jesus, she wishes to distinguish for her audience three kinds of wisdom: clerical wisdom and Christian teaching (*pfeffelichú wisheit und christanlichú lere*), wisdom from the natural senses (*von naturlichen sinnen*) and wisdom from grace (*von gnaden*). Even the most positively disposed reader, in struggling to understand this distinction, has to admit that the three senses of wisdom remain elusive (DFL; N 114–117). In light of this, we should not be surprised to find that evidence of traditional thought regarding visions is certainly not overwhelming. Nonetheless, indications do exist that Mechthild was familiar with and touched by this thought.

Perhaps the most important question we can ask is whether it is possible to find in her writing something corresponding to Augustine's division of visions into corporeal, spiritual, and intellectual, since this mode of considering visions left such an indelible mark on his intellectual heirs. At first glance, our search for this distinction seems to bear fruit in Chapter 3 of Book VI (N 232–233) where Mechthild describes the three places where God speaks to the soul: in the senses, in the soul, and in heaven. God, the devil, and all creatures have access to the senses and enter as they please, but only God can enter the soul. When he does, it happens without the knowledge of the senses. When Mechthild mentions God's raising the soul to the third place – heaven, where it enjoys his marvels (*da ir sines wunders gelusten mus*), her description leaves one uncertain whether she is referring to an ecstatic state or to the reward of the blessed or to both. Despite some similarities, Mechthild's three places do not correspond to Augustine's distinction. It is especially the absence of any clear reference to that peculiarly Augustinian concept *visio spiritualis* that undermines any claim of correspondence.

An earlier passage in Book II yields evidence of a connection that is more convincing. Here, in a dialogue with Lady Knowledge, Lady Soul asserts that Paul would have never been raised to the third heaven and would have remained Saul if he had found truth in the first or second heaven. Lady Knowledge then explains the nature of the three heavens. In the first, made by the alluring but deceptive art of the devil, thoughts roam amid the troubled and deceived senses. Here the devil can appear as a respendent angel, or even as divine; but the soul does not find the natural object of her love.[20] The second heaven is made of the holy desires of the senses and the beginning of love. The soul lacks light to see God but senses a boundless sweetness. Because the soul is still joined to earthly senses, humility is necessary; otherwise, the devil will bring his light. What happens then is not from God.[21] Finally, in the third heaven, the soul receives the true light. It sees truly and

---

20 "Vrou sele, ein himmel ist, den het der túfel gemachet mit siner schoenen valschen list. Da wandelnt die gedenke inne mit trurigen sinnen und dú sele lit alstille, wan si vindet nit ir naturen minne. Da blibet dú sele ungetroest und betrúget die einvaltigen sinne" (DFL II, 19; N 51).

21 "In disem himmel ist enkein lieht, dú sele siht da gottes nit; mere si smekket ein

knows how God is all things in all things.[22] In this passage, despite the role attributed to the devil which Augustine might not allow, the correspondences of the three heavens to Auguntine's threefold distinction are striking. Especially the second heaven, with its mixture of corporeal senses and lofty spiritual desires exhibits slightly reworked aspects of Augustine's *visio spiritualis*.

The probability of a more immediate connection to the bishop of Hippo's *Literal Interpretation of Genesis* increases greatly when we examine a passage from this work which we have not yet considered. Toward the end of Chapter 12, as he is bringing his thoughts on Paul, his ecstatic vision, paradise, and the three heavens to a rhetorically fashioned conclusion, he himself connects his previously carefully articulated distinction (*corporalis*, *spiritualis*, and *intellectualis*) to Paul's mention of the three heavens. The first heaven is corporeal, containing all that is on the waters and the earth. The second is where one sees in spirit things that are like corporeal things. Finally, in the third heaven, the mind, purified and torn from the senses, sees things as they are in heaven, even the substance of God.[23] While discrepancies between the two authors' words and ideas make it unlikely that Mechthild's thought proceeds from an immediate study and assimilation of this passage from Augustine, the similarities are too pronounced to be fortuitous. However it may have happened, Augustine's interpretation of the three heavens found its way into Mechthild's writing.

Mechthild, like Augustine, is also aware of the proximity of visions and dreams. Especially toward the end of her life, after she had become part of the Helfta community and when her ability to transmute her spiritual life into poetry was definitely on the wane, the frequency of night visions with dreamlike characteristics increases.[24] Augustine, in discussing the similarities between visions and dreams, had maintained that it was often impossible to distinguish between them without divine assistance. And, indeed, one night as Mechthild received an infusion of divinely inspired knowledge and sweetness, this proximity of dream and vision

unbegrifliche suessekeit, die ir alle irú lider durgat. Si hoert ouch eine stimme von etlichen dingen, die si doch gerne wil, wan si ist noch gemenget mit irdenschen sinnen. Ist denne die tieffi aller diemuetekeit da nit, so bringet der túfel dar sin lieht; das denne da geschiht, das ist von gotte nit" (DFL II, 19; N 52).

22 "Ist aber die volle diemuetekeit da, so muos dú sele vúrbas varn in den dritten himmel, da wirt ir gegeben das ware lieht. . . . In disem lieht sihet si sich al umbe, wie der si, der sich iro wiset, und was das si, das man ir zú sprichet. So siht si werlich und bekennet, wie got ist allú ding in allen dingen" (DFL II, 19; N 52).

23 "Si ergo coelum primum recte accipimus hoc omne corporeum generali nomine quidquid est super aquas et terram; secundum auten, in similitudine corporali quod spiritu cernitur, sicut illud unde animalibus plenus in ecstasi Petro discus ille submissus est; tertium vero, quod mente conspicitur ita secreta et remota et omnino abrepta a sensibus carnis atque mundata, ut ea quae in illo coelo sunt, et ipsam Dei substantiam, Verbumque Deum per quod facta sunt omnia, in charitate Spiritus sancti ineffabiliter valeat videre et audire . . ." (Cap. 34, n. 67; PL 34, 483).

24 See, for example, the experiences described in DFL VII, 13, 14, and 53; N 267, 267–268, and 299–300.

becomes for her a source of doubt. The devil appears and insinuates that her experiences have been nothing but empty dreams. She successfully repels his insidious assault only to have him suggest thoughts of pride stemming from the privilege of divine favor she enjoys (DFL VII, 7; N 262–263). Her doubts about the validity of her experiences are just part of an encounter with the enemy of humankind, but they fit into the pattern of self-doubt that is a clear undercurrent in her last years. Thus, their relationship to Augustine's thought may be largely accidental, though the similarity clearly exists.

Finally, one might ask whether Mechthild at all tries to classify her visions according to the Augustinian way of evaluating them. Does she assign different values to different kinds of visions? And how would a knowledgeable contemporary react to the kinds of visions she claims to have had? Regarding this second question, we can respond that an informed reader of the time would have assumed from her writings that she had experienced both spiritual and intellectual visions, as Augustine understood these terms. The majority of her most vividly described visions – for example, those portraying heaven, hell, and purgatory, as well as those describing appearances of dead persons or important biblical figures, such as John the Baptist, Enoch, and Elias – certainly fall into that strange category of *spiritualis*, which describes the world of material images that are not directly dependent on material objects. Mechthild is often at her poetic best in depicting this kind of vision in great detail. However, if we are to believe her, not all her visions can be reduced to this category. Her occasional comments about the incapacity of language to describe her experiences and her aforementioned appropriation of Pauline phrases, if taken seriously and not simply as clichés, force the reader to place her among those who have been favored with the highest kind of vision – intellectual vision.

What about Mechthild herself? What value did she place upon her visions and upon herself as a visionary? She leaves little doubt that she considers her book to be extremely important. However, in her frequently expressed view, her book, and her visions as well, are God's doing, not hers. When one asks how visions should be viewed in the ultimate system of values, her response places her in the mainstream of traditional asceticsim: "One should do everything in equal measure to honor God. My most commonplace taking care of a natural need I would rank as high in God's sight as though I were in the highest state of contemplation that a person can attain."[25] Intention imparts value to an act. In achieving divine pleasure, the exalted visionary really has no advantage over the most ordinary of persons.

---

[25] "daz man allú ding glichlich gotte ze eren tuo, wan min snoedeste notdurft wil ich vor gotte also hohe reiten, als ob ich were in der hohesten *contemplacie*, da ein mensche in komen mag. Warumbe? Tuon ich es in einer liebin gotte ze eren, so ist es alles ein" (DFL I, 27; N 21).

# PRACTICES

# BEATRICE OF NAZARETH (c.1200–1268)
## A SEARCH FOR HER TRUE SPIRITUALITY

### RITAMARY BRADLEY

*Her Formation*

BEATRICE OF NAZARETH spent her childhood with her family in Tienen, not far from Brussels. Her mother died when Beatrice was seven. Her father and several of his children devoted their time and resources to the monastic life. Beatrice received her own initial formation among some beguines in the town of Zoutleeuw, where she also attended a coeducational school with a curriculum in Latin and the liberal arts. She continued her studies in the Cistercian monastery of Florival, and was received as a novice and subsequently professed there at the age of sixteen. Her abbess sent her to Rameya for a year to learn the art of manuscript writing. There she became attached in a bond of love to Ida of Nivelles, who was her spiritual mentor. This relationship developed into a deep and lasting friendship, which continued after Beatrice left Rameya. Ida's death in 1231 was the occasion for Beatrice to begin her memoirs, later expanded into an autobiography. She died at the age of sixty-eight, when she was prioress of Nazareth.[1]

Five to ten years after her death an anonymous monk wrote her *Vita.*[2] He claimed to have access to her diary, which has since disappeared.[3]

---

[1] See Martinus Cowley, *Lives of Ida of Nivelles, Lutgard and Alice the Leper* (Lafayette, Oregon: Guadalupe Translations, 1987) l; and Roger DeGanck, "Chronological Data in the Lives of Ida of Nivelles and Beatrice of Nazareth," *Ons geestelijk erf* 57 (1983): 14–29. I wish to acknowledge the help I received from Roger DeGanck, Frank Willaert, the Trappistines of Our Lady of the Mississippi Abbey, and several others in interpreting the texts. An earlier form of this study was given at the International Seminar on Thirteenth-Century Cistercian Nuns, New Melleray Abbey, Dubuque, Iowa, May, 1987.

[2] There are four extant Latin manuscripts of the *Vita*: Brussels, Koninklijke Bibliotheek, 4459–70, f. 66R–130V; and 1638–49. f. 317 R–367 R. Ghent, Universiteitsbibliotheek, 165. Vienna, Ostereichische Nationalbibliothek, Ser. nova, 12706–07, 2. TL f. 296R–335V [olim Fideicommiss-Bibliothek, 9363]. The critical Latin edition is by Leonce Reypens, *Vita Beatricis.* De autobiografie van de Z. Beatrijs van Tienen O. Cist. 1200–1268 (Antwerp: Uitgave Van Het Ruusbroec-Genootschap, 1964). A translation of the Latin life is by Roger DeGanck, *Beatrice of Nazareth.* A Thirteenth-century Biography (Kalamazoo, Mich: Cistercian Publications, 1991).

[3] "It is possible that, following the Latin version of her *Vita*, the original Flemish diary was

## Her Cultural and Spiritual Heritage

It seems likely that Beatrice separated herself from the excessive penitential mode common among thirteenth-century Cistercians. In many ways, however, she shows the influence of her times. She was writing at a period when the courtly love tradition was in vogue in society at large. Religious writers, however, did not necessarily adapt to the moral and romantic codes of that movement, but they did find it in the spirit of the times to write about love rather than about wars and military conquests. Hence, it was in harmony with the literary culture of the age to see Christ in his humanity as a loving person reflecting Trinitarian love rather than to imagine God as a king or head of armies.

St Bernard taught the first Cistercians that the feeling part of the soul is the deepest part and that faith, hope, and charity awaken the image of God within the soul. For Bernard's friend, William of St. Thierry, however, the affective part is not the core of the soul, but through the development of the affective part, the intellect comes to a deeper knowledge of God. The intellect remains itself, but is raised above itself by grace.[4] Cistercian women visionaries especially stressed that through wisdom, which is Christ, the Scriptures become food – a food which delights and nourishes.[5]

There is lack of agreement as to whether or not the spirituality of Cistercian nuns differs from that of the monks. Edmund Mikkers approaches this question by insisting that in defining spirituality one must consider the exterior life situations of the monasteries and also the theological assumptions. There is some reliable source material now being explored for the study of the external monastic conditions. Mikkers sums up the doctrinal part of Cistercian spirituality briefly: (1) it held a realistic, and at the same time, optimistic view of human nature: the human soul, even though wounded, remains open to God, capable of a desire for God, and with the help of grace can return to God by conversion, for the image of God is never lost; and (2) the way back to God is Christ through imitation of his life and sufferings and sharing in his resurrection. In Christ one reaches God through the Holy Spirit, experiencing joy, jubilation, peace and tranquility of spirit. A major source of this doctrinal stance was the Rule of St Benedict and the *Consuetudines*, the first and fullest commentary on the Rule.[6]

Though the first generation of Cistercians transmitted the spirituality of St

discretely (sic) destroyed, since it may have contained theological speculations regarding the Trinity which were considered dangerously close to pantheistic heretical thinking." Jerome Kroll and Roger De Ganck, "The Adolescence of a thirteenth-century visionary nun," *Psychological Medicine* 16 (1986): 746.

4　See Andrew Louth, "William of St. Thierry and Cistercian Spirituality," *Downside Review* (Oct., 1984): 262–263.

5　See Caroline Bynum, *Holy Feast and Holy Fast* The Religious Significance of Food to Medieval Women (Berkeley: University of California Press, 1987).

6　"Spirituality of Cistercians – A Methodological Approach." Typescript.

Bernard to monasteries of nuns, this golden age of spiritual theology lasted no longer than a century, from about 1150–1250. In 1244 the abbot of Clairvaux (Stephen of Lexington) founded a theological college in Paris, where the most gifted Cistercian students were then sent to study scholastic theology. In monasteries of men this decision dealt the death blow to monastic theology, but it survived among the nuns, nourishing their spirituality with its central emphasis on scriptural exegesis.[7] Hence there would have arisen during Beatrice's lifetime a basic difference between men and women in their theological orientation.

The chaplains serving the women's houses influenced the nuns through confessions, spiritual direction, and preaching. But the biographies of the nuns, when written by the chaplains, have little value as sources of feminine spirituality. This is because the purpose of these treatises was to present – not the facts of a particular life – but a pattern of Cistercian ideals. This pattern included a high regard for severe penitential practices. It is always doubtful if the biographies correspond to the reality of feminine monastic life. The biographer-clerics seem often to have been "handlers" who put their own "spin" on whatever events underlay their subject matter. Fortunately in the case of Beatrice there exists a substantial text which she herself composed: *The Seven Experiences of Loving.* [8]

## The Central Theme of her Spirituality

*The Way of Desire:* Beatrice's spirituality, as revealed in the text of *The Seven Experiences of Loving,* is one of holy desire, pursued faithfully throughout her life. She traces the path of this desire for God as it works to remove obstacles to love, motivates her service of love, shapes her experience of love in this life, and culminates in hope for the enjoyment or fruition of love in eternity. Two Scriptural texts give the context for this desire: the text in Matt. 25:20–21, in which the faithful servant who used well his five talents hears a summons into the joy of the Lord; and the text from Phil. 1:23: "I long to depart this life and be with Christ." Beatrice is able to say in summary in harmony with these two Scriptural passages: "This is truly love's work, to desire what is supremely best, and to pursue that state in which it can love the most." (*The Seventh Experience*).

7  Paul Verdeyen, "Cisterciens," in "Pays-Bas," *Dictionnaire de Spiritualité* 12, Part I, col. 713–716.

8  Quotations from Beatrice's text are from *Beatrijs van Nazareth. Van Seuen Manieren van Heileger Minnen.* Vitgegeven naar het Brusselse handschrift. Ingeleid en van aantekeningen voorzien door, ed. H. W. J, Vekenman and J. J. Th. M. Tersteeg. Klasiek Letterkundig Pantheon 188 (Zutphen: Thieme et Cie, 1971). (With the assistance of various translations in English and French). Three manuscripts of the *Seuen Manieren* are extant: Brussels, Koninklijke Bibliotheek, 3067–73, f. 25R–40V; the Hague, Koninklijke, 70 E 5, f. 190Va–197Rb; and Vienna, Osterreichische Nationalbibliothek, 15258, f.252R–271V.
For a comprehensive bibliography of Beatrice, see Frank Willaert, *Bibliographie zur deutschen Frauenmystik des Mittelalters,* von Gertrud Jaron Lewis et al (Berlin: Erich Schmidt, 1989) 325–350.

*The Seven Experiences* is an exposition of how this holy desire is directed, how it grows, and how it is rewarded. *The First Experience* is "an active longing which proceeds from love." This form of desire serves to remove obstacles to love and leads towards that "purity, liberty, and nobility" in which the soul came forth from the Creator, formed according to his image and likeness. The soul "desires to lead its whole life so as to work, grow, and ascend" to greater knowledge and love of God. The soul checks on "what is lacking to its desire" so that in fidelity "it can serve love with a free conscience, a pure spirit, and a clear intelligence."

In *The Second Experience* desire is described as an aspiring to perform faithfully every service for the honor of love, without seeking for any other satisfaction or reward. The soul at this time is "ardent in desire," and "with its whole being it desires to serve the Lord." In *The Third Experience* the soul suffers from its lack of love and its inability to perform every service. Seemingly the soul thinks of the Scriptural text, "in my flesh I am filling up what is lacking in the afflictions of Christ on behalf of his body, which is the church." (Col. 1:24). But the soul knows that this "filling up what is lacking" is beyond human capacity. "With full will and strong desire" the soul is unable to supply what is deficient in its own works. Such knowledge, though, does not dampen its desire, which it cannot satisfy, and it continues to "desire and to sigh for love," and does what it can.

*The Fourth Experience* of loving is a turning point. Here the "active longing" and self-scrutiny give way to a spontaneous awakening of love in the soul. Immersed and absorbed in the abyss of love, the soul feels drawn towards love "with great desire." In *The Fifth Experience* a new kind of spontaneous activity is manifested: love rises in the soul like a storm, which leads it at one time to the exercise of love, at another into feeling overwhelmed by love, and at still another into a desire to rest in the experience of possessing and being embraced by love. The soul's heart and sense strongly incline towards this condition of supremely "desirable happiness." Here activity and rest inter-penetrate each other: While being universally operative and active in both exterior and interior business the soul is still mindful of what is in its heart and may even be outwardly at rest. Not satisfied with this renewal of its own powers the soul is impatient in its desire for love. Love grows, not as enjoyment, but as suffering, in a form reminiscent of the sufferings of the crucified Christ, including the very withering of marrow, the opening of veins, and the drying of the throat from thirst. A new desire arises: to break the bond of suffering, without rending the unity of love, which is so far above comprehension that the soul can receive no enjoyment from it. As these divine gifts are given to it "with increase of desire," the soul is "drawn to approach closer to the light of truth, and to purity, nobility, and the enjoyment of love." The desire which tears the soul apart knows no satiety, but healing is in the wound itself.

In *The Sixth Experience* the soul receives some of the rewards and fruits of its lifetime of holy desires: it experiences the cessation of competing desires, and now begins to know "freedom of conscience, sweetness of heart, keenness of the senses, nobility of soul, loftiness of mind, and the beginning of eternal life." But Beatrice cautions that those who desire to attain this state must do so with fear, remaining faithful, and exercising love "with longing" – with desire. Only then will love reign within them, bringing that peace where all desires are in proper order. Then God and the soul act in concert, like a bird flying with its own energy and gliding and also by the upholding of the element in which it moves.

Lastly, in *The Seventh Experience* the soul is lifted up "by vehement desire," experienced even in the senses. Now the soul could not cease to love even if it tried: it must "necessarily desire" love intensely. The soul is drawn by these desires into "the deep abyss of the Divinity, which is wholly present in all things and remains incomprehensibly above all things . . . immutable perfect being, all-powerful, all-intelligent, almightily operating." The soul seeks its Beloved, knows him, loves him "and so desires him" that it cannot attend to anything else: with its whole being it desires to see, possess, and enjoy him. Moved by a desire to transcend its own nature, the soul is led into the company of the blessed seraphs. Then with the apostle Paul the soul is filled with vehement desires and is grievously impatient to be free and "to live with Christ." She exclaims: "O holy desire of love, how strong is your power in a loving soul." In heaven the soul will be "made one spirit with Christ in inseparable faithfulness and eternal love." In its desire to see, possess, and enjoy God, the soul chooses the Divine One both above, and also in, everything that exists. It is at this point that Beatrice can say – for this is truly love's work: "to *desire* what is supremely best, and to pursue the state in which it can love the most." In the end the soul will be received with love by its Beloved, in that home to which it has directed all its desire during this time of exile.

Such is the pattern of Beatrice's seven experiences of love, all of which are forms of desire. She is thus clearly situated in the spiritual tradition which described the Christian life in terms of desire.[9] Desire is the matrix of the monastic teaching of Gregory the Great, and of those who drew on his teaching throughout the Middle Ages. Jean LeClercq summarizes Gregory's doctrine of desire as it is set forth in the *Moralia*:

> St. Gregory is the doctor of desire; he constantly uses terms like *anheleare, aspirare, suspirare*, which express a tendency towards transcendence, "sublimation" . . . desire for God is ardent, it is also patient . . . The importance given to desire confers on St. Gregory's doctrine an extremely dynamic quality. It is concerned with constant progress, for desire, as it becomes more intense, is rewarded by a certain possession of God, which increases it still more. The result of this desire is peace rediscovered in God, since desire is itself a possession in which fear and love are reconciled. In the desire which, here below, is the very shape of love, the Christian finds God's joy, and union with the glorified Lord . . . the soul becomes fruitful in the service of God.[10]

9 See "DIEU (DÉSIR DE)," in "Connaissance mystique et désir de Dieu," *Dictionnaire de Spiritualité* t. 111, col. 929.

10 *The Love of Learning and the Desire for God.* Trans. Catharine Misrahi (New York: New American Library of World Literature, 1962) 39–40.

Beatrice has conveyed this traditional doctrine of desire in such a way as to suggest a lived experience. Absent are the conflicts so often expressed in monastic literature between action and contemplation, between acquiring virtue and living solely by love. Beatrice does not dwell on temptations, nor on the dangers of pride, nor on the practice of penance.[11] Desire for God is truly and comprehensively the matrix which leads to her growth in love and union with Christ. All other means to transformation are integrated into this constant impulse of the whole person – body, mind, and spirit.

Beatrice's spirituality is further marked by a pattern of flux and reflux, and of cyclical growth. Such a pattern occurred in some of her antecedents, especially in Gregory of Nyssa (c.330–95). The ascent of the soul, according to Gregory, is not by distinct stages, but rather by growth cycles in each of which there is always both an active and contemplative dimension. His fundamental conception of the mystic way is "progressive transformation into Christ."[12] Gregory's mystical writings exhibit an "insistence theologically on the paradoxical character of contemplative union: he defines it as an ecstatic going out of oneself in quest of the Divine, which is at the same time a penetration into the inmost regions of the soul where the image of God is implanted."[13] This theory is especially manifest in Gregory's *Commentary on the Song of Songs*, a work which "had a profound though indirect influence on medieval spirituality, since it was a major source for St Bernard's widely popular sermons on the text."[14]

## Contrasts between the Vita and the Vernacular Text

The preceding analysis of Beatrice's spirituality, however, is based solely on a study of *The Seven Experiences of Loving*, a vernacular text which is the work of Beatrice herself. A different picture emerges if one uses as documentation the Latin *Vita*.[15]

Frank Willaert summarizes the spirituality implicit in the Latin *Vita*, linking it with what is ascribed to other female mystics of the thirteenth century:

> As with so many other female mystics in the thirteenth century, Beatrice's spiritual life was characterized by a stern ascesis, by the imitation of Christ, a

11 In the *Vita*, however, her biographer attributes such themes to her in detail.
12 Rosemary Ann Lees, *The Negative Language of the Dionysian School of Mystical Theology. An Approach to the Cloud of Unknowing* (Salzburg: Institut für Anglistik und Amerikanistik, 1983) I:58.
13 Lees 86.
14 Lees 104, note 15.
15 Frank Willaert, "Beatrijz von Nazareth," typescript. See also H. Vekeman, "Vita Beatricis en Seuen Manieren Van Minne," *Ons Geestelijk Erf* 46 (1972): 3–54. Despite the difference of literary form between the *Vita* and the *Seven Experiences* Vekeman believes that there is a unity between the two works, though the latter is distinctive in its use of the *minne* as a key word.

strong devotion to the Eucharist and ecstatic phenomena like the gift of tears, irrepressible laughter and visions.[16]

The *Vita* also contains reports of striking experiences, thoughts, and complex meditation schemes.

But we must approach with extreme caution the text of the *Vita* and not accept uncritically the portrait of Beatrice which it conveys. Medieval writers of saints lives, as we know, were not striving to be faithful to historical fact but were trying to create a narrative which would lead readers to admire and imitate the holy person. They generally drew on a body of accounts of miracles, divine interventions, and even language which served their didactic purposes. The *Vita*, it seems to me, is in many respects such a piece of hagiography.

The author of the *Vita* writes in convoluted sentences, marked by rhetorical verbosity.[17] He may have believed that the differences between the two perspectives were due to the differences in the Latin language and the vernacular.[18] But in fact over the years Beatrice had arrived at a new synthesis of her spiritual life under the unity of the *minne*, a synthesis achieved some time after coming to Nazareth.[19]

What the *Vita* author may have done to the now-lost autobiography of Beatrice can be inferred from a comparison of her own work, *The Seven Experiences of Loving*, with the passage which corresponds with it in the biography, in Book three, chapter 14, entitled "The Love of God and its Seven Degrees." The author seems to have superimposed on the text a medieval anti-feminist stereotype of woman, albeit the holy woman. Medieval writers frequently assumed that the fullness of human nature existed only in the male. For example, John Ruusbroec, (1293-1381), writing in the next century, sets forth this view in the Prologue to *The Spiritual Espousals*:

> "See, the bridegroom is coming. Go out to meet him" (Mt.5:6) . . . The Bridegroom is Christ, human nature is the bride, whom God . . . placed in Paradise. But then came an evil doer . . . who deceived the woman. They both deceived the man, in whom human nature existed in its entirety[20]

Other components of the medieval stereotype of the woman are well known: the woman was regarded as weak in reason and overpowering in passion; the holy woman was seen as given to excessive outward expressions of her devotion, which

16 Willaert, typescript.
17 DeGanck, *Life of Beatrice of Nazareth*, xxv.
18 ". . . I am only the translator of this work. Of my own I have added or changed little; rather I have only given a latin coloring to the vernacular words as they were given to me in diary-notes." *Vita* Prologue, in *The Life of Beatrice of Nazareth*, p. 4. He also claims in the Prologue to be: "Weaving my writing in a simple way for the sake of simple people" (p. 3).
19 H. Vekeman, "Vita Beatricis en Seuen Manieren Van Minne," *Ons Geestelijk Erf* 46 (1972): 3-54.
20 "Prologue," *The Spiritual Espousals in John Ruusbroec* trans. James A. Wiseman. Classics of Western Spirituality (New York: Paulist Press, 1985) 41.

was related to the supposed carnality of her nature. These views were reflected in the biographies of women, and, as Carolyn Bynum notes:

> Male biographers romanticized and sentimentalized female virtue far more than male, especially by describing it (as does James de Vitry . . . [in a passage quoted in her text]) in heightened and erotic imagery.[21]

It is therefore important to study the writings of the women themselves when such texts exist. In the case of Beatrice we have the advantage also of a specific text by a woman retold and revised by her male biographer. I will show briefly, with only a few examples, how the passage in the *Vita*[22] differs significantly from the corresponding text as written by Beatrice.

First, however, we may note that some English translations of *The Seven Experiences of Loving* , when based on the Latin text supplied by Leonce Reypens, have followed him also in omitting two short passages from what Beatrice wrote.[23]

The first passage affected is in *The Fourth Experience*, which reads in part: "In this the soul feels a great closeness to God, a substantial clarity, a wonderful delight, a noble liberty and a ravishing sweetness." The omitted lines add: "and a great impulse of a stronger love and an abundant fullness of greater delight." Since through the word "impulse" the passage focuses again on desire, it is a loss to overlook these additional lines.

In *The Sixth Experience* the omission may be more significant since it does not merely intensify the total sense of the section but adds a new thought. The passage begins: "Sometimes it also happens that love is vehemently stirred up in the soul, and it rises like a storm with a great uproar and a great frenzy, as though it would draw the soul outside itself into the exercise of love and into the exhaustion of love." The omitted lines add: "And strongly is the soul also pulled into the longing of love to accomplish the great and pure deeds of love."

These added words signify that the soul is not simply passively submitting to the motions of love but is being awakened in all her powers to carry out and express that love in charity towards the neighbor. Again Beatrice's contemplative experience bridges the sense of God's powerful presence and the living of that experience in a concrete way.

The *Vita* biographer, however, made much more radical changes in Beatrice's writings than simple omissions of the type we find in these modern instances.

---

21 Caroline Walker Bynum, *Holy Feast and Holy Fast: The Religious Significance of Food to Medieval Women* (Berkeley: University of California Press, 1987) 29.

22 *The Life of Beatrice of Nazareth*, Bk. 3, chap. 14, pp. 288–331.

23 For example, Sister Josepha Carton, "The Seven Steps of Love by Beatrice of Nazareth," *Cistercian Studies* 15 (1984): 31–42; and Edmund Colledge, *Medieval Netherlands Religious Literature* (London, Leyden, New York: House and Maxwell, 1965) 19–29. The lines are included, however, in a French translation by Dom J. Kressemakers, who used the Louvain, 1926, critical edition of the *Vita*, as edited by L. Reypens and J. van Mierlo. See "Beatrix de Nazareth (1205–1268)," *La Vie Spirituelle* Supplement 19 (1929): 320–332.

DeGanck speculates that in one instance the biographer modified Beatrice's text because he found the original words "too strong" for the "simpleminded to whose comprehension he adapted her *Vita*." [24]

Furthermore, the overall tone, mentality, and spirituality of the *Vita* adaptation differs basically from Beatrice's *Seven Experiences*. For the biographer life is a journey, marked off by conventional stages of progress and differing speeds of walking or flying. At the end of the journey is the actual presence of God, known in this life dimly as in a mirror.

For Beatrice the pattern of life is that of flux and reflux, similar to – though this is not her specific image – the tides of the sea. The yearning search for God is broken into two phases: that of striving with deliberate intention to serve God and that of an awakening of a powerful, once-dormant love within the soul. This second phase is the awakening of the Christ-life which becomes the directive force within her, without destroying the freedom of her internal and external powers. The fruition of this love is joy in the heavenly homeland.

The *Vita* amplifies the journey metaphor by bringing in the familiar concept of the two feet: the foot of cognition and the foot of the will[25] This imagery embodies a dualism of reason and will, while for Beatrice the sole fountain of all cognition, desire, and activity is love, and all her powers are integrated. Love is a teacher, love is the teaching, and those who are taught are learning love: "Love teaches such activity to those who cultivate love."

Again, in the *Vita* the contemplative experience is presented as passive: "mercy poured into the Beloved's heart as into a most pure vessel a certain nectar-like taste of love without any additional effort of body and spirit." For Beatrice the experience is one of awakening, of a mutual indwelling of God and the soul: the soul is simultaneously in God – "the abyss of love" – and God is in the soul, which is like "a full vessel."

Along the same lines the *Vita* author speaks of love as if it disorients and disables the woman: "The fifth experience was a certain madness of holy desire and love . . . rioting so strongly within her that, raving like some roaring, untamed beast, it struck the whole framework of her body and acted like a madman within the house of her heart as if it wished to break out and seize with violence that which it so much desired."

---

24 "Beatrice in her sixth *maniere* stresses love's totality, exclusive of all that is not included within it: 'then Love makes the soul so bold and free that in all its actions and omissions, in its work and rest, it fears neither men nor demon, neither angels nor saints, nor God himself.'. . . Beatrice's biographer, who read her treatise with his own thought patterns, found these words about not fearing God too strong, at least for the simpleminded to whose comprehension he adapted her *Vita*. He, therefore, wrote in his Latin translation of the sixth *maniere* that 'she feared neither man nor demon or the angelic nor even the divine judgment.'" *Towards Unification with God*, 459–60.

25 For an overview of this metaphor see Vincent Gillespie, "Mystic's Foot: Rolle and Affectivity," *The Medieval Mystical Tradition in England*, ed. Marion Glasscoe (Exeter: Univ. of Exeter, 1982) 199–230.

In Beatrice's words, however, love is not a strong, destructive beast; rather, love is stirred up in the soul like "a storm with a great uproar and a great frenzy." This force[26] is not destructive but creative: "and strongly is the soul also pulled into the longing of love to accomplish the great and pure deeds of love." The image implied here may well be that of a storm at sea which would incite a besieged sailor to act with irrational risk, courage, and loving concern.

Elsewhere Beatrice implies too that love unleashes a spontaneous power of action. Love does not act upon the soul, as a scalpel on flesh, but is operative within it: She is not wax imprinted passively with the divine image, but she is like a fish or a bird: "Like a fish swimming in the broad river, and like a bird flying boldly in the vastness and height of the sky, so does the soul feel its spirit moving freely in the breadth and vastness and height of love." A fish or a bird moves by a power from within, alternated with a restful gliding through the vastness that is God.

It is in passages such as these that we observe the *Vita* author overlaying the life of Beatrice with stereotypes of the woman: unable to exert self-control, centered in her emotions rather than in her deeds, beset by illness and physical weakness, primarily either exerting herself immoderately in ascetical exercises, or passively receiving the actions of God. Her self-image and the restrained account of her actual experience is quite different from the hagiographer's portrait, which may have been shaped to teach ascetical practices and humility to an audience of nuns who did not know Beatrice herself.

These are only samples of the contrasts between the two texts. But these contrasts are basic enough to justify some scepticism concerning the biographies about holy women for which there is no reliable documentation to substantiate or correct what the hagiographer says. With regard to Beatrice the only fully reliable source indicating what her spirituality was like is in her own text of *The Seven Experiences of Loving*. The *Vita*, then, remains a source for determining the character and mentality of its author and perhaps of its original audience. It should not be relied upon for an understanding of Beatrice's mature spirituality, or her own perspective on her entire life.

## IMAGERY IN BEATRICE

It is futile, though, at this point to pursue further contrasts between these two texts since they come from different thought-patterns and differing purposes. Let us instead look intensively at some aspects of Beatrice's own text, dealing with it as a poem, which uses language evocatively and with multiple meanings. In such a poetic text the meaning of a word often evolves, and this evolution resolves a conflict posed in the experience of the poet.

[26] It is called "orewoet" by both Beatrice and Hadweych (Roger DeGanck). Vekeman and Tersteeg translate "orewoet" as "razenmij"-madness. But the context suggests impetuousness, spontaneity, and escape from the restrictions of reason under the impulse of love.

## *Variations on Fear*

First, let us look at the specific references to fear. This word is selected because God as Wisdom is an important help to understanding Beatrice's much-studied word, *minne*, and fear is the source of wisdom as a human quality. In Beatrice's text the concept of fear moves from denoting a rival of love to embodying the fullness of perfection. The word is especially significant since it is used in connection with one of the few Scriptural quotations in the poem and with the only direct patristic allusion – to St Augustine.

Fear is first mentioned in association with the desire of the soul to "serve love with a free conscience, a pure spirit and clear intelligence," "without impediment from its past misdeeds." Fear, she says, could not be a source of this holy desire. Fear, rather, "makes one work and suffer, act and desist from acting" and hence does not inspire free, spontaneous activity. This false fear leads the soul to see God as one easily angered and presenting himself as a "just judge." This judge, before whom no one is perfect, is then imagined as ready to inflict punishment – either eternal or in the form of afflictions in this life.

We must keep this passage and its context in mind in order to understand a later statement, where Beatrice says that love makes the soul so bold and free that it fears no one – not even God himself." (*The Sixth Experience*). The soul does not fear God in the sense that it does not see him as an exacting giver of rules and laws, one easily excited to wrath, confronting the cowering penitent as a judge, issuing decrees of eternal punishment and eternal pain. Rather, one sees God as love and knows that love does not consist in "pain and sorrow." But while saying that the one who loves God need not fear him as a judge, she speaks in paradox in affirming that it must nevertheless be "with fear" that we seek God – that is, we must fear ourselves. And such fear-free loving, far from eliminating suffering, brings about great labors and many pains, the bearing of trouble and experiencing of contempt. (*The Sixth Experience*).

> [The soul] well knows and feels that love does not consist in labor and sorrow in those in whom it reigns. But all who desire to attain love must seek it with fear, and follow it faithfully and exercise it with longing, and this they cannot do if they spare themselves in great labors, and many pains, in bearing trouble and in suffering contempt.

Such a passage as this, too, indicates that Beatrice's experiences of love are interwoven with the events of her own life – with separations, misunderstandings, human conflicts and the like. Ecstacies and states of union do not seem to be something separate from what happens to the holy woman on the strictly human plane.

In a further development of the motif of fear she says that the soul will not be dominated by fear of these inevitable sufferings which follow upon yearning for love and seeing God as love. Even the longing to be dissolved and to be with Christ is not rooted "in fear of future troubles." Yet such troubles will continue to come in the form of "a blessed martyrdom, a sharp torment, a long-drawn-out evil, a murderous death, a dying life." These are powerful words descriptive of life's most severe vicissitudes.

Yet the soul will indeed fear. (*The Seventh Experience*). She will follow "in fear and in cares" the paths which Love teaches her to travel.

In the final paradox, the soul "will not fear" – but this is only when it has entered "into the joy of the Lord." The Scriptural text cited is Matthew 25:21, the parable of the talents: the story of the servant who, unlike the one who merely hid the Master's money, worked zealously to multiply it. The additional reference is to St Augustine, who says in a sermon drawing on this very text:

> When it is said, "Henceforth I call you not servants," He is to be understood as speaking of that servant who abideth not in the house forever, but is characterized by the fear which love casteth out [1 John 4:18]; whereas, when it is here said, "The servant is not greater than his lord: if they have persecuted me, they will also persecute you," that servant is meant who is distinguished by the clean [pure] fear which endureth forever [Ps. 19.9.]. For this is the servant who is yet to hear, "Well done, good servant: enter thou into the joy of thy Lord" [Matt. 25:21].[27]

*Relation to Suffering:* Fear does not extend to suffering, for Beatrice says specifically in *The Third Experience* that the soul is "unafraid in labor and sorrow." Though fostered in an environment which put great stock in self-imposed penance, Beatrice does not fasten on voluntary suffering as a way to improve the divine image in the mirror of the soul. Her most vivid descriptions of suffering evoke the sufferings of Christ on the Cross, indicating the deep reality of her union with God (*The Fifth Experience*). Such suffering is welcomed, for, as she says in *The Second Experience*, the soul delights in finding "something to do or to suffer for the service and the honor of love." In *The Third Experience* the soul knows that "the filling up of the measure" [of the sufferings of Christ] surpasses all human strength.

It is implied that this suffering is for others because of the soul's union with Christ. And there are two intercessory prayers specifically for others. In *The Sixth Experience* Beatrice asks that God in his goodness will grant that all may attain "freedom of conscience, sweetness of heart, loftiness of mind, and the beginning of eternal life." And in *The Seventh Experience* she prays that God will lead us all to that eternal glory "where the only activity will be praising and loving."

But fear in this treatise does not take the shape of facing the darkness, or

---

[27] *On the Gospel of St John*, Tractate 88.1, *Nicene and Post-Nicene Fathers* 7, ed. Philip Schaff (New York: Charles Scribner's Sons, 1908) 356. See also in the same volume Tractate 85.3: "In some wonderful but indescribable way, we may as servants have the power not to be servants; servants, indeed, with that clean fear which distinguishes the servant that enter into the joy of his lord, but not servants with the fear that has to be cast out, and which marketh him that abideth not in the house forever" (p. 352).

specifically the dark night, as described by many mystics, at least in the sense of a dread of non-being or annihilation. Rather, there is deep pain before the avalanche of being: Love is the only force that enables her to stand up to it, to withstand its abundance, to grow large enough to receive it.

## The Servant Image

Next it is appropriate to look at Beatrice's references to the servant, references inter-related with what she says about fear. There is repeated mention of serving in the text: in *The First Experience*, the soul desires "to serve Our Lord faithfully"; and in *The Second Experience*, "it sets itself the task to serve our Lord freely out of love alone." This state of growing freedom is carefully delineated: "To her, it is enough that she serve him and the Lord allows her to serve him lovingly, without measure . . . faithfully performing every service." The soul then "becomes so ready to serve" it is pleasant for it to find something to do or to suffer for the service of love. In this phase of relationship to God the soul is like a "noble maiden," eager to serve without measure.

In *The Third Experience* of loving the concept of serving is transformed into a desire "to yield to love in all service and all obedience and all loving submission." "In this state the soul is very ready for every service." But still unsatisfied the soul conceives an impossible desire: that it alone "could serve . . . love in accordance with Love's dignity." Frustrated, it simply "does what it can."

Then with *The Fourth Experience* there is a more distinct change: the anguish at being unable to serve adequately disappears. There is no longer any striving to serve and perfect her service: love acts within her, in joy and sorrow. The soul has become a friend, lover, bride. From here on the soul moves swiftly towards the end where she will enter into the joy of the Lord (*The Seventh Experience*). Only one further mention of serving occurs, and that indicates that none of life was lost nor none goes without its reward. These two phases of life are drawn together into one: the soul "will gaze with eagerness upon what it has so tenderly loved, and it will possess for its own blessedness him whom it has so faithfully served, and it will with full delight have fruition of him whom it has often embraced in the soul with love." Thus seems to be realized the scriptural promise of Christ to his disciples, "I no longer call you slaves . . . I have called you friends" (John 15:13–15). Out of the one source and energy, love, has come first service and then identification in love. The reward is also love, for love is its own reward.

Herein, it appears, we find the basic structure of Beatrice's text. She introduces love as the source of all. This love first begets a life of service, with the soul growing more and more disassociated from that role. Then the soul is given a new form of love: love lives within it. Lastly love is the reward, both of the first phase of faithful service, and of the second phase of a life lived wholly from the impulse of love.

In this second phase it is clear that the soul identifies with Christ, and that Christ lives his own life, including his sufferings, within her. This closeness to Christ is embodied no longer in the figure of the noble handmaid, but in the image of the housewife (*The Sixth Experience*). This figure, it is important to note, is associated with "a certain divine power and wisdom," and the soul is likened to a housewife in that she orders her house – the house of her own interior – "wisely." The soul "has become love, and love within it rules strongly and powerfully."

This conflation of the images of servant, of handmaid, of housewife, of loving spouse, along with the figure of Wisdom, also occurs explicitly in Augustine. He, like Beatrice, as in this passage from his commentary on the Psalms, also refers to Christ as the Power and the Wisdom of God, making clear that the imagery is respectively masculine and feminine, that the person relating to God is corporate and ecclesial more than individual, and that fear no longer rules:

> "Behold, even as the eyes of servants look unto the hand of their masters, and as the eyes of a maiden unto the hand of her mistress: even so our eyes wait upon the Lord our God". . . . We are both servants, and a handmaiden: He is both our Master and our Mistress . . ." . . . for He is the Power and the Wisdom of God . . . [When] thou hearest the Power of God and the Wisdom of God, lift up thine eyes to the hands of thy Mistress; for thou art both servant and handmaiden; servant, for thou art a people; handmaiden, for thou art the Church. But this maiden hath found great dignity with God; she hath been made a wife. . . . As there is no one else who can be preferred to Christ, let her love without apprehension.[28]

In harmony with this commentary from Augustine is his further explication of the words of Jesus at the Last Supper: "Henceforth I call you not servants but friends. For the servant knows not what the Lord does."[29] Augustine's sense of the biblical meaning of servant is an appropriate sub-text for interpreting Beatrice's imagery on the same theme.

*The Figure of Wisdom*: In evoking her experience of God Beatrice also uses the figure of Wisdom, a concept Augustine associates with the servant reference in the commentary on the Psalms cited above. Wisdom, a feminine power in the Hebrew scriptures, is made manifest in Christ in the New Testament.

The image of God reflected in the mirror of the soul – purity, liberty, and nobility in Beatrice's text – is likewise among the marks of the Wisdom figure in the Scriptures: First, she is pure: "Wisdom pervades all things by reason of her purity"; "Naught that is sullied enters into her" (Wisdom 7:25). "She is the spotless mirror of the might of God" (Wisdom 7:26). She is also free: "an initiate into the mysteries of God's knowledge, *making choice* of the works he is to do" (Wisdom 8:4–5). And she is noble: "Her closeness to God lends luster to her *noble* birth." (Wisdom 8:3). Her role overall is to live with the servants of God, to guide them on the way, and to lead them to their reward: "She entered into the soul of

---

[28] Augustine, "On the Psalms," Psalm 123.4, *Nicene and Post-Nicene Fathers* 8:597.
[29] "On the Gospel of John," Tractate 85, chapter 15, 14–15, *Nicene and Post-Nicene Fathers*, ed. Philip Schaff (New York: Charles Scribner's Sons, 1908) 7: 351–352. Tractate 88, chapter 15: 20–21, 7:356.

the Lord's servant . . . she gave the holy ones the recompense of their labors, conducted them by a wondrous road." (Wisdom 10:16–17). These are concepts permeating the text of the Seven Experiences."[30]

*Minne.* The concept of Wisdom is also an important component in the meaning of *minne* as used by Beatrice. This difficult word, with its overtones from many forms of love, has been widely explored by scholars but without definitive conclusions. A study group, engaged for over a year in studying the term *minne*, specifically in Beatrice, concluded that "she projects in the word the totality of her experience of divine love . . . expresses the existential value of love of God . . . makes us understand this love in its reality."[31] *Minne* interlocks with the desire for God, for "The longing for the likeness of God becomes a longing for *minne* . . . *Minne* is discovered to be the cause of the desire [for God] and the final aim of it."[32] Over a decade later Roger DeGanck after surveying studies on *Minne* summarizes his insights concerning the concept thus: "Though God is *Minne* and Christ is *Minne*, *Minne* itself is neither God nor Christ. . . . [Beatrice] felt that she herself had become *minne*, as she wrote in her fourth *manière*: 'The soul feels . . . that its will has become *minne* . . . that it [the soul] has wholly become *minne*.' "[33] "To encompass the manifold aspects of God, his love for himself, for his creation, and for Beatrice in particular, and the equally manifold aspects of her reciprocal love for God, his creation, and herself, she personalized *minne*, in the sense that *minne* represents a syntactical, not autonomous, personal entity. . . . With her whole being Beatrice responded affectively and effectively to *Minne*."[34] DeGanck notes carefully that Beatrice's biographer, in the Latin *Vita*, renders *minne* sometimes by *dilectio*, sometimes by *amor*, and at other times by *caritas*, "a carelessness which indicates that he did not fully understand what Beatrice meant by *minne*."[35]

What remains to be stressed is the association which Beatrice makes between love, including *minne*, with wisdom. The Sacred Text offers a precedent for such a linking, by conflating wisdom with love for a spouse and for a divine teacher:

> I sought to take her for my bride/ and was enamored of her beauty./ She adds to nobility the splendor of/ companionship with God./ Even the Lord of all loved her./ For she is instructress in the understanding of God.
>
> (Wisdom 8:2–4).

---

30 See entry on "Sophia" in *Encyclopedia of Religion*, ed. M. Eliade (New York: Macmillan, 1986) vol. 13; and on "Wisdom" in volume 15.

31 See *Beatrijs van Nazareth. Van Seuen Manieren Van Heileger Minne* H. W. J. Vekeman and Th. M. Tersteeg, Thieme et Cie (Zutphen, 1971).

32 H. Vekeman, *Citeaux* 4 (1968) p. 316. He says further: "Feelings and desires become signs and signals of the divine world, inviting man to reach the plenitude of love by the recovery of His image and likeness." Summary of study group on *minne*.

33 *Towards Unification with God*, 469–70.

34 *Towards Unification with God*, 470.

35 *Towards Unification with God*, 454.

*Vox Mystica*

In Beatrice's text there is also such a conflation of the theme of Wisdom with the metaphor of the spouse and bride. And though the author of the *Vita* frames his treatise in the metaphor of the bride, with verses from the *Song of Songs*, in Beatrice's own text the bridal/spousal metaphor is subordinate to the Wisdom motif. This point can be established by an examination of the metaphor of the bride.

*Bridal/spousal Image:* When medieval hagiography superimposed the female stereotype on the life history of a holy woman, the bridal/spousal metaphor was pervasive. Even when the woman mystic did not especially stress this image, her works were often classified as if she did.[36] It is often assumed that the woman sees her soul in relation to the male Christ, considered as her bridegroom, superior to an earthly husband. But since this metaphor was a widely-used convention, it is important to find out to what degree the woman herself saw Christ from such a perspective. We must treat the occurrence of the metaphor with that same critical judgment which comes into play when the biographer tells us his subject died at the age of thirty-three, in order to suggest to us through metaphor that the person ended life in union with Christ.

Central to the bridal metaphor, of course, is the influence of commentaries through the ages on the *Song of Songs*. Yet from the time of Origen writers cautioned against taking the bridal and spousal metaphors literally. Origen, for example, warns:

> ... you must not understand ... the Word of God in a corporeal sense, simply because He is called the Bridegroom, which is an epithet of male significance. Nor must you take the Bride's embraces in that way, simply because the word "bride" is of feminine gender.[37]

From the beginning commentators noted, as does Origen, that the church as a corporate personality is the bride.[38] And when the individual speaks of himself as bride, the implied relationship is with the church.

---

[36] See, for example, the discussion of Beatrice and Hadewych in "Contemplation, VI, Au xiiie Siècle, 2. Le thème nuptial de mystique du nord," cols. 1972–1973; "*Dictionnaire de Spiritualité*, 2, cols. 1972–3; and also, in tome 3, "Dieu (Connaissance mystique, Hadewych)," cols. 893–894; and "Beatrice de Nazareth," cols. 894–895. Of Beatrice it is said: "Le caractère nuptial y est plus prononcé que chez Hadewijch, mais moindre que chez saint Bernard, dont l'influence est moins apparente que celle de Richard de Saint Victor."

[37] Origen, *The Song of Songs Commentary and Homilies*, trans. R. P. Lawson, Ancient Christian Writers 26 (New York: Newman Press, 1956) 200–201. Note also: ". . . although the 'Word' of God is of the masculine gender in Greek, and neuter with ourselves [from Rufinus, the translator], yet all these matters with which this passage deals must be thought of in a manner that transcends masculine and neuter and feminine, and everything to which these words refer. And this applies not only to the 'Word' of God, but also to His Church and to the perfect soul, who likewise is here called 'the Bride.' For thus says the Apostle: '*For in Christ there is neither male nor female, but we are all one in Him.*' "

[38] "For the *mulieres religiosae*, as for their mentors, the incarnation of Christ meant his whole human existence on earth and even his glorified humanity, which, although glorified, remains humanity. . . . Both aspects of Christ are considered when Christ – 'the lover of

72

In Beatrice's text the bridal and spousal metaphors are less explicit than they are in the writings of her male predecessors, for example in those of Gregory of Nyssa. In Gregory the bride searches for her Beloved in the angelic world, coming to the insight that God transcends all and cannot be apprehended:

> Hence she [the Bride] gets up again and in spirit traverses the entire spiritual and transcendental world, which she here calls a "city". . . . In her search she surveys the entire angelic army. And not finding among the good things there the object of her quest, she reasons thus with herself: Is it possible that my Beloved can be comprehended? "Have you seen him whom my soul loveth?". . . by their silence they show that what she seeks is incomprehensible to them.[39]

Beatrice, in a more restrained passage, says that the soul enjoys the "sweet society of the heavenly spirits," because they, too, "overflow with superabundant love" and they are "in clear knowledge, possession and fruition of their Love" (*The Seventh Experience*).

She reflects in conceptual terms on God's transcendence and immanence: the Divinity is "incomprehensibly above all things" and also "totally present in all things." Her union with God is fully Trinitarian as well as Incarnational: God is "all powerful, all intelligent, all mightily operating," and the response of the soul is a desire "to be dissolved and to be with Christ." It is in such a context that she speaks of the soul being united "to its Bridegroom." There is no specifically feminine feeling involved but simply the enjoyment of the Divine Lover in bonds of devotion, fidelity, and fruition.

The only other explicit spousal reference is in the introduction to *The Sixth Experience*, where she refers to the soul simply as "the Lord's bride." Far from being passive in this section, the bride grows in freedom and in a spontaneous power of action felt from within: love is a source of action and great works.

In fact, the motif of the bride in Beatrice's text is less individual than it is ecclesial, based on the gender-free reality that each individual soul baptized into Christ's body is the whole church while remaining uniquely personal. Andrew Louth's description of the "mutual co-inherence of the mystical and the ecclesiological" seems to describe well what Beatrice intends:

men,' it should not be forgotten – is seen as the bridegroom of the Church, his mystical Body, and of the individual soul." Roger DeGanck, *Beatrice of Nazareth in Her Context*, Cistercian Studies Series, 121 (Kalamazoo, Mich.: Cistercian Publications, 1991) 232.

See *Canticle of Canticle* I.2–4 and Origen's commentary on this passage: "Let us see if the inner meaning also can be fittingly supplied along these lines. Let it be the Church who longs for union with Christ; but the Church, you must observe, is the whole assembly of the saints. So it must be the Church as a corporate personality. . . . The kisses are Christ's, which he bestowed on His Church . . . ." pp. 59–60.

[39] Lees 17.

The mutual co-inherence of the mystical and the ecclesiological is, indeed, a striking feature of many of the Fathers, though it is a pervasive colouring rather than a specific theme. We noted this with Origen for whom the *Song of Songs* is the song of the soul united with God, but also the song of the Church. ... We have seen this co-inherence in Denys the Areopagite in our attempt to correlate his mystical theology and his doctrine of the hierarchies. It is, however, perhaps most developed in Gregory of Nyssa. In his two principal treatises on the mystical life we have what seems at first sight to be a single figure ascending to God – Moses, in *The Life of Moses*, and the bride, in the *Commentary on the Song of Songs*. But, if we look more carefully, we see that Moses is not solitary, he is ascending the mount on behalf of the people of God, and indeed in Gregory's *Life* is always surrounded by his people. Nor is the bride alone in her search for the Beloved, but accompanied by a band of maidens.[40]

There seems to be in Beatrice, too, this "colouring" which renders the bridal metaphor ecclesial as well as personal. What she says of suffering, for example, and her two short intercessory prayers near the end of the treatise indicate that she is not only concerned with herself but with the Body of Christ and hence with the people of God.

## CONCLUSION

Beatrice's highly-condensed text, then, differs radically from the more diffuse *Vita*. Her imagery is not specifically feminine, as this term is defined in the stereotypes of women mystics. Rather it is closely linked with the classical approaches of the Fathers, such as Gregory the Great in the doctrine of desire and in broad ways with Gregory of Nyssa and Augustine. Her use of *minne* is not alone a sign of her passionate experience but is merged with the multiple meanings of Wisdom in both testaments. Her "seven experiences of loving" are not distinct stages in the spiritual life but experiences of growth cycles, peaking with a more spontaneous love, which is rooted in identification with Christ. These marks point to the originality of Beatrice's approach, along with its integration with the mysticism of the past.

[40] Andrew Louth, *The Origins of the Christian Mystical Tradition. From Plato to Denys* (Oxford: Clarendon Press, 1981) 201.

# ST AUGUSTINE'S *JUBILUS* AND RICHARD ROLLE'S *CANOR*

### ROBERT BOENIG

WHAT WE MEAN BY the word *music*, living in this post-Brahmsian, post-Cagian, post-Elvisian world, is not quite what those others, those medieval women and men, meant. For us it refers primarily to an aural experience, mediated by human voices and human hands, however filtered through electronics and compressed into the CD. Even those among us who have written Ph.D. dissertations on, say, twentieth-century serial or atonal music would, I wager, still describe what they analyze as primarily sounds – however abstract and theoretical their analyses might be. Until the high Middle Ages, however, music theory had surprisingly little to do with musical sounds, for the study of music, epitomized by the basic text, Boethius's *De Musica*,[1] was primarily concerned with mathematical relationships as a means of decoding the order of the cosmos. Music – at least as it was presented in books and taught as part of the university quadrivium – turned its scornful back on the church singers and especially the secular minstrels who produced pleasing sounds.[2] A musician was a philosopher who did not listen to music, or at least

---

[1] For a translation of Boethius, see Calvin M. Bower, trans., and Claude V. Palisca, ed., *Anicius Manlius Severinus Boethius: Fundamentals of Music* (New Haven: Yale University Press, 1989). For an assessment of Boethius as music theorist, see Henry Chadwick, *Boethius: The Consolations of Music, Logic, Theology, and Philosophy* (Oxford: Clarendon Press, 1981), pp. 78–101. See also Calvin M. Bower, "The Role of Boethius' *De institutione musica* in the Speculative Tradition of Western Musical Thought," pp. 157–74 in Michael Masi, ed., *Boethius and the Liberal Arts: A Collection of Essays* (Bern: Peter Lang, 1981); and Alison White, "Boethius in the Medieval Quadrivium," pp. 162–205 in Margaret Gibson, ed., *Boethius: His Life, Thought and Influence* (Oxford: Blackwell, 1981).

[2] In Book I of his *De Musica*, for instance, Boethius writes, "We propose . . . that we should not grant all judgment to the senses – although the whole origin of this discipline [i.e., music] is taken from the sense of hearing, for if nothing were heard, no argument whatsoever concerning pitches would exist. Yet the sense of hearing holds the origin in a particular way, and, as it were, serves as an exhortation; the ultimate perfection and the faculty of recognition consists of reason, which, holding itself to fixed rules, does not falter by any error. . . . Although basic elements of almost every discipline – and of life itself – are introduced through the impression of the senses, nevertheless there is no certain judgment, or comprehension of truth, in these if the arbitration of reason is lacking." See Bower, *Fundamentals*, pp. 16–17.

would not admit it if he did.[3] "Can a minstrel be saved?" asked Honorius Augusto-dunensis in a treatise whose intent was to weigh carefully the pros and cons of the various professions from the point of view of the spiritual health of their followers. "No" is the simple, brutal, one-word answer.[4]

In the high Middle Ages music treatises did turn to more practical matters. The mathematics were still there, as were references to cosmology, usually taken from Boethius, but the emphasis was more on defining chant and the Church modes and the placement of the semitones within the hexachoard.[5] The aesthetics of music was a topic rarely pursued, and the treatises dealt almost entirely with singing within the Church, only occasionally mentioning musical instruments.[6]

St Augustine, whose Manichean ideas about life's other pleasures – especially those attending sex – hover ghostlike over much of Western culture, set the terms for this ascetic rejection of music by musicians. The interplay of his ideas about music with those of the fourteenth-century English mystic Richard Rolle indicates some important things about both the centrality of music to Rolle's mystical agenda and also the emergence of *practical* as opposed to *philosophical* music among the theorists of the early fourteenth century – his exact contemporaries.

---

3 Boethius puts the matter bluntly: "Now one should bear in mind that every art and also every discipline considers reason inherently more honorable than a skill which is practiced by the hand and the labor of an artisan. For it is much better and nobler to know about what someone else fashions than to execute that about which someone else knows.... How much nobler, then, is the study of music as a rational discipline than as composition and performance! It is as much nobler as the mind is superior to the body; for devoid of reason, one remains in servitude.... Just how great the splendor and merit of reason are can be perceived from the fact that those people – the so-called men of physical skill – take their names not from a discipline, but rather from instruments; for instance the kitharist is named after the kithara [i.e., cithara], the aulete after the aulos, and the others after the names of their instruments. But a musician is one who has gained knowledge of making music by weighing with the reason, not through the servitude of work, but through the sovereignty of speculation." See Bowers, *Fundamentals*, pp. 50–51.

4 Quoted in Christopher Page, *The Owl and the Nightingale: Musical Life and Ideas in France, 1100–1300* (Berkeley: University of California Press, 1989), p. 8.

5 For the standard treatment of chant, see Willi Apel, *Gregorian Chant* (Bloomington: Indiana University Press, 1958). For standard textbook treatments of chant, see Richard H. Hoppin, *Medieval Music* (New York: Norton, 1978), pp. 57–187; David Fenwick Wilson, *Music of the Middle Ages: Style and Structure* (New York: Macmillan, 1990), pp. 37–96; and Giulio Cattin, *Music of the Middle Ages I* (Cambridge: Cambridge University Press, 1984). For the technical aspects of the placement of the semitone, see Dolores Pesce, *The Affinities and Medieval Transposition* (Bloomington: Indiana University Press, 1987).

6 An interesting example is the anonymous *Summa Musicae* of circa 1200. It is a practical manual for singers, whose concluding chapter rehashes Boethius's cosmological distinction between *musica mundana* and *musica humana* and in its course covers the modes and affinities. The instruments fall into the corner of Chapter 4, "Concerning the division of music into 'natural', 'instrumental,' 'celestial' and 'human' " – indication that the author's interest is more in Boethian cosmology than in the sounds the instruments themselves make. See Christopher Page, ed. and trans., *Summa Musice: A Thirteenth-Century Manual for Singers* (Cambridge: Cambridge University Press, 1991).

St Augustine's attitudes towards music change over the course of his life[7] in a way even more complicated than those about sex. As is generally known, he rejected sex with his conversion to Christianity in his early thirties. He had previously lived with a woman to whom he was not married, but as a good Manichee who preferred spirit to matter, and was thus unwilling to beget material children, he habitually interrupted his sexual intercourse with her before conception could take place. As a new Christian he wrote his treatise *On Virginity* valorizing total sexual abstinence as the preferred state for spiritual growth. In one sense his musical life closely parallels his sex life: as an unconverted student of rhetoric, he went to the theaters, delighted in the music, especially the sounds of the harp (or *cithara* as it was termed in Latin), responding to its sounds, as he admits, libidonously. As Bishop of Hippo he condemns music, especially that of the *cithara*, as morally dangerous. Can a minstrel be saved, writes Honorius. The answer is an Augustinian "No."

But in between these two musical Augustines, one young and the other old, stands a middle-aged man who sought for a while to baptize music for Christian uses. There is no equivalent Augustine for sexual matters, and his loss is grievous. The maturity of this musical Augustine's attitudes is impressive, and what he says is important for the history of mysticism. This man is also the forefather of Rolle. For him music provides direct mystical access to God; had the later Augustine not condemned practical music so roundly, pre-fourteenth-century music theory might not have taken such a philosophical detour. The attitudes of these three Augustines need some explication.

In his *City of God* (II:4), Augustine looks back to his wanton youth and describes the power of music to lead him both to lustful desires and to pagan religion:

> I myself, when I was a young man, used sometimes to go to the sacrilegious entertainments and spectacles; I saw the priests raving in religious excitement, and heard the choristers; I took pleasure in the shameful games which were celebrated in honor of gods and goddesses, of the virgin Coelestis, and Bere-cynthia, the mother of all the gods. And in the holy day consecrated to her purification, there were sung before her such productions so obscene and filthy for the ear . . . that not even the mother of the foul-mouthed players them-selves could have found [themselves] one of the audience.[8]

In Book III of the *Confessions*, he relates his sinful joy in going to the theater and uses a musical metaphor to describe the temptations besetting him: "To Carthage I came, where there sang all around me in my ears a cauldron of unholy lies."[9]

---

[7] See Herbert M. Schueller, *The Idea of Music* (Kalamazoo, Michigan: Medieval Institute Publications, 1988), pp. 239, 252.

[8] Marcus Dods, trans., *The City of God by Saint Augustine* (New York: Modern Library, 1950), p. 43.

[9] Edward Pusey, trans., *The Confessions of Saint Augustine* (New York: Washington Square Press, 1962), p. 30.

As an early convert, though, he cannot shed a certain psychological tendency of music to move him towards love – now the love of God, perhaps, but still love:

> How did I weep in your hymns and canticles, touched to the quick by the voices of your sweetly-attuned church! The voices flowed into my ears, and the truth distilled into my heart, whence the affections of my devotion overflowed and tears ran down, and happy was I therein.[10]

But the old Augustine, recounting the experiences of the young, is uneasy about them. As he states in Book 10 of the *Confessions*:

> However, when I recall the tears which I shed at the song of the Church in the first days of my recovered faith, and even now as I am moved not by the song but by the things which are sung, when sung with fluent voice and music that is most appropriate, I acknowledge again the great benefit of this practice. Thus I vacillate between the peril of pleasure and the value of the experience, and I am led more – while advocating no irrevocable position – to endorse the custom of singing in church so that by the pleasure of hearing the weaker soul might be elevated to an attitude of devotion. Yet when it happens to me that the song moves me more than the thing which is sung, I confess that I have sinned blamefully and then prefer not to hear the singer.[11]

Not quite St Bernard, who railed against what he perceived as the ornamental excesses of Gothic architecture, not quite Oliver Cromwell, whose Roundhead followers went about the countryside of seventeenth-century England breaking stained glass windows, Augustine is here profoundly ambivalent about the aesthetics of music.

This ambivalence pushed him in later life into what we might term with some accuracy a puritanical attitude towards music. He counsels Christians to avoid the theater and revels, where music is used licentiously[12] – this is what, perhaps, we may expect. But he also sought to de-aestheticize, if you will, music within a church context. In his *Confessions*, he writes:

> And safer to me seems what I remember was often told me concerning Athanasius, bishop of Alexandria, who required the reader of the psalm to perform it with so little inflection of voice that it was closer to speaking than to singing.[13]

Before Augustine rose to what we may alternately term the mystical heights of abandoning all sensual pleasure for the Word of God or the philistine low point of

---

10 *Confessions*, p. 158, slightly modernized. Compare James McKinnon, *Music in Early Christian Literature* (Cambridge: Cambridge University Press, 1987), p. 154.
11 Quoted in McKinnon, *Music in Early Christian Literature*, p. 155.
12 Schueller, *Idea*, p. 255. See *City of God* II, chapters 20 and 25. See also his *Sermons* 9.4.5 and 198.1 and *Retractions* 1.3.2.
13 *Confessions* 10:33, quoted in McKinnon, p. 155.

the ex-Manichee who would deny pleasures to others, he sought to redeem music for use in the Church. He did this in two ways, one cosmological, philosophical, and mathematical, one affective, even mystical.

In his commentaries on the Psalms he, of course, ran into the obstacle of musical instruments. The Psalter, as we all know, commends the playing of musical instruments for the worship of God. With echoes of the licentious cithara of his theatergoing, pubescent past in his ears, Augustine cosmologized them, particularly the psaltery, whose example may serve us here. He treats this instrument, which of course gave its name to the Psalter, well, preferring it to the cithara.[14] The psaltery, strung in Old Testament times with ten strings, becomes a cosmological metaphor for the moral universe. The strings are stretched over the sound board like the sinews of Christ's body on the Cross. They are the Ten Commandments, which may be divided into three for the Trinity and seven for humanity in that we are composed of the four elements together with heart, soul, and mind. Music, with its attendant mathematics, becomes, in other words, a method of creating analogies which explain the cosmos. How the sound of a psaltery delights is far from Augustine's ear and mind, but he is not ready to abandon or, worse, condemn the instrument as a demonic force leading to lechery and damnation. He has not yet, in other words, heard of the use to which Chaucer's Handy Nicholas puts his psaltery in the Miller's Tale.

Augustine stands behind the greatest of all cosmological interpretations of the psaltery, of course, one closer to Rolle's time and one usually interpreted as "mystical." Joachim of Fiore, the twelfth-century abbot famous for his interpretations of the Apocalypse, which the fourteenth-century Franciscan Spirituals read as prophecies of their own advent as heralds of the end of time,[15] took Augustine's psaltery for the title of one of his prophetic descants, the *Psalterium decem chordarum*[16] (*Ten-Stringed Psaltery*). In this characteristically prophetic work, Joachim envisions the Trinity as a psaltery, whose basically triangular shape lends itself readily to this interpretation. God the Father is at the top, God the Son at lower left, and God the Holy Spirit at lower right. The lines stretching from the Father to the other persons of the Trinity are the psaltery's pegs, to which the strings are attached. The ten pegs to the left joining the Father and the Son represent humanity and the nine orders of angels. The ten pegs to the right, between the Father and Holy Spirit, represent

---

14 For Augustine's extended treatments of cithara and psaltery, see his *In psalmum* 32:2 and *In psalmum* 56:16 (PL 36, 279–80 and 671). See also Schueller, *Idea*, pp. 253–54.

15 For the influence of Joachim on the Franciscan Spirituals, see Bernard McGinn, *Visions of the End: Apocalyptic Traditions in the Middle Ages* (New York: Columbia University Press, 1979), pp. 158–167.

16 Joachim of Fiore, *Psalterium decem chordarum* (Venice: Bindoni and Pasyni, 1527, rpt. Frankfurt: Minerva, 1964). For explications of Joachim, see Henry Bett, *Joachim of Flora* (Merrick, New York: Richvoid Publishing, 1976); Bernard McGinn, *The Calabrian Abbot: Joachim of Fiore in the History of Western Thought* (New York: Macmillan, 1985); and Delno C. West, *Joachim of Fiore in Christian Thought: Essays on the Influence of the Calabrian Prophet*, 2 vols. (New York: Burt Franklin, 1975).

the theological virtues – faith, hope, charity, and the rest. The psaltery in the hands of Joachim of Fiore and his interpreters is, in other words, Augustinian in his cosmological mode; it is an image of the moral universe.

This cosmological Augustine, of course, wrote a long if fragmentary treatise, *De musica*,[17] about that art's place in the educational curriculum. In his treatise Augustine writes his famous dictum, a cliché for the rest of the Middle Ages: *musica est bene modulandi scientia* – "music is the art of measuring." The treatise is actually more about poetry than music, and that I suggest is a significant fact. He defines the various types of poetic feet and talks about numbers as a structuring principle of the cosmos. Music for the now-Christian but still pre-puritan Augustine, is primarily a method for measuring time. *De musica* is in fact an important preliminary treatment of time leading up to the magisterial definition of it in *The City of God*. God's creation of time orders the universe as the flow of rhythm and meter structures a musical composition.[18]

This middle Augustine, cosmological and mathematical as he may have been, had not yet lost his sense of affective music. In two passages from his writings on the Psalms he eloquently describes the power of music to move the worshipper to mystical heights when she or he sings the wordless part of the liturgy known as the *jubilus*:

> . . . this is to sing well to God, to sing in jubilation. What is it to sing in jubilation? To be unable to understand, to express in words, what is sung in the heart. For they who sing, either in the harvest, in the vineyard, or in some other arduous occupation, after beginning to manifest their gladness in the words of songs, are filled with such joy that they cannot express it in words, and turn from the syllables of words and proceed to the sound of jubilation. The *jubilus* is something which signifies that the heart labors with what it cannot utter. And whom does jubilation befit but the ineffable God? For he is ineffable whom you cannot speak. And if you cannot speak him, yet ought not to be silent, what remains but that you jubilate, so that the heart rejoices without words, and the great expanse of joy has not the limits of syllables.[19]

Notable here are Augustine's rejection of words in favor of wordless music, particularly in view of the old Augustine's preference for "that which is sung" – i.e., the words, over the "song" and his recommendation of a type of singing that is more like speaking – doubtless the more to highlight the meaning of the words. Notable also here is Augustine's likening the singing of the *jubilus* in church to secular music done outside of it – not perhaps that of the licentious theater, but at least the

---

17 See Robert Catesby Taliaferro, trans., *St. Augustine: On Music, Books I–VI* (Annapolis: St John's, 1939).

18 For a discussion of *De Musica*, see Schueller, *Idea*, pp. 241–50; and R. O'Connell, *Art and the Christian Intelligence in St Augustine* (Cambridge, Massachusetts: Harvard University Press, 1978), pp. 178–88.

19 *In psalmum* 32:II, *PL* 36, col. 283; translated in McKinnon, *Music in Early Christian Literature*, p. 155.

singing that graces the workplace. For this Augustine pure music, not necessarily only that employed for religious purposes, has the capability of moving the singer's affections.

The second passage is even more significant from a mystical and affective point of view:

> One who jubilates does not speak words, but it is rather a sort of sound of joy without words, since it is the voice of a soul poured out in joy and expressing, as best it can, the feeling, though not grasping the sense. A man delighting in his joy, from some words which cannot be spoken or understood, bursts forth in a certain voice of exultation without words, so that it seems he does indeed rejoice with his own voice, but as if, because filled with too much joy, he cannot explain in words what it is in which he delights. You observe this even in those who sing improperly. Now our jubilation will not be such as theirs, for we ought to jubilate in justification, while they jubilate in iniquity; we, then, in confession, they in confusion. Yet that you might understand what I say, call to mind what you well know, that it is especially those who perform some task in the fields who jubilate. Mowers and vintagers and those who gather other products, happy in the abundance of harvest and gladdened by the very richness and fecundity of the earth, sing in joy. And between the songs which they express in words, they insert certain sounds without words in the elevation of an exultant spirit, and this is called jubilation.[20]

Again we see the emphasis on the pure music of the workers and on wordlessness. But even more important is the mystical spontaneity, in which the worshipper loses control in jubilation – she/he "bursts forth" in song. Given what we have already seen as the new convert Augustine's tendency to burst into tears at the singing of hymns in church, we are not too far from the mark in assuming that there is something autobiographical about these passages. Perhaps music played as large a role as St Ambrose in Augustine's conversion. But he learned to suppress this joy in pure music as he got older. Was it loss or was it gain?

Richard Rolle seems never to have lost this joy in music. I suggest that he learned much from this affective Augustine while his later critics, Walter Hilton and the author of *The Cloud of Unknowing*, preferred the older Augustine. The terms of debate, in other words, between three of the major fourteenth-century English mystics were set long before that century, back almost a thousand years before as that learned clerk Austin moved along his own time line towards his own apocalypse. When Hilton and the *Cloud*-author criticize Rolle, they do so in Augustinian terms; what they perhaps fail to realize is that what they criticize is also Augustinian.

Like Augustine, Rolle also wrote commentaries on the Psalms, and like the

---

[20] *In psalmum* 99:4; *PL* 37, col 1272; quoted in McKinnon, *Music in Early Christian Literature*, p. 158.

Church Father and many others, he too was attracted to the cosmological significance of the psaltery. His English gloss on Psalm 56:8 reads:

> *Exurge gloria mea, exurge psalterium et cythara. Exurgam diluculo.* "Rise my ioy,
> rise psauteri and harp. I sal rise in þe dawynge." þat es, Jhesu þat is my ioy,
> make me to rise in ioy of þe songe of þi lovynge, in mirthe of þi lufynge, and
> þat it so be, "rise psauteri," þat es, gladnes of thoght in lyf of contemplacioun,
> and "þe harp," þat es, purgynge of alle vices with tholemodenes in angwys, and
> so "I sal rise in þe dawynge," þat es, in þe general resurreccioun with ioy.[21]

Here the psaltery is again associated with things specifically celestial, not terrestrial.
Contemplation is, of course, the sole activity of the seraphim who circle God's
throne. In his comment on Psalm 150, Rolle also associates the psaltery with
heavenly worship:

> *Laudate eum in sono tubae, laudate eum in psalterio et cithara.* "Praise him in
> the sound of the trumpet, praise him on the psaltery and harp." "Praise him in
> the sound of the trumpet," that is, for the highest brilliance of praise which is
> in you. "Praise him on the psaltery," that is, for all the things of heaven. And
> "on the harp," that is, for all things on earth; it was he who made heaven and
> earth. *Laudate eum in tympano et choro, laudate eum in cordis et organo.* "Praise
> him on the tabor, and the crowd, praise him on strings and organs." "Praise
> him on the tabor," that is, on flesh changed to immortality and incapacity for
> suffering, for the tabor is made of dried skin. "And on the crowd," that is, in
> peaceful companionship and unison of voices. "Praise him on the strings," that
> is, on flesh freed from all corruption, for by strings he refers to all musical
> instruments which sound with strings. To the strings he adds "organs," which
> are manufactured like a tower, with different pipes, in such a way that each
> does not give sound by itself, but they all sound together in most harmonious
> diversity, as happens in organs. Therefore, holy men must attend in harmony,
> not discord. Harmony, as with different voices, not discordant [with each
> other], is a sweet song.[22]

Following Augustine, he associates the cithara or harp with earthly things and the
psaltery with celestial. The references to the other musical instruments align Rolle
with Augustine and Joachim for the cosmological use he makes of them. But in a
departure from the two earlier commentators, he remembers their mystical affect as
well: "Harmony . . . is a sweet song."

This emphasis on the sweetness of music brings us close to he very center of
Rolle's thought. In the Prologue to his English Psalter, he transforms Augustine's

---

[21] Hope Emily Allen, ed., *English Writings of Richard Rolle, Hermit of Hampole* (Oxford:
Clarendon Press, 1931), p. 15.
[22] Rosamund S. Allen, ed. and trans., *Richard Rolle: The English Writings* (New York: Paulist
Press, 1988), p. 84.

psaltery with his mathematical analogy between its ten strings and the Ten Commandments into something affective:

> A great fullness of spiritual comfort and joy in God comes into the hearts of those who recite or devoutly intone the psalms as an act of praise to Jesus Christ. They drop sweetness in men's souls and pour delight into their thoughts and kindle their wills with the fire of love, making them hot and burning within, and beautiful and lovely in Christ's eyes. And those who persevere in their devotion he raises up to the life of meditation and, on many occasions, he exalts them to the melody and celebrations of heaven. . . . This book is called The Psalter, a name which it takes from a musical instrument known in Hebrew as *nablum*, the Greek form is *psaltery* . . . and this consists of ten strings, and gives out sound from the upper part when it is touched by hand. In the same way, this book gives instruction on keeping the Ten Commandments. . . .[23]

Again, Rolle accepts Augustine's cosmological and tropological psaltery, but he places the fingers on its strings and insists on the sweetness of heavenly melody.

This passage, as many, many others in Rolle's *oeuvre*, presents his three themes of heat, sweetness, and song – or *calor, dulcor,* and *canor* – which for him define the affective power of mysticism. The pervasiveness of these affective themes has driven one very distinguished historian of medieval mysticism and religion, Dom David Knowles,[24] to drive him out of the canon of true mystics under the assumption that true mysticism of necessity rejects affective sensations in favor of the *via negativa* charted by Pseudo-Dionysius, Meister Eckhart, *The Cloud of Unknowing,* and John of the Cross. This of course is a definition matter little to our point. More to the point is Nicholas Watson's[25] recent extraction of *canor* from the other two as the structuring element in Rolle's mystical career.

Regardless of such privileging or de-privileging of *canor*, Rolle treats music as something literal rather than metaphorical, something affective rather than philosophical. One other passage among many will serve to set the terms of Rolle's *canor* and enable us both to see what so upset Hilton and the *Cloud*-author and to understand what it shares with Augustine's *jubilus*. In a famous passage from his *Form of Living*, Rolle defines the three degrees of love and invests the highest with *calor, dulcor,* and *canor*:

> . . . in this degree the sweetness of him [Jesus] is so invigorating and enduring, his love so burning and cheering that he or she who is in this degree can as easily feel the fire of love burning in [the] soul as you can feel your finger burn if you put it in the fire. . . . Then the song of praising and of love has arrived. Then your thought turns into song and into harmony. Then you feel

---

23 Allen, *Richard Rolle*, pp. 66–67.
24 David Knowles, *The English Mystical Tradition* (New York: Harper, 1961), chapter 4.
25 See Nicholas Watson, *Richard Rolle and the Invention of Authority* (Cambridge: Cambridge University Press, 1991).

compelled to sing the psalms which previously you recited; then you have to spend a long time over just a few psalms. Then death will seem to you sweeter than honey. . . .[26]

Notice here the dispersal of all three of the themes – heat, sweetness, and song. Rolle insists on a literal interpretation of sorts: the soul's heat burns one as a finger is burnt in a fire. Notice also the inversion of Augustine's own experience of music. Where Augustine felt the joy of the *jubilus* as a young convert moved to tears, and then late in life preferred his psalms recited in a manner more like speaking than singing, Rolle will have the mystic sing the psalms when previously they were merely spoken. If the late Augustine felt the pleasures of music distracted the worshipper from the meaning of the words, Rolle seems to imply the opposite – mere recitation is no affective means of experiencing the joys of heaven.

Rolle continues his definition of *canor* in the same chapter of *The Form of Living* in similar reverse-Augustinian terms:

> . . . no one possesses [this song] without being in this third degree of love, to which it is impossible to attain except in a great surge of love . . . it comes from heaven and God gives it to whichever person he wishes to, but not without great prevenient grace. Whoever has it finds all the vocal talent and all the musicianship on earth nothing more than wailing and whining by comparison.[27]

Where Augustine moved from earthly music of the theater to a surge of emotion in singing hymns to spoken words without music, Rolle moves towards that surge of emotion as the highest state of love.

There was, as the modern media might have put it, a conservative backlash to Rolle's affective mysticism. Walter Hilton, for instance, asserts with some slight indication of a stamp of the foot: ". . . the fire of love is not in the body, for it is only in the spiritual desire of the soul . . . but some are simple, supposing that because it is called fire it should be hot like material fire, and therefore I say what I have said."[28] The author of *The Cloud of Unknowing* agrees: "But the consolations, sounds, gladness and sweetness which come suddenly from outside . . . I beseech you to hold all these suspect."[29]

Now this disagreement, which has been usually depicted as an intramural tiff among three of the five major Middle English mystics, is, I suggest, more than that, for it has a social context that historians of mysticism have not yet explicated. The fourteenth century marks a movement of music away from the mathematical and into the affective that in some ways mirrors Rolle's movement away from

---

26 Allen, *Richard Rolle*, p. 171.
27 Allen, *Richard Rolle*, p. 172.
28 John P. H. Clark and Rosemary Dorward, trans., *Walter Hilton: The Scale of Perfection* (New York: Paulist Press, 1991), p. 98.
29 James Walsh, SJ, ed. and trans., *The Cloud of Unknowing* (New York: Paulist Press, 1981) p. 213.

Augustine's growing musical asceticism. Treatises about music theory in that century still contain great amounts of mathematics and occasional references to cosmology, but their intents and purposes have largely changed. There are treatises about how to tune musical instruments like the *vielle* and *rebec*,[30] and there are long explanations about how to measure music to make the new style in polyphony possible.[31]

Richard Rolle's exact contemporary was Guillaume de Machaut, whom no less than Igor Stravinsky has called the greatest of all composers. His and Phillipe de Vitry's are the names usually associated with the so-called *ars nova*, the new-style of polyphonic music whose aim was to delight the ear – sometimes at the expense of the words. The characteristics of *ars nova* composition were exaggerated syncopation, hocket (or the shifting of melody from one voice to another, creating a kind of hiccoughing sound), and the simultaneous singing of more than one text. *Ars nova* compositions delight the ear – unless one is interested primarily in the words. *Ars nova* composers wrote for the Church and soon themselves felt the same sort of conservative backlash that we have seen met Rolle's affective mysticism from the later English mystics.

Jacques of Liege, for instance, in his *Speculum Musicae* attacked the *ars nova*, especially the work of Johannis de Muris. Finally Pope John XXII, also Rolle's exact contemporary, issued a bull attacking affective music:

> The competent authority of the Fathers has decreed that, in singing the offices of divine praise through which we express the homage due to God, we must be careful to avoid doing violence to the words, but must sing with modesty and gravity. . . . But certain exponents of a new school, who think only of the laws of measured time, are composing new melodies of their own creation . . . these composers, knowing nothing of the true foundation upon which they must build, are ignorant of the Modes, incapable of distinguishing between them, and cause great confusion. The mere numbers of the notes, in these compositions, conceal for us the plain-chant melody. . . . These musicians run without pausing, they intoxicate the ear without satisfying it . . . by creating a sensuous . . . atmosphere. Thus it was not without good reason that Boethius said: "A person who is intrinsically sensuous will delight in hearing these indecent melodies, and one who listens to them frequently will be weakened thereby and lose his virility of soul.[32]

The reference to Boethius is significant, as is the association between the sensual delights of music and indecency. We are not far away, in other words, from the

---

[30] For instance, Jerome of Moravia's *Tractatus de Musica*; see Christopher Page, *Voices and Instruments of the Middle Ages* (Berkeley: University of California Press, 1986), pp. 126–133.

[31] For instance, Johannes de Muris's *Ars nove musice* and Philippe de Vitry's *Ars nova*; see Hoppin, *Medieval Music*, pp. 353–74.

[32] See Robert F. Hayburn, *Papal Legislation on Sacred Music* (Collegeville, Minnesota: The Liturgical Press, 1979), pp. 20–21.

theater of Augustine's youth. Perhaps ironic is the Pope's condemnation of "measured time." The new composers needed a system of measuring notes to keep the several lines of their pieces together. Remember that Augustine, foremost among the Fathers to whom the Pope appeals, called music in his *De musica* the art of measuring time. Augustine was, of course, speaking metaphorically, using music as a means of explicating God's ordering of the cosmos. The *ars nova* composers are here subject to criticism for taking Augustine's musical metaphor literally and creating sensual effects with it.

Rolle heard his heavenly music of course in his own soul, not in the cathedrals of France. But the criticism he faced was part of the larger debate over the use of the senses in apprehending God. From the point of view of people like Jacques of Liege, Pope John XXII, Walter Hilton, and the author of *The Cloud of Unknowing* his mistake was preferring a younger Augustine to an older. But the Pope's bull failed to stop musical history in its tracks: the glories of Dufay, Josquin, Tallis, Palestrina, Bach, Mozart, and Messien were still to come. Perhaps then we can learn something from Rolle in his reverse chronological reading of Augustine: the *jubilus* which Augustine grew to distrust and its close kin, Rolle's *canor,* are perhaps not as untrustworthy as some have made them.

# "GOOSTLY FREEND IN GOD":
## AELRED OF RIEVAULX'S *DE SPIRITUALI AMICITIA*
## AS A SOURCE OF THE *CLOUD OF UNKNOWING*

### EDWIN L. CONNER

Here we are, you and I, and I hope a third, Christ, is in our midst. There is no one now to disturb us; there is no one to break in upon our friendly chat, no man's prattle or noise of any kind will creep into this pleasant solitude. Come now, beloved, open your heart. . . .[1]

Farewel, goostly freend, in Goddes blessing & myne! & I beseche almighti God, that trew pees, hole counseil, & goostly coumforte in God with habundaunce of grace, euirmore be with thee & alle Goddes louers in eerthe. Amen.[2]

THE SENTENCES from Aelred of Rievaulx translated in the first epigraph begin the Ciceronian dialogue *De spirituali amicitia*, Aelred's most original contribution to Christian spirituality. The lines dramatize vividly the theme of spiritual friendship as Aelred conceived it. By the end of the fourteenth century, when the anonymous author of *The Cloud of Unknowing* had written all the known works attributed to him and had probably passed on to complete the form of living which he called "Perfect," spiritual friendship as an intellectual tradition had flourished all over England and was in decline.[3] However, Aelred's salutary influence on English monasticism is still evident in the letters of spiritual direction written by the *Cloud*

---

[1] Aelred of Rievaulx, *Spiritual Friendship*, trans. Mary Eugenia Laker (Kalamazoo, Michigan: Cistercian Publications, 1977), p. 51. Quotations of Aelred's *De spirituali amicitia* in English translation will refer to this edition and will be cited by book and paragraph number.

[2] *The Cloud of Unknowing and The Book of Privy Counselling*, ed. Phyllis Hodgson, Early English Text Society O.S. no. 218 (London: Oxford University Press), 75.133.4–7. Quotations of the *Cloud* will be taken from this edition and will be cited, as here, by chapter, page number, and line number. I have regularized the peculiarly Middle English alpahbetical characters according to modern usage.

[3] Extant copies show the universal dissemination of Aelred's work within England. Four short redactions in the fourteenth century (one attributed to St Augustine) had followed Peter of Blois's popular thirteenth-century version. These appear to have enjoyed considerable popularity among both religious and lay folk before the mid-century decline in interest. See Douglas Roby's "Introduction" in Laker, ed., pp. 39–40.

author. Indeed, Aelred's great work is an unacknowledged, if relatively minor source of the *Cloud* author's unique achievement.[4] One may argue that because of the tradition of spiritual friendship in general and his familiarity with Aelred in particular, the fourteenth-century master could compose letters expressing an authentic personal relationship with his correspondent. Because of the accepted tradition of spiritual friendship and the letters that arose out of it, he could publish the most warmly humane, appealingly intimate, and rhetorically skillful manual of the austere and solitary *via negativa* in the late Middle Ages.[5] The paradoxical accomplishment is, I think, a secret of the work's perennial appeal, even, or perhaps especially, in an age of unbelief. There is evidence in the *Cloud* of the author's knowledge of Aelred's celebrated work, and, given that evidence, there is a basis for acknowledging Aelred's direct and indirect contribution to *The Cloud of Unknowing*.

The most concrete evidences of the *Cloud* Master's familiarity with Aelred's work are three: (1) the formula he uses for addressing his disciple, "Goostly freende in God" (1.13. 1, 8); (2) a series of apparent allusions to the *De spirituali amicitia* in Chapter 9; and (3) the discussion of spiritual friendships under the category of "special beholdings" in Chapters 25 and 26. Less conclusive but also evident is a certain understanding in the *Cloud* of the relation between the author's four degrees of Christian living and Aelred's three phases of friendship. If the argument regarding this source and influence is valid, we may draw certain conclusions regarding the *Cloud of Unknowing* as a whole. What follows is the case for these assertions.

---

[4] I have found no acknowledgement of Aelred as a source for *The Cloud of Unknowing* among the best accounts of the work's sources: besides Phyllis Hodgson's introductions to her editions, John P. H. Clark, "Sources and Theology in the *Cloud of Unknowing*," *Downside Review* 98 (1980): 83–109; Kent Emery, Jr., "The *Cloud of Unknowing* and *Mystica Theologia*," in *The Roots of the Modern Christian Tradition*, ed. E. Rozanne Elder (Kalamazoo: Cistercian publications, 1984), 46–70; Alistair Minnis, "The *Cloud of Unknowing* and Walter Hilton's *Scale of Perfection*," in *Middle English Prose: A Critical Guide to Major Authors and Genres*, ed. A. S. G. Edwards (New Brunswick: Rutgers University Press, 1984), 61–81; James Walsh, "Influence, Sources, and Doctrine" in *The Cloud of Unknowing*, ed. and trans. Walsh, The Classics of Western Spirituality (Ramsey, N.J.: Paulist Press, 1981), 12–47.

[5] Letters of spiritual friendship constituted an epistolary sub-genre in the Middle Ages even before Aelred, but Aelred's influence served to humanize and individuate the relationship expressed in such letters well beyond what had been done before him. On spiritual friendship before Aelred, see Adele M. Fisk, *Friends and Friendship in the Monastic Tradition*, Cidoc Cuaderno 51 (Cuernavaca, Mexico: CIDOC, 1970). On medieval letters of friendship, see Jean Le Clerq, "L'amitie dans les lettres au moyen age," *Revue du moyen age latin*, 1 (1945), 391–410; and Le Clerq, *The Love of Learning and the Desire for God*, trans. C. Misraeli (New York: Fordham University Press, 1960), 226–27.

I

The phrase "Goostly freende in God," apparently original in English with the *Cloud* author, establishes at the outset the exact relationship in which Master and Disciple are joined: the same kind of relationship that Aelred and his friends in the dialogues enjoy – a friendship between master and novice grounded at once in a shared devotion to spiritual perfection and in the personal ties between two individuals.[6] "And so," in Aelred's definition, based on Cicero, "spiritual friendship among the just is born of a similarity in life, morals, and pursuits, that is, it is a mutual conformity in matters human and divine united with benevolence and charity" (1.46). The idea is precisely expressed in the appellation "Goostly freend in God," identifying, in this instance, two individuals affectively united by a common form of living, an agreement in morals, and a common calling – the uncommon desire for a life of solitary contemplation as a means of union with God. The personal and ethical bonds between master and disciple (matters human) are hardly less important to a spiritual friendship than their common devotion to the work of contemplation.

But spiritual friendship is for Aelred but one kind of friendship distinguished from two other kinds, the carnal and the worldly: "The carnal springs from mutual harmony in vice; the worldly is enkindled by the hope of gain; and the spiritual is cemented by similarity of life, morals, and pursuits among the just" (1.38).[7] Carnal friendship is based on the regard of one's friend as a corporeal being to whom one is carnally attracted. Aelred shares with Augustine the confession that the friendships of his youth were of this nature, and he likewise repents of them.[8] Indeed, "this type of friendship belongs . . . especially to the young people, such as they once were, Augustine and the friend of whom he was then speaking. And yet this friendship except for trifles and deceptions, if nothing dishonorable enters into it, is to be tolerated in the hope of more abundant grace, as the beginnings, so to say,

---

6  Aelred was master of novices at Rievaulx for years before his election as Abbot, and the dialogue form in his works perhaps suggests something of the quality of the spiritual conferences that he held in this capacity. However, both this literary form and his admiration for Cicero's use of it obviously are rooted in the profound importance that his own special friendships held for his life. The interlocutors in the dialogues are apparently given the names of living friends. And by nearly all accounts the most deeply moving passage in the *Spiritual Friendship* is Aelred's narration of personal memories of the two most intimate friendships of his life, both with men who were dead at the time of writing. See p. 9, 1.6–7, and 4.119–27.

7  This distinction among kinds of friendship originates with Aristotle in the *Nicomachean Ethics* 8.1–6, whence Cicero ultimately derived it.

8  *Confessions* 6.6–10.

9  In the *Cloud*, the powers of the soul, which the Master discusses at some length in an Augustinian, Victorine vein, must be "illuminid by grace" and thus redeemed from their fallen state (64.116.14).

of a holier friendship" which may come "with the growing seriousness of maturer years and the illumination of the spiritual senses" (3.87). Aelred and the *Cloud* author share a common devotion to Augustine's *Confessions* and dialogues, including the *De Magistro*, a source of the Augustinian doctrine of the "illumination of the spiritual senses," which both writers discuss.[9] But the *Cloud* writer's more particular debt to this passage from Aelred is expressed in a chapter in which he alludes quite specifically to the Aelredian distinction among kinds of friendship, and to remembrances of spiritual friends living and dead. In arguing the necessity of relegating to the Cloud of Forgetting "the minde of the holiest creature that euer God maad," the Master says that this act

> is more profitable to the helthe of thi soule, more worthi in itself, & more plesing to God & to alle the seintes & aungelles in heuen – ye!, *& more helply to alle thi freendes, bodily & goostly, quik & dede* – . . . & beter thee were for to haue it & for to fele it in thin affeccion goostly, then it is for to haue the iye of thi soule openid in contemplacion or beholding of alle the aungelles or seyntes in heuen, or in hering of alle the mirthe and the melody that is amonges hem in blisse. (9.34.5–14; italics added)

This passage appears to allude particularly to Aelred's distinction between friendships carnal or corporeal ("bodily") and spiritual ("goostly"), even to the extent of implying the same generous approval that Aelred bestows on tolerating carnal friendships because of the hope they offer of becoming spiritual friendships. There also appears to be a recollection here, fast on the heels of this Aelredian distinction, of Aelred's vivid remembrances of friends both "quik and dede."

Phyllis Hodgson's note to this passage invites comparison with Hilton's *Scale of Perfection* 1.47. She quotes it as follows:

> Soothly I had liefer feel and have a soothfast desire and a clean love in mine heart to my Lord Jesus Christ, though I see right little of him with my ghostly eye, than to have without this desire all bodily presence of all men living, all visions or revelations of angels appearing, songs, and soundings, savours and smells . . . all the joys of heaven and earth.[10]

If the prevailing judgment that the *Cloud* was written after its author had read Book I of the *Scale* is correct, Hilton is doubtless the main source of the passage. However, the *Cloud* author has altered his source precisely in such a way as to refer not only to the emphasis among Rolle's followers on sensory manifestations, as Hilton apparently does, but to refer also to Aelred's emphasis on the categories of friendship and on the memories of friends living and dead. These references are not in the Hilton passage. The *Cloud* author by these alterations places in the perspective of his own teaching these differences with Aelred and Rolle.

There is still more to the *Cloud* author's adaptation of this passage that makes it

---

[10] London, 1927: p. 89; Hodgson, p. 189.

refer to Aelred as Hilton's passage does not. Aelred, at the end of his dialogue, concludes the detailed and moving reminiscences of his two most intimate friends, both now deceased, as follows:

> What more is there, then, that I can say? Was it not a foretaste of blessedness thus to love and be loved; thus to help and thus to be helped; and in this way from the sweetness of fraternal charity to wing one's flight aloft to that more sublime splendor of divine love, and by the ladder of charity now to mount to the embrace of Christ himself; and again to descend to the love of neighbor, there pleasantly to rest? And so, in this friendship of ours, which we have introduced by way of example, if you see aught worthy of imitation, profit by it to advance your own perfection. (3.127)

The essential idea here is that in the greatest spiritual friendships there is a "foretaste" of the union with Christ by love, in love, and as love, for as Aelred boldly affirms in his amendment of 1 John 4.16, "Deus amicitia est" (1.69–70). But the perfection of this love and this "friendship" with Christ, the ultimate "spiritual fruit of friendship," awaits "the fullness of all things in the life to come." Then,

> with the dispelling of all anxiety by reason of which we now fear and are solicitous for one another . . . and, above all, with the destruction of the sting of death together with death itself, whose pangs now often trouble us and force us to grieve for one another, with salvation secured, we shall rejoice in the eternal possession of Supreme Goodness; and this friendship, to which here we admit but few, will be outpoured upon all and by all outpoured upon God, and God shall be all in all. (3.134)

Characteristically, Aelred describes the affective union with God in terms of the communion of the saints, the final stage in the cultivation of spiritual friendships. The *Cloud* author, after referring to "thi freendes bodily and goostly, quik and dede," offers a more direct route to a more immediate end – not a vision of the Communion of Saints, but the ecstatic union with God in this life the fullest possible foretaste of the beatific vision in the life to come. The "blynde steryng of loue vnto God for Himself" is better than the remembrances of past friendships or the distractions of present friendships (both carnal and spiritual), and it is better "then it is for to haue the iye of thi soule openid in contemplacion or beholding of alle the aungelles or seyntes in heuen, or in hering of alle the mirthe and the melody that is amonges hem in blisse."[11] The *Cloud* author does not deny the doctrine of the communion of the saints, but he holds out the love of God for himself as a path preferable to the love of spiritual friends for the sake of God, and preferable even to the communion of saints, a joy ancillary to that of perfect union with God.

---

[11] The reference to the celestial "melody" is probably one among many glances at another spiritual path, that of Richard Rolle, as specifically expressed in Rolle's idea of the celestial *canor*.

After this series of apparent references to the *De spirituali amicitia* in Chapter 9, a discussion of spiritual friendships under the category of "special beholdings" (in Chapters 25 and 26) should not surprise us. I believe that is what we have. The argument of Chapter 25 is "That in the tyme of this werk a parfite soule hath no special beholding to any o man in this liif." A "special beholding" is a particular regard forming the basis of a relationship such as "freende or fo, sib or fremmyd" (25.59.16). The detachment from special beholdings does not exclude all spiritual friendships. It permits any friendship which the cause of *caritas* requires:

> I say not bot he schal fele somtyme – ye! ful ofte – his affecion more homely to one, two, or thre, then to alle these other: for that is leueful to be for many causis as charite askith. For soche an homly affecion felid Criste to Ihoun, & unto Marye, & vnto Petre bifore many other. Bot I say that in the tyme of this werk schal alle be iliche homly vnto hym: for he schal fele than no cause, bot only God. So that alle schul be louyd pleinly & nakidly for God, & as wel as himself. (25.60.8–15)

Just before the passage in which Aelred recalled his dead friends, he too had discussed the "homly affecion" of Christ for particular friends, recalling that John was a closer friend than Peter, and the care of His mother was commended to John, but the Church was commended to Peter. "To Peter he gave the keys of his kingdom," but "to John he revealed the secrets of his heart" (3.117). For both Aelred and the *Cloud* author, the Exemplar has established a role for "homly affecions" and special friendships in this life. But, characteristically, the *Cloud* author amends Aelred's emphasis on the special friendship of Jesus and John to affirm that the friendship of Jesus with Peter was "bifore many other." Both writers acknowledge that Mary Magdalene was a special friend of the Lord. These three were the objects of the "homly affections" of Jesus, as distinguished from the more impersonal *caritas* he feels toward all his disciples.

Thus the anonymous Master does not repudiate spiritual friendships – they are "leueful to be" – but he emphasizes that "alle shall be louyd pleinly and nakidly for God" and "as charite askith," so that the friend "schul fele no cause, bot only God." And insofar as "alle schal be iliche homly vnto hym," the *Cloud* master has simply taken Aelred's idea of spiritual friendship and raised the standard, so that it is now identical to what Aelred says is the perfection of spiritual friendship among the blessed: "and this friendship," says Aelred, "to which here we admit but few, will be outpoured upon all and by all outpoured upon God, and God shall be all in all" (3.134).[12] The more stringent standard of spiritual friendship taught by the

---

[12] Indeed the *Cloud* author does have other spiritual friends. He says he has "ben sterid many day bothe to fele thus & think thus & sey thus, as weel to som other of my specyal freendes in God, as I am now vnto thee" (Chap. 47, p. 189). We may take him at his word that whatever intimacy he feels toward them – and surely nothing is more intimate than the deepest affections of the heart – it is *caritas* that moves him in relation to them all.

*Cloud* is no less than a direct attempt to realize the communion of saints in this life as the soul is united to God in pure *caritas*, all the while realizing that the perfection of such a work awaits the perfection of the soul in the life of the world to come. In the meanwhile, spiritual friendships in Aelred's sense go "under the Cloud of Forgetting" with all other remembrances of God's creatures. This is a particularly difficult part of the "ful grete trauayle" of the contemplative's work, but a small price to pay for the unspeakable bliss of the ecstatic union (26.61.13–14).

II

Insofar as the *Cloud* author identifies his disciple as a spiritual friend in God, their identities and relationship may be understood not only in terms of the four forms of living which the *Cloud* describes, but also in terms of three stages of friendship that Aelred discusses. The first sentences of the *Cloud's* first chapter establish perhaps the most important distinctions in the work:

> Goostly freend in God, thou schalt wel vnderstonde that I fynde, in my boistous beholdyng, foure degrees & fourmes of Cristen mens leuyng; & ben theese, Comoun, Special, Singuler, & Parfite. Thre of theese mow be bigonnen & eendid in this liif; & the ferthe may by grace be bigonnen here, bot it schal euer laste withouten eende in the blis of heuen. (1.13.8–13)

The master identifies his disciple and himself in terms of these degrees or forms of living, each of which has specific implications for the nature of the friendships cultivated in each form. "For first thou wote wel that when thou were leuyng in the comoun degre of Cristen mens leuyng in companie of thi wordely [*sic*] freendes" (1.18–19). "Wordely" or "Worldly" friendships, we should recall, are Aelred's third category of friendships, with the "carnal" and the "spiritual." Then the Godhead in his eternal love, who made the disciple out of nothing and redeemed him from his fallen state,

> might not suffre thee be so fer fro him in forme & degree of leuyng. & therfore he kyndlid thi desire ful graciously, & fastnid bi it a lyame of longing, & led thee bi it into a more special state & forme of leuyng, to be a seruaunt of the special seruauntes of his. (1.14.2–5)

This "Special" form of living is not specified, but is presumably a religious vocation, whether lay or ordained, of a communal nature. In the Cistercian tradition especially, after Aelred, spiritual friendship assumes a pre-eminent role in the life of the community. But in any religious community, a "seruaunt of the special seruauntes of his" is in the form of living most suitable to cultivating spiritual friendships. The friendship between Master and Disciple begins in this stage and displaces, or at least assumes priority over, the "companie of thi wordely freendes" – and gradually over other friendships as well, except such as "charite askith." For now the Disciple has received a vocation to the third degree or form of living:

93

Seest thou nought how lystly & how graciously He hath pulled thee to the thrid degre & maner of leuyng, the whiche hight Synguleer? In the whiche solitari forme & maner of leuyng, thou maist lerne to lift up the fote of thi loue, & step towardes that state & degre of leuyng that is parfite, & the laste state of alle. (1.14.10–15)

The perfect degree or form of living is not attained until the soul is transformed and perfected in Heaven, just on the other side of the Cloud of Unknowing, the nature of which is that it stands between the soul and the vision of God throughout one's mortal life, to be removed only in the life to come. So the Singular life – the life of the solitary contemplative – is the highest form of living which one may complete in the mortal state. In this form of living, again, the contemplative retains only such friendships "as charite askith."

In the Common life, "liuing in companie of . . . wordely freendes," one is clearly in the form of living in which Aelred's "worldly" and "carnal" friendships abound, as the *Cloud* author implies. The *Cloud* author is not concerned with those in this form, with the peculiar exception of those in the active life who are drawn in their *apex affectionis* to such contemplation as their lives afford them:

Bot yif it be to thoo men the whiche, though al thei stonde in actyuete bi outward form of leuyng, neuertheles yit bi inward stering after the prive sperit of God, whos domes ben hid, thei ben ful graciously disposid, not contynow-ely as it is propre to verrey contemplatyues, bot than & than to be parceners in the hieghst pointe of this contemplatyue acte. Yif soche men might se [this book], thei schuld by the grace of God be greetly counforted therby.

(Prologue 3.1–7)

But the Common life and its worldly and carnal friendships are not conducive to the contemplative work, which this book is about.

In the Special form of living, spiritual friendship has its natural context: with others in a religious vocation, particularly in a community, spiritual friendship may be nurtured, may even flourish. This is the point at which Aelred's experience of the three phases of true or spiritual friendship began. He describes the three phases concisely: spiritual friendship "can begin among the good, progress among the better, and be consumated amony the perfect" (2.38). That it may "begin among the good" means that "the beginnings of spiritual friendship ought to possess, first of all, purity of intention" (2.59) – not, that is, the carnal attraction or hope of gain that motivate carnal and worldly friendships. The "solid foundation" of spiritual friendship is "the love of God" (3.5) – the precise idea expressed in "Goostly freend in God." The beginning of spiritual friendship should also show "the direction of reason and the restraint of moderation" (2.59). "Purity of intention" implies that a spiritual friend "may expect nothing from your friendship except God and its natural good" (3.61). Given the proof of this purity of intention and of other qualities essential to friendship – particularly loyalty, discretion, and patience – a spiritual friendship may "progress among the better." Such, of course, is the nature of the very special friendship between the *Cloud* Master and his Disciple. We may only speculate about the beginnings of their friendship, but at least we know that both have received a vocation from the Special form of living to the Singular, and that this vocation deepens both the personal and spiritual bonds between them.[13] That their relationship is a spiritual friendship that "progresses among the better" as it advances the spiritual perfection of each, more than fulfilling Aelred's requirements, need not be belabored.

In Chapter 16, the Master begins to distinguish the work of the solitary contemplative (the third degree) from that of the communal religious (the second degree). And here, in a traditional use of the story of Mary Magdelene's relationship to Jesus, the Master wishes to insist on the necessity of a further refinement in love, wherein all trace of the carnal disappears, just as Mary's love for the man Jesus is transformed into the love of God. Jesus forgives Mary's sins, he says, not primarily because of her sorrow in repenting, but "for sche loued mochel" (16.45.4). "& therfore," he says,

> sche heng up her loue & hir longing desire in this cloude of unknowing, & lernid hir to loue a thing the whiche sche might not se cleerly in this liif, bi the light of vnderstondyng in hir reson, ne yit uerely fele in swetnes of loue in hir affeccion. (16.46.15–18)

That is, the greatness of her love of the man Jesus is transformed, by grace, into a greater love, the love of God. The author uses the scriptural story with a nice sense of its nuances to make his theological point, but the wonderful conclusion to the chapter shows his extraordinary sensitivity to the story's human dimensions:

> Ye! & ful oftymes I hope that sche was so deeply [affecte] in the loue of his Godheed that sche had bot right lityl specyal beholdyng unto the beute of his precious and his blessid body, in the whiche he sate ful louely, spekyng & preching before hir; ne yit to anything elles, bodyly or goostly. That this be soth, it semith by the Gospelle. (16.46.20–47.2)

There is a distinct note of uncertainty in the Master's expression of hope, and it is the uncertainty that always characterizes friendships in this mortal life, as both the *Cloud* Master and Aelred were acutely aware. This uncertainty means a constant threat of distraction from the work of the contemplative, and so for the Cloud author friendship itself, as a "special beholding," is finally an impediment to the work. But for both writers, friendship "progresses among the better" to a point as near perfection as one may come in this life.

Indeed, even to Aelred, spiritual friendship is "consummated among the Perfect"

---

[13] In Chapter 23, the Master exhorts his disciple to have faith that God will support those in the Singular form of living, and he says that God will "stere other men in spirite to yeue us oure needful thinges that longen to this liif, as mete and clothes with alle theese other" (23.57.3–5).

by God's grace in the communion of the saints, a consummation devoutly to be wished but impossible in this mortal coil. It is possible only "with the destruction of the sting of death together with death itself," because the consummation of friendship occurs when "with salvation secured, we may rejoice in the eternal possession of Supreme Goodness" (3.134). Thus, Aelred's third phase of friendship coincides entirely with the *Cloud* Master's fourth form of living and is appropriately named with the same word, the "Perfect." For both masters, this stage is completed only in the life to come, when the union with God in love is perfected with a union in knowledge, and the blessed *aspectus* of the intellectual vision completes the ecstatic *affectus* of the union in love.

### III

If we accept the evidence for the *Cloud* author's references to Aelred and the tradition of spiritual friendship, what are the consequences for our understanding of the *Cloud of Unknowing*? There is perhaps very little consequence regarding the theology or practical teachings of the work. However, a more thorough analysis of the work in the light of this evidence could possibly tell us more about its origins, particularly about the author and addressee themselves. We might also learn something more about the work's rhetorical artistry. The tradition of spiritual friendship offers a key to the qualities of the work as a literary masterpiece of its kind.

In defining the character and uniqueness of the *Cloud* we may better understand how, why, and when it was written as it was. For it could not have been written before Aelred's work had its impact on the monasteries, nor before the great resurgence of eremitic vocations in the fourteenth century, at a time when the intellectual tradition of spiritual friendship was still alive but in decline. The author of the *Cloud* could thus, as a religious, represent one of the finest fruits of an eclipsing social tradition among religious, at the moment that he was in the spiritual vanguard of his fragmented age.

In defining the intended audience of the *Cloud*, we may also understand why, for the author, there was no important distinction between the particular friend he was writing and the wider audience he hoped to reach. In the tradition of spiritual friendship, it is understood that true friendship grows into a disinterested love for all souls, ultimately reciprocated in the communion of the saints. It does so, both in Aelred and in the *Cloud* author, because of the very nature of spiritual friendship. For as its names implies, it is not only *amicitia*, like the best secular friendships, but *caritas*. As long as the requirements of *caritas* are obeyed, there is no essential conflict between the privacy required by the most intimate exchanges between friends and the public good of a community of souls united by the same vocation, a community like that of the Carthusian eremites.

But whether we grant the Carthusian provenance of the *Cloud* or not, we must acknowledge a stronger Cistercian influence than has yet been credited, even given the degree of Bernard's influence demonstrated by John P. H. Clark in 1980. For at least some of the Augustinian and Cistercian influence on the theology of the *Cloud* is filtered through Aelred and the tradition of spiritual friendship. As a result there may be occasion to re-consider the role of a possible Cistercian background for the *Cloud* author, or possibly his assuming such a background in his young disciple.[14] If the latter case is true, then the author's references to Aelred and matters of spiritual friendship may be understood as part of a necessary weening of his disciple from particular influences in his religious background which have served their purpose. However, given the author's ease – indeed, excellence – in the mode of spiritual friendship, it appears no less likely that he himself left a Cistercian community for the more austere rule of an eremitic Carthusian.

Finally, if we acknowledge a role in the *Cloud* for the formal tradition of spiritual friendship, then it is entirely appropriate to study the work in the context of the epistolary genre of spiritual friendship, a genre that St Anselm had cultivated even before Aelred's work. Kent Emery has argued the case for naming the genre of the work as mystical theology, but that is not its literary genre, because the work's purpose is not that of theological exposition, but spiritual direction as practical instruction in contemplation. The work is rhetorically sophisticated, with a well-defined practical purpose; a well-defined audience; a mastery of tone, style, and distance; a carefully controlled persona; a structure appropriate to its nature as a letter of spiritual direction – in short, a mastery of the use of language equal both to the author's spiritual advancement and the task he has set himself, "in the which a soul is oned with God." The challenge in such a task is as much a challenge to one's linguistic mastery as to his intellect.

I am not prepared to say what redaction of Aelred's *Spiritual Friendship* the *Cloud* author knew. I suspect from the absence of quotations that he had an early, general, and longstanding familiarity with the work, but was not writing with a manuscript of it at hand. His use of Aelred suggests, rather, that the work was in his background, and he had moved beyond it, just as he had moved well beyond the third degree of Christian living.

A great source of the spiritual beauty of the *Cloud* is its presentation of the austere, rigorous detachment of the Negative Way not at all in an austere and detached manner, but with the personal warmth and intimate embrace of a good friend. There is nothing of these qualities in the Pseudo-Dionysius, and the addition of them is not all due to the Latin tradition of Pseudo-Dionysian redaction and commentary. Not even Bernard's influence accounts fully for these qualities. We may, of course, infer that they are simply qualities of the author's personal style, but if we acknowledge Aelred as a source on empirical grounds, as I believe we should, we may also recognize that the *Cloud* author claimed for his own a tradition of spiritual friendship in which his personal style had a meaning well beyond itself, and a living tradition in which this style may well have taken shape.

14 Cf. Fr. Walsh's discussion in the "Introduction" to his translation of the *Cloud*, pp. 3, 13, et passim.

That he chose, presumably, an eremitic life, and a role as spiritual director to beginners in such a life, meant that with his more spiritually advanced perspective on the friendships to which he admitted but few, he could write a masterpiece of practical spiritual friendship as well as of contemplative prayer. I believe he accomplished just that.

# CHAUCER'S MOMENTS IN THE "KNEELING WORLD"

## BEVERLY BOYD

IN AN ASSESSMENT OF structural and semantic approaches to the Prioress's prologue and tale, the eminent Japanese medievalist Michio Masui calls attention to
the fact that prayers, shorter or longer, appear throughout Chaucer's works.[1] He
cites Sister M. Madeleva's *A Lost Language* in observing, ". . . the first and last thing
that Chaucer wrote was prayer," assuming *An ABC* the first piece written, the
"Retraction" which follows the Parson's tale the last.[2] With Sister Madeleva he
believes that Chaucer had moments of living in the "kneeling world" suggested by
his passages of prayer.[3]

Although I have more than once faulted Sister Madeleva for drawing inaccurate
parallels between religious practices of the Middle Ages and their pre-Vatican II
expressions in more recent times, the points made by Madeleva and by Masui are
worthy of further consideration, for, as a person of his time, Chaucer was part of a
society permeated by Catholicism. Many have tried to prove that he was devout, or
that he was sympathetic with the Wycliffite heresy, or that he was a hedonist to
whom religion meant little or nothing.[4] Nevertheless, mysticism appears in his
writings, as a mode proper to medieval Catholicism, regardless of the "slice of life"
about which he wrote. Fragment I of his *Canterbury Tales*, for all its ecclesiastical
rogues of the General Prologue, and ensuing fabliaux, is not incompatible with
moments in the "kneeling world" or with even deeper personal spirituality.

It is easier to approach the mysticism in Chaucer's writings though his free-
standing lyric poetry than through his narratives, since, as E. T. Donaldson has
established, Chaucer wrote narrative through the voice of a *persona*, a literary
characterization of himself not always drawn as true portraiture.[5] The distinction

---

1  *Studies in Chaucer's Language of Feeling* (Tokyo: Kinseido, 1988), p. 97. Professor Masui
   died after this paper had been submitted.
2  *A Lost Language and Other Essays on Chaucer* (New York: Sheed and Ward, 1951), p. 26.
3  Masui, p. 98.
4  These points of view are summarized by Roger S. Loomis, "Was Chaucer a Laodicean?"
   *Essays and Studies in Honor of Carleton Brown* (New York: New York Univ. Press, 1940), pp.
   129–48. See also Madeleva, *Chaucer's Nuns and Other Essays* (New York: Appleton, 1925),
   pp. 1–42; *A Lost Language*, p. 16.
5  *Speaking of Chaucer* (New York: Norton, 1970), pp. 1–12.

between narrative and lyric, moreover, is not always clear, for some of Chaucer's best lyric passages belong to the *Canterbury Tales* and are prefatory to, or woven into, these works. Another complication is the fact that much of Chaucer's writing, including lyrics and lyric passages, is translated from works by other authors. One such piece, *An ABC*, which exists in the Chaucer canon as a free-standing lyric, will be considered first, because, although a translation, it is a prayer rather than an instruction or a commentary on religious virtue, and therefore not simply religious but mystical.

Elsewhere, I have described *An ABC* as an adaptation rather than a literal translation.[6] Indeed, it is an adaption that deals quite ruthlessly with its exemplar, found in the *Pèlerinage de la vie humaine* by the Cistercian monk Guillaume de Deguilleville (c.1330), though the Riverside editors call the translation "close but skillfull."[7] The skill lies in maintaining the alphabetical artifice while translating Guillaume's French. But not only does the English version omit the last two stanzas of the French poem, which cover *et cetera*: it introduces imagery not present in the original, such as the lovely but commonplace *flos flora* epithet in Chaucer's line 4: "Glorious virgine, of alle floures flour. . . ." The freedom of his translation may be seen by comparing the two texts as printed together in Skeat's edition.[8] Chaucer's *An ABC* consists of eight-line stanzas of five-beat lines rhyming ababbcbc (total, 184 lines), far simpler than Guillaume's complicated twelve-octosyllabic-line stanzas rhyming aabaabbbabba (total, 274 lines involved in Chaucer's translation). *An ABC* must have had a fairly wide readership, for the Riverside editors list sixteen manuscript copies.[9] This is especially interesting because Speght (1602), who was the first to include the piece in a printed edition of Chaucer's works, says that the poem is thought to have been translated for the Duchess Blanche of Lancaster (and hence before her death in 1369).[10] There is no evidence for this, though *An ABC* is certainly an early work.

The device of an alphabet, in which each of Guillaume's stanzas starts with a letter in alphabetical sequence, is less strained when understood in terms of the metaphor that begins stanza 11, translated by Chaucer "Kalenderes enlumined ben they / That in this world ben lighted with thy name." The reference is to the illumination (use of gold) in calendars found in liturgical books and other manuals of worship because they record commemorations of the ecclesiastical year next to

6 "Our Lady According to Geoffrey Chaucer: Translation and Collage," *Florilegium* 9 (1990), 147–54.
7 *The Riverside Chaucer*, gen. ed. Larry D. Benson (Boston: Houghton Mifflin, 1987), p. 633. All quotations from Chaucer's works are from this edition unless otherwise specified. The principal edition of Guillaume's complete poem is that of J. J. Stürtzinger (London: Roxburghe Club, 1893).
8 W. W. Skeat, ed., *The Works of Geoffrey Chaucer*, 2nd ed., 7 vols. (Oxford: Clarendon, 1972), I, 261–71.
9 *Riverside Chaucer*, p. 1185.
10 (London: printed by Adam Islip [S.T.C. 5080]), fol. 347 [Sig. Oooo.i]. I am indebted to the Henry E. Huntington Library for permission to examine this book.

their dates, indicating rank by color-coding, gold being used for feasts of the highest rank, including major feasts of the Virgin Mary, the specific reference of Guillaume's poem. While his device of addressing Mary through an alphabet of verses may lack appeal in a later age, his epithet of her devotees as calendars illuminated with her name springs from the essential occupation of monastic life, liturgy. For the liturgy, especially the liturgy of the canonical hours, many books were then needed, the service being put together by date and liturgical commemorations, by means of an ordinal, a book of cues and rubrics, now more commonly called an ordo. Liturgical calendars were in the Roman style, arranged vertically by kalends, nones, and ides, days of the week denoted next to the dates by letters of the alphabet (hebdomidal letters), the Sunday letter of a given year, calculated from tables and probably announced to the general public, being a matter of common knowledge.[11] Guillaume's poem extends the idea of hebdomidal letters in his poem with a full alphabet, though alphabets as literary devices are common in medieval literature.

In reading Chaucer's *ABC*, the voice must be understood as originally Guillaume's and therefore Cistercian, which is not to deny the presence of the translator in the English work. This is very important, for Cistercian spirituality was and is highly marian. For all its apparent artifice, the *ABC* is profoundly spiritual, a *crie de coeur* from a soul conscious of ideal purity seeking release from temptations of the flesh though Mary's intercession and hoping for her advocacy at the Last Judgment. Anticipation of the Last Judgment is familiar in confessional literature, which on that account abounds in legal terminology, as the Riverside editors have noted of Chaucer's poem.[12] But *An ABC* should not be read as an indicator of any legal bent on Chaucer's part, as, for example, when he writes in lines 36–43,

> But merci, ladi, at the grete assyse,
> Whan we shule come bifore the hye justyse.
> So litel fruit shal thanne in me be founde
> That, but thou er that day me wel correcte [vice],
> Of verrey right my werk wol me confounde.

There are no legal terms here or elsewhere in Chaucer's *ABC* that require or suggest a specialized knowledge of law.

This passage is especially notable in the present context because it involves the Virgin Mary in the role of advocate, assigned to her because of the theology of the hypostatic union (Christ as God/man), which made her, as mother of a son of such origins, an irresistible intercessor for her devotees, even if they should happen to be complete reprobates with nothing but a single *Ave Maria* to their credit. Long

---

11 Beverly Boyd, *Chaucer and the Liturgy* (Philadelphia: Dorrance, 1967), pp. 9–25.
12 *Riverside Chaucer*, pp. 1076–77.

before Shakespeare created Portia, medieval folklore portrayed the Virgin Mary pleading the causes of apparently lost souls against claims by the Devil.[13]

F. N. Robinson is mistaken in saying that *An ABC* reveals very little about Chaucer.[14] Chaucer never put away the main theme of this early work. The hymn to the Virgin Mary which Dante assigns to Bernard of Clairvaux in *Paradiso* XXXIII likewise fascinated Chaucer, and eventually he interpolated his own translation of it into the prologue of his Second Nun's tale, between its "Idleness prologue" and its rhapsody on the name Cecilia Chaucer translated from his hagiographical sources.[15] Chaucer's marian lyric forms no really thematic connection with any of these materials, though as a prayer for inspiration it has its own reason for being. Captioned *Invocacio ad mariam*, whether by his scribes or by Chaucer himself, the *Invocacio ad mariam* is what Dante had made it: Bernardine and therefore Cistercian in spirit, though there is no evidence that Bernard himself composed the poem which Dante translated into Italian. Indeed, beloved poetic works, such as *Jesu dulcis memoria*, once thought to have been written by Bernard, have been ascribed to others and the mysticism of that saint is evidenced by his prose.[16] This, however, raises no question about the Bernardine and Cistercian spirit of Dante's poem, which forms the second, third, and fourth stanzas of the Second Nun's *Invocacio ad mariam*, while the remaining stanzas rehearse not only Dante's regret (through the voice of Bernard) for human weakness, and prayer for Mary's intercession at the Last Judgment, but also these same points as Chaucer had found them in Guillaume de Deguilleville's alphabetical praise of Mary. Chaucer evidently had a consciousness of the Last Judgment throughout his life, not an unusual aspect of medieval Catholicism; that event motivates his Retraction, again through the intercession of Mary.

Chaucer's supreme mystical expression returns to Dante's Bernardine hymn to Our Lady, from which he borrows in the prologue to the miracle of the Virgin told by the Prioress. Robert A. Pratt was undoubtedly correct in describing the Prioress's prologue as Chaucer borrowing from himself.[17] The intertextuality of the Prioress's prologue with the psalms and with the Church's marian devotions, especially its marian liturgy, has long fascinated scholars, Sister Madeleva's works on the subject

---

[13] Beverly Boyd, ed., *The Middle English Miracles of the Virgin* (San Marino, Calif.: Huntington Library, 1962), *passim*.

[14] *The Complete Works of Geoffrey Chaucer: Student's Cambridge Edition* (Boston: Houghton Mifflin, 1933), p. 613. The comment is not repeated in subsequent editions.

[15] *The Divine Comedy*, ed. and trans. Charles S. Singleton (Princeton: Princeton Univ. Press, 1975), 3 vols., 2 parts each. For discussion of the hagiographical sources of the Second Nun's prologue, see *Riverside Chaucer*, pp. 942ff.

[16] Matthew Britt, O.S.B., ed., *The Hymns of the Breviary and Missal*, rev. ed. (New York: Benziger, 1955), pp. 90–92. For a brief discussion of Bernard's life and writings, see E. Rozanne Elder, "Bernard," *Dictionary of the Middle Ages*, gen. ed. Joseph R. Strayer, vol. 2 (New York: Scribner's, 1983), pp. 190–94.

[17] "Chaucer Borrowing from Himself," *MLQ* 7 (1946), 259–64.

being justly famous.[18] This is not to deny that the main direction of present-day scholarship has been the violence and anti-Semitism of the tale itself, which Chaucer inherited from the society in which he lived, however one may prefer to cast him in a different sociological mold.[19]

The Prioress's miracle of the Virgin, as she tells it, is a mixture of lyric and narrative modes, though the lyric element is not sufficiently structured for the piece to be a *chantefable* (the form known also as Menippean satire, followed by the *Consolatio* of Boethius, which Chaucer also translated). Both prologue and tale are highly emotional, both in their exultation of Mary and in their praise of holy innocence as seen in the child murdered for singing *Alms redemptoris mater* in a ghetto. The theme of holy innocence is cued by the paraphrase of Psalm 8 with which the Prioress's prologue begins:

> O Lord, oure Lord, thy name how merveillous
> Is in this large world ysprad – quod she –
> For noght oonly thy laude precious
> Parfourned is by men of dignitee,
> But by the mouth of children thy bountee
> Parfourned is, for on the brest soukynge
> Somtyme shewen they thyn heriynge.

*Laud* means praise, a function of prayer as are petition and adoration. The Prioress's second stanza says that she intends to tell a story in praise of the Lord, invoked in Stanza I, as well as of Mary, though she notes that she cannot thereby increase the honor of her who ". . . hirself is honour and the route / Of bountee, next hir Sone, and soules boote." These matters are important, for it is they, and not the emotional tone of the prologue and tale, which can be defined as mysticism. Both come together, however, in the three invocations that open the third stanza:

> O mooder Mayde, O mayde Mooder free!
> O bussh unbrent, brennynge in Moyses sighte,
> That ravyshedest doun fro the Deitee,
> Thurgh thyn humblesse, the Goost that in th'alighte. . . .

These invocations use imagery familiar in liturgy and other contexts.[20] They are prayer, and they are passionate. Assigned to the Prioress by Chaucer's pilgrim persona, who claims at the end of the General Prologue to have witnessed the Canterbury pilgrimage, the composer is nevertheless Chaucer, writing the language of prayer and hence of mysticism.

[18] *Chaucer's Nuns and Other Essays: A Lost Language and Other Essays.*
[19] The debate on this controversial subject is fully discussed in Paul G. Ruggiers, gen. ed., *A Variorum Edition of the Works of Geoffrey Chaucer*, vol. 2, *The Canterbury Tales*, Part 20, *The Prioress's Tale*, ed. Beverly Boyd (Norman, Oklahoma: Univ. of Oklahoma Press, 1987), *passim.*

The Prioress's prologue now begins the paraphrase of Dante's Bernardine hymn, through Chaucer's own translation of that sublime passage as implanted in the Second Nun's prologue, to which, as I have already said, it is scarcely related; in fact it seem insisted upon, as if Chaucer were determined to have it included. Lines 477–80 have often been paralleled with the fourth stanza of the Second Nun's *Invocacio ad mariam*, but the comparison bears repeating here:

> For somtyme, Lady, er men praye to thee,
> Thou goost biforn of thy benyngnytee,
> And getest us the lyght, of thy preyere,
> To gyden us unto thy Sone so deere.

The Second Nun says (lines 50–56),

> Assembled is in thee magnificence
> With mercy, goodnesse, and with swich pitee
> That thou, that art the sonne of excellence
> Nat oonly helpest hem that preyen thee,
> But often tyme of thy benygnytee
> Ful frely, er that men thyn help biseche,
> Thou goost biforn and art hir lyves leche.

However indebted to his sources, the maker (to use Chaucer's own name for his art) is certainly the historical Geoffrey Chaucer, author of the *Canterbury Tales* and creator of his persona-pilgrim. He was undeniably interested in marian poetry from the earliest evidence of his literary career, whether or not his *ABC* was translated at the request of Blanche of Lancaster. His interest might be seen as simply topical, but one of his younger contemporaries, Thomas Hoccleve, who had Chaucer's portrait copied into his own *Regement of Princes*,[21] makes a point of Chaucer's marian devotion in the introductory stanzas 712–13 which begin his tribute to Chaucer of stanza 714, facing the portrait:

> The firste fyndere of our faire langage,
>   Hath seyde in caas semblable, and othir moo,
> So hyly wel, that it is my dotage
>   For to expresse or touche any of thoo.
>   Alasse! my fadir fro the worlde is goo –
>     My worthi maister Chaucer, hym I mene –
>     Be thou advoket for hym, hevenes quene!
>
> As thou wel knowest, O blissid virgyne,
>   With lovyng hert, and hye devocioun

---

20 Madeleva, *opera cit.*; Boyd, *Chaucer and the Liturgy*, pp. 60–75.
21 *The Regement of Princes and 14 of Hoccleve's Minor Poems*, ed. F. J. Furnivall (London: EETS, e.s. 72, 1897). I have normalized u-v and capitalization, according to present-day English usage, and I have removed Furnivall's diacritical marks.

> In thyne honour he wroot ful many a lyne;
>   O now thine helpe and thi promocioun,
>   To God thi sone make a mocioun,
>     How he thi servaunt was, mayden marie,
>     And lat his love floure and fructifie.

This essay makes no claim that Chaucer was more devout than other fourteenth century Englishmen. It does propose that there is a strain of mysticism in his works from the earliest item extant to the end of his life; that its first expression is marian and Cistercian; and that Dante's marian hymn assigned to the Cistercian mystic Bernard of Clairvaux had a profound influence on at least two of the *Canterbury Tales*. One poet who knew Chaucer and who was likewise a layman knew that he had a special love for the Virgin Mary which should merit her intercession at the hour of his judgment, exactly what Chaucer had asked for himself in his Retraction at the end of his *Canterbury Tales*.

# WOMANLY MEN AND MANLY WOMEN
# IN THOMAS À KEMPIS AND ST. TERESA

## ELIZABETH PSAKIS ARMSTRONG

THE WORD "virago," now reduced to a simple pejorative, was once a concession, made within the patriarchal notion of women as inferior, to the possibility that a woman could be perfected: she had only to act and think more like a man. Both Ovid and Virgil use the word to describe Athena, the warrior-Goddess who has, perhaps, her nurture in the father's thigh to thank for her gifts of manly reason and prowess. Stoic philosophers praise the virtues of strong and courageous women, and early Christian theologians like Jerome and Chrysostom adopt the notion of "virago" to their formulation of a doctrine on sex which extraordinarily privileges virginity and chastity. The rewards for renouncing sex, great for both genders, has remarkable effects on women: even a celibate, married woman, Jerome says, becomes manly by living with her husband as a sister, or better, as a brother. Such a wife is praised in a letter to her husband: "You have with you a companion, once of the flesh, now of the spirit, once a subject, now an equal, once a woman now a man." "Habes tecum prius carne, nunc in spiritu sociam . . . de femina virum, de subiecta parem. . . ." (Ep. 71 "Ad Lucinum Baeticum"). Although the idea that males are so absolutely the superior gender that the best woman is a man is not palatable to modern feminists, it is easy to see that the idea of woman become man is not in the same class of vilifying rhetoric which marks misogynist texts. Working also from Pauline texts about heaven's effects upon gender, Jerome means to allow women, once they have given up sex, the same dignity and worthiness he would grant to men who have given up sex.

The later history of the virago has usually not been far from comedy and farce – the stories of Socrates's wife, for instance, are part of a long tradition that survives in the American slang "battle ax," a warrior-woman who wears the pants in a marriage and "henpecks" her husband. Christine de Pisan's fifteenth-century *City of Ladies* is one of the very few attempts to rescue the idea of virago from corruption as well as from the kind of praise of women Boccaccio offers in *Concerning Famous Women* where satires on the infrequency of laudable behavior in women deconstruct the theme. The idea of gender reversal in men has a more benign history in medieval times, beginning especially if ironically, in the twelfth century which accommodated also the most vehement anti-feminist treatises ever written. Caroline Bynum's meticulous study of monastic literature shows us a dense pattern

107

of feminine/female images used to define the ideal nature of the monastic community, the abbots like mothers to their monks, tenderly nurturing them as a mother breast feeds a baby. God himself becomes lavishly double-gendered during this century, as the concept of God the disciplinary Father is aligned with the opposite concept of a motherly Christ. These feminizations, particularly among the Cistercians, though Bynum does not see that they ameliorate women's actual social condition, do, she says, "reveal . . . a sense (not without ambivalence) of a need and obligation to nurture other men, a need and obligation to achieve intimate dependence on God" (168). Cistercian abbots were "called upon to respond with qualities that medieval men considered feminine. Anxious, even guilty about ruling, these religious leaders tried to create a new image of authority (both their own and God's) that would temper that authority with compassion" (158). Contemporaneous with this opulent imagery of nurturing is the prosaic use of womanliness as a humility topic. By corroborating his culture's stereotyping of women, a monk could signal his humility by calling himself a "weak woman" (Bynum 138). The lexicon which temporarily smiled upon the idea of a manly woman had no space for a word approving the idea of a womanly man – no one coined a word, gynago? – for so odd a case as that. The patriarchy, of course, did not seem much interested in examining any outré or critical notions of manliness – was the comic stereotype of the *miles gloriosus* the only popular characterization of foolish and corrupt manliness?

This essay must put aside for another time these intriguing questions about the history of gender reversals for its specific interest in the difficulty, given this tradition, in interpreting St. Teresa's occasional but always startling advice to the nuns of her Order to be courageous and brave, like men. Does this direction, some of us still ask, suggest some psychological antipathy to her own sex? Is it perhaps tainted with that historical misogyny that can praise women no higher than to say that they are like men in virtue? Is Teresa like Catherine of Siena whose fondness for the word "virilmente" shows her, some scholars say, to be "glaringly sexist"? (Noffke 21). Although I cannot hope to answer the larger questions in this cultural riddle (which is, in any case, being splendidly treated by Bynum and Peter Brown as well as by Teresian scholars like Jodi Bilinkoff) I think I can add another kind of "no" to these questions by comparing Teresa's voice on gender to a like voice in Thomas à Kempis's *Imitation of Christ* which also treats matters of gender as matter of fact, not polemic.

The word "sexist" is not only anachronistic but irrelevant to the kind of interest these writers bring to questions of gender. That interest, though it is engaged within the two discourses in different ways, has a precisely similar goal: both Thomas and Teresa encourage their audiences to shed those attributes of gender which create barriers between them and Christ. Their purpose is to change behaviors and attitudes which are tuned to the world's wish and convenience into behavior fit for God. Thomas sees a major danger for men is that the pursuit of reason and the love of learning are often full of aggressive arrogance that leads far from the ideals of Christian humility. But Teresa sees the danger for women in their habits of acquiescence, timidity, and love of comfort that destroy the rigor and dedication necessary to a contemplative life. As Thomas counsels men to be quiet and obedient, Teresa counsels women to have a "holy daring" (*Way of Perfection*, 16.12). Thomas's opening premise is that men's natural desire for knowledge (he uses that famous Aristotelian phrase from the *Metaphysics* to open Chapter 2 of Book 1) can lead them to love the authority and ascendancy over other men which knowledge can give them. Teresa's premise is that women naturally desire to take the way of least resistance, to take it easy, to listen always to their bodies' merest signals of discomfort, to be, in short, passive in mind and in body both. What in these characterizations our age would call sexist, seems merely to be the unexciting circumstances of real living, the habits of mind and body which men and women teach each other. These ties to gendered behavior are treated like other ties to the social and political way of the world – love of possessions and of rank – and must be cut away like them. Thomas's man is not only educated but has a academician's love for learning. He has a great deal of trouble withdrawing himself from arguments because he feels that his own opinions and ideas are always right, and he is apt to think of the religious community as he would the secular one, as an opportune place to rise in power and authority. He finds it almost impossible to see himself as a humble servant to anyone or anything. It is on this ordinary middle to upper class male's attachment to his birth-right privileges and responsibilities that Thomas sets his gaze. Everything he says is drawn from the very roots of Christian/stoic thought and action, but Thomas's rendition of the spiritual implications of these ancient traditions of obedience, service, of abasement of self and contempt of the world is nonetheless striking for its quiet if relentless presentation.

Thomas opens the *Imitation* with the crucial topic – "Of what use is it to discourse learnedly on the Trinity, if you lack humility and therefore displease the Trinity? Lofty words do not make a man just or holy; but a good life makes him dear to God" (1.1). "Learned men always wish to appear so, and desire recognition of their wisdom" (1.2); "At the Day of Judgement, we shall not be asked what we have read, but what we have done; not how eloquently we have spoken, but how holily we have lived" (1.3). And in a wry variation on the *Où sont les neige d'antan* topic – "Where are now all those masters and doctors whom you knew so well in the full flower of their learning?" (1.2). The academician is apt to be more interested in pressing his ideas on his companions than on loving and obeying them. We should not "cling to our own opinions", he says, or "rely on the rightness of [our] views. . . . If your opinion is sound, and you forego it for the love of God and follow that of another, you will win great merit. I have often heard that it is safer to accept advice than to give it (1.4). We must be patient with the faults of others, realizing that "We wish to see others severely reprimanded; yet we are unwilling to be corrected ourselves" (1.16).

Thomas dismantles the very center of learning's citadel: "Old habits are hard to break, and no one is easily weaned from his own opinions; but if you rely on your own reasoning ability rather than on the virtue of submission to Jesus Christ, you will but seldom and slowly attain wisdom. For God wills that we become perfectly obedient to Himself, and that we transcend mere reason on the wings of a burning love for Him" (1.13). The mildness and matter-of-factness of this statement is striking – the chapter stops there with the words "on wings of burning love"; and in the original Latin, without the wings: "et omnem rationem per inflammatum amorem transcendere" (Pohl 1904, 26). This is the fact, he implies, take it and consider it in itself; he does not further entice the reader with descriptions of either renunciation's or love's rewards.

And, then, Thomas cuts the monk off from what he might be thinking is a safe place of allowable power, the assumption of authoritative roles within the community. Those, too are dangerous – it is better "not to be one's own master," he says; "safer to obey than to rule" (1.9).

This is the text's center from beginning to end – to convince the man accustomed to authority and power that there is no power he can safely employ or reserve if he wishes to become a lover of Christ. It is perhaps the centrality of the message, the plainness of a delivery shorn of (conventional) violent metaphors of struggle and of heroic endurances and suffering, that call attention to how much a monk's life resembles any traditional woman's life. He obeys instead of rules, tolerates rather than instructs, submits instead of commanding. He is advised not to long for much freedom, encouraged to stay at home, not to go out to gossip: "It is easier to remain quietly at home than to keep due watch over ourselves in public" (1.20). He advises:

> Avoid public gatherings as much as possible, for the discussion of worldly affairs becomes a great hindrance, even though it be with the best of intentions, for we are quickly corrupted and ensnared by vanity. But why is it that we are so ready to chatter and gossip with each other when we so seldom return to silence without some injury to our conscience? The reason why we are so fond of talking with each other is that we think to find consolation . . . and to refresh a heart wearied with many cares . . . [but] this outward consolation is no small obstacle to inner and divine consolation. (1.10)

It is interesting that in this chapter the translator has chosen to preserve the feminine gender of the Latin word "anima".

Scattered throughout this meticulously detailed description of submission are encouragements to act manfully – "arm yourself manfully" (1.19); "Accinge te sicut vir (Pohl 1904, 33); "fight most manfully" (1.25); "virilius" (Pohl 1904, 53); "advance manfully" (2.4); "viriliter" (Pohl 1904, 86); "manfully bear the cross" (1.12). In the even and certain flow of the text's description of the safety which rests in quiet, silence, obedience, humility, these admonitions, rather than striking sparks of irony, seem to mark a redefinition of manliness. They implicitly recognize that the virtues central to Christianity have always reversed society's preference for aggression and ascendancy in males. The sense of the following passage suggests the realignment:

> It is no great matter to associate with the good and the gentle, for this is naturally pleasant to everyone. All men are glad to live at peace, and prefer

those who are of their own way of thinking. But to be able to live at peace among hard, obstinate, and undisciplined people and those who oppose us, is a great grace, and a most commendable and manly achievement. (2.3, 71)

Non est magnum cum bonis et mansuetis conversari: hoc enim omnibus naturaliter placet; et unusquisque libenter pacem habet et secum sentientes magis diligit. Sed cum duris et perversis aut indisciplinatis aut nobis contrariantibus pacifice posse vivere, magna gratia est et laudabile nimis, virileque factum. (Pohl 1904, 64–65)

If the man can successfully live this reversal, then he activates the miracle of the Christian/stoic paradox. Conquering himself by stilling his opposing nature, he becomes "master of the world, a friend of Christ, and an heir of Heaven" (2.3, 71); "Isti est victor sui et dominus mundi, amicus Christi et heres caeli" (Pohl 1904, 65). He "manfully bears the cross" by being able to endure trials and suffering in silence and peace.

As the *Imitation of Christ* constantly encourages its audience to give up what the world grants them, the *Way of Perfection* urges its audience to seize for Christ what the world denies them. Thomas implicitly revises the image of manliness fostered by the world, but Teresa explicitly revises the image of femininity.

Recent studies of Teresa demonstrate how she became a craftswoman of the art of simultaneously writing two texts, one addressed to the men above her in the hierarchy of the church, the other to the nuns of her communities. Her language, which used to be criticized for being too informal and colloquial, is now seen to be graced by those same characteristics. Alison Weber calls it a "low register language [which] could count as a disavowal of any homiletic presumption before her male audience; at the same time her verbal informality constituted a gesture of solidarity toward the beleaguered nuns of the early Carmelite reform" (Weber 78). Part of the beleaguerment had something to do with the fact that Spanish churchmen seemed more comfortable with the soft nuns they were used to than the hermit nuns Teresa had in mind to create. Teresa's reforms may have seemed to be turning convents into amazonian battalions. For she, like Thomas, favors the most absolute model of withdrawal from worldly attractions in the Desert Fathers and first martyrs of the young Church. Thomas calls them to his audience's mind: "These all hated their lives in this world, that they might keep them to life eternal. How strict and self-denying. . . . How long and grievous the temptation. . . . How often they were assaulted by the Devil. . . . How valiant the battles they fought. . . . How pure . . . their intention . . . !" (*Imitation*, 1.18). And in *Way of Perfection*, Teresa says, "Let us remember our holy fathers of the past, those hermits whose lives we aim to imitate. What sufferings they endured! What solitude, cold, and hunger, and what sun and heat, without anyone to complain to but God! Do you think they were made of steel? Well, they were as delicate as we . . . so what if we die?" (11.4). What this life demands, she says, is fortitude, courage – "I want you to be like strong men, not weak women, with a strength that will amaze men" (7.8). Strength, courage, determination – these words repeat throughout her text; they must be like soldiers, or, they must be, she says, choosing a more apt comparison, standard bearers in a battle to which they carry no actual arms. It is clear to her that women can too easily assume the role their culture has assigned them as fragile, soft, and sentimental. We need to remember the ordinary allowances made in unreformed convents of the time for wealthy nuns to live in suites of rooms with servants and dogs, meeting friends in parlors like salons where Chaucer's Prioress would have felt at home. It was just such a convent that Teresa fled to build her own reformed order. And, on the other hand, she recognizes how hard it is to take on a whole cultural tradition: "Is it not enough, Lord, that the world has intimidated us...so that we may not do anything worthwhile for You in public or dare speak some truths that we lament over in secret?" 93.7). Her commentary on misogyny is not a dominant theme in the *Way*, but she certainly sees it as a factor which keeps women (whom, she points out, Christ never despised) from the Church's work: "The world's judges are sons of Adam and all of them men" is one of her trenchant, Alison of Bath-like observations (3.7).

But, then, Teresa concedes in a complex way to the notion that women are weak, though in *The Way of Perfection*, when she talks about weakness to her nuns, it is to call them to the strengths she knows they have. She works in a careful way to make them aware of the kinds of behavior and attitude that cannot suit the hermit life. Because these subjects, particularly the ones that locate themselves around the attributes of women's bodies, were all anciently and scabrously treated in misogynist literature, part of the pleasure in Teresa's text for us is in seeing those topics emptied of venom and disgust. In Chapters 10 and 11, the whole subject of physical mortification and of illnesses (which recent studies such as Donald Weinstein's and Rudolph M. Bell's have isolated as peculiarly numerous among women) is treated to what must be its most practical and comic presentation. The first thing we must do, Teresa says, is "rid ourselves of love for our bodies, for some of us are by nature such lovers of comfort that there is no small amount of work in this area" (10.5). This love takes on odd implications when there is, as was true at the time, too much anxiety about the severity of penances, but really, she says, none of us has to worry about that: "I find for myself that the Lord wishes that we be sickly; at least in my case . . . since I would have looked after my comfort anyway. He desired that there be a reason for my doing so" (10.6). Her list of excuses nuns give for their absences from services sounds remarkably like our own self-apologies for not keeping exercise programs: "we stay away [from Choir] one day because our head ached, another because it was just now aching, and three more so that it won't ache again" (10.6). Or: "Once there was a nun who complained to me about a head-ache, and she complained a great deal about it. When it came time to examine her, the head didn't ache at all, but she felt an ache somewhere else" (10.7).

Women, she says, cannot be good nuns if they are always submitting to these rounds of complaints and she makes it clear that she is talking about those menstrual biological cycles. Certainly a nun can be "truly sick:"

But with regard to some of the weaknesses and little illnesses of women, forget

112

about complaining about them, for sometimes the devil makes us imagine these pains. They are things that come and go. If you do not lose the habit of speaking and complaining about everything – unless you do so to God – you never finish lamenting. I insist so much on this because I think it's very important and a reason why monasteries have mitigated their observance.

(11.2)

*They are things that come and go*: her focus here, steady on the fact that she is speaking to women, then turns to a sharp and witty observation about human bodies of either sex: "A fault this body has is that the more comfort we try to give it the more needs it discovers. It's amazing how much comfort it wants" (11.2). But, she observes, returning to women's issues, secular women must suffer silently for "fear of annoying their husbands," so she says, "learn how to suffer a little for love of God without having everyone know about it!" (11.3) . . ."If our body has mocked us so often, shouldn't we mock it at least once?" (11.5). It's important to notice that Teresa does not ever follow the tradition of valorizing chastity and virginity through disgusting descriptions of the trials of married life, as is done in such works addressed to women as *Ancrene Wisse*. Her intent here and everywhere when she makes the comparison between secular and religious life is to maintain a bond (in their capacity for endurance) between women in the world and in the cloister.

When she turns from the biological and female to the social and feminine dimension of women's lives, specifically the capacity for tender lovingness, she takes up another much treated topic. Monastic literature has always been full of warnings to both sexes against too exclusive and fervent friendships within the community. But, on the other hand, it is women's capacity for love, particularly nurturing love that societies across the ages have approved and encouraged. Of this quality Teresa says: "I believe this excessive love must be found among women even more than among men" (4.6). It is dangerous because it drains away from Christ the love that rightly is owed to him. The impulse to bind oneself to affective relationships, though it seems so natural and virtuous, she insists must be reoriented to Christ. The easy phrases of affection must be abolished: ". . . all the tender words that can be uttered . . . should not be used in this house, those like 'my life,' 'my soul, my only good,' and other similar expressions addressed now to one, now to another, of the Sisters. Keep these words of affection for your Spouse . . . if they are used a lot among ourselves, they will not be so touching when used with the Lord" (7.8).

It is this topic that elicits her strongest statement on gender. The unconsidered demonstrations of affection, the careless words of love are just the kind of woman-ish ("mujeres") behavior she wishes her hermit-nuns to avoid.

They are very womanish, and I would not want you, my daughters, to be womanish in anything, nor would I want you to be like women but like strong men. For if you do what lies in your power, the Lord will make you so strong that you will astonish men. And how easy this is for His Majesty since He made us from nothing!

113

Y sin esto, no hay para qué; *es muy de mujeres*, y no querría yo, hijas, lo fueseis en nada, ni lo parecieseis, *sino varones fuertes*; que si ellas hacen lo que es en sí, el Señor las hará tan varoniles, que espanten a los hombres. ¡ Y qué fácil es a Su Majestad, pues nos hizo de nonada!"  (7.8)

Weber's translation of "espanten" as "frighten" not "astonish" makes this passage even more obviously comic (85). Perhaps it is here, in her playfulness with this metamorphosis of "womanish" into manliness, with those distinctions by gender which society has always considered of the soberest importance, that we see how determined Teresa is, if not to eradicate distinctions, to reduce their significances. The playfulness is a clear indication that she does not place much serious weight on either sex's gendered qualities as virtues in themselves – they are useful only as they can lead one to God.

It is, in any case, impossible to charge Teresa with treason against her sex as Celia does Ganymede/Rosalind in *As You Like It*, for looking at women as men can look at them. The idea that the best woman is a man is nowhere even implicit in Teresa. And it may be true that no one who has written about women has ever treated their disabilities so circumstantially, so forthrightly and yet so therapeutically. The famous Teresian quality of liveliness and humanity is strong in the conclusion she draws from her discussion of womanish attitudes. If her daughters and sisters can mock womanly tendencies – both physical and emotional, female and feminine – they are rewarded by becoming "lords" of their bodies.

> And believe that this determination is more important than we can realize. For little by little as we grow accustomed to this attitude we shall, with the Lord's help, remain lords of our bodies. Now, then, conquering such an enemy is a very important means to enduring the battle of this life . . . the benefits . . . are so great that no one would feel [oppressed who] could remain in this calm and dominion.  (11.5)

What a wonderful phrase that is – "calm and dominion." ("sosiego y señoría"). The rewards of the spiritual life enter the dynamic of gender in an even more creative way later:

> They say for a woman to be a good wife to her husband she must be sad when he is sad, and joyful when he is joyful, even though she may not be so. See what subjection you have been freed from, Sisters! The Lord, without deception, truly acts in such a way with us. He is the one who submits, and He wants you to be the lady with authority [la señora], to rule; He submits to your rule.  (4)

This passage is like the similar passage in the *Imitation* (2.3) quoted above where Thomas says that the reward for a man who can find the "secret of endurance" in "humble forbearance" is to be restored to his ascendency as "master of the world." It is, of course, the given that Thomas's characterization of the "good and peaceful man" is drawn on the ancient and perennially vital stoic model. Thomas's monk is

114

strong and silent, immune to the world's passions and pastimes, steady in his recourse to intellectual calm and philosophic/spiritual peace. For Thomas's monks, gender reversal is a continuation, even though certainly in another key, of stoicism's precepts. But a nun who discards ancient biological and social stereotypes enters largely uncharted territory. Hers is a *vita nuova*, a parabolic shift as rift-making as the reversal of precedence in the vineyard story of the Gospel (Matthew 20.1–16). At the very least, she is freed from the emotional subjection to men which caused her to live in the shadow of their feelings.

If Thomas cannot urge his monks to be less than men as forthrightly as Teresa urges her nuns to be more than women, he is as intent upon creating a new man as she is a new woman. But some readers of both texts cannot help thinking that Teresa's nuns have a more interesting and lively time in their new lives than do Thomas's monks. Centuries of the world's doubts about women are laughed away as Teresa envisions her hermit-warrior nuns in a brave new world where anything is possible: "I don't say that we shouldn't try [to reach the highest forms of contemplation]; on the contrary, we should try everything" (17.7).

## WORKS CITED/CONSULTED

Bilinkoff, Jodi. *The Avila of St Teresa*. Ithaca, NY: Cornell UP, 1989.

Boccaccio, Giovanni. *Concerning Famous Women*. Trans. Guido Guarino. New Brunswick, N.J.: Rutgers UP, 1963.

Brown, Peter. *The Body and Society*. N.Y: Columbia UP, 1988.

Bynum, Caroline. *Jesus as Mother*. Berkeley, CA: U of California P, 1982.

Christine de Pisan. *City of Ladies*. Trans. Earl J. Richards. NY: Persea Books, 1982.

Erickson, Carolly. *The Medieval Vision*. NY: Oxford UP, 1976.

St Jerome. *Lettres*. Vol. 4. Ed. Jérôme Labourt. Paris: Societé d'édition des Belles Lettres, 1954.

Noffke, Suzanne. Trans. *Catherine of Siena: The Dialogue*. NY: Paulist Press, 1980.

Teresa of Avila. *The Way of Perfection*. Trans. K. Kavanaugh and O. Rodriguez. Washington, D.C.: Institute of Carmelite Studies, 1980.

——— *Obras Completas*. Ed. P. Silverio de Santa Teresa. Madrid: M. Aguilar, 1945.

Thomas à Kempis. *Imitatione Christi*. Ed. Michael Pohl. Freiburg: Herder, 1904.

——— *The Imitation of Christ*. Trans. Leo Sherley-Price. NY: Penquin Books, 1952.

Weber, Alison. *Teresa of Avila and the Rhetoric of Femininity*. Princeton, N.J.: Princeton UP, 1990.

Weinstein, Donald and R. M. Bell. *Saints and Society*. Chicago: U of Chicago P, 1982.

# HOLY THEATRE/ECSTATIC THEATRE

## MARY E. GILES

IF SUCH PHENOMENA as medieval morality plays or the *autos sacramentales* of the seventeenth-century Pedro Calderón de la Barca were our exclusive sources for understanding the relationship of theatre and religion, we probably would conclude that the two are linked only insofar as drama represents religious dogma. But drama and religion may meet on less obvious levels than propaganda or moral instruction. The conjunction of "holy theatre" as understood by the modern playwright, Peter Brook, and the "ecstatic theatre" of late medieval visionary women, for example, offers one possibility for approaching the relationship with minimal attention to dogma and primary emphasis on the nature of dramatic and religious experience and how they intersect in our lives. The comparison of these seemingly disparate forms of theatre is also appealing as a means to legitimate the artistry of ecstatic texts as well as to underscore their socio-religious implications for medieval visionary women.

In the first decade or so of the sixteenth century a Spanish woman named Sor María of Santo Domingo, also known as the Beata (blessed one) of Piedrahita, became famous for ecstasies in which she answered questions posed by learned men, discoursed on theology, and represented events from the gospels.[1] Born between 1470 and 1489, Sor María had been especially devout as a child, given to visions and raptures and harsh ascetic practices. As she matured, the physical phenomena increased in kind and frequency; she fasted for extraordinarily long periods, miraculously bled from her side on Fridays, received the host on her tongue without being present physically at mass, and was enraptured alone or in the company of religious and secular folk. She even was ecstasized on public occasions, most notably when she was summoned by the king to the royal court at Burgos, where her public raptures bolstered her fame as an ecstatic and visionary.

We have some record of Sor María's ecstasies in a small volume of printed transcriptions of her enraptured discourse.[2] Thought to be the work of her religious

---

[1] For information on Sor María of Santo Domingo see Mary E. Giles, *The Book of Prayer of Sor María of Santo Domingo. A Study and Translation* (Albany: State University of New York Press, 1990).

[2] José Manuel Blecua, ed., *Libro de la Oración de Sor María de Santo Domingo* (Madrid: Hauser y Menet, 1948).

117

confessor, the transcriptions had been ordered by Cardinal Cisneros for the primate's spiritual edification. Of the selections that have come down to us, the longest is a contemplation that Sor María experienced on Easter, in which she ecstatically represented the events at the empty sepulchre. The contemplation is unmistakably dramatic in Sor María's portrayal through dialogue and narration of the Blessed Virgin Mary, Jesus, Mary Magdalen, and the apostles Peter and John and as she sets herself within the play to witness the events she dramatizes. The dramatic nature of this contemplation gave rise to the term "ecstatic theatre" in my earlier study of Sor María.[3] In considering the possible linkage of theatre and ecstatic discourse since that study I have been attracted to twentieth-century "holy theatre" as a possibly valid term for a comparison that might further clarify the dramatic aspects of Sor María's contemplations and urge appreciation for her actions as being courageous and creative.

Selecting the "holy theatre" associated with such playwrights as Antonin Artaud, Peter Brook, Jacques Copeau and Jerzy Grotowski for comparison to the ecstatic theatre of Sor María is not meant to imply a direct influence of the one on the other. The purpose of the comparison is to sharpen rather than blur distinctions in the belief that uniqueness of expression earns our highest regard as students of religion and literature and that distinctions as well as similarities spur the critical imagination to seek for connections where they were not thought to exist. Since the subject matter of the present volume presupposes the reader's greater familiarity with mystical literature than with contemporary theatre, I would like to initiate the analysis by setting forth three aspects of holy theatre as possible topics for comparison to Sor María's ecstatic discourse. These aspects in turn generate an explication first of modern theories of catharsis and then the theatre of Jerzy Grotowski.

In a general sense modern theatre is said to challenge Aristotelian concepts on two fronts, first on the notion of mimesis and second on theatre as literature. With respect to the former concept, modern theory rejects the view that the purpose of theatre is to represent a universal action that might happen in favor of the idea that performance is a fragmentary, changeable event occurring in a specific time. The effect of this shift from universal to particularized action is, as Timothy J. Wiles explains in *The Theatre Event*, "to move art from reflecting reality to being a kind of reality of its own."[4] The second threat to Aristotelian theory comes from according privileged status to the performance such that the meaning of the text is registered not in an independent written script but in a moment-by-moment performing that itself becomes the text. One effect of so-called performance theatre is to give prominence to the actor, especially in his relationship with the audience, at the expense of accoutrements like staging and costuming.

The broad lines of Sor María's contemplations foreshadow modern theatre in three ways: the non-mimetic nature of her discourse; the absence of a literary text;

---

3  *Ibid.*, 95–104.
4  Timothy J. Wiles, *The Theatre Event. Modern Theories of Performance* (Chicago & London: The University of Chicago Press, 1980), 4.

the performer's affective relationship with the audience. These lines of comparison emerge more sharply in connection with the affective nature of catharsis, with particular attention to the theatre of the Polish playwright, Jerzy Grotowski.

In an essay on the subject of catharsis, Philip Auslander sees the desire to penetrate the surface of experience as characteristic of both Peter Brook and Jerzy Grotowski and their predecessors, Jacques Copeau and Antonin Artaud.[5] From Copeau and Brooke is derived the notion of a communal theatre whose intent is to bring "its spectators into emotional harmony with one another by celebrating their common identity as human beings."[6] For Artaud and Grotowski theatre is therapeutic, "designed to accomplish spiritual renewal by unmasking repressed psychic materials."[7] Whatever its manifestations, holy theatre is concerned with changing the affective state of the audience; in this respect, notes Christopher Innes in *Holy Theatre: Ritual and the Avant Garde*, holy theatre may be today's successor to classical tragedy.[8]

Whether catharsis is regarded as primarily educative in the Aristotelian sense – the dramatic experience teaches the audience a disciplined use of emotions so as to attain a balanced inner state – or therapeutic, that is, enabling the spectator to relive and heal unresolved psychological pain, modern theorists agree that the final cause of drama is catharsis. The dynamic of catharsis, however, is expanded to include the director, the actor and the audience.

The two forms of catharsis carry two kinds of communication, the first symbolic, the second causal.[9] In the first mode the symbol of an affective state is an image that leads the spectator to conceptualize the state and to understand the image discursively. Essentially, all spectators form the same concept. The second mode does not produce a universal concept and significance; the image causes an affective state in the spectator that varies from person to person. The theatre of Copeau and Brooke is both symbol and cause while that of Artaud and Grotowski is more causal; no one of the dramatists strives to impart discursive meaning.

These concepts of theatre do not exactly inform the ecstatic theatre of Sor María for the reason that the intentionality of Sor María as "author" of her performance is not known as is the purpose of holy theatre according to its practitioners. Sor María left no account, as does Grotowski, for example, to prove that she was conscious of herself as purposefully creating a performance. Were there such an account, the nature of her ecstasy would have incurred even more suspicion than appears in the records of the informal inquisitorial proceedings to which Sor María

---

5  See Philip Auslander, " 'Holy Theatre' and Catharsis," *Theatre Research International* 9 (1984): 16–29.
6  *Ibid.*, 16.
7  *Ibid.*
8  Christopher Innes, *Holy Theatre: Ritual and the Avant Garde* (New York: Cambridge University Press, 1981).
9  For this discussion on theories of catharsis I am indebted to Philip Auslander in the article already cited. In turn Auslander mentions his indebtedness to T. J. Scheff, *Catharsis in Healing, Ritual, and Drama* (Berkeley: University of California Press, 1979).

was subjected on four occasions. Ecstasy in the Christian tradition is a graced event, befalling its subject unexpectedly and outside of her control. Any hint of the subject's controlling or willing the phenomenon would cast serious doubts on its genuineness. Sor María was not without suspicion in this respect; documents cite witnesses who asserted that she seemed to go in and out of ecstasy at will, as when she "performed" for royalty and nobility at court. On the other hand, there was sufficient testimony to the genuineness of her ecstasies, meaning that they were God-given rather than self-induced, to sway the examiners to her side. Eventually, she was exonerated, though ordered to remain enclosed in her monastery.[10]

But if the intentionality of Sor María with respect to her ecstatic performing is not determinable, the effects on her spectators are a matter of record. Even those detractors who decried her behavior as scandalous at best had to admit that ecstasized discourse could be beneficial, as when some listeners were moved to pious weeping while others changed their lives. A partial conclusion to the question of catharsis in the case of Sor María is that her theatre was predominantly causal, rousing in her spectators emotions that were appropriate to her actions. Thus, if she sorrows at the sorrowing Virgin, asking us as readers/spectators to behold Mary's grief, the effect is to draw us into the emotion, perhaps but not necessarily producing an effect that cuts below the surface of emotions. When, for example, Sor María weeps over the crucified Christ who suffered because of our sins, her sorrow turns to exhortation as she implores herself and her audience to repent:

> Woe to him who is hardened in the habit of sin! How far he is from help, for his corrupt will does not permit him to see the truth and makes him loathe virtue. And to what coldness, confusion and callousness do the passions of such a person bring his soul, made so dead and deaf? Oh what a great thing it is for a sinner to burn in his God at least to be freed of passions! So love your God if only for this rest and freedom even though you might not have to love Him for His own sake.[11]

A fuller response to the question of whether and in what form the ecstatic theatre of Sor María is cathartic may lie in a comparison to the theatre of Jerzy Grotowski; I selected Grotowski as a term for comparison because he explicitly acknowledged the relationship of religion and theatre, affirming the possibility of creating a "secular *sacrum* in the theatre."[12] "The theatre," he said, "when it was still part of religion, was already theatre" in that "it liberated the spiritual energy of the congregation or tribe by incorporating myth and profaning or rather transcending it."[13]

Grotowski's indebtedness to religion and spirituality is evident in several

---

[10] See the study by Giles for details on the four proceedings.
[11] *Ibid.*, 167.
[12] Jerzy Grotowski, *Towards a Poor Theatre* (London: Methuen & Co. Ltd, 1969), 49.
[13] *Ibid.*, 22–23.

dimensions of his theatre, as when he applies the phrase *via negativa* to what he calls "poor" theatre, meaning a theatre that is denuded of sound scores, staging and costumes, thus being reduced to the essential encounter between spectator and actor. The phrase further denotes a process of disciplining the actor in such a way that blocks are eliminated rather than skills acquired; ultimately "impulse and action are concurrent" and "the body vanishes, burns, and the spectator sees only a series of visible impulses."[14] In the disciplined actor the appropriate state of mind is passive readiness in which "one does not *'want to do that'* but rather *'resigns from not doing it.'"*[15] Or, the actor is a clear channel through which outside forces can penetrate and operate.

Grotowski gave the name "holy" to the actor who in the effort to become a clear channel submits to a kind of training that requires him to be skinned psychically and to be penetrated in existential nakedness. The actor works in public with his body, making a public spectacle of himself through what Grotowski called an "outrageous sacrilege."[16] Revealing himself in his psychic nakedness by casting off socially acceptable masks, the holy actor exposes and thus sacrifices the innermost core of his personality. *Apocalypsis cum figuris* is a compelling demonstration of the actor's submission to the *via negativa* and to self-sacrifice as the principal actor assumes the bodily and philosophical function of Christ: he is made the scapegoat of the other actors and the audience, both of whom become the victimizers. Thus, the victimization of the central actor playing the fool is the victimization of the actor himself who is the Christ-figure of the simpleton.[17]

The purpose of the actor's self-sacrifice is to unmask and heal his inner self and to move the audience as well to psychic penetration in a kind of communal catharsis. In order to involve the audience in psychic penetration, Grotowski limited the number of spectators, situating them in such ways that they physically and emotionally had to participate in the action. The spectator was no ordinary theatre-goer bent on an evening's diversion; he was, in Grotowski's words, one "who has genuine spiritual needs and who really wishes, through confrontation with the performance, to analyze himself."[18]

A comparison of Sor María to Grotowski, with primary reference to the *Apocalypsis cum figuris*, reveals a strong connection between his "poor" theatre and her ecstatic performances. As readers of her "text," we must make conscious efforts to imagine a landscape beyond the frontiers of the written word. The imaginative effort includes letting the words evoke images of the bodily Sor María as she speaks, gestures and moves. We must appreciate as well the enormous effort demanded of the woman to create before her spectators a physical, emotional and spiritual reality that was in no wise mediated by props or staging or by the

---

[14] *Ibid.*, 16.
[15] *Ibid.*, 17.
[16] *Ibid.*, 34.
[17] For an excellent analysis of *Apocalypsis cum figuris* see *The Theatre Event*.
[18] *Ibid.*, 40.

participation of other people. She had no theatrical space as such, no co-actors, no text, even in the minimalist sense of lines from world literature that would be recited from memory, as in the case of *Apocalypsis cum figuris*. In her "empty space" Sor María created the happening through her physical self – the voice, the gesture, the larger moving of the body as when, according to witnesses, her body became positioned as if she were nailed to the cross. As readers, we infer her movements from passages such as the following in which Sor María implores the spectators to gaze with pity upon the sorrowing mother of Jesus: "Now see the living mother who saw her son die. See with what love and tears she washes and sweeps the cell while waiting for her Beloved."[19] Ultimately Sor María had only herself.

Not only was Sor María physically alone in her space, but she was psychologically alone as well. Although she enjoyed fame as a visionary, she was at the same time the subject of gossip and informal examination at the hands of male religious superiors. Part of the reason why she scandalized people is that the Dominican monastery to which she was attached as a member of the third order was embroiled in a controversy over reform. Her compatriots advocated a radical reform in the direction of austerity, much like that of Savonarola and the Dominican brethren in Italy. The fact that the Italian reformers had a visionary woman who pronounced oracularly in favor of strict reform probably inspired the Spanish Dominicans to seize upon Sor María for similar prophetic duties. Because the push for a Savonarola-like reform was promoted by a minority of the Spanish Dominicans, Sor María's behavior looked suspicious to the conservative majority. The point is that when Sor María "performed" ecstatically, her credibility as God's oracle had to be created in the moment through her words and gestures, silence and stillness. The spectators might well include skeptics, disbelievers and enemies of the reform, whose reasons for being present were to find proof that she was a fraud and, in some cases, to use that proof to discredit the reform movement. She created in an atmosphere of political agendas that were hostile at least in part. Granted that I am indulging my imagination, but I have to believe that more than naivite or craving for fame supported this uneducated peasant woman as she allowed herself to be a public spectacle. I am inclined to believe that courage marked her steps as she readied herself for public exposure and as she bore its consequences in the examinations that probed intimate details of her private religious life.

As a "performer," Sor María did not have the safety net of the holy actor, who, even though victimized by fellow actors and the audience, nonetheless actively trains for that event in the hope that self-disclosure will occur. Morever, the holy actor may carry into the performance a history of accomplishment and the knowledge that, however real the skinning, he can refuse to go on with the performance.

Theoretically, Grotowski, might take issue with this last statement, for he demanded of his actors a giving of themselves that is reminiscent of the asceticism of the spiritual athlete (the desert anchorites come to mind). The holy performance,

19 *Ibid.*, 151.

he asserted, "demands a mobilization of all the physical and spiritual forces of the actor,"[20] giving oneself "in one's deepest intimacy, with confidence, as when one gives oneself in love."[21] Giving, he continued, must be done "fully, humbly and without defense."[22]

Although the "giving" that Grotowski describes appears to transcend the aesthetic realm for the spiritual one, there is, nonetheless, an aloneness that differentiates the ecstatic woman from the holy actor. The holy actor has the company of other actors who share the vision of psychic penetration and self-sacrifice and who also allow themselves to be exposed. More significantly, he has the guiding touch of the playwright-director who is the concrete, perceptible author of the vision. Even though Sor María's supporters spoke and wrote in her defense, at times incurring the suspicion of their religous superiors, they were not bodily exposed as was she. Their limbs – to be graphically explicit – were not contorted into the position of Christ on the cross in full view of other people. They did not put their body "on the line" as did this woman who was a fraud in the eyes of misogynist religious men. Finally, the actor could pull back if the self-sacrifice became too painful, whereas the enraptured woman was bound to live by the terms and consequences of her "performance," even when they dictated public disgrace, abandonment by colleagues, and banishment from public life to monastic enclosure.

The *via negativa* of the holy actor and his ecstatic counterpart is similar, however, if not identical: in both there is evident a spontaneity and passive readiness that presupposes some kind of spiritual training for some purpose. Just as Grotowski believed that the true nature of human beings is hidden beneath layers of behavior and beliefs that we adopt in order to be socially acceptable, so the visionary and the mystic believe that the Imago Dei lies deep within the soul and that the purpose of the spiritual journey is to bring to the conscious level the divine spark or image within. The holy actor is to unlearn acting techniques so as to encounter his naked self; the ecstatic unlearns beliefs, images, people, books, in short, all the mediators of the divine so that in spiritual nakedness she may meet God. And while the holy actor is to experience as the necessary state of mind "a passive readiness to realize an active role,"[23] the ecstatic speaks of being made utterly open and passive, alert to that which presents itself to her, unsummoned and uncontrolled. To emphasize the fact of Sor María's passivity, we note that when questioned about her behavior, the visionary woman told her examiners that she was not responsible for her words and actions during ecstasy, nor could she remember what she said. Pure spontaneity, therefore, is the hallmark of both the holy actor and the ecstatic visionary.

The *via negativa* for Sor María – and I am not suggesting that she studied or practiced apophatic theology – was a life lived as a passive subject. First, Sor María

20 *Ibid.*, 37.
21 *Ibid.*, 38.
22 *Ibid.*
23 *Ibid.*, 17.

was subject to religious superiors, ranging from the village priest of her childhood who testified to her exceptional piety, to the reformers who encouraged her public prophecies and accompanied her to Toledo, Burgos and elsewhere, to the confessor who insisted on spending nights in her cell, even atop her bed, in order, he explained, to protect her from her infirmities and the insidious attacks of the devil. Ultimately, she found herself subject to the religious examiners and their final order that she quit her role as peripatetic prophet and get back to the monastery where she belonged. Whatever the source of the extraordinary phenomena that marked her life, Sor María became on their account a woman in the public eye whose behavior ignited gossip in court and cloister.

Second, as suggested above, Sor María was subject to phenomena that by her account and the testimony of her supporters happened to her beyond her control. Although skeptics wondered about the ease with which she seemed to go in and out of ecstasy, she herself was convinced that the visions, colloquies with heavenly beings, miraculous communion, supernatural fasts and bleeding from the side were visited upon her by God himself. The physical pain that Sor María suffered during ecstasy, as when she bled from her side, indicate that, unless she was masochistic, she was being subjected to less than desirable experiences. Certainly the devil's attacks were no occasion for celebration. Once, she admitted, the devil "had thrown her down a well where she managed to stay alive by praying the Creed aloud until her sisters heard her and rushed to rescue her."[24] As modern readers who are inclined to scoff at such tales, we must remember that to Sor María the devil and his ruses were real enough as were the physical injuries he inflicted on her. Terrorized by fear that she would be subjected to who knows what deviltry, she understandably longed for the psychological solace and physical protection afforded by the presence of another human being in her cell at night.

Thus, for Sor María the *via negativa* was not a discipline assumed at will and, by implication, set aside voluntarily as well. The role of ecstatic visionary seems to have been thrust upon her at an early age and in time came to exact heavy recompense for whatever good fortune and fame it brought her. In this respect she occupies terrain similar to that traveled by mystics for whom the interior landscape is necessarily dark and painful.

The holy actor, on the other hand, actively travels the *via negativa*, consciously training for the cumulative self-exposure that is the hallmark of catharsis; in this respect he is like the spiritual pilgrim who ascends the mountain in the active night of the senses and spirit – to borrow an image and its roadmap from St. John of the Cross. The act of self-exposure bears the signs of passivity when there comes upon the actor, spontaneously and, in a way, unexpectedly, the moment when the other actors and the audience make of him a victim. If and how this experience of being *acted* upon becomes a way of living for the actor, I cannot judge from reading

[24] *Ibid.*, 32.

about holy theatre; but I accept the possibility that self-sacrifice in the theatre may effect a conversion of sorts.

The comparison of holy theatre and ecstatic theatre is on firmer ground in the matter of text: no script in the conventional sense exists for either *Apocalypsis cum figuris* or Sor María's contemplations. The only script existent prior to the performance of *Apocalypsis cum figuris* was a compilation of lines from literature, including Sacred Scripture and the writings of T. S. Eliot, Shakespeare and Simone Weil, while Sor María had no prepared text whatsoever. Granted she derived material from Scripture, but she did not recite passages as if committed to memory. Consider, for example, her dramatization of the events at the empty tomb, when the Virgin Mary is portrayed sorrowfully awaiting her Beloved Son.[25] The script for the scene cannot be a verbatim retelling of Scripture since the sorrowful mother is not mentioned as being present at the empty tomb in any one of the gospels. Her presence is, however, central to the "*Planctus Maríae*" that liturgically comes from the early days of the Church.[26] Although Sor María may have been influenced, consciously or not, by liturgically-based representations of the sorrowing mother at the empty sepulcher, her ecstasized dramatization is no mere reproduction of a written or oral text. As Sor María beckons her reader/spectator to behold her characters and to participate in their emotions, she creates a something that is going on right now, principally referrent only to itself, akin to what Richard Schechner calls an "actual".[27] Sor María does not recreate a text: rather she creates a script unique to the moment, one that comes into existence as she begins to speak and move and goes out of existence with the stilling of her voice and body. In both theatres, then, the performance in the moment takes precedence over a text, irrespective of its form.

Similarly, *Apocalypsis cum figuris* and the contemplations were the subject of transcribing, which resulted in a gestural script of the Grotowski play and a verbal one of Sor María's ecstatic performance. In an attempt to evoke the power of the performances of *Apocalypsis cum figuris* that he attended and convinced that "the gestural text provided a whole layer of meaning which qualified the literary quotations and the pantomimed myths and sacraments,"[28] Konstanty Puzna wrote a description of the play as being performed. Whereas Puzna transcribed gestures, Sor María's transcribers dealt with her words. The chief transcriber explained that he would confer with others about what the ecstatic woman had said and then they would agree among themselves on the transcription of her oral text.

The absence of a gestural text in the case of Sor María does not mean that bodily movements and facial expressions were insignificant. On the contrary, from an imaginative reading of the transcription we can infer a visual dimension. Granted the "audience" experienced the power of her words as they issued forth

---

[25] The full text is in *The Book of Prayer of Sor María of Santo Domingo*, 147–168.
[26] *Ibid.*, 99–101.
[27] Richard Schechner, "Actuals," *The Theatre Quarterly* 1 (1971).
[28] *The Theatre Event*, 170.

spontaneously from Sor María's lips, enveloping the people in attendance, who, however they were positioned relative to the woman, were within the soundings of her voice. At the same time, the audience witnessed the crucified body of Sor María/Christ, following the movements of her body as she urged them to look now here, now there. The voice they heard was embodied; the body whose power to evoke emotional response they watched. Thus in Sor María's ecstatic discourse the visual and the oral collide, as they also do in *Apocalypsis*.

The point has been made that orality has greater potential for stirring the human spirit than does the visual; the visual requires the viewer to move analytically, in linear fashion, whereas sounds flooding the listener open up the capacity for intuition and collapse lineal time.[29] The descriptions of Grotowski's theatre with its emphasis on gesture attest to its profound emotional impact on the audience, actor and playwright alike and suggest that a rethinking of the relative values of sound and sight with respect to affectivity may be in order. Perhaps the prudent course here is not to declare in the abstract that either the verbal or the gestural has greater affective potential but to acknowledge that in the art of performing is an incalculable potential for evoking emotional response such that we cannot predetermine if and to what degree an audience will be moved emotionally, nor can we qualify or quantify the experience. Wiles recognizes the elusive nature of affective experience when he notes that "the affectivity of theatre and the value of its catharsis do not seem to be transportable outside the realm of the art experience."[30]

Affectivity may not be measurable in either holy or ecstatic theatre, but evidence points to its being a desirable experience in both. The affective experience of which we are speaking must be more than "skin deep." For Grotowski the larger purpose of the holy actor's self-exposure, or sacrifice, is to create the possibility of communal catharsis whereby the audience – which need be composed of only one spectator – undergoes a psychic penetration as well. Realized through the naked communion of actor and audience, the ideal of inner healing is no less than a psychic penetration.

Transformation is also at the heart of ecstatic theatre. Clearly Sor María is transformed before her audience as limbs move and words pour forth without conscious effort on her part. She and God unite in such intimacy that He speaks through her, conforming her will to his; she is made one with God. For this transformation no audience is requisite, as in Grotowski's holy theatre, where the fact of theatre as being "what takes place between spectator and actor"[31] makes necessary the presence of at least one person at the performance.

Nonetheless, there is a communal dimension to ecstatic theatre as well as to holy theatre. The fact of the written text attests to the communal experience, for there would be no text without an audience and one that was influenced by the ecstatic

---

29 See Walter J. Ong, *The Presence of the Word* (New Haven & London: Yale University Press, 1967) and *The Technology of the Word* (London and New York: Methuen, 1982).
30 *Ibid.*, 173.
31 *Towards a Poor Theatre*, 32.

utterances. Remarks by the editor of the *Book of Prayer* and testimony by witnesses at the informal examination prove that the effects of Sor María's ecstasies were transformative, as has been noted already.

At this point I would like to refer back to the question of Sor María's intentionality. Did Sor María intend to affect the men and women in attendance? In terms of the ecstatic nature of her discourse and her belief that the raptures were God-given, she does not have the explicit purpose of a Grotowski vis-à-vis her "performance"; she did not consider herself an artist as such. But she was purposeful in the matter of evangelization and reform, and her ecstasies abet this purpose. Sor María was aware of herself as being an oracle for reform both within the Dominican Order and in the larger order of Spanish society, having corresponded with Cardinal Cisneros, who proclaimed her to be no less than living gospel, and enjoying the company of reform-minded men and women. As surely as she saw a reformist role for herself that assumed public exposure, so did she pronounce in favor of a reform that would purify the hearts of men and women and set them on a straight course with Jesus Christ. Consider her authority as she replies in the person of God to a question about the success of converting Indians in the New World:

> "If the fire is not lit or if it drifts to places where it is quickly extinguished, how can the rotten wood be lit that is mired in the slime of sin? First the fire must be lit where there is greater means and capacity for it so that where there is not such great means and capacity it may last and not die out so quickly. Therefore, when the marvelous flame of My love begins to shine in despoiled Spain, many other men of Mine will go forth who will not act like those who are there now."[32]

These observations on holy theatre and ecstatic theatre reveal several similarities, especially between the holy actor and the ecstatic woman. Just as the holy actor undergoes a psychic skinning so does Sor María experience a spiritual skinning as she is exposed bodily to public view and there is exposed as well the deepest center of the heart where pulsates the desire to live in conformity with God's will. So also is the transformative nature of the two experiences alike: the purpose of the actor's psychic penetration is communal catharsis while the effect of Sor María's self-exposure may be a communal transformation whereby her spectators are awakened to the desire to love and serve God that grounds their existence.

Although holy theatre and ecstatic theatre are not identical, nor was the intention of the essay to prove exact correspondence, the similarities that emerge from the comparison are significant in terms of assessing both the artistry of ecstatic discourse and the interconnectedness of aesthetic and spiritual experience. The centrality of the body in both theatres suggests that attempts to evaluate the aesthetics of ecstatic discourse ought to concentrate on determining how for the visionary woman her body becomes the primary locus of meaning as it does in holy

[32] *Ibid.*, 178.

theatre. One approach is to read the text with an eye to discerning the presence of the body in the connotations of words and in the emptiness surrounding them. Another way is to read imaginatively so that the words are enfleshed in images of gesture and movement.

Locating the value of the text as text in the primacy of the body creates an aesthetic that exposes the fragile boundaries of an already beleaguered canon. And if analogy is an accepted instrument for argumentation, then the comparison of holy theatre and ecstatic theatre promotes the effort to "re-vision" the canon. The fact that holy theatre with its unmistakable emphasis on the body is established within the canon of dramatic literature argues for similar treatment of a discourse that analysis shows to be comparably artistic in several aspects, including respect for the body as the source, the means, and the fruit of creativity.

Attending to words as being embodied, which means to imagine a gestural text in the spirit of Puzna's transcription, has socio-religious implications that corroborate recent interpretations of medieval women's texts. Accordingly, visionary women defined themselves existentially through the body, validating their spiritual authority to themselves and other people in spite of and, paradoxically, because of the misogyny and vilification of matter embedded in Christian tradition.

With respect to the interconnectedness of aesthetic and spiritual experience, the comparison demonstrates that in the journey of both holy actor and ecstatic woman the discipline and suffering they endure find ultimate blessing in a life transfused with meaning; as a kind of preparatory asceticism requiring commitment and perseverance, their way may be paradigmatic of our own struggle to create a life with meaning and purpose through the vocations, professions, and relationships by which we define ourselves. Second, the transformative effects of holy theatre as seen in the light of ecstatic theatre reveal a spiritual potential to human experience that is not restricted to the conventions of institutional religion; as such, holy theatre reminds us that in undergoing the mystery of psychic transformation we are being opened to the larger mystery of the sacredness of all life.

# COMMUNITIES

# 'A REASONABLE AFFECTION'
## GENDER AND SPIRITUAL FRIENDSHIP IN MIDDLE ENGLISH DEVOTIONAL LITERATURE

ANNE CLARK BARTLETT

> Respondeo dicendum quod necessarium fuit feminam fieri, sicut Scriptura dicit, in adiutorium viri: non quidem in adiutorium alicuis alterius operis, ut quidam dixerunt, cum ad quodlibet aliud opus convenientius iuvari possit vir per alium virum quam per mulierum; sed in adiutorium generationis.[1]

SOMETIME AT the end of the fifteenth century, a close friendship developed between James Grenehalgh, a Carthusian brother from the celebrated English foundation of Sheen, and Joanna Sewell, a nun at the nearby Bridgittine house of Syon.[2] Their alliance is documented rather enigmatically in the margins of several devotional manuscripts that the prolific Grenehalgh annotated, apparently with Sewell in mind. Using her initials and his own characteristic trefoil, as well as sporadic marginal commentary, Grenehalgh called attention to specific passages that appear designed both to further Sewell's spiritual development and to reflect upon the changing circumstances of their relationship. That Grenehalgh saw himself as Sewell's spiritual adviser and friend is clear from the many instructional sections that he marks with her initials, and with such comments as: "Follow not the book [i.e. Hilton's *Scale of Perfection*] in this, but rule according to discretion and take counsel,"[3] and "Let it seem hard to you, and too bitter, to be allied eternally with the devil; so let it seem sweet to you to labor a while in the service of

---

[1] "I respond that one should say that it was necessary for woman to be created, as the Scripture says, for the help of man, not however, in some other work, as some have said, since in any other work it would be more fitting for man to be helped by another man than by a woman, rather [woman was created] for her help in procreation." Thomas Aquinas, *Summa Theologiae* (Rome: Marietti Taurini, 1950), I, q. 92, a. 1. Unless otherwise noted, all translations of Latin and Middle English texts are my own.

[2] This summary relies on Michael Sargent's fascinating essay, "James Grenehalgh: the Biographical Record," *Kartäusermystik und -mystiker*, Analecta Cartusiana 55 (1982), pp. 20–54. For a complete account of Grenehalgh's literary activities, see Sargent's *James Grenehalgh as Textual Critic*, 2 vols. (Salzburg: Institute für Anglistik und Amerkanistik, 1990).

[3] Sargent, "James Grenehalgh," p. 30.

Christ, that afterward you may joy with Christ without end."[4] Such marked passages urge Sewell to abandon temporal pleasures, to attune her spiritual senses, and to fix her attention on the promised delights of the afterlife.

One of the most striking of Grenehalgh's marginal exhortations is a remark that glosses a discussion by Richard Rolle concerning the fleshly enticements that can distract the soul from its contemplation of God. The highlighted passage, from *Contra amatores mundi*, is well worth citing in its entirety:

> I meditated attentively, that I might discover such [love], and I did find a little, for eternal love sustains those who are despised by the world, left without family, and surely raises the impoverished above the earth. Affirming this, the Prophet says, 'For my father and my mother left me, but the Lord took me up.' To this delight in eternity the rich do not ascend, nor do the powerful of the world attain it, nor truly the cloistered monks who are occupied with the love of fleshly friends or of whatever other earthly affairs; for at the beginning divine love casts a man down, makes him humbly subject to all, forces us to forsake *(renuere)* vain joys, and always directs us to desire true joys.[5]

At the close of this section of the text, Grenehalgh appends a terse personal reminder commenting on Rolle's remarks: *"Sewellam renue,"* [forsake Sewell]. At some point, then, Grenehalgh undoubtedly had come to categorize his attachment to the Syon nun among the "fleshly friends" and "vain joys" that Rolle claims divert professed religious from their pursuit of ascetic perfection and must therefore be abandoned.

Whether he was willing and able to "forsake Sewell" is another question. Sometime between 1507–8, Grenehalgh was removed from Sheen and placed as a guest in the Charterhouse at Coventry, farther from Syon, where he continued to annotate manuscripts with his own and Sewell's initials. His further editorial work indicates that he subsequently lodged at several other English Carthusian houses.[6]

How can we understand this incident? Sargent contends that Grenehalgh's removal from Sheen resulted from accusations of incontinence or insubordination lodged against him by his monastic superiors, and the passages that Grenehalgh marks certainly support this interpretation. Sargent also suggests that the reference to Sewell as a recluse testifies to her incarceration, since this term was rarely used to describe Syon nuns.[7] He concludes that "however they may have met, [their relationship] can only represent a relaxation of the Carthusian discipline, as well as the Bridgittine . . ."[8]

However, the marginal glosses, annotations, and recorded events associated with this episode are much more ambiguous than this interpretation suggests. Does the

---

4 Sargent, "James Grenehalgh," p. 33.
5 Translation in Sargent, "James Grenehalgh," p. 34.
6 Sargent, "James Grenehalgh," pp. 24–5.
7 *James Grenehalgh as Textual Critic*, p. 106.
8 *James Grenehalgh as Textual Critic*, p. 92.

reference to Sewell as *reclusa* indicate that she was imprisoned, as Sargeant contends, or does it merely mean that she decided to pursue a more strenuous form of religious observance? Did Grenehalgh's superiors at Sheen misunderstand the nature of his relationship with Sewell? Were his departure from the house and subsequent wanderings motivated by some factors unrelated to his friendship with the Syon nun? The available documents cannot answer these questions conclusively, but they do hint at the complexity of the representation and practice of mixed-sex spiritual friendships among late medieval English female and male religious.

Late medieval English monastic houses attempted in various ways to regulate contact (innocent or otherwise) between the sexes.[9] Along with most monastic

---

9  The relations between medieval English nuns and monks needs much further historical examination. Eileen Power's *Medieval English Nunneries* still provides the standard contextual reference for many recent literary studies. (For example, see Elizabeth Robertson's *Early English Devotional Prose and the Female Audience* (Knoxville: University of Tennessee Press, 1990), esp. pp. 22–30.) Unfortunately, Power's work is misleading, since it examines only episcopal injunctions, it ignores correlating data from male houses, and it confirms its conclusions by citing anti-monastic satirical literature. Graciella S. Daichman's more recent comparison of the representation of English and Spanish convents merely repeats Power's evidence and interpretations. See *Wayward Nuns in Medieval Literature* (Syracuse: Syracuse UP, 1986). Jacqueline Murray's study of clerical bequests to women introduces a more productive approach to gender relations in late medieval England. See "Kinship and Friendship: The Perception of Family by Clergy and Laity in Late Medieval London," *Albion* 20 (1988): 369–85. Murray shows that the spiritual friendships of religious women and men "sometimes superseded [their] family attachments" (376). Margaret Aston has shown how separation of English worshippers by sex, as well as by social status was the norm throughout the Middle Ages. See "Segregation in Church," in *Women in the Church*, Studies in Church History XXVII, ed. W. J. Sheils and Diana Wood (Oxford: Basil Blackwell, 1990), pp. 237–94. Virtually all other analyses of the relations between English nuns and male religious focus on the earlier Middle Ages or Anglo-Saxon period. Sharon Elkins argues that mixed-sex friendships flourished during the monastic expansion of the eleventh and twelfth centuries, but that they declined after the expansion concluded. However, this conclusion needs to be reevaluated in light of data from later centuries. See Elkins, pp. 105–16. Sally Thompson's *Women Religious: the Foundation of Medieval English Nunneries After the Conquest* (Oxford: Clarendon Press, 1990) surveys the foundations of women's monastic houses during the eleventh and twelfth centuries. Jane Schullenburg documents a "golden age" of double monasteries in seventh-century England, but ends her investigation at 1100. See "Women's Monastic Communities, 500–1100: Patterns of Expansion and Decline," *Signs* 14 (1989): 261–92. Unfortunately, a survey of late medieval archival evidence on gender relations in English monastic houses is beyond the scope of this essay. Some recent studies of French monasticism offer useful approaches to this topic, although their findings cannot be applied wholesale to English convents. Constance Berman argues that the extent of permissible relations between women and men throughout the Middle Ages has been underestimated, due to the willingness of modern readers to accept misogynistic rhetoric either at face value, or to view prescriptive discourse as the chief index of social values and behaviors. See "Men's Houses, Women's Houses: the Relationship Between the Sexes in Twelfth-Century Northern France," in *The Medieval Monastery*, ed. Andrew MacLeish (St

legislation, both the Bridgittine and Carthusian statutes explicitly prohibit physical contact between women and men, except under special circumstances. Carthusian monks were officially forbidden from speaking to or hearing the confessions of women.[10] It was considered a "lyght defaute" for a Syon nun to look at monks during the divine services,[11] a "greuous defaute" to speak alone with any males except those in charge of the gates of the convent,[12] and a "more greuous defaute" (classed with rebellion against the English sovereign and challenging the veracity of the revelations of St Bridget) for a Syon nun to be found "in any suspicious place, speaking with any brother."[13] For the latter category of sins, the accused could be imprisoned if she denied her guilt and sought to appeal the verdict or the assigned penance.[14] The Syon statutes do not attempt to distinguish specifically between various forms of mixed-sex contact. Rather, they insist that all conversation between men and women should be sober, quiet, and discreet: ". . . they shall speak soberly and piously that which is to be spoken, not multiplying unprofitable words for no good purpose, nor dissolutely crying out in a loud voice; but softly, discreetly, and with a quiet brevity, they shall say that which is to be said; and immediately take their leave and go their ways."[15] Such legislation approves only the briefest and most instrumental communication between nuns and their monks, priests, and laybrothers. Strictly followed, these monastic prohibitions would leave written communication as the only available channel for mixed-sex relationships. Such regulations explicitly forbid at least one variety of the familiarity that Sewell and Grenehalgh appear to have enjoyed, however briefly. For example, one of Grenehalgh's annotations records what appears to be a meeting between the two on the eve of St Valentine's Day, 1504.[16]

It is difficult to determine how strenuously such statutes were enforced. Mentorships between male ecclesiastics and female postulants were commonplace in the late Middle Ages, particularly at Syon Abbey, where books of spiritual instruction

---

Cloud: North Star Press, 1988), pp. 43–52. Penelope Johnson compares the records of women's and men's foundations, in order to correct the conventional assumption (perpetuated by Power's study) that nuns were considered inferior members of the medieval ecclesiastical community. See *Equal in Monastic Profession: Religious Women in Medieval France* (Chicago: University of Chicago Press, 1991), esp. pp. 62–102. Another fascinating form of ascetic gender relations is the practice of *syneisacticism*, the testing of celibacy by sleeping chastely with a member of the opposite sex (allegedly performed by ancient monks, as well as by Robert of Arbrissel, founder of the Order of Fontevrault). See Elkins, p. 153; and Jacqueline Smith, "Robert of Arbrissel, Procurator Mulierum," in *Medieval Women*, ed. Derek Baker (Oxford: Basil Blackwell, 1978), pp. 175–84.

10 Sargent, p. 28.
11 *The Rewyll of Seynt Sauioure*, ed. James Hogg, 4 vols. (Salzburg: Institut Für Anglistik und Amerikanistik, 1980), p. 4.
12 Hogg, *The Rewyll of Seynt Sauioure*, p. 8.
13 Hogg, *The Rewyll of Seynt Sauioure*, p. 11.
14 Hogg, *The Rewyll of Seynt Sauioure*, p. 14.
15 Hogg, *The Rewyll of Seynt Sauioure*, p. 73.
16 *James Grenehalgh as Textual Critic*, p. 86.

travelled freely across the Thames between Syon and Sheen.[17] Many Middle English devotional authors drew on biblical, patristic, and hagiographic models in their enthusiastic representation of chaste relationships between women and men (both lay and religious)[18] On the other hand, a counter-tradition of ascetic misogyny rejected mixed-sex friendships altogether. Bernard of Clairvaux set a precedent for many later writers when he argued in his *Sermones in cantica* that "it is easier to raise the dead than to be alone with a woman and not to have sex."[19] Events including the nun of Watton's pregnancy[20] and the scandalous relationship of Heloise and Abelard testify to the difficulties faced by female and male friends in a celibate and often deeply antifeminist religious culture.

Some Middle English devotional texts for female audiences offer well-known warnings about the sexual risks associated with friendship between women and men. The early thirteenth-century *Life of Saint Margaret* gives a particularly vivid voice to this principle of sexual segregation. In answer to Margaret's query about the his nature, a demon replies:

> I've thrown down many who confidently expected to escape my guile, and this is how. Sometimes I let a pure man stay near a pure woman – I don't throw myself at them, or fight, but let them completely alone. I let them talk about God and debate the nature of goodness, and love each other truly without evil wishes or any wicked desires – so that each of them will truly trust both their own and the other's will, and so feel more secure, sitting by themselves, having a good time together. Then, using this security, I attack them, shoot very

17 See Michael Sargent, "The Transmission by the English Carthusians of Some Late Medieval Spiritual Writings," *Journal of Ecclesiastical History* 27 (1976), p. 228.
18 On the mutually dependent relations between Marie d'Oignies and Jacques de Vitry, Lutgard of Aywières and Thomas de Cantimpré, and Beatrice of Nazareth and her chaplain, see Brian Patrick McGuire, "Holy Women and Monks in the Thirteenth Century: Friendship or Exploitation?" *Vox Benedictina* 6 (1991): 342–73. On Heinrich Suso and his female friend, collaborator, correspondent, and "spiritual child," see Jeffrey F. Hamburger, "The Use of Images in the Pastoral Care of Nuns: the Case of Heinrich Suso and the Dominicans," *Art Bulletin* 71 (1989): 20–46. On the conjunction of friendship and gynephobia in hagiography, see John Coakley, "Friars as Confidants of Holy Women," in *Images of Sainthood in Medieval Dominican Hagiography*, ed. Renate Blumenfeld-Kosinski and Timea Szell (Ithaca: Cornell UP, 1991), pp. 222–46.
19 PL 183:1091. Though clearly, this remark tells us more about medieval misogynistic conventions (or perhaps about Bernard himself) than about medieval gender relations. Richard Rolle adopts this line of reasoning in *Incendium Amoris*. Richard Mysin's Middle English translation (made for another "Margaret") advises "cautiously flee women, and always keep your thoughts far from them; for even though a woman may be good, still the devil is always at work. . . ." See *The Fire of Love and the Mending of Life or the Rule of Living*, ed. Ralph Harvey, EETS o.s. 106 (London: Kegan Paul, 1896), p. 65. Elsewhere, however, Rolle recommends friendships between women and men, and certainly put this position into practice in his relationship with Margaret Kirkeby.
20 See Giles Constable, "Aelred of Rievaulx and the Nun of Watton," in *Medieval Women*, esp. pp. 206–9.

secretly, and before they know it, wound their unwary hearts with a highly poisonous drug. Lightly, at first, with loving looks, with burning glances at each other, and with playful talk, I incite them to more – for such a long time that they are toying and trifling with each other. Then I strike into them thoughts of love . . . and in this way, when they let me, and don't resist at all, nor bestir themselves, nor stand strongly against sin – I lead them into the fen, into the foul lake of that dirty sin.[21]

This admission encodes gender relations as a spiritual hazard, a slippery "continuum" that elides neat categorizations between sexual and non-sexual attachments, and thus easily can progress from chaste affection into uncontrollable appetite.[22]

Moreover, for many medieval authors, even those writing for female readers, women bore the primary responsibility for male sexual temptation. The *Ancrene Riwle*, for example, insists that women should hide themselves from men because their faces and bodies constitute a figurative pit into which men fall and perish: "You uncover this pit, you who do anything by which a man is bodily tempted by you, even though you may be unaware of it . . . unless you are absolved, you must, as they say, suffer the rod, that is, feel pain for his sin."[23] Such texts support Sharon Elkins's contention that in England, spiritual friendships between female and male religious declined after the end of the expansion of women's monasticism at the end of the twelfth century,[24] and it is therefore not surprising that Nicholas Watson can accurately describe Richard Rolle's mid-fourteenth-century willingness to associate with and mentor pious women as unusual.[25]

We might expect late medieval English devotional literature to accept and repeat these restrictions and suspicions regarding mixed-sex activity. However, many of the texts for women readers written and compiled during the late-fourteenth, fifteenth, and early sixteenth centuries – especially those disseminated by Carthusian houses – reject the "ideal" of sexual segregation (implicitly or explicitly), and promote, though with some ambivalence, spiritual friendship between cloistered

[21] Trans. Anne Savage and Nicholas Watson, in *Anchoritic Spirituality: Ancrene Wisse and Associated Works* (New York: Paulist, 1991), pp. 297–98.
[22] See Eve Kosofsky Sedgewick, *Between Men: English Literature and Male Homosocial Desire* (New York: Columbia UP, 1985); and Adrienne Rich, "Compulsory Heterosexuality and Lesbian Existence," in *The Signs Reader: Women, Gender, and Scholarship*, ed. Elizabeth Abel and Emily K. Abel (Chicago: Chicago UP, 1983), pp. 139–68. For a relevant analysis of the ambiguous language of *amor* and *amicitia* in a stanza from *Troylus and Criseyde* which appears in a Middle English devotional text, see Lee Patterson, *Negotiating the Past: the Historical Understanding of Medieval Literature* (Madison: University of Wisconsin Press, 1987), pp. 115–53.
[23] Trans. M. B. Salu, *The Ancrene Riwle (the Corpus MS: Ancrene Wisse)* (Exeter: University of Exeter Press, 1990), p. 25.
[24] See Elkins, *Holy Women in Twelfth-Century England*, pp. 105–61.
[25] *Richard Rolle and the Invention of Authority* (Cambridge: Cambridge UP, 1991), pp. 47, 229.

women and men.[26] Treatises such as *The Tree, The Twelve Fruits of the Holy Ghost, Speculum Devotorum,* and *The Chastising of God's Children,* to name a few, represent female and male religious as parallel partners in intellect, zeal, and worth before God, equal sharers in monastic labor. In contrast to the dire warnings against mixed-sex contact offered by a tradition of ascetic, and typically misogynistic medieval piety, these texts insist that spiritual friendship between women and men is a rational and virtuous alliance, not an invitation to moral disaster.

These works displace concern over sex and gender with a focus on religious vocation, developing what I call a "discourse of familiarity,"[27] which is modelled in part on the generic conventions of the Latin epistle of spiritual friendship, which circulated primarily between male correspondents and communities. The term "familiarity" encompasses both the Latin meaning of *familia* (family), and the looser senses of proximity and intimacy. Middle English devotional texts for women employing this discourse adapt several conventions drawn from an earlier tradition of spiritual friendship between men. These include the author's humble address to readers and his protestations of unworthiness; his characterizations of female audiences as "ghostly sisters," members of the author's monastic household; the development of a rhetoric of gender equality; and occasionally, explicit refutations of misogynistic commonplaces. This discourse challenges the traditional medieval hierarchy of God, man, and woman, no doubt offering what must have seemed an attractive alternative to the ascetic, and often misogynistic piety of earlier English devotional literature for female audiences. Such a view of friendship assumes that each member of a mixed-sex relationship must be considered a spiritual and intellectual equal, and is therefore responsible for edifying and instructing the other. Seen in this way, the texts annotated by James Grenehalgh of Sheen for Joanna Sewell, may well provide only the most well-known example (apart from that of Richard Rolle and Margaret Kirkeby) of a commonplace development of cloistered spiritual friendship between women and men organized around devotional literature in late medieval England.

Latin letters of *amicitia* regularly use certain formal and thematic conventions of friendship.[28] A correspondent might use elaborate greetings that convey his extreme pain over the absence of his reader, and his longing for the sweetness of his companionship and spiritual embraces, all while complaining of the inadequacy of his own writing skills to convey these sentiments. The letter might typically

---

26 An expanded treatment of this topic appears in my book, *Male Authors, Female Readers: Representation and Subjectivity in Middle English Devotional Literature* (Ithaca: Cornell UP. 1995).

27 Brian Patrick McGuire, *Friendship and Community: the Monastic Experience 350–1250* (Kalamazoo: Cistercian Publications, 1988). McGuire distinguishes between *amicitia,* an intense spiritual love between individuals, and *familiaritatem,* a less intense communal ideal of friendship. The male-authored Middle English devotional texts under consideration here fall primarily into the latter category.

28 See Giles Constable, *Letters and Letter Collections,* Typologie des sources du moyen age occidental, fasc. 17 (Turnholt: Brepols, 1976), pp. 15–16.

concern the vicissitudes of monastic life, seeking to strengthen the reader's commitment to his religious vocation.[29] They illustrate Aelred of Rievaulx's claim that fraternal intimacy between monks represents the zenith of the religious life on earth and a foretaste of the joys of the after world. In his *Speculum Caritatis*, Aelred lists the benefits of monastic friendship:

> . . . to have someone to whom you can unite yourself in the embrace of an intimate and sacred love *(amor)*, to have someone in whom your spirit can rest, to whom your soul pours itself out, to whose dear conversation, as to comforting songs, you can flee from melancholy; to the fold of whose dear friendship, whose loving breast you can approach, safe from all the temptations of the world, and if you unite yourself to him without delay in all the meditations of your heart, by whose spiritual kisses, like healing balm, you will discharge the weariness of all of your stressful concerns, who will weep with you in troubles, rejoice with you in good fortune, seek an answer with you in times of doubt; who with the chains of love you will bring into the secret places of your mind. . . .[30]

Aelred further maintains that the cloister is spiritual friendship's optimal setting, and he states categorically that "without friendship, absolutely no life can be happy."[31]

In his writing for female audiences, Aelred vehemently discourages relationships with men (or indeed with other women). However, a few centuries later, male-authored Middle English devotional treatises for women were borrowing the conventions of monastic spiritual friendship, formerly the domain primarily of male readers and writers. Citing Aelred, *The Chastising of God's Children* assures its audience that friendship is a

---

[29] McGuire, *Friendship and Community*, p. 232.

[30] I have used Ruth Mazzo Karas's excellent translation, in "Friendship and Love in the Lives of Two Twelfth-Century English Saints," *Journal of Medieval History* 14 (1988), pp. 317–18. Cf. *Aelred Opera Omnia*, ed. A. Hoste. CCCM I Brepols: Turnholt 1971, p. 159.

[31] Aelred of Rievaulx, *On Spiritual Friendship*, trans., Mary Eugene Laker (Kalamazoo: Cistercian Publications, 1977) p. 112. It is important to note here that Aelred does not extend his belief in the value of spiritual friendship to women. If the male readers of *On Spiritual Friendship* learn that the pre-lapsarian Adam and Eve were the first spiritual friends, female audiences gain a far different view of mixed-sex friendship. Aelred's *De Institutione Inclusarum* warns women that the visits of male friends can easily lead to a loss of chastity, that the gradations delineating social and sexual relations are dangerously ambiguous and slippery. For example, male acquaintances pose a grave danger to female chastity, because: "the more you see the same face or hear the same voice the more indelibly does it engrave itself on your memory. . . . Listening to the same man's voice can be a cause of great danger to many people." Aelred of Reivaulx, *A Rule of Life for a Recluse*, trans. Mary Paul Macpherson, in *Aelred of Rievaulx: Treatises and the Pastoral Prayer*, ed. M. Basil Pennington (Kalamazoo: Cistercian Publications, 1971), p. 52.

. . . a reasonable affection. This reasonable affection comes from a spiritual apprehension of another person's virtue, just like when we discover a virtue or spiritual gift associated with any man or woman, by the person's reputation or by the reading of the person's biography, and it moves our souls to a tender softness of love. This affection stirs a person to a gentle compunction and calls to mind, with the pleasant spiritual joy of meditation, the virtuous deeds that have been performed in the past. We respond similarly when we hear about the glorious passion of the martyrs and of the lives of the other saints. In addition, it is a reasonable affection when we are moved to love one man or woman more tenderly than another, on account of their virtuous living or teaching or example, which edifies us spiritually and stirs us to better living . . . but the holier that this love is, the more helpful, reasonable, and profitable it is.[32]

Middle English treatises that develop a discourse of familiarity commonly address their readers amiably as "ghostly sisters," or "religious sisters." This is often seen as a mere convention, but occasionally, individual copies of these texts allow us to glimpse the traces of a relationship between a writer, compiler, or translator and an audience, by showing how an individual work was adapted for an intended reader. For example, where most copies of a particular treatise address both women and men, one copy might be altered to address a female reader. This is the case with one text of the widely-read *The Mirror of Saint Edmund*, which begins: "to my dear sister and friend."[33] One similarly addressed copy of William of Flete's *Remedy Against the Troubles of Temptation* (which nevertheless maintains male pronouns throughout the text) notes apologetically, "sister, always when I speak of a man in this writing, take it for both man and woman, for so it is meant in all such writings."[34]

Other Middle English texts illustrate that these are not isolated examples. Many treatises are obviously replies to prior and continuous communication. *The Tree* responds to the request of a nun for spiritual guidance. A sequel, *The Twelve Fruits of the Holy Ghost* appears sometime later, with an apology and an acknowledgment that: "it is now long ago that I wrote to you that epistle of exhortation. . . ."[35] Similarly, the *The Chastising of God's Children* is the result of written communication between a nun and monk. It begins: "Dear sister, I understand by your writing about diverse temptations and trials, that you have suffered and still suffer . . . from the malice of the old serpent . . . I am sending you some remedies that I have found

32 Ed. Joyce Bazire and Eric Colledge, *The Chastising of God's Children and the Treatise of Perfection of the Sons of God* (Oxford: Basil Blackwell, 1957), pp. 193–194.
33 A. I Doyle, "A Survey of the Origins and Circulation of Theological Manuscripts in English in the Fourteenth, Fifteenth, and Early Sixteenth Centuries With Special Consideration of the Part of the Clergy Therein," Ph.D. Diss., 2 vols., Cambridge University, 1953. I.46.
34 Carl Horstmann, ed. *Yorkshire Writers: Richard Rolle of Hampole and His Followers*, 2 vols. (London: Swan Sonnenschein and Co., 1895) II.109.
35 Ed. J. J. Vaissier, *The tree & the xii frutes of the holy goost* (Groningen: J.B. Wolters, 1960), p. 36.

in the writings of the holy doctors."[36] The *Speculum Devotorum* apparently arose from face to face contact. It begins by reminding its reader of their last meeting together: "Ghostly sister in Jesus Christ, I believe that you have not forgotten that when we spoke together last I promised you a meditation of the passion of our Lord, which promise I have not forgotten in the meantime, but by the grace of God I have performed it as well as I could."[37] This admission is particularly significant since this text was written by a Carthusian who, as I have suggested, would technically not have been allowed to speak with women, even to hear their confessions.[38]

Like the Latin letters of spiritual friendship, these devotional texts are frequently prefaced by elaborate displays of authorial humility. The author of the *Speculum Devotorum* apologizes profusely for his "inability" and "ignorance," and asserts that "I have put nothing [in this text] . . . of my own wit but what I hope may truly be comprehended by ready reason and a good conscience."[39] The *Chastising of God's Children* begins with a similar disclaimer: "[a]lso, my sister, I dread to write of such lofty matters, for I have neither the affect nor the intellect to declare them either in English or in Latin, and especially in English, for it far surpasses my intellect to convey to you in any way the terms of divinity in the vernacular. Also I am unworthy to have that spiritual knowledge through which I should know or have inner understanding of what theologians mean in their holy writings."[40] Certainly these are all familiar rhetorical *topoi* in writing for male audiences,[41] reminding us of earlier deferential protestations like that of Peter of Celle who, while an abbot, calls himself an "old man who still studies his alphabet," and "the tiniest ant [carrying] some cut-up granules to the insignificant little hut which is my treatise."[42] Such *topoi* in literature for female audiences, though, signify far more than just the simple incorporation of Latin devotional *formulae* into vernacular texts. Such modes of address to female audiences have several possible functions: they provide a textual space for the elaboration of a communal model of conduct that

---

36 Quoted in Doyle, I. 185.
37 *The Speculum Devotorum of an anonymous Carthusian of Sheen, edited from the Manuscripts Cambridge Univ. Library Gg 1.6 and Foyle, With an Introduction and Glossary*, ed. James Hogg (Salzburg: Institute für Anglistik und Amerkanistik, 1973), p. 1.
38 Ian Doyle argues that the author must have finished the text before he took final orders and, as I've shown, Michael Sargeant believes that, especially in view of the close relationship between James Grenehalgh and Joanna Sewell, the discipline at Carthusian houses must have been somewhat lax. I prefer to view this phenomenon in a more positive light, as the (perhaps secretive) substitution of edifying practices for overly-harsh ecclesiastical directives.
39 *The Speculum Devotorum*, pp. 4, 6, 10.
40 *The Chastising of God's Children*, p. 95. For similarly humble assertions, see also Nicholas Love's *The Mirrour of the Blessyd Lyf of Iesu Christ*, p. 13; Richard Rolle's *Ego Dormio*, pp. 61–62; and Walter Hilton's *The Scale of Perfection*, pp. 78, and 160.
41 See Ernst Curtius, *European Literature and the Latin Middle Ages*, trans. Willard Trask (New York: Harper and Row, 1953), pp. 83–85, 159, and 407–13.
42 Peter of Celle, *The School of the Cloister*, trans. Hugh Feiss (Kalamazoo: Cistercian Publications, 1987), p. 68.

seems to have been routinely forbidden, or at least discouraged, by religious authorities; they offer some compensation for the ubiquitous warnings of preachers, bishops, and poets against personal contact between female and male religious; and they may document a type of intimacy that flourished in practice, despite being forbidden in theory.

A particularly notable feature of Middle English texts incorporating a discourse of familiarity is their rhetoric of sexual equality. Treatises such as *The Chastising of God's Children* and *The Twelve Fruits of the Holy Ghost* aim at a kind of reciprocity that implicates the male author in his own advice, and targets moral flaws among both sexes, rather than singling out women as weaker and inherently more sinful than men. These Middle English texts refuse to validate conventional misogynistic stereotypes. For example, *The Chastising of God's Children* prefaces a discussion of true and false visions by explaining that "many men and women have been deceived by revelations and visions. . . ."[43] The English adaptor declines to represent women as the primary victims of false apparitions, even though medieval authors traditionally did so. Holding up Eve as an example, theologians commonly argued that women were more gullible and less reasonable than men, and therefore more susceptible to deception.[44] Rather, *The Chastising* argues that spiritual discernment is not a gender issue, but rather one of religious vocation. Both women and men are susceptible to trickery, but professed religious are more so, because "good men and women who strive to be perfect are more tempted those who live carelessly . . ., for at the peak of a mountain there is the greatest wind."[45] Similarly, the author of *The Tree* refuses to legitimate another commonplace antifeminist stereotype, the loquacious woman. He argues that the virtue of silence applies equally to men and women: ". . . speak sparingly . . . So it is that our lord gave to a man and a woman two ears and one tongue, so that they should be quick to hear and slow to speak. . . ."[46] Clearly, this advice derives from a monastic tradition of silence applicable to both sexes, rather than from the negative stereotypes so prevalent in earlier English devotional writing for women.

The conventional assumption that women are inherently more vulnerable to sexual transgression than men are is another stereotype rejected by Middle English devotional treatises employing a discourse of familiarity. For example, *The Twelve Fruits* exhorts its female reader that the devil is "as weak as a mouse, if he is resisted with a good will."[47] This text urges female audiences to resist temptation valiantly, because their chastity is "the most dreaded battle to demons, among all the earthly conflicts of this fighting church . . ., because the devil finds no mark of his lust in

---

43 *Chastising of God's Children*, p. 169.
44 See Eleanor Commo McLaughlin, "Equality of Souls, Inequality of Sexes: Women in Medieval Theology," in *Religion and Sexism*, ed. Rosemary Reuther (New York: Simon and Schuster, 1974) esp. pp. 217–19.
45 *Chastising of God's Children*, p. 97.
46 *The Tree*, p. 10.
47 *The xii frutes*, p. 149.

the flesh of virgins, and therefore he is most afraid of them."[48] If chastity were the only virtue that the author saw as necessary or attainable for women, this advice could easily be construed as a misogynistic trope. Barbara Newman points out that the twelfth-century literature of spiritual formation does in fact view women in this way.[49] However, this male author sees all twelve of the fruits of the Holy Spirit that he describes as important and attainable for female readers.

Because such texts do not focus obsessively on female celibacy, they refuse to erect an impermeable boundary between the enclosed woman reader and the world. For example, *The Tree* encourages its audience to have personal contact with visitors to their convents or anchorholds, "[o]n certain days and times when people desire to speak with you. . . ."[50] Although the author delivers the conventional monastic warnings about gossip and humility ("avoid all kinds of idle tales, or gracefully take your leave"),[51] the visitation of neighbors is presented as a matter of institutional protocol and vocational obligation, rather than as a potentially dangerous site for a supposed feminine moral weakness. The focus of such passages is on the community's need for the reader's spiritual instruction,[52] rather than on her need for protection from their sexual advances or the threat to their chastity that she would supposedly represent. Similarly, *The Tree* concedes that contact between women and men can cause gossip, though the author regards this as an inevitable condition of religious life, rather than a problem of female sexual weakness. He advises: "[t]hough you are in religion, you must beware of slander, for it creeps out of a monastic house marvelously."[53] This concern also appears in Book One of *The Scale of Perfection*, which acknowledges its reader's desire for solitary contemplation, but which also urges her not to neglect her duty to provide her visitors with counsel and prayer.[54] Again, this relative permissiveness contrasts with earlier literature that advocates strict enclosure, and maintains the inevitable danger of female contact with the world, and specifically with men.

The most unusual element of texts using a discourse of mixed-sex familiarity is their occasional explicit refutation of misogynistic commonplaces. For example, explaining how sobriety keeps the soul and body from death, the author of *The Twelve Fruits* strategically mistranslates an obviously misogynistic passage: "lust is bitterer than death, as Solomon says, 'Inveni amariorem morte mulierem,' which means, "I haue found a bitterer enemy than death, and that is truly lust, for lust kills not only the body but also the soul."[55] Obviously, a Latin reader would know

---

[48] *The xii frutes*, p. 145.
[49] See "Flaws in the Golden Bowl: Gender and the Literature of Spiritual Formation in the Twelfth Century," *Traditio* 45 (1989–90), esp. pp. 131–39.
[50] *The Tree*, p. 13.
[51] *The Tree*, p. 13.
[52] *The Tree*, p. 13.
[53] *The Tree*, p. 12.
[54] Walter Hilton, *The Scale of Perfection*, trans. John P. H. Clark and Rosemary Dorward (New York: Paulist, 1991) p. 103.
[55] *The xii frutes*, p. 139.

that the correct translation of this quotation is "I have found woman a bitterer enemy than death," and that the author has substituted non-gender-specific "lust" for the misogynistic "woman." No doubt a male author concerned with maintaining a spiritual friendship with his female reader would have considered this Latin quotation a bit inappropriate. At the same time, the mistranslation does seem somewhat ingenuous: the Latin itself is simple, and would probably be accessible to readers with only the most rudimentary knowledge of Latin. Yet it is also easy to imagine that female audiences who were able to notice this substitution would have applauded this apparent editorial decision.

The fifteenth-century version of the Life of Saint Margaret included in Bokenham's *Lives of Holy Women* offers another example of the revision of texts for female readers. It excises completely the tirade against mixed-sex friendships that I mentioned at the beginning of this essay. In Bokenham's version, the demon tells Margaret only his name and lineage, and volunteers that "when we were unbound,/ We filled all the environs of the earth,/ Seeking out those whom we might annoy and tempt,/ For this tendency remains with us always."[56] Although it is not clear that Bokenham worked directly from a copy of Margaret's *vita* that contained the demon's speech, the omission of the tirade against friendship certainly would be appropriate, since this copy of the text was commissioned by Thomas Burgh and given to a house of nuns at Cambridge.[57] Including such a condemnation of friendship between women and men in this gift (itself a marker of spiritual friendship) would clearly have been inappropriate.

The *Chastising of God's Children* attacks misogyny more directly, offering an *exemplum* of the "abbot poule" being disciplined by God for his avoidance of women, when he went with another monk to visit an anchorite. "As they went along, it happened suddenly that they met a woman, and immediately, Paul turned and fled, with great speed home to his monastery, and he would listen to no pleading or prayer of the first monk. Even though he did what he did out of piety, it exceeded the observances of his rule. And therefore, he was struck with such a palsy that none of his limbs were able to rest, neither his hands nor his feet; and he could control neither his his eyes, nor his tongue, nor his ears. All of his limbs had lost their strength. And afterward, it happened that no care might ease his suffering except the care of women. And all this lasted about four years, until he died. . . . And thus was that holy man chastised for a little trespass done against the observance of his rule."[58] This vignette represents "the abbot Paul" 's gynephobia as a breach of his monastic observance. It is easy to see why an author concerned with

---

[56] Osbern Bokenham, *Legendys of Hooly Wummen*, ed. Mary S. Sarjeantson, EETS o.s. 206 (London: Oxford UP, 1938) p. 21.

[57] Bokenham, p. xx.

[58] *Chastising of God's Children*, pp. 164–165. The apparent source for this story is John Cassian's *Collations*, VII.26. For a discussion of similar *exempla* in the writings of the desert fathers, see Aline Rouselle, *Porneia: On Desire and the Body in Antiquity*, trans. Felicia Pheasant (Oxford: Basil Blackwell, 1988), pp. 151–52.

female monasticism would have condemned Paul's actions. Such reluctance to associate with women would have presented extreme difficulties for nuns, especially when, as Penelope Johnson has pointed out, virtually all medieval convents had to be in effect double houses, since they regularly needed the services of priests, perhaps scribes and legal witnesses, as well as laybrothers.[59] Moreover, Paul's punishment for this error, the "palsie," implies that, in this text, misogyny is figured as a spiritual disease. Avoiding *cura monialium* (the care of female religious) brings a sickness that only *cura a monialibus* (care *by* nuns, or women) can cure.

This is not to suggest that these texts are free from the misogynistic commonplaces of other medieval treatises. For example, The *Speculum Devotorum* insists that "a virgin should not tarry long out in the open, nor hold conversations in public places,"[60] or she will invite assault, revealing the same conception of Woman as sexual *provocateur* that the *Ancrene Riwle* maintains. Likewise, the *Speculum Devotorum* offers this gloss on the story of Jesus at the Temple: "Also, ghostly sister, take heed how our meek lady, preferred Joseph before herself, saying 'your father & I [have sought you, sorrowing],' and not 'I and your father have sought you . . .' [this shows how a woman should] be meek and not prefer herself before men in anything, especially those women who have husbands."[61] Similar ambivalence about gender relations runs through most of the texts I've discussed here. Nevertheless, their primary tendency is to address the author as a spiritual friend, in Penelope Johnson's term, "equal in monastic profession."

No doubt late medieval female readers found these texts appealing. The attraction of the discourse of familiarity for both monastic and laywomen is documented in copies of texts in which the names of original addressees have been erased, and those of subsequent readers substituted, for example, a copy of *Disce Mori*, in which the treatise's original recipient, "Alyce" is erased, and "Dorothy Slyght" (a Syon nun) is written in; or the copy of Rolle's *Form of Living* in which the name "Cecily" (probably Cecily, Duchess of York) is written over that of Margaret Kirkeby.[62] These substitutions illustrate the very literal identification of later audiences with the earlier female spiritual friends to whom treatises were addressed. And as Katherine Shrevelow notes, such identifications "read[y] the reader to receive and, presumably to act on the text's teaching . . . they interact with its reader's predilections to create a receptivity that strengthens and supplements the [work's] didactic message."[63] As they were copied and disseminated outside their original epistolary context, these texts conveyed the idealized gender positions

[59] See Johnson, p. 7.
[60] *Speculum Devotorum*, pp. 50–1.
[61] *Speculum Devotorum*, p. 138.
[62] See A. I. Doyle, I. 78; and Vincent Gillespie, "Vernacular Books of Religion," in *Book Production and Publishing in England, 1374–1475*, ed. Jeremy Griffiths and Derek Pearsall (Cambridge: Cambridge UP, 1989), pp. 327–28.
[63] "Fathers and Daughters: Women as Readers of the *Tatler*," in *Gender and Reading: Essays on Readers, Texts, and Contexts* (Baltimore: Johns Hopkins UP, 1986), p. 108.

offered by mixed-sex spiritual friendship, along with their doctrinal information, to subsequent female readers.

Though devotional literature for women has only recently begun to receive the attention that it deserves, its literary and social conventions clearly both structure and reflect the institutional and cultural components of women's experience in the Middle Ages. One of the most important of these is the discourse of familiarity, which makes available to English female religious and laywomen an aspect of the monastic literary and social traditions to which they had previously had only limited – if any – access. Furthermore, the relationship of these devotional texts for female audiences to historical practices involving women invites much further investigation. What specific contributions did the extension to women of the ideals of spiritual friendship make to the development of female monasticism in late medieval England? What happened to English nuns and monks who attempted to act on the heterosocial ethic of these texts? How did monastic spiritual friendship function for lay readers? And, since it appears in translated treatises as well as native English texts, how does this discourse correspond to the traditions of spiritual friendship between women and men in the Rhineland, Italy, France, and the Low Countries? Although these questions remain open for future speculation, it is clear that the discourse of familiarity in Middle English texts for female readers must have presented an appealing alternative to the philosophy of sexual segregation advocated by much medieval religious literature.

# THREE (RECUSANT) SISTERS[1]

## ANN M. HUTCHISON

WHEN THE AGENTS of Henry VIII finally closed the door of Syon Abbey, the celebrated English Bridgettine house founded in 1415 by Henry V on the banks of the Thames near his palace at Richmond, they came away without the keys. Nor, for that matter, did they manage to acquire the seal, or even any record as to whether the nuns or brethren of this double house formally took an oath to maintain "the king's new title".[2] On May 4, 1535, Richard Reynolds, one of Syon's most distinguished priest-brothers, had been executed for his refusal to do so; his example undoubtedly set an important precedent for the community. In a letter to Cromwell dated 17 December 1535, Thomas Bedyll reported that "one Agnes Smythe, a sturdy dame and a wylful, hath labored diverse of her susters, to stope that we shuld not haue theire convent seale".[3] That such strength of character and determination to continue living under Bridgettine Rule are not unique to Sister Symthe, can be seen at various times in the unbroken history of this English monastery, the only house to survive the dissolution.[4]

Thus, when the community left Syon Abbey in November 1539, it was as the result of a legal quibble, rather than voluntary surrender.[5] Though pensions were

---

[1] This is a more formal version of a paper given at a special conference of Bridgettine scholars inside the enclosure of Syon Abbey in the presence of Lady Abbess and three members of the community, 7–8 September, 1991. I would like to thank York University, Toronto, for awarding me a grant which made this trip possible. I would not, however, have known of the existence of this unique house had I not been led to it by Valerie Lagorio, who in 1985 gave me an important reading list when I was faced with a major career change, and it is to Valerie that I would like to dedicate this paper with grateful thanks for her tireless help, constant encouragement and, above all, her enthusiasm.

[2] David Knowles, *The Religious Orders in England*, III (Cambridge: University Press, 1959), p. 221.

[3] Quoted in G. J. Aungier, *The History and Antiquities of Syon Monastery, etc.* (London: J. B. Nichols & Son, 1840), p. 87.

[4] As Aungier (p. 88, n. 1) and other more recent historians have pointed out, there is no surrender in the Augmentation Office.

[5] The only contemporary accounts of the "suppression" are notes among Cromwell's "Remembrances" for the year 1539, and an entry under 25 November 1539 in Wriothesley's chronicle stating that: "the home of Syon was suppressed into the Kinge's hands and the ladies and brethren putt out which was the virtuest house of religion in

assigned, the majority of the community dispersed in small groups. Seven such groups went to live in private houses in England, and a larger number, led by Catherine Palmer, went abroad to seek refuge with the Bridgettines in Flanders. In 1546, at the death of the abbess, Agnes Jordan, at Denham in Buckinghamshire, Catherine Palmer returned from Flanders to collect those who wished to join the community there.[6] Sometime after the accession of Mary, the community was invited to come back to its former home, Syon Abbey. They began to return in November of 1556; on March 1, 1557, Catherine Palmer's position as abbess was confirmed by the Pope, and on August 1 of the same year the community was once again enclosed. Their restoration was, however, short-lived, for not long after Mary's death Elizabeth let it be known that she would reestablish the Protestant Church, and so sometime in July of 1559, the Spanish Ambassador escorted Catherine Palmer and the English Bridgettines abroad once more.

In 1578, almost 20 years later, the Bridgettines, who had already moved from place to place in the Spanish Netherlands at least four times, were based at Malines, or Mechlin, when they made the momentous decision to send about a dozen of the younger nuns back to England.[7] There were two pressing reasons: one was to protect the young women from the antics of the marauding Calvinists, who had been commiting outrages against religious houses in the area (Syon itself had already been invaded once in 1576); and the other was to try to raise funds among English supporters for the impoverished, and perhaps even starving, community. Details of the lives and adventures of three of these nuns survive; their stories reveal information not only about life in England in the early recusant period, but they also offer an unexpected glimpse of life inside an enclosed monastery.

Two sets of documents provide this information: "The Life and Good End of Sister Marie", preserved in British Library, Additional MS 18,650, which tells the story of Mary Champney and, more briefly, of Anne Stapleton; and two letters written by Elizabeth Sander after her return to the convent in Rouen in 1587.[8] The "Life" must have been written very soon after Mary Champney's death in London

---

England". Quoted in Syon's journal, *The Poor Souls' Friend* (hereafter *PSF*), Jan–Feb (1962), 12, 19; see also Knowles, *op. cit.*, pp. 220–221. It is worth noting that Wriothesley's aunt, Sister Agnes Wriothesley, had been one of the Syon "ladies" (d.1529).

6  See *PSF*, May–Jun (1962), 79–86.

7  Details of the Bridgettines in exile can be found in *PSF* (1964), *passim*, and in J. R. Fletcher, *The History of the English Bridgettines of Syon Abbey* (South Brent, Devon: Syon Abbey, 1933).

8  I am currently completing an edition of BL Additional MS 18,650, hereafter referred to as "Life". Elizabeth Sander's (also spelled Sanders, or Saunder[s]) first letter is preserved in the Englefield Correspondence at the English College, Valladolid. The original of the second is lost, but the text was preserved in a Spanish translation which was retranslated into English by Adam Hamilton (*PSF*, 1894). Both letters were printed in *PSF* (1966), Jan–Feb, 11–22 and Mar–Apr, 43–54. I am grateful to Peter Paul Bogan for allowing me to see his edited version of the second letter (March 1987). His notes, garnered from information in the Farm Street Archives, were especially useful.

on April 27, 1580 by someone who had been close to her during her time in England. It seems to have been intended for circulation among Catholics in England, partly to enlist their support for the exiled convent (the surviving manuscript is certainly a copy, not the original), and partly to encourage them in their adherence to the Catholic faith. The tone, therefore, tends at times to be somewhat hagiographical, and perhaps to a modern reader, in places intolerant, but nevertheless, the narrative itself is engrossing, especially when dealing with Mary's imminently approaching death.

The letters of Elizabeth Sander were written at the request of Sir Francis Englefield, an important benefactor of Syon, who was then in Madrid.[9] He wanted to know both about conditions in England at the time and, more particularly, who had sheltered and given assistance to Sister Elizabeth. This was crucial information for the priests who were being trained on the continent before being sent back to minister to English Catholics. The first letter did not immediately reach Sir Francis (though he must have received it later, since it still survives in the Englefield Correspondence at Valladolid), and so Elizabeth wrote a second account. Unlike the "Life", which is very guarded about names and places, the letters, written from the safety of the convent in Rouen, provide details that can, to some extent, elucidate aspects of the "Life". On the other hand, the letters are written at the end of Elizabeth's event-filled, nine-year sojourn in England, so that there appear to be lapses in memory, as well as contradictions in the details of the accounts given in the two letters. Taken together, however, the "Life" and the letters become important resources: they are of immense value in helping to reconstruct some of the details of the "adventures" endured by the nuns in England; they offer a perspective of the Catholic underground in England, especially London of 1578 to 1580 – the period just before the well-documented arrival of the Jesuits; and they give insight into the devotional life of the Bridgettines and the faith that gave them such courage.

Evidence of the high regard in which these young Bridgettines were held by contemporaries, can be found in a letter sent from England by "A. Dolm" and preserved in the Douay Diaries in the entry for February 1579: "Many of the wisest sort hath fownde greate fault with the sending over of the younge nonnes, whome God of his aboundante mercy hath delivered from a thousand periles of body and sowle, no doubte of it to his honoure and the confowndinge of his enemies. For there passinge greate constancy in there fayth, singuler modesty in

---

9  Sir Francis Englefield, a devout Catholic and confidential adviser to Princess Mary, succeeded Sir William Paulet as Master of the Court of Wards in 1554, after Mary had become Queen. In December 1558, soon after the accession of Elizabeth, his appointment was terminated, though he continued to enjoy the "fees and other advantages". In April 1559, he left England, under licence, supposedly for two years, but he remained in Spain in voluntary exile until his death nearly forty years later. See Joel Hurstfield *The Queen's Wards: Wardship and Marriage under Elizabeth I* (London, New York, Toronto: Longmans, Green and Co., 1958), pp. 244–245.

ther behaviour and wise and discreete awnswers the[y] are thorow owte the Realme talked of and commended yea, even of ther enemies".[10]

By chance, at the time the decision was made to send the younger nuns to England, there was a detachment of English soldiers nearby. Having learned of the existence of the English convent and fearing for their safety, the officers came forward with an offer of safe conduct, and, in addition to arranging their passage, they provided the young nuns with food and money. From Mary Champney's "Life", as well as from the record of the arrest of five of the nuns on their arrival at Dover, we learn they they travelled disguised as Dutch women. They were first taken by water to Antwerp, and from there, sometime in September or October of 1578, sent singly or in groups from a nearby port to a suitable port in England.

Sisters Mary Champney, Elizabeth Sander and Anne Stapleton seem to have travelled on their own. In her first letter, Elizabeth Sander describes her arrival at Gravelines, where in response to questions from the examining constable she "smyled, gyving no word att all" (Letter 1, p. 11), and then after spending one night there sailed to Billingsgate. From there she went to Fulham, which must have been a preappointed rendezvous, since her letter describes her surprise at finding none of the others there. After about a week, however, Anne Stapleton arrived "very syck". According to Elizabeth, Anne arrived on St Simon and St Jude's day (October 28), and Elizabeth remained to tend to her until St Thomas's day (December 21), when she was sent away, as she relates "much agaynst myne owne mynde" (Letter 1, p. 11), since Anne was so near death. In fact, she died three days later.[11] By this time, however, the arrest of the five nuns at Dover and of three more on their arrival at Colchester had become known to their contacts, and must have indicated the need for caution. Indeed, when Mary Champney arrived, and we learn from the life that she was the last, it was determined that her initial stay in the London area be brief, for "greate feare was taken of her detection" (fol. 10r–v).

Although Elizabeth Sander's remarks about Anne Stapleton are confined to the beginning of her first letter, we do learn more about her from the author of the "Life", who gives a brief vignette in order to reinforce the profile being drawn of the kind of young woman who chose to become a Bridgettine. Anne Stapleton is described as "a proper, fayre, yonge gentlewoman", brought up in exile by her father (fol. 5).[12] At about the age of fifteen or sixteen, as a result of an extraordinary dream in which the Lord called her to the service of "his holye Mother and the xij

---

10 See *The First and Second Diaries of the English College, Douay* (London: David Nutt, 1878), p. 149. The letter goes on to mention the serious condition of Sister Anne Stapleton, "very sore syke of a burninge fever". Since we know that she died on Christmas Eve 1578, this helps us determine when the letter was written. It also suggests that Anne was very likely a sister, or close relative of Thomas Stapleton, a well-known figure at Douai (Douay), who had been a student, lecturer, and – for one year – rector there.

11 In his history, Fletcher suggests that Elizabeth was sent away for reasons of safety, that is, to avoid enquiries at the time of a death (p. 60).

12 Since we know that Thomas Stapleton's father took his family to Louvain soon after Thomas had departed for Douai, this information in the "Life", in conjunction with the

Apostles", she gave up the pleasures of her secular life, such as "playing vpon the virginalls", and offered herself as a novice to the Bridgettines. The author goes on to detail the composition of the Order, noting that it was "no dowte a very heavenlye order" since the rule and "all the substance" of the service was revealed to St Bridget by Christ (fol. 5v).[13] Though this information must have been included to impress the potential supporters of Syon, it is nevertheless interesting to note what aspect of the Order was considered of particular appeal. In conclusion, we are told that Sister Anne had only been professed for four years when she died at the age of twenty-three. This must mean that her profession took place in 1574 when she was eighteen or nineteen.[14]

Mary Champney too, we learn from the "Life", became a Bridgettine as a result of a dream or vision. Her story is even more dramatic than Anne Stapleton's, and though there is no direct reference to the *Vita* of St Bridget herself, there seems to be an attempt to suggest parallels. Obviously a highly sensitive and very devout child, Mary, at the age of twelve, had a vision in her sleep of being clothed by a bishop in what was – though unknown to her – the habit of a Bridgettine nun. This vision made a lasting impression, though it was "taken but for a dreame" (fol. 2r–v). In the meantime, Mary was put into service "as a waytinge gentlewoman" with a person who had to go abroad "for some urgent busines" (fol. 2v). While abroad, she was encouraged to become a nun, but at this stage Mary was quite uncertain about her vocation, and, in addition, she had become intensely homesick for England.

A second vision, this time a waking vision which occurred during Mass, eventually helped determine Mary's future: at the elevation, the figure of Christ appeared over the chalice and blessed her "with his twoo fingers (as the use of the Bishopps is)" (fol. 3). This vision too made a lasting impression, and though she did not immediately vow to become a nun, she did agree to undertake the necessary training. For this she was placed with nuns near Antwerp – perhaps the English Carmelites, or maybe the Falcon Sisters who often gave the Bridgettines shelter.[15]

mention of Anne in the letter sent to the English College at Douai, reinforces the speculation concerning Anne's possible relationship to Thomas.

[13] The Rule was revealed all at once to Bridget shortly after her husband's death while she was still in Sweden; the lessons of the service, or *Sermo Angelicus*, were dictated by an angel over a period of about a year and a half soon after Bridget's arrival in Rome; the remainder of the service, or *Cantus Sororum*, was divinely revealed to one of Bridget's confessors, Master Peter of Skänning, who put the service into proper liturgical form. See the introduction of A. J. Collins' edition of *The Bridgettine Breviary of Syon Abbey*, Henry Bradshaw Society 96 (Worcester: The Stanbrook Abbey Press, 1969).

[14] Eighteen was the minimum age for women; for men, it was twenty-five (Rule 22). For a modern edition of the Rule, see *Sancta Birgitta Opera Minora I: Regula Salvatoris*, SFSS, Andra Serien, Latinska Skrifter, VIII: 1, ed. S. Eklund (Lund: Berlingska Boktryckeriet, 1975); for a facsimile of a Middle English translation, see *The Rewyll of Seynt Sauioure*, 2, ed. J. Hogg, Salzburger Studien zur Anglistik und Amerikanistik 6 (Salzburg: Universität Salzburg, 1978).

[15] See Peter Guilday, *The English Catholic Refugees on the Continent 1558–1795*, Vol. I

From these nuns, the "Life" tells us, Mary was "to learne her Songe and her Grammer, for vnderstandinge of her lattin service, for her preparacion to be fitt for Religion" (fol. 3).

Sometime during her training, Mary was taken to visit the Bridgettines, who were then nearby at Mishagen. Abbess Palmer had apparently heard about this young woman and wished to meet her. The visit must have occurred soon after 16 March 1568, the date on which the site was purchased for Syon.[16] The minute she saw the abbess, Mary went into a kind of trance-like state, for she recognized the habit from her dream of many years before. When eventually she was able to speak, she begged for admission to the Order. Though the Lady Abbess and Confessor General were kind to her,[17] they were firm about receiving her "in due tyme", as the "Life" puts it (fol. 3v). Meanwhile, she was told to remain as she was, at liberty, for some months, and then, if she still desired to become a Bridgettine, to come and make her petition again. This she apparently did, and then, after being "a probationer for the first yeare" (fol. 3v), she became a fully professed sister of the Order in 1569, at the age of twenty-one (fol. 2).

Just a year after her profession, Sister Mary had yet another vision; this time it concerned a matter of discipline. As the author of the "Life" describes the incident that led up to this second vision, we are given a brief glimpse into the more domestic side of the community. Sister Mary, preparing to move into the cell of an older nun who was moving elsewhere, asked if she could have the "fine picture" and "prettie deske" already in the room, "the one, dailie to beholde there all her privatt deuotions" and the other, "for her ease and comodyte" to write upon (fol. 3v–4). One night not long after, St Bridget's daughter, St Katherine, appeared to Mary as she slept, and, reminding her that she had broken the rules of her profession, brought a disciplining rod from under "her glorious garment" and administered "fiue stripes . . . as she thoughte, upon her shoulders" (fol. 4).[18] The next morning, she took the desk and the picture to the Lady Abbess, and thereafter,

---

(London, New York, etc.: Longmans, Green, and Co., 1914), p. 28; no date is given, however, for the establishment of the Carmelite house.

16 The purchase was made with the help of Dr Nicholas Sander, brother of Margaret, then the Prioress (the 11th; she died in Mechlin on 4 March 1575), and Elizabeth. For further information on the Sander family, see T. M. Veech, *Dr. Nicholas Sanders and the English Reformation 1530–1581* (Louvain: Bureau du Recueil, Bibliothèque de l'université, 1935), especially Ch. 1.

17 The Lady Abbess was Catherine Palmer (d. 19 December, 1576), and the Confessor General, Henry Hubert (d. 30 April, 1575).

18 The first chapter of the Rule stresses poverty and the fact that no personal possessions are permitted. In the Additions (Ch. 2), one possible penalty for "lyght defautes" is "fyue lasches"; see *The Syon Additions for the Sisters from the British Library MS. Arundel 146* in *The Rewyll of Seynt Sauioure*, 4, ed. J. Hogg, Salzburger Studien zur Anglistik und Amerikanistik 6 (Salzburg, Austria: Institut für Anglistik und Amerikanistik, Universität Salzburg, (1980), pp. 5–6.

according to the account, never had more than "her booke and her beades for the daye tyme to praye on, and her strawe bed at nighte to lye on" (fol. 4v).

The author of the "Life" depicts Sister Mary's devotional life as fervent: she was "the first in the Quier, and the last out agayne"; she was able both to recount saints lives and, "to any good purpose, as aptlie to applie them"; with respect to *The Scale of Perfection*, which is cited as "a golden booke and sufficient to shape a saynte", she was "as prompte as coulde be"; she knew "the histories of holie scriptures"; and she was "a greate reuerencer of any good preacher" (fol. 6v). In this last connection, particular mention is made of the sermons of a Mr Hyde – a mention all the more remarkable in an account which otherwise witholds names. He is credited with great prescience, since well before the "disaster" of 1576, he had encouraged the community to keep up their choir, no matter what calamity might befall. Since we discover that Sister Mary was the Chauntress at this time (fol. 8), it is perhaps not surprising that Mr Hyde is singled out, for he must have struck a highly sympathetic cord.[19]

Such fervent devotion does not seem to be unique to Sister Mary. According to the "Life", it was usual for most members of the community to receive Communion "almost euery daye, or at leaste euerye seconde daye", even after the time when the Choir had had to be abandoned (fol. 8v). The account does, however, seem to endow Mary Champney with an almost saintly aura. She is described, for example, as having had "the grace of teares", which was often manifested during the period of private meditation at the end of a service (fol. 8v). Like St Bridget, she preferred the rigours of a "cowche of strawe" and a "flannell smocke", even in her last illness, rather than the comfort of cushions and linen (fol. 7). As much as possible, she tried to observe the dietary rules of the Order: "4 dinners in the weeke of fleshe, and never eate any fleshe at nighte"; but she also, we are told, recognized the need to "lett . . . judgment . . . temper our fastinge", and though we are given a portrait of a woman who is very much her own person, and who, it is hinted, is quick to be angry (fol. 6), in this matter at least she showed "obedience . . . & humilitie in takinge counsell" (fol. 7r–v).

The "Life" also gives a more general sense of the atmosphere that prevailed among English Catholics in 1580. As she lay on her death bed in London, Sister Mary was asked to add her special efficacy to daily prayers for "the speedie conversion of Englande" and for "Godis cheife prisoner", who, though unnamed, was clearly Mary, Queen of Scots (fol. 8). The author also includes reference to prayers for the building "up agayne" of Syon "more bewtifully, accordinge to Father Renoldes hope and prayer", and mentions the secret hope, held by some, that Syon "shoulde be erected againe in the northe partes of Englande" (fol. 8).

---

[19] Mr Hyde is most likely Leonard Hide (1550–1608), who was ordained at Douai in 1577; see G. Anstruther, *The Seminary Priests, A Dictionary of the Secular Clergy of England and Wales 1558–1850*, I (Durham: Ushaw College, [1969]), pp. 164–166; see also A. Bellenger, *English and Welsh Priests 1558–1800, A Working List* (Bath: Downside Abbey, 1984), p. 74. I would like to thank Dr Jan Rhodes of Durham University Library for this identification.

The central focus of the last two-thirds of the "Life" is the description of Mary Champney's final days in April of 1580. At "Shrovetide", she had been moved back to London (I think, to the house in Fulham where Sister Anne had died, since the author of the "Life" included her story, and also because a pair of Anne's black beads is later offered as a gift) when the moist air of the country had aggravated the condition of her lungs.[20] While she was in London, or nearby, Sister Mary seems to have had frequent visitors, despite the gravity of her illness. These visitors included priests, bachelors of divinity and other devout Catholics, both men and women. From the "Life", one has the sense that this venue was a hub of Catholic activity, and unlike the atmosphere at the time of Sister Mary's first arrival in London, when fear of detection caused her to be hurried away to the country – or that at the time of Sister Anne's death, less than two months after her arrival, which had caused Sister Elizabeth to be sent away – now the presence of priests seems to have been continuous. In addition, two other Bridgettine nuns (apparently based in different parts of the country, since they arrived separately) were sent for to attend Sister Mary at her death, and there is no mention of fear for their safety.[21]

Among the visitors Sister Mary received was George Gilbert, a founder and mainstay of the Young Catholic Association and a well-known supporter of the Catholic cause. In the "Life", he is referred to not by name, but as "a vertuous youthe", and he seems to have been a frequent visitor to Sister Mary, for she greeted him with warmth and familiarity (fol. 13v). Gilbert was asked to give Sister Mary a last consolation in the form of a gift to Syon. We gather from this example, as well as elsewhere in the "Life", that during her brief sojourn in England she had been both diligent and successful in collecting alms for Syon. In particular, Gilbert was asked for assistance in printing books, since "all their portable bookes for theyr private use ar so rudelye written . . . & none of their service bookes were ever yet in prynte" (fol. 14v). In addition, he was asked to pay for the printing of *The Scale of Perfection*, "which is an other of their bookes as needefull to be renewed for the mendynge of the olde prynte" (fol. 14v). Gilbert readily agreed to do so, and also to give two hundred pounds toward new professions, of which he left a pledge of

[20] Fletcher had identified the country house as Lyford Grange, the moated manor house of Mr Francis Yate in Berkshire. We know from Elizabeth Sander's letters that she and a number of the others stayed there, and at the time of Campion's arrest in July 1581, Sisters Catherine Kingsmill and Juliana Harman were apprehended there.
[21] Fletcher has suggested that the Fulham house belonged to Thomas and Magdalen Heath, well-known members of the recusant community (p. 58). He has further suggested that Sister Mary was taken to die at the house of Lord Vaux in Hackney (p. 59); but Lord Vaux did not rent the Hackney house until 1583, when, following his imprisonment, he was placed under observation. Perhaps during this period, before the arrival of the Jesuits, when surveillance increased, the Heath's house would have been a relatively safe place. Another possibility, since the house where Mary died must have been considered very secure, is that it might have been the Fulham house of Dr Adam Squire, son-in-law of the Bishop of London, who sheltered many Catholics and was in the pay of the Young Catholic Association.

five pounds "in angells to be sent to hir Covent [*sic*]" (fol. 14v). Though there is no trace of a printed edition of *The Scale* from that date, records indicate that Gilbert was indeed very generous to Syon.

Sister Mary's courage in the face of approaching death from tuberculosis is recounted in moving detail. Once again, like St Bridget, Sister Mary seems to have had a premonition of her impending death, and the author of the "Life", registers no surprise, but notes that: "it is no straunge thinge amonge them in their order to haue some warninge somtyme of their ende neere approchinge, whensoever their tyme is come to goe (as they call it) to their Lorde . . ." (fol. 11). The author then remembers having heard that Sister Mary had had a warning vision about five or six years before. In addition, it is suggested that she had "some privy meaninge" in equating the illness that wracked her whole being with pain with Christ's Passion. She is even quoted as equating their ages: "I am juste xxxiijth yeares olde, even as my deere Lorde & Spowse was at his crucyfyinge" (fol. 11). The author muses on this parallel and remembers having heard that when Mary had first come to the house in her illness, she had confided that she had learned in a vision "that she or an other deere frende of hers shoulde shortlye paye theire dett and tribute" (fol. 11v). In a further aside, the author notes that shortly after Sister Mary's death, "Sister Katherine" (perhaps Catherine Kingsmill) narrowly escaped death and that she was "still to this hower in very feeble case" (fol. 11v) – thereby witnessing to the veracity of Sister Mary's visions.

The arrangements for the funeral, which, according to the "Life", were discussed with Sister Mary by "a certeyne frende of hers" (fol. 15) – presumably a priest – seem, in the circumstances, to be fairly elaborate. Mourners were "in readiness", alms had been collected, "a whole Colledge of Preistes" had been gathered "to solemnize" the service, and a sermon had been written. For the burial itself, a "white stammell", or smock, along with her veil and crown had been prepared; and other necessaries, such as "the sweete powders" for embalming, a winding sheet, tapers, and "a sweete close coffin" (fol. 15v) of alabaster had been provided by her "worshipfull frendes" (fol. 16), so that she could be buried "reverentlie" (fol. 16v). After the funeral, "a bride cuppe, full of good spiced cakes & sweete wyne" had been planned so that those present could "rejoyce agayne after mourninge" (fol. 15v). The account in the "Life" concludes with a description of Sister Mary's death in the afternoon of 27 April. Even then, there was a group of considerable size gathered around her: the two nuns, who had been summoned to her side; "a learned preiste", who "never was from her"; her "cheife Confessor & comforter in all extreames", who had by chance arrived at the crucial time; and joining these four in the prayers being said around the bed were "one or two preistes more & other vertuous gentlewomen" (fol. 16). The number of people involved and the scope of the arrangements suggest the high regard in which Sister Mary herself must have been held, and is further testimony to the excellent reputation of the Bridgettines.

The "adventures" of Sister Elizabeth also demonstrate the calibre of the women who became Bridgettine nuns as well as their esteem in the Catholic community. Her intelligence and courage in dealing with the authorities, already witnessed during her interrogation at Gravelines, were tested again and again during her nine-year stay in England, at least six years of which were spent in various prisons. After leaving the bedside of Anne Stapleton, she first went to her sister's house at Adingdon for Christmas, and then on "heerying of Sr. Julyans [i.e., Juliana Harman] beyng with Mr. Yate" (Letter 1, p. 12), she went to Lyford Grange for a year and a half, that is, from January 1579 until about June or July of 1580. Fear of "troubles" there led to her departure for the house of another sister, Mrs Henry Pitts, near Alton in Hampshire.[22] There, Sister Elizabeth joined her sister and her nephew in helping to distribute copies of Campion's *Challenge*.

As a result of this work, Sister Elizabeth was arrested toward the end of August by a "Mr. Pessquod", who took her that night to Alton, where she was questioned the next morning by "Sr Rychard Norton, a Justice".[23] When she was arrested at her sister's house, her room was thoroughly searched and a "chalice" and "masse booke" were found, so that the questioning chiefly concerned the identity of the priest who had said mass for her and the whereabouts of his vestments, which had not been discovered, even after an exhaustive search. It is clear from the account that Sister Elizabeth's response that: "I knew of no pryst, albe, or vestment, and that the chalice and booke was myne owne, for I brought ytt over with me" (Letter 1, p. 12), was not believed, for she was taken next to Winchester to be questioned.

At Winchester she underwent an extensive interrogation by "one Wattsone", who brought a clerk to record her answers. It seems that with the Jesuits at large in the countryside, the presence in England of Elizabeth Sander, the sister of Nicholas, a well known activist, had given the authorities the jitters, for they considered her to be a participant in what they feared to be a grand scheme to restore England to the Catholic faith. Unable to substantiate these fears, yet clearly not believing what Sister Elizabeth told him, Watson tried a variety of techniques to lead her to reveal the information he wanted. Sister Elizabeth kept firmly to her story and would not allow herself to be tricked, so that eventually she was taken to a higher court. In her second letter, she describes the process eloquently and in a way that indicates the depth and firmness of her faith: "they brought me before more judges than Annas and Caiphas, Pilate and Herod; for they did not rest till they brought me before all the magistrates, whom they call Justices, who are very numerous in that country". To their "impertinent questions", she gave "but one short answer, saying that I was a woman and a nun", which, as she pointed out, ought to indicate that she "would not disturb the kingdom". Otherwise, she

---

[22] The "troubles" may possibly have been related to the arrival of the Jesuit priests, Parsons and Campion, in mid-June of that year, for almost immediately they both became active preachers, dividing the various parishes of England between them – Berkshire, as is well know, fell to Campion. See above n. 20.

[23] In her second letter, she states that this is the second time she was apprehended. It is interesting to speculate about her first arrest: is she referring to the incident at Gravelines? or is this just a lapse of memory?

reports, and especially to questions she considered "dangerous", she "kept silence" (Letter 2, pp. 43–44).

During the next few years,[24] Sister Elizabeth was condemned to a harsh existence in the Winchester prison of Bridewell, where she was kept along with hardened criminals, and often deprived of food and the company of others. She was continually urged to go to church, and from time to time she was fined for not going – though since she had no money, she could not discharge this debt, with the result that she was sentenced to imprisonment for life. Amidst such hardship, her courage never failed her, and she also, as she recounts, received secret gifts of food and other necessaries from Catholics confined in the same prison (Letter 2, p. 44).

Once Syon became safely settled in Rouen, sometime in the early 1580s, the Lady Abbess and Confessor General,[25] wrote to the nuns urging them to return: "as well with sweet entreatyng, as also with expresse comaundments uppon our obedyence to God, our Religion, and unto them" (Letter 1, p. 17). Sister Elizabeth's attempts to comply with this request met with unexpected obstacles. Since she was a prisoner, she could not lawfully go back, and the priests and other Catholics whom Sister Elizabeth consulted at various times, were adamant that she not cause scandal by behaving unlawfully. In her own mind, she felt her allegiance was to her superiors and not to English law, and so she felt no qualms about taking up the suggestion of offering a bribe, using alms collected by fellow prisoners. Once her identity became known, not to mention the fact that she owed hundreds of pounds in fines, this route too became closed to her, and so she gave up and decided, as she wrote, to consider the prison her convent (Letter 2, p. 47).

Fate, in a number of guises, did, however, intervene. The first instance, caused by Elizabeth's having slipped out of prison to hear mass at a neighbouring house and of her being arrested there, resulted in her transferral to a less harsh, but higher prison, Winchester Castle, over which her former jurisdiction had no authority, so that her fines were eradicated. From this prison, a bribe did procure her release, though in a most extraordinary manner – by rope, down the side of the castle in the middle of the night. Once again, however, she was advised not to cause scandal, nor to bring harm to the sympathetic governor's wife. If the manner of her escape seems astonishing, her return on horseback, accompanied by a servant, with money in her pocket, seemed to both officials and fellow prisoners absolutely astounding, and to Sister Elizabeth, a great embarrassment. In the long term, however, it turned out for the best, for it enhanced her reputation and allowed her to be accorded greater liberty, and eventually a more carefully planned escape took place, while the governor himself willingly turned a blind eye.

Yet, even now sister Elizabeth was only at liberty a brief time before pursuivants

---

[24] Letter 1 says "six", Letter 2, "three"; three is the more likely figure.

[25] At the time of the letter from Rouen, Father Willan (d. 22 February, 1583) was still the Confessor General, and Bridget Rooke, the Abbess. Elizabeth actually refers to Father Willan by name (Letter 1, p. 17), which helps date their letter (i.e., sometime between late summer or early autumn 1580 and early 1583).

raided the house of her cousin, Mrs Mary Lusher, with whom she had taken refuge. A bribe procured her temporary release, and Sister Elizabeth, taking advantage of this freedom, went to London to consult another cousin, Erasmus Sander. Once again, however, she was unlucky, for as the result of the vigilance of an astute spy, she was arrested almost as soon as she arrived; or, as Elizabeth herself described it, it was "as if the pursuivants had been spirits following me in the air" (Letter 2, pp. 51–52). Erasmus Sander, however, understood "the ways of the pursuivants" (p. 52), and, with suitable bribes, was able to arrange for the release of his cousin and his sister. The problem then became how to keep Sister Elizabeth safe until passage to France could be arranged. His ingenious solution was to put her into London's debtors' prison, known as the Counter, under the assumed name of Elizabeth Neale.

Somehow hearing of this, Francis Yate was horrified, and not thinking the Counter a fitting place, he removed Sister Elizabeth once more to Lyford Grange. After about five or six weeks (Letter 1, p. 21; Letter 2, p. 52), trouble struck once again, but this time it was Mr Yate who was arrested and Sister Elizabeth was forced to flee. Disguising herself for a second time as Elizabeth Neale, she spent the remainder of her time in England at the house of a poor widow in London. Eventually, through the influence of a friend of the Queen's secretary, Sir Francis Walsingham, and money collected from Mr Yate and other supportive Catholics, a passport was obtained for her under her assumed name. A letter sent from Rheims, which tells of her safe arrival, is dated 27 May 1587, and so we know that she got back sometime before then. At the end of her second letter, Sister Elizabeth mentions that some of the other sisters who had been in different English prisons returned at about the same time as she; "their arrival", she notes, "increased our gladness and consolation" (p. 53). No record survives to reveal the identity of these nuns, and so far there is no evidence of the existence of other accounts.

From the stories of Anne, Mary, and Elizabeth, however, we discover how astonishingly well three such unworldly women, women who had chosen to belong to an enclosed contemplative order secluded from the world, were able to cope with entirely unfamiliar and challenging events. Unlike their Chekhovian counterparts, the three Russian sisters who longed for "life" in Moscow, but never left the quiet of their country retreat, Anne, Mary and Elizabeth, from diverse backgrounds but sisters in their faith, were forced by circumstances to leave the serenity of their cloister and were brought face to face with the harsh realities of a world actively engaged in destroying their Church and the foundations of their faith. From each of the three sisters we are given a perspective on what it meant to be a Bridgettine nun in the sixteenth century, and we also see the strength of the commitment which has carried this foundation forward from medieval times, through the dissolution, to the present day.

# MUSIC AND DANCING
## IN THE FOURTEENTH-CENTURY SISTER-BOOKS[1]

### GERTRUD JARON LEWIS

WHILE AUSTERE, life of the medieval women monastics was not without joy and beauty. In the case of the cloistered Dominicans that the Sister-Books deal with, we find frequent references to music, especially to singing, and also to dancing. They are contained in accounts of visionary experiences as well as in tales about sisters bursting out in an exuberant dance of joy and singing during the normal course of events, as this paper is about to show. The basis for this study is a *corpus* of nine different texts[2] (two originally written in Latin, the others in Middle High German) from different women's monasteries in the German-speaking area of the

---

[1] This essay is based on material in my forthcoming book, '*The Sister-Books': By Women, For Women, About Women*. Toronto: PIMS 1995.

[2] The primary texts are cited according to the editions listed below (with the appropriate abbreviations):

A. J. König, ed., "Die Chronik der Anna von Munzingen. Nach der ältesten Abschrift mit Einleitung und Beilagen," *Freiburger Diözesan Archiv* 13 (1880) 129–236

D. Ruth Meyer ed., "Das 'Diessenhofener Schwesternbuch': Untersuchung, Edition, Kommentar" (unpublished diss., München, 1991)

E. Karl Schröder, ed. *Der Nonne von Engeltal Büchlein von der Genaden Überlast*, Litterarischer Verein in Stuttgart (Tübingen 1871)

G. F. W. E. Roth, ed., "Aufzeichnungen über das mystische Leben der Nonnen von Kirchberg bei Sulz Predigerordens während des XIV. und XV. Jahrhunderts," *Alemannia* 21 (1893) 123–148 (i.e. the second half of Roth's edition, which ought to be entitled "Aufzeichnungen der Nonnen von Gotteszell bei Schwäbisch Gmünd"]

K. F. W. E. Roth, ed., "Aufzeichnungen über das mystische Leben der Nonnen von Kirchberg bei Sulz Predigerordens während des XIV. und XV. Jahrhunderts" *Alemannia* 21 (1893) 103–123

O. H. Zeller-Werdmüller/ J. Bächtold, eds., "Die Stiftung des Klosters Oetenbach und das Leben der seligen Schwestern daselbst, aus der Nürnberger Handschrift," *Zürcher Taschenbuch*, n.s. 12(1889) 213–276

T. Ferdinand Vetter, ed., *Das Leben der Schwestern zu Töss beschrieben von Elsbet Stagel, samt der Vorrede des Johannes Meyer und dem Leben der Prinzessin Elisabet von Ungarn*, Deutsche Texte des Mittelalters 6 (Berlin, 1906)

U. Jeanne Ancelet-Hustache, ed. "Les *vitae sororum d'Unterlinden*. Edition critique du

Dominican province of Teutonia; they were composed very roughly between 1310 and 1350. The Sister-Books deal with the foundation history and the spiritual life of women's cloistered communities. Partly by way of legendary cliches, the authors communicate their spiritual fervor, theological interests, and the pursuit of knowledge. We find, moreover, routine details of the daily life of asceticism behind the cloister walls.

Though the Sister-Books are decidedly not a reflection on women's attitude to music and dancing, references to music are so pervasive that we are led to imagine these women's monasteries vibrating with liturgical melodies much of the time. And in fact, this picture probably comes close to reality. For singing was an integral part of the women's communal life from its very beginning. The sisters spent many hours practicing liturgical chants which they sang regularly at the seven canonical hours and at mass. Singing played such an eminent role in the sisters' daily life that it even showed up in dreams (cf. D. 152).

Choral music is one of the dominant themes in this entire literary *corpus*. Singing in choir typically refers to the sisters' celebrating the liturgy, that is, the divine office and mass. Mass is normally, and certainly on the solemn feast days, sung by the priest and the women. (One text reveals that the nuns sang the table blessings at mealtime, cf. G. 145.)

We gather from the Unterlinden book that the choir nuns who could sing well stood in front while the others were assembled in the rear of the church choir (U. 413). The Töss author also speaks of parts being distributed among the sisters to read and sing (T. 51). The nuns' choir, divided into two halves, is, in the contemporary musical texts, referred to as "the choir at left" and "the choir at right,"[3] "usually seated opposite each other."[4] These two halves alternate in singing the texts of the divine office.[5]

How seriously the sisters take their singing in choir is illustrated with the example of Anna von Klingnau in Töss who was quite ill, but who, nevertheless, "was always eager for choir. And when she could not stand, she sat in her stall and sang" (T. 37).

We find formulations like the one in the Unterlinden text, *ad matutinem, alacriter cantans* ("cheerfully singing at Matins" U. 360), and terms such as *complet*

manuscrit 508 de la Bibliothèque de Colmar ," *Archives d'Histoire Doctrinale et Littéraire du Moyen Age* 5 (1930) 317–517

W. Karl Bihlmeyer, ed., "Mystisches Leben in dem Dominikanerinnenkloster Weiler bei Eßlingen im 13. und 14. Jahrhundert," *Württembergische Vierteljahreshefte für Landesgeschichte*, n.s. 25 (1916) 61–93

3 Hildegard Wachtel, "Die liturgische Musikpflege im Kloster Adelhausen seit der Gründung des Klosters 1234 bis um 1500," *Freiburger Diözesan-Archiv* 66 n.s. 39 (1938) 61f.

4 Anne Bagnell Yardley, " 'Ful weel she soong the service dyvyne': The Cloistered Musician in the Middle Ages," in Jane Bowers and Judith Tick, *Women Making Music: The Western Art Tradition: 1150–1950* (Urbana: University of Illinois Press, 1986), p. 22.

5 An Engeltal sister, we read, was reprehended for having inadvertently sung both parts (E. 14).

*singen* ("singing Compline") that occur throughout. That the sisters apparently sang with voice and heart is convincingly shown in the following statement by Katherina von Unterlinden: "Standing in choir at Matins and at mass at her proper place, [Rinlinda] cried copiously and sang the psalms" (U. 461). The psalms were routinely sung as well as traditional hymns, such as the *Veni creator spiritus*. As is still characteristic for many religious orders, "during Compline . . . the *Salve Regina* was sung" (T. 16), thus concluding the day with a hymn to Mary.[6] Of the Engeltal women we even hear that, during the time before the rule of the strict enclosure was enforced (in 1298), they were invited out to sing the Pentecost mass in a chapel in Reichnek; and the liturgy inspired their noble founder, who had invited them, to miraculously sing the mass along with them, although "he had never learned the letters" (E. 6).

Singing the liturgy is considered so important that the sisters need to be trained for it. Both in Unterlinden and Engeltal, Benedictine sisters, the so-called black nuns (*ein swartze nunne*, E. 26), teach the Dominican women "how to chant the divine office" (U. 365). And they were eager to sing well, as the Unterlinden chronicler states about her community's early days (U. 339f.), while she complains – by way of admonishing her monastic readers – that in later years the singing was, at times, "morose" (U.397). Humbert of Romans' mid-13th century constitution for the Dominican sisters equally specifies that reading and singing the office should be done attentively, that nobody should "disturb the choir when [they are] beginning a responsary or any antiphon," and that nobody should offend by "singing badly."[7] The important office of the *cantrix* in the Dominican community includes "organizing the choir, designating soloists, choosing the correct chants for the liturgical occasion, taking care of the liturgical books, making up the weekly rotational chart, and assembling the music for such occasions as local saints' days."[8] It is, therefore, little surprising that we read of Kathrin von Stein, *cantrix* in the Diessenhofen community, that she was overly exhausted from her demanding work to the point that one day she felt she could not get up for Prime. But when the first bell for this canonical hour was sounded, her conscience gave her no peace:

> She heard a voice like an army trumpet that said: Get up! Get up! Then she got
> up right away and went into the choir and began [singing]: *Jam lucis orto*
> *sidere*, for she was a chantress . . . (D. 172, no. 50)

---

6 The origin of the *Salve Regina* (attributed in legends to angels) is in dispute, but it may go back as far as the tenth century. It is documented as a procession song at Cluny in 1135. Translated into the vernacular in the sixteenth century, it has been a favorite Catholic hymn ever since. (Cf. *Lexikon für Theologie und Kirche* 9 (1964/1986) 281f.)

7 "Constitutions Revised by Humbert of the Romans [1259]," trans. by the Dominican Nuns of Our Lady of the Rosary, Summit, N.J. in *Early Documents of the Dominican Sisters*, (Summit, N. J., 1969), vol. II, 24.

8 Yardley, *op. cit.*, p. 20.

The Unterlinden sister Mechtild, who was forced to move about on crutches because of an illness, is described as having been the best chantress this monastery ever had:

> ... the Lord had given her a strong and exceedingly sweet voice. ... For thirty years she held the office of chantress in choir, and she practiced it incessantly with the greatest alertness. Walking on both sides of the choir, she diligently admonished and solicited the sisters, not only through words but also through her example, so that they sang the psalms loudly and festively. ... At that time everything that was said and sung in choir was orderly and without mistakes. (U. 437, 1–15)

The value of liturgical singing is undisputed under all circumstances, for it is looked upon as chanted prayers. The Töss author praises Ite von Wezzikon for her diligence in singing in choir even though "she did not sing well" (T. 18). Some sisters sing so fervently that we hear of one, for example, that while "she sang in choir in great devotion, a sister saw a golden pipe going up from her mouth to heaven", while at another time "a red rose" was seen before her mouth (D. 120f.). And one Christmas Day, the Diessenhofen author tells us, her entire singing community was honored:

> ... a sister saw a golden plate come down from heaven into the choir. And all the sisters who sang were listed on it. And when Matins was over, the plate went up to heaven again. (D. 132, no. 27d)

This miraculous sign was perceived to be an expression of divine pleasure in the nuns' liturgical singing. Singing was understood as divinely sanctioned and deserving of reward (D. 126).

Besides the regular rehearsals, much time and energy in these communities was also spent on copying the texts and melodies for choir (T. 51).[9] And while no traces of medieval Dominican women's own compositions or arrangements have yet been found (as they have been of Hildegard von Bingen), Wachtel states that the Dominicans, in particular, are known to have introduced a number of new sequences (usually sung in D and G major) during the 13th century to supplement the existing hymns.[10] It is not unlikely, then, that besides copying the centuries-old sacred chants, some sisters composed new works in these women's scriptoria.

As far as the sisters' own participation in music is concerned, the texts exclusively speak of vocal music. And even here, the accent apparently lies on the word rather than the tune. When St Augustine in his *Confessions* speaks of "the pleasures taken in hearing," he emphasizes that psalm singing, for example, should be "nearer to

---

[9] In her musicological study of four codices of choir books from the thirteenth/fourteenth century in Adelhausen, Wachtel gives a detailed description of all the contents including the musical notation (cf. *op. cit.*, pp. 18–48 and 81 f.).

[10] Wachtel, *op. cit.*, p. 80.

speaking than to singing."[11] The medieval church made a sharp division between acceptable music when produced by singing words and the pure sound of instrumental music. As R. G. Weakland explains, "The rejection of all musical instruments from Christian worship is consistent among the Church Fathers. Instruments were associated with pagan, orgiastic rites. . . ."[12] Internal evidence in the Sister-Books perhaps reflects this bias by giving no indication whatsoever that musical instruments were played in any of these communities. But the fact that the playing of instruments in the monastery is not directly mentioned does not imply that no favorable references are made to instrumental music, as visionary accounts show. Furthermore, through external evidence (that is, from a contemporary document referring to the Oetenbach community), we learn that people standing by the monastery church heard "violin playing and polyphonic singing in the choir" (*do gigent und kûnternet*[13] *man im kor*).[14]

Given the Dominican women's life-long immersion in a musical atmosphere, it is little surprising that music is said to either have outright influenced visions[15] or to have played an important part in many visionary experiences reported in the Sister-Books. Thus, Metzi von Waltershoven in Adelhausen talked about a vision in which the child Jesus sang for her (A. 176). And a liturgical vision scene attributed to the Töss sister Mechthilt von Stanz starts as follows:

> Once she was again in her stall and heard a beautiful sweet singing, and those were the words: *Sanctus. sanctus* and *Alleluia*, and then a miracle happened . . .
>
> (T. 67, 26–29)

Significantly the reported auditory experiences do not stop at chanting but comprise the sound of instrumental music. The texts speak of "the sweet sounds of harps (*manigen suessen harfen klang*," e.g. T. 82) and organ music (K. 122).

Music in such miraculous experiences is said to be supernatural, for heaven itself is imagined as "singing before [the] Holy Trinity" (E. 15) with choirs of angels and singing cherubim and seraphim (W. 77). Thus, an Unterlinden sister supposedly was delighted with "celestial melodies" for two years and greatly consoled in her illness by the grace of hearing heavenly music (U. 382 f.). The sound of celestial music also has great healing power (U. 458). And often "the sweetest heavenly harmony" and/ or the singing of angels are said to coincide with visions which then, in fact, became multi-sensory experiences.

---

[11] St Augustine, *Confessions*, trans. William Watts 1631 (London/ New York: Heinemann, 1912), vol. II, 164–167.

[12] R. G. Weakland, "Music, Sacred, History of," *New Catholic Encyclopedia* 10 (1967) 106.

[13] This verb is apparently connected with *kunterbunt* which originally meant "polyphonous" (Der Große Duden *Etymologie* (Mannheim: Bibliographisches Institut, 1963), p. 378).

[14] Quoted by Annemarie Halter, *Geschichte des Dominikanerinnen-Klosters Oetenbach in Zürich 1234–1525* (Winterthur: Keller, 1956), p. 65.

[15] Cf. Yvonne Rokseth, "Les Femmes musiciennes du XIIe au XIVe siècle," *Romania* 61 (1935) 475.

Some of the most beautiful passages in the Sister-Books are reserved for describing the heavenly music, also referred to as the song of the spheres, which some sisters are granted to hear in very special cases (cf. U. 400: *celica armonia*).[16] Heilrade von Horburg perceiving "heavenly music" was so overcome with "joy and exultation" that "her soul, as it were, began to dance in her body" (U. 458). The Unterlinden sister Elisabeth von Senheim is described as having had the following "out of this world" experience:

> One day as she was deep in prayer, God suddenly granted her [the ability] to hear with her bodily ears singing voices making a sweet and magnificent harmony resound through the air. The beauty and charm of these voices was so great and ineffable that no musical sound nor any songs of this world could be compared with it. Delighted by this magnificent heavenly melody, she was filled with sweetness and wonderful devotion. (U. 451, 1–19)

And Adelheit von Hiltegarthausen in the Gotteszell monastery, after having been taught in a vision a superb *jubilus* is said to have heard the music of the spheres (*das firmamenten klanck*):

> And there she was led to the rotation of the firmament, and from there came such sweet sound and music that it exceeded all senses. Later, when she came to, she told her intimate friends everything: If all the string music that this world could play and all the sweetness that anybody ever heard sounded together it would still not resemble that loveliest of sounds she had heard there . . . (G. 131, 6–13)

The hyperboles the author uses in this account leave little doubt that the music of the spheres is understood as the supreme *auditio spiritualis*.[17]

Angels play such an important role in music that the terms angels and music are next to inseparable in the Sister-Books. Nuns often report having heard angels singing along with the monastic choir, as the following passage from the Gotteszell book indicates:

> Once, on the Second Sunday in Advent, when they stood [in choir] at Matins and sang the antiphon *Benedicite montes et colles*, she heard the angels in the air sing the same antiphon with the community (G. 139, 18–22; and cf. E. 38).

---

[16] St Augustine, in his work *De Musica*, speaks of *carmen universitatis* ("the song of the universe"), which is a notion later resumed by Bonaventura (+ 1274) in his *mundum quasi carmen pulcherrimum*. (Cf. the discussion of "die Welt als Lied" by Ernst Robert Curtius, "Zur Literarästhetik des Mittelalters I," *Zeitschrift für Romanische Philologie* 58 (1938) 20.)

[17] Reinhold Hammerstein's hypothesis (*Die Musik der Engel. Untersuchungen zur Musikanschauung des Mittelalters* (Bern/ Munich: Francke, 1962) p. 54) that such heavenly music can only be perceived by visionaries in the image of music already known to them should perhaps be amended to say that such auditory experiences are presumably rooted in music the visionaries are familiar with but at times carried further by means of their musical imagination.

An Engeltal sister heard the angels sing in polyphony:

> Once on All Angels' Feast, [Diemut Ebnerin] heard the angels sing the respon-
> sary *Te sanctum Dominum*, and when they came to the verse *Cherubim*, they
> sang with three voices. And that, she said quite sweetly, went beyond the
> human senses [*waz uber menschlich sinne*]   (E. 32, 35–33,3).

And since a very similar passage of "a beautiful *Kyrie eleison* sung [by angels] with
three voices" is found in the same text (E. 27f.), we may infer that the Engeltal
women, among others, sang some polyphonic choral music themselves.[18]
Although, as Maria V. Coldwell explains,[19] the composition of polyphonic music
requires an in-depth musical training and skill, polyphony was, in fact, used in a
number of women's monasteries as early as the twelfth century. Manuscript studies
have brought to light, among others, a fourteenth century mansucript of the Swiss
Maigrauge Abbey (MS. 4) with a "three-voice troped Agnus" and a "two-voice
Kyrie."[20]
   Visual and auditory experiences that include angels represent a topos in medieval
religious prose and single out the person involved as having attained a saintly
status.[21] Such sensations could easily be triggered by the liturgy itself, especially by
the *praefatio* in the mass where the community of faithful is exhorted to sing along
with the angels in heaven. Some authors, in fact, make a direct reference to the
*Sanctus*, such as:

> [Heilrade von Horburg] heard . . . with her bodily ears, as it were, two or three
> times, but at different times, a crowd of holy angels intoning an ineffably sweet
> melody on high and presenting in a most joyful rhythm with resonant voices
> the *Sanctus sanctus sanctus Dominus Deus Sabaoth*   (U. 458, 38–459, 4).

The effect on the sister is again said to be "a *jubilus* of heart."
   Similarly the Weiler author relates the following:

> [One sister] heard that angels above the choir sang the *Sanctus* with the
> community; and they made the most beautiful sounds of all with their voices
> and ringing with their wings   (W. 82, 12–14).

Angels with wings [Is. 6:2] do not otherwise occur in the Sister-Books but are here
needed for the special musical effect. Hammerstein interprets the notion of angels

---

[18] Hammerstein (*op. cit.*, p. 59) is hesitant to make this connection because of the three-part
   division of the chanted *Kyrie* which may have caused the writer to speak of the "three
   voices". He does not, however, quote the first example cited, i.e. E.32f.
[19] Maria V. Coldwell, "Jongleresses and Trobairitz: Secular Musicians in Medieval France," in
   Bowers, *op. cit.*, p. 43.
[20] Yardley, *op. cit.*, pp. 26f.
[21] Cf. Hammerstein, *op. cit.*, p. 60.

accompanying the sisters' liturgical singing as a reflection of "the mystical desire to unite the heavenly and earthly liturgy."[22]

Angelic melodies are often a part of the auditory revelations the Sister-Books report, for which the following Unterlinden passage serves as a typical illustration:

> One day, deep in prayer, [Elisabeth von Senheim] was suddenly divinely given to hear with her bodily ears, voices singing, resounding a heavenly harmony most sweetly and very clearly through the air. The sweetness and delightful beauty of these voices was so great and ineffable that no kind of musical instrument nor any song of this world could be compared with it. Most delighted by this heavenly magnificent melody, she was affected with sweetness and wonderful devotion  (U. 451, 11–19).

An Engeltal sister who had to miss the divine office during an illness is said to have heard the angels sing the liturgy to her instead; "then she became so immeasurably glad that she broke out into a *jubilus*" (E. 28). Angels are also heard singing as an aftermath of a rapture, as the Engeltal author says about Elisa's vision: "And then for three days, she heard the angels singing" (E. 40). For another sister, this period lasted for several months (E. 28).

The singing of angels as well as "the sweetest string music" is frequently interpreted as a foreboding of death. Elisabeth von Kirchberg speaks of a visionary anticipating her death where "our Lord" asks Mary to "play the organ (*rur die orgeln*)" for the reception of her soul in heaven (K. 122).

Music and angels singing can also be heard, we are told, at the time of death itself. Thus, some Engeltal women are said to have perceived "the sweetest string music in the clouds" at the death of some sisters (E. 38, 42). Also, while the community gathered around a dying sister sings during their vigil, angels are often imagined to have joined in with the sisters. At the death of Anne von Tettikon, "the angels were heard singing at two places in the monastery" (D. 123). Angels also sing during the Requiem for the dead and at some funerals, the authors explain.

Furthermore, to singing angels is attributed the function of escorting a sister's soul to heaven after her death – the topos of the so-called *Seelengeleit*.[23] In Engeltal Anne Vorhtlin was supposedly accompanied on her way to heaven by "sweet string music" (E. 37), while at Töss, sister Richi witnessed how a deceased sister "was led by angels with beautiful singing to the heavenly kingdom" (T. 84).

The legendary happy death, which is so often portrayed in the Sister-Books, frequently presents the dying person herself singing. The Engeltal author even recites the words of a long song in rhyming couplets (based on similar traditional poems) that a sister sang on her death bed. Part of the passage reads as follows:

> Jubilate, meditate,
> Jubilate, contemplate,

---

[22] *Ibid.*, p. 57.
[23] *Ibid.*, pp. 83f.

> Jubilate, speculate,
> Jubilate, be at peace.

And the text continues:

> She steadily sang these words at her death, and especially on the day she died
> and the day before. She scarcely stopped singing for as long as it would take
> someone to read the seven psalms  (E. 30, 2–8).

Singing and even dancing to the tunes of songs – which, like laughing in death, are
clichés adapted to these texts – is also found illustrated in the Unterlinden book:

> . . . [Sophie von Rheinfelden] immediately burst into song, as if drunken with
> heavenly wine, [chanting] the heavenly *jubilus* and began to sing with a serene
> face some songs of God and the glorious virgin, and she continued for hours.
> When her voice sounded this way, the entire community of sisters came to see
> with amazement this blessed sister dancing and singing the psalms [*tripudian-
> tem et psallentem*] at the threshold of death . . .  (U. 434, 35–435, 4)

The text continues that Sophie eventually, while dying, sang nothing but a repeated *Amen* in a variation of tunes which might be an allusion to the festively sung
*Amen* during liturgy.

It is in connection with death that instrumental music is occasionally mentioned. The Engeltal sister Berhte Makerin is quoted as saying: "I will not die until
King David comes to play my soul out [of my body] with the tunes of his harp" (E.
23). And, indeed, Berhte is ready to die after she "heard the sweetest string music
that ever a human being has heard" (E. 24).

Other than the ones already mentioned, there are very few examples in the
Sister-Books of someone spontaneously breaking out in song. One suspects, nevertheless, that some singing exceeded the liturgical context. For the Unterlinden
author deems it necessary to state by way of an example that one should not seek
one's own glory in singing but seek only the glory of God because all else will be
punished after death (U. 361). Sophie von Klingnau in Töss is shown to sing while
working:

> When she sat in the work room with the community, she often sang very sweet
> words of our Lord; and the sisters were very eager to hear this
> (T. 59, 37–60, 1).

The only non-liturgical song in the Sister-Books is of a didactic nature, admonishing the listeners to turn away from false love. Mezzi Sidwibrin, the paragon of
simplicity in the Töss community, sings a song about *falsche minne*, while spinning
in the common work room:

> Wise heart, detest the love
> that must vanish through suffering.
> Remain in the very best [love]

> that will persist with joy.
> If caught in false love, rid yourself of it.
> May God make you abhor it.   (T. 29, 15–20)

Equally, the aged sister Hedwig von Regensburg in Engeltal is said to have sung a pious song whenever she was happy (E. 22), while Sophie von Neitstein after a rapture sang a song "of which nobody understood a word" except for the final word "Mary" (E. 25). The Adelhausen sisters are said to have sung God's praises while they were suffering serious food deprivation; and the author adds, that their singing was recompensed when God sent his angels to serve them a meal (A. 163).

We are thus to believe that even non-liturgical singing within the cloister is restricted to religious content.

While the reader is at times left with the impression that these texts show very little room for genuine self-expression in any of the art forms – except perhaps for a rare poem – , the following scenes strike a different note.

Thus the Adelhausen sister Adelheit von Brisach showed a surprising reaction after having been charged with heresy in the chapter of faults. For she left defiantly, "in a happy mood, dancing and singing" (A. 154). And we note that, while the song quoted is a psalm, she sang it in a non-liturgical and rather undignified manner.

The Adelhausen author also tells us the story of Adelheid Geishörnlin who, after an exhilarating spiritual experience, was so filled with "superabundant joy and sweetness" that she spontaneously jumped up and started whirling around the altar like a spinning-top (*das si vff fuor vnd zwirbelet vmb den altar*), not being able to contain herself in her exultation (A. 166). The Engeltal sister Alheit von Trochau is described "jumping and singing" for joy when she passed by a statue in the monastery choir (E. 13).

While these spontaneous eruptions into song and dance are technically still within a religious context (and might, indeed, have been inspired by biblical passages, such as 2 Sam. 6:14 and Luke 15:25), they are yet quite different from the measured liturgical movements or chanting in its proper setting. Moreover, these scenes become especially noteworthy when we take into account that church authorities, especially during the thirteenth/fourteenth century, cast a very suspicious eye on dancing;[24] for the church felt she had to combat the "medieval passion for dancing" by speaking out against dancing as an "indecent habit."[25]

There is finally one passage in the Sister-Books with a hidden allusion that dancing in these women's communities may not have been as infrequent as the rare passages, that directly mention dance, lead us to suppose. For when the Kirchberg author tells us about Mechthild von Waldeck's extraordinary spiritual experience and explains that it made her soul dance inside her body, she writes:

[24] Cf. Rokseth, *op. cit.*, p. 476.
[25] Wolfgang Hartung *Die Spielleute. Eine Randgruppe in der Gesellschaft des Mittelalters* (Wiesbaden: Steiner, 1982), p. 64.

. . . and the experience of God went into her soul so that it jumped up. And it seemed to her in true experience that her soul inside showed all the gestures that our sisters did on the outside when they were jubilant [*jubilirten*]. And innumerably often she could not contain herself so that we became aware of it. (K. 119, 20–25)

What the author refers to by way of a negligible simile, as it were, is the fact that the cloistered women habitually expressed their feeling of joy in spontaneous dancing, that is, they "jubilated" by jumping up and making gestures; in other words, they abandoned themselves in dancing with joy. While the writer really tries to show the inner spiritual joy in Mechthild, she does so by comparing it with her community's joyful dancing that her contemporary audience of nuns, no doubt, is familiar with.

The question of why we do not hear more about such beautiful scenes is easily answered. On the one hand, church authorities frowned on dancing; on the other hand, the description of explicit dancing scenes, as much as they would be of interest to a reader today, simply exceeded the scope and intent of the Sister-Books. The reader is thus provided with only accidental glimpses of impulsive artistic expressions of deep emotions. They suffice, however, to permit us a brief insight into the joyous spontaneity of these women typically expressed in singing and dancing.

# TEXTS

# LETTERS FROM MECHTHILD OF HACKEBORN TO A FRIEND, A LAYWOMAN IN THE WORLD

## TAKEN FROM
## THE BOOK OF SPECIAL GRACE
## BOOK IV, CHAPTER 59

*Translated by* MARGOT H. KING

### Chapter 59
*Of those things which she wrote to a laywoman friend*

My dearest daughter in Christ:

The Lover of your soul holds your hand in his right hand and is touching each of your fingers with his fingers. It this way it will be shown to you how he works in your soul and how you ought to follow him by imitating his example. His little finger signifies his very humble way of life on earth when he "came not to be served but to serve" (Mk 10, 45) and to be subject to every creature. Place your finger on his: that is to say, when you are puffed up with pride, recall the humiliation and subjugation of your God, praying that through his humility, you may subdue all pride and self-will that which springs from the personal love by which humans love themselves.

His ring finger signifies the fidelity of his heart which cares for us most solicitously in the manner of mothers, relieving our burdens and hardships by the ineffable fidelity of his heart and protecting us from all ills. Join your finger to this one, thereby acknowledging how much unfaithfulness you have shown towards this most sweet and most faithful Lover when you absented your soul from him. He created you for his praise and love so that your soul might have full enjoyment in eternal delights with him alone of whom you are reminded only rarely and then only tepidly.

His middle finger signifies his eternal, highest and divine love which inclines him so wondrously and efficaciously to the soul. His heart is not permitted any rest until it is poured into the whole soul like a flooding waters which seek a place into which they can overflow. Place your finger on his, that is to say your will, for if you cannot love him every moment, at least give him the desire to do the deed; in this way you [are indicating that] you wish to direct the love of all the saints and of all creatures towards him alone.

173

His index finger signifies the wondrous and inscrutable order of divine providence which foresees with mercy all the future of humans and calls them back with great wisdom and respect when they go astray, either because of good fortune or of adversity. Willingly place your finger on his, that is to say, believe that everything which happens to you (no matter whether it brings happiness or sadness), springs from his exceedingly great love and that it has happened thus for your advantage so that you would not have wanted anything else to have happened or have wished for anything else for yourself. Therefore, offer him every praise and thanks-giving.

The thumb signifies his divine omnipotence and the potent protection of his paternal benevolence through which he offers resistance and checks all adversities to a faithful soul although he does allow some things to happen insofar as they contribute to its sanctification and to the exercise of virtue. Join your finger therefore to him, that is to say be strong in the exercise of virtue and resist vices manfully. Do not lack confidence in the mercy of God, even if he permits you to suffer in anything or even if he withdraws the consolations of his grace from you.

## Good Consolation to the Same Woman

O faithful soul which lovingly cherishes God, consider diligently and lovingly the law which Jesus, the royal child, the son of the fatherly benevolence, gave you when he chose you as a bride for himself and bestowed himself upon you as a delectable groom who consummated those nuptials from himself and by himself. On that day of such solemnity and of his heart's joy, he clothed himself, for love of you, with a rose-coloured vestment which love had coloured for him in the blood of his own heart. He also placed a garland of roses upon his head encircled with most noble pearls, that is to say, with the drops of his most precious blood. The gloves which he wore on his hands were so deeply pierced that he could hold nothing at all and instead he passed on to you all that he had previously hidden from the world. His noble couch was the hard cross on which he leapt with such joy and burning love: no bridegroom has ever experienced such delight in his couch of ivory and silk. He is still waiting for you with unutterable and raging desire on this bed of love until he can have full enjoyment of your embraces. But if you wish to be his bride, for your part you must completely renounce all delight and approach him on his bed of sorrow and indignity and join yourself to his wounded side.

Consider diligently the nature and reason of the precious pledge he laid up for you when he opened for you his most sweet heart, the treasury of his divinity, by giving you to drink the excellent nectar of love which heals every languour of your soul. This goodly pledge is of priceless value because it contains all grace, all virtue and all good. He does not wish, I say, to take this pledge from you because by it he has confirmed his promise. Like a king who has not yet brought his bride into his own house and who leaves a wealthy city or town as a pledge to his friends, so has the bridegroom, thy lover, given a most precious gift, namely his own divine heart, to God the Father as a pledge that he will never forsake you, his own bride. Moreover he offers it for you each day on the altar in order to show the love with which he has predisposed for you from everlasting.

Therefore daughter of the eternal Father, chosen bride of his co-eternal only Son, and beloved friend and longed-for resting place of the Holy Ghost, cherish such a one whose heart is so full of cherishing love by whom you are lovingly cherished and who is himself all love. Be faithful to him who is faithfulness itself. If anything troubles you, receive it as if it were a golden chain which God has placed on you and with which he draws you to the love of his Son. Then immediately lift yourself up completely – and your heart as well – as if you were consenting to be drawn in this way, that it may be still more drawn towards him. Make yourself ready through gratitude and patience and observe diligently how God wishes to work salvation in your soul through this.

Consider as well what may be lacking to you in virtue. If you stand in need of humility or of any other virtue, open with the key of love the most precious receptacle of all virtues – that is, the divine heart of Christ – and pray to the Lord of virtue to give you his noble virtues by which you may subdue every temptation of vice. And if thieving evil thoughts approach, run to your armoury and take from it the ever-bright arms – that is the passion and death of your Lord – and fix them as strongly as you can in your heart by continual remembrance of them, so that the whole horde of thoughts may be put to flight and utterly routed. Moreover, when despairing thoughts assail you, run to the receptacle of inexhaustible loving-kindness which wishes that no one perish (2 Pet 3:9) but to come to an acknowledgement and love of the truth, except only those who freely choose to be damned. Remember that God is more ready to receive the person than the person is to come to God. And God desires this above all, that all persons be so disposed that he may be able to pour his grace upon them without ceasing and ever increase in them every good gift.

### A Letter to the same Woman:
### An Excellent and Good Teaching

The Lover of humans, the Lord Jesus Christ desires with a great desire that the soul be united to him, especially that soul which wishes to be consoled by him and yearns to experience his delights, and he desires that it should cast away all consolation or delight in creatures that does not attract or impel it to the love of God. For when a person has anything that they love or in which they take delight, let them think within themselves that God has given this to them this in order that they thereby may be moved to love him. If they feel, however, that they are making no progress in the love of God because of this thing, but that the thing which they love comes oftener into their hearts than God, they ought to remove it – whether it be for a person or any other creature – if they do not wish to lose their close relationship with God. This close relationship with God is exceedingly delicate and it does not suffer in any way to have anything [esteemed] above it or with it. Jesus himself, the Son of the Father's love, wishes to be loved alone in your heart, to be the only one in your heart, the most beloved and the most intimate.

### To the Same Woman:
### A Useful Admonition

God has given his divine heart to the soul so that it may give its own heart to him in return. If someone happily and trustingly does this, [God's] power will so support the heart of this person that it will not be able to fall into any great sin. Let a person therefore pay close attention to the heart of God by considering attentively what would please it the most. And when they are sad, let them fly immediately with confidence to the treasure committed to them and there seek to be consoled. If, however, divine grace so disposes and they are not consoled, nevertheless let them praise God and give thanks from their heart because this greatly pleases God in a faithful soul: that it seeks not its own but rather the things which belong to Jesus Christ and it does not its own consolation before God's honour.

# OF THREE WORKINGS IN MAN'S SOUL
## A MIDDLE ENGLISH PROSE MEDITATION
### ON THE ANNUNCIATION

STEPHEN E. HAYES

COPIOUS MINOR WORKS of medieval devotional writings in Middle English (to say nothing of Latin and the vernaculars) remain unedited or even unprinted, and in a all too many cases either unidentified or poorly catalogued. This article presents an edition and study of one such text, a brief Middle English prose meditation on the Annunciation, entitled in the Trinity College Cambridge MS *Of Three Workings in Man's Soul* and ascribed in only that manuscript to Richard Rolle of Hampole, the fourteenth-century English mystic (d.1349) whose reputation for piety caused dozens of anonymous works to be ascribed or otherwise attributed to him.

In the first written notice of this meditation in 1927, Hope Emily Allen, the great Rolle bibliographer, called it "a somewhat dilute work of mysticism, written . . . either by a 'second-hand mystic' or by an original mystic in an off-moment."[1] What Professor Allen could have meant by 'dilute mysticism' it is hard to know precisely, since nowhere did she set out systematically a definition of mysticism or of the difference between mystical writings and writings which are simply devotional.[2] And 'second-hand mystic' (referring to the generations of mystics following

---

[1] *Writings Ascribed to Richard Rolle, Hermit of Hampole, and Materials for His Biography* (New York: MLA, 1927), pp. 364–66; Allen prints portions of the text from the Trinity College manuscript (O.8.26). A fragment of the text from Trinity College Cambridge, Ms Dd.5.64 was printed by C. Horstman, *Yorkshire Writers: Richard Rolle of Hampole and His Followers*, 2 vols. (London, 1895–96), 1: 82. For other manuscripts, see my discussion below. The meditation is item M.5, O.15 in P. S. Jolliffe, *A Check-List of Middle English Prose Writings of Spiritual Guidance* (Toronto: Pontifical Institute of Mediaeval Studies, 1974); and no. 5 in R. E. Lewis, N. F. Blake, and A. S. G. Edwards, *Index of Printed Middle English Prose* (New York: Garland Publishers, 1985).

[2] In her introduction to *Writings* (p. 5) Professor Allen states: "It should be said at once that Rolle was the simplest possible type of mystic, and accordingly the term 'mysticism' is used in the present work in the broadest possible meaning." Her promised second volume to the edition of *The Book of Margery Kempe*, had it appeared, may have attempted to refine the issue; cf. J. C. Hirsh, "Hope Emily Allen and the Limitations of Academic Discourse," *Mystics Quarterly* 18 (1992): 94–102. The problem is by no means a settled one; see Valerie Lagorio, "Problems in Middle English Mystical Prose," *Middle English Prose. Essays on*

177

the "Ricardians" Walter Hilton [d.1396] and *The Cloud of Unknowing* author) is even less helpful a term today than it was sixty-eight years ago, as suggested, for example, by one recent critic's convincing argument to move the composition of such a front-rank devotional work as Julian of Norwich's *Revelation of Love* to a significantly later date than previously had been thought.[3] A closer look at the present meditation showed it to be on the whole greatly more interesting than Professor Allen was willing to give it credit, and I am grateful to the Master and Fellows of Trinity College, Cambridge and to the British Library, London for permission to print texts from their collections here.

I. The meditation[4] may be divided into three sections. The first two sections act as a preface to the meditation proper. In the first, the author treats the differences between thought, or simple cognition; thinking, or thought ordered to a specific end, otherwise called meditation; and contemplation, a mystical state of love-knowing in which divine truths are apprehended affectively, unmediated by the mental concepts formed by the imagination in meditation, and which the English mystics call "ravishment" (ed. lines 279, 305).[5] This progression is a late-medieval popular version of the Platonic ascent, especially as it was modified and transmitted by Pseudo-Dionysus the Areopagite and popularized in the writings of Hugh, Richard, and Thomas Gallus of St Victor.[6] For the distinction between thought, meditation, and contemplation, the source of which is named in the incipit, the author translates a few key sentences from Richard of St Victor's *Benjamin major*, a twelfth-century treatise on contemplative prayer found widely in medieval monastic and university libraries. In the following quotation from that work, italics indicate where the Middle English author has rendered his Latin source more or less faithfully: "By means of inconstant and slow feet, thinking wanders here and there in all directions without any regard for arriving. Meditation presses forward with great activity of soul, often through arduous and rough places,

*Bibliographical Problems*, eds A. S. G. Edwards and D. Pearsall (New York: Garland Publishing, 1981), pp. 129–148 (esp. pp. 130–36).

3  For this argument, see Nicholas Watson, "The Composition of Julian of Norwich's *Revelation of Love*," *Speculum* 68 (1993): 637–683.

4  Both Professor Allen and Carl Horstman observe that this piece is written as an epistle. However, given that the epistolary form was often a literary pretext, that Rolle's English epistles, for example, circulated widely as independent treatises divorced from their epistolary context, that the immediate recipient of this text is unknown, and that the author refers to his work as "þis tretice" (l. 322), I prefer the term "meditation" after the subject matter of his treatise.

5  See Wolfgang Riehle, *The Middle English Mystics*, trans. Bernard Standring (London: Routledge and Kegan Paul, 1981), pp. 94–96.

6  On the influence of these authors in medieval England, see especially Alastair Minnis, "*The Cloud of Unknowing* and Walter Hilton's *Scale of Perfection*," *Middle English Prose: A Critical Guide to Major Authors and Genres*, ed. A. S. G. Edwards (New Brunswick, NJ: Rutgers University Press, 1984), pp. 61–81 (pp. 63–69); and the articles by Thomas Bestul cited below, note 10.

to the end of the way it is going. Contemplation, in free flight, circles around with marvelous quickness wherever impulse moves it. Thinking crawls; meditation marches and often runs; contemplation flies around everywhere and when it wishes suspends itself in the heights. *Thinking is without labor and fruit; in meditation there is labor with fruit; contemplation continues without labor but with fruit.* In thinking there is wandering; in meditation, investigation; in contemplation, wonder." In the Latin: "*Cogitatio est sine labore et fructu. In meditatione est labor cum fructu. Contemplatio permanet sine labore cum fructu.*"⁷ By the thirteenth-century Richard of St Victor was an established authority on contemplation, and his theory of the meditative ascent, broadly and in particulars, underlies numerous subsequent treatments of the subject. Dante Alighieri, for instance, placed Richard in Paradise in the company of Isidore of Seville and the Venerable Bede, calling him "di Riccardo, / che a considerar fu più che viro" ('that Richard who in contemplation was more than man,' X.131–32).

The second section, on the role of grace in contemplation, appears to start from the Victorine treatise as well, where Richard uses the biblical story of the Ark of the Covenant allegorically to show that contemplation is God's gift only to those whom He deems merit it, in what manner and for however long He chooses. As Richard explains in the *Benjamin major*: "The Ark of the Lord was shown to Moses on the mountain by a showing from the Lord; but afterward in the valley it was known familiarly and seen often . . . [O]ther persons who rarely and as though fortuitously have ecstasy of mind in their contemplations begin at some time to have it familiarly. Hence it is that at long last Moses habitually went within the veil to the Ark of the Lord, which he first learned to see in the cloud only at the calling and showing of the Lord": "Moysi quidem arca Domini ex Dominica revelatione est in monte ostensa, postmodum autem in valle familiariter nota et frequenter visa. Alii item quod rarum, et velut fortuitum habent (in suis videlicet contemplationibus mente excedere) incipiunt aliquando familiare habere. Hinc est quod Moyses ad arcam Domini intra velum familiariter tandem intravit, quam ad solam Domini vocationem et revelationem prius per nubem videre accepit."⁸ Summarizing Richard's teaching, *The Cloud of Unknowing* – a late fourteenth-century treatise on meditative prayer, and one of only three known Middle English works to translate from the Latin Victorine source (including the present meditation) – glosses: "herby maist þou see þat he þat may not com to for to see & feel þe perfeccion of þis werk [of contemplation], bot wiþ grete trauayle, & ӡit it is bot seeldom, & may liӡtly be disceyuid ӡif he speke, þink & deme oþer men as he feliþ himself: þat þei mowe not com to it bot seeldom, & þat not wiþouten greet trauaile."⁹

---

7  PL 196: 66–67; English trans. G. A. Zinn, *Richard of St Victor* (New York: Paulist Press, 1979), pp. 155–56. Cf. Riehle, *Middle English Mystics*, pp. 67–75, on peripatetic metaphors for the approach to God.

8  PL 196: 169; trans. pp. 309–10.

9  *The Cloud of Unknowing and related treatises*, ed. Phyllis Hodgson, Analecta Cartusiana 3 (Exeter: Catholic Records Press, 1982), p. 71; subsequent references are to this edition.

Although a "detached didactic voice instructing the reader in the techniques of meditation through precept and example"[10] is a convention of this genre from the earliest examples, the naming of the Victorine source and borrowings from it suggest that the meditation may also draw from Richard of St Victor the position from which this didactic voice speaks. According to Richard: "[S]ome persons advance to the same grace [of contemplation] by instruction from another more than by their own keenness of mind, who nevertheless in their contemplations often rise up as far as ecstasy of mind. For this reason it is read that Bezeleel did build the ark, although he never went into it. . . . Behold: In this work we who take up, as it were, the office of Bezeleel take the trouble to impart instruction to you for the pursuit of contemplation and to sweat greatly in making this ark": "Illud vero notandum quod quidam ad hanc gratiam propria industria et sine alicujus doctrinæ magisterio promoventur, qui tamen in suis contemplationibus usque ad mentis excessum nullo modo rapiuntur. Quidam autem ad eamdem gratiam ex aliena traditione magis quam proprio mentis acumine proficiunt qui tamen in suis contemplationibus sæpe usque ad mentis excessum assurgunt. . . . Ecce nos in hoc opere quasi Beseleel officium suscepimus qui te ad contemplationis studium instructionem reddere et quasi in arcæ operatione desudare curavimus."[11] In such meditations as form the focus of the present text, it is sometimes the Virgin Mary who speaks with this voice of authority.[12] This last point is important to our understanding of the composition and integrity of the present meditation since it answers the question why material drawn ostensibly from Richard of St Victor's *Benjamin major*, with its medieval title *De arca mystica*, prefaces a meditation on the Annunciation. For, as Marina Warner points out, a number of Old Testament echoes in the Lucan account of the Annunciation reinforce the typology that made the Virgin Mary the New Ark of the Covenant.[13]

That the gift of contemplation is granted exclusively to those in whose souls desire for contemplation and humility when they receive it are balanced is the

10 Thomas H. Bestul, "Chaucer's *Parson's Tale* and the Late-Medieval Tradition of Religious Meditation," *Speculum* 64 (1989): 600–619 (602). On the influence of the Victorine school in England, see *idem*, "Devotional Writing in England between Anselm and Richard Rolle," *Mysticism: Medieval and Modern*, ed. Valerie Lagorio, Analecta Cartusiana 92: 20 (Salzburg: Institut für Anglistik und Amerikanistik, Universität Salzburg, 1986), pp. 12–28; and "The *Meditationes* of Alexander of Ashby: An Edition," *Mediaeval Studies* 52 (1990): 24–81 (esp. 43–46).
11 PL 196: 169; trans. p. 309.
12 For example, see Alexandra Barratt, "The Virgin and the Visionary in the Revelation of St. Elizabeth," *Mystics Quarterly* 17 (1991): 125–36.
13 *Alone of All Her Sex. The Myth and the Cult of the Virgin Mary* (New York: Alfred A. Knopf, 1976), pp. 11–12. Warner describes Luke's account as "a veritable labyrinth of Old Testament reminiscence": e.g., "The verb he uses to describe the action of 'the power of the Highest' on Mary is very particular – 'overshadow' – a verb that explicitly picks up the mysterious image that closes the Book of Exodus, when the *shekinah*, the cloud that is the spirit of God, covers the Ark of the Covenant 'and the glory of God filled the tabernacle' (Exodus 40:34)."

sentence of the meditation which follows and a standard devotional topos. Indeed, the particular tableau here recommended has a lengthy history as a meditation device, especially as it was used in the later Middle Ages in conjunction with the Lady Psalter (so named because it interprets the Psalms typologically in reference to the Virgin) or the *rosarium*, as the author of this piece recommends (ll. 225–226, 228).

Visual representations of the Annunciation in which Mary is depicted as a contemplative, housed within a cell or temple, meditating on Isaiah's *virgo concipiet* (7.14), occur as early as Byzantine art and in their basic lines show the probable influence of the Pseudo-Matthew's *Liber de ortu beatae Mariae* popularly attributed to St Jerome.[14] From the twelfth century onward, meditation on this scene became increasingly more popular as meditative writings developed a certain level of sophistication and convention and the contemplative came to be identified as the mystical handmaiden, ministering to the pubescent Virgin and her unborn son. Bernard of Clairvaux touches on the scene briefly in his *Homilia in laudibus virginis matris* (Hom. 2), wherein the reader is directed not only to visualize the angel's visitation but to imagine himself present:

> Gather round this virginal chamber and, if you can, enter your sister's chaste inner room. Behold, God has sent down for the Virgin. Behold, Mary is being spoken for by the angel. Put your ear to the door, strain to listen to the tidings he brings. Maybe you will hear soothing words to comfort you.[15]

Bernard's friend, the Englishman Aelred of Rievaulx, in a treatise on meditation written for an anchoress under his spiritual direction, similarly conducts her:

> ferst goo in-to þy pryue chaumbre wit oure lady Marie, wher schee abood þe angel message, and þer, suster, abyd þe angel comyngge, þat þu mowe isee whanne he comeþ in, and hou graciously he grette þilke gracious mayde; and soo þu, as it were irauesched of al þy wittes . . . cry þu as lowde as þu my3t grede to þy lady and sey: *Aue maria, gratia plena, dominus tecum; benedicta tu in mulieribus et benedictus fructus ventris tui Ihesus, amen.* And þis rehersyngge ofte and many tyme be-þenke þe how much was þilke fulsumnesse of grace in Marie, of whom al þis wordle borwede and beggede grace, whanne Godys sone

---

14 See Isa Ragusa and Rosalie B. Green, *Meditations on the Life of Christ: An Illustrated Manuscript of the Fourteenth Century* (Princeton: Princeton UP, 1961), p. 393; and D. M. Robb, "The Iconography of the Annunciation in the Fourteenth and Fifteenth Centuries," *Art Bulletin* 18 (1936): 480–526. Cf. Susan Groag Bell, "Medieval Women Book Owners: Arbiters of Lay Piety and Ambassadors of Culture," *Signs* 7 (1982): 742–768: "The developing association of the Virgin with books . . . coincides with the rise in numbers of women book owners during the fourteenth and fifteenth centuries" (762). Given the regular, early appearance of books or scrolls in depictions of the Annunciation, certain aspects of Bell's thesis are difficult to support.
15 *Magnificat. Homilies in Praise of the Blessed Virgin Mary*, trans. Marie-Bernard Saïd and Grace Perigo (Kalamazoo: Cistercian Publications, 1979), p. 16.

was maad man, ful of grace and sooþfastnesse. . . . [T]ake good heede of þis mayde þat þu scholdest folwe, and of þys maydenes sone Crist, to whom þu art iweddid;

this in the late-fourteenth-century Middle English translation of Aelred's Latin from the Vernon Manuscript.[16] In the fifteenth-century translation from Bodley 423:

whan thy soule is purged clerly from alle vnclene thoughtes, than entre in-to that pryue chambre where oure blessed Lady praide deuoutly vnto the tyme the aungel grette hir, beholdyng bisely hou she was occupied with redynge of suche prophecies in the whiche weren profecyed Cristis comynge thorugh a maydens birthe. Abyde there awhile and thou shalt se hou the aungel cometh and gretith hir, seieng thus: *Aue Maria gracia plena, dominus tecum.* Al-though thow be astonyed of this seconde comynge, natheles dresse the vpward and grete oure Lady with the aungel and saye, *Aue Maria gracia etcetera.*[17]

Occurring as it does at the beginning of the medieval canonical Life of Christ, this meditation also frequently commences the individual's devotional progress, though with certain variations. Those qualities of the Virgin that were emphasized were as dependent upon a rich tradition of accumulated Marian tropes as they were upon the specific visionary or devotional context. Three better-known examples in Middle English from the late-fourteenth and early-fifteenth centuries, St Bridget of Sweden, Dame Julian of Norwich, and the lay woman Margery Kempe, demonstrate. St Bridget (in the Middle English translation of her *Revelations*, I, x) places herself outside of the scene as the Virgin narrates Gabriel's appearance to her:

But onone þare aperid ane aungell of God, as a man of soueraine bewte, noght clethed, and he said to me, "*Aue gracia plena et cetera*: haile, full of grace, þe lorde is with þe. Þou art more blissed þan all oþir women." When I had herd þis, I was astoned, merueilinge what þis suld betaken, or whi he profird to me swilke a salutacion. I wist wele and trowed miself vnworthi ani swilke, for I held me noȝt worthi ani gude; bot I wiste wele it was noȝt vnpossibill to God for to do what him liked. Þan saide þe aungell againne, "Þat sall be born of þe is hali, and it sall be called þe son of God; and as it hase plesed him, so it sall be." Neuirþeles I held me noȝt worthi, ne I asked noȝt of þe aungell, "Whi or when sall it be?", bot I asked þe maner, "How it sall be þat I, vnworthi, be þe modir of God, þe whilke fleshli knawes no man." And þe aungell answerd to me as I saide, "To God is noþinge vnpossibill, but what he will be done, sall be done." – Eftir þe whilke worde of þe aungell, I had þe most feruent will þat might be had to be þe modir of God. And þan spake mi saule þus for lufe: "Lo, I here redi: þi will be done in me." At þe whilke worde anone was mi son

16 *Aelred of Rievaulx's* De Institutione Inclusarum, *Two English Versions*, eds. John Ayto and Alexandra Barratt, EETS 287 (London: Oxford UP, 1984), pp. 39–40.
17 *Ibid.*, p. 18.

conceiued in mi wombe with unspekeabill gladness of mi saule and of all mi partis.[18]

The vision is much more intimate for Bridget than it is for Julian of Norwich, who meditates on the scene as though on a static tableau:

> I saw her ghostly in bodily lykenes, a simple mayden and a meeke, yong of age, a little waxen aboue a chylde, in the stature as she was when she conceivede. Also god shewed me in part the wisdom and the truth of her sowle, wher in I vnderstode the reuerent beholding, that she beheld her god, that is her maker, marvayling with great reuerence that he would be borne of her that was a symple creature of his makyng. And this widome and truth, knowing the greatnes of her maker and the littlehead of her selfe that is made, made her to say full meekely to Gabriell: Loo me here, gods handmayden. In this syght I did vnderstand verily that she is more then all that god made beneth her in wordines and in fullhead; for aboue her is nothing that is made but the blesssed manhood of Christ, as to my sight.[19]

Margery Kempe, whose meditation may have been inspired by Bridget's, participates in the tableau with characteristic directness, first offering herself in place of Mary's mother to care for the infant Queen of Heaven, then clipping the angel Gabriel's wings, so to speak, by announcing to Mary the fulfillment of the Isaiahan prophecy within her:

> An-oþer day þis creatur schuld ȝeue hir to medytacyon, as sche was bodyn be-for, & sche lay stylle, nowt knowyng what sche mygth best thynke. Þan sche seyd to ower Lord Ihesu Crist, "Ihesu, what schal I thynke?" Ower Lord Ihesu answeryd to hir mende, "Dowtyr, thynke on my Modyr, for sche is cause of alle þe grace þat þow hast." And þan a-noon sche saw Seynt Anne gret wyth chylde, and þan sche preyd Seynt Anne to be hir mayden & hir seruawnt. & anon ower Lady was born, & þan sche besyde hir to take þe chyld to hir & kepe it tyl it wer twelve ȝer of age wyth good mete & drynke, wyth fayr whyte clothys & whyte kerchys. And þan sche seyd to þe blyssed chyld, "Lady, ȝe schal be þe Modyr of God." The blyssed chyld answeryd & seyd, "I wold I wer worthy to be þe handmayden of hir þat xuld conseive þe Sone of God." Þe creatur seyd, "I pray ȝow, Lady, ȝyf þat grace falle ȝow, forsake not my seruyse." The blysful chyld passyd awey for a certeyn tyme, þe creatur being stylle in contemplacyon, and sythen cam a-geyn and seyd, "Dowtyr, now am I be-kome þe Modyr of God." & þan þe creatur fel down on hir kneys wyth gret reuerens & gret wepyng and seyd, "I am not worthy, Lady, to do ȝow seruyse." "ȝys, dowtyr," sche seyd, "folwe þow me, þi seruyse lykyth me wel."[20]

[18] *The Liber Celestis of St Bridget of Sweden*, ed. Roger Ellis, EETS 291 (Oxford: Oxford UP, 1987), pp. 18–19.

[19] *A Book of Showings to the Anchoress Julian of Norwich*, eds. E. Colledge and J. Walsh, 2 vols. (Toronto: Pontifical Institute of Mediaeval Studies, 1978), 2: 297–98.

[20] *The Book of Margery Kempe*, eds. S. B. Meech and H. E. Allen, EETS 212 (Oxford: Oxford UP, 1940 [for 1939]), p. 18.

By far the most widely-circulated example in Middle English is the Die Lune section of Nicholas Love's *Mirror of the Blessed Life of Jesus Christ*, in the main a translation of the Latin *Meditationes vitae Christi* now attributed to John Caulibus. For the relevant portion, Caulibus's work conjoins a revelation to St Elizabeth of Hungary on the early life of the Virgin with the pseudo-Matthian *Liber de ortu beatae Mariae*. Additionally, as with the Passion section of Love's *Mirror*, this section of the *Mirror* circulated separately in at least eight manuscripts as "A Short Reule of the Liif of Oure Lady,"[21] and in one manuscript of the meditation at hand it is written into the folios immediately following the text.

II.  The meditation edited here is extant in four manuscripts, which for clarity's sake I will call MSS 1, 2, 3 and 4. These are, respectively: Trinity College Cambridge, 0.8.26 (s. XV med.),[22] ff. 73v–78v, the base text for my edition; Magdalene College Cambridge, Pepys Library 2125 (s. XIV ex./XV in.),[23] ff. 80v–82v; Cambridge University Library, Dd. 5. 64 (s. XIV ex.),[24] f. 42v; British Library, Sloane 1009 (s. XV ex.),[25] ff. 25v–26v, the text of which is here printed parallel with MS 1. MSS 1 and 2 contain complete texts which in general agree fairly closely. MS 1, in Northern English, comes from Lincolnshire near the Yorkshire border, whereas MS 2, in Central Midlands Standard English, is considerably more southern, probably from Gloucestershire. The differences between the two are slight and are of a kind that may well have come about through successive copying. MS 2 at least can not be a copy of MS 1, since at one point it supplies a crucial line of text missing from MS 1, probably as the result of eye-skip (ll. 60–61). Regardless, MS 1 throughout presents better readings, though in a few

---

21 See Elizabeth Salter, "The Manuscripts of Nicholas Love's *Myrrour of the Blessed Lyf of Jesu Christ* and Related Texts," *Middle English Prose: Essays on Bibliographical Problems*, pp. 115–127 (p. 127), who cites Mss. British Library, Harley 1022, 2330, Royal 8.C.i; Oxford, Bodley 938, Ashmole 41; and Cambridge, Magdalene College, Pepys 2125 (MS 2, below); to which can be added Westminster School 3 and British Library Add. 11748. The texts in Harley 1022 and Bodley 938 are printed by Horstman, *Yorkshire Writers*, I: 158–61.

22 Numbered 1401 in M. R. James, *The Western Manuscripts in the Library of Trinity College, Cambridge: A Descriptive Catalogue*, 4 vols. (Cambridge, Eng.: Cambridge UP, 1900–1904), 3: 418–20. My thanks to Professor Linne R. Mooney for sharing draft description of this manuscript's Middle English contents for the forthcoming *A Handlist of Manuscripts Containing Middle English Prose in the Library of Trinity College, Cambridge*.

23 For description, see Rosamond McKitterick and Richard Beadle, *Catalogue of the Pepys Library at Magdalene College Cambridge. Volume 5. Manuscripts. Part i: Medieval* (Cambridge: D. S. Brewer, 1992), pp. 54–61. In what follows, my own examination of this manuscript from microfilm supplements their careful description.

24 See Allen, *Writings Ascribed, passim*, for description.

25 For description, see J. M. Manly and E. Rickert, *The Text of* The Canterbury Tales, *Studied on the Basis of All Known Manuscripts*, 8 vols. (Chicago: University of Chicago Press, 1940), 1: 515–18.

places I have used MS 2 to supply or correct readings in MS 1. Variants from MSS 2 and 3 are recorded in the textual apparatus.

MS 3 preserves only a fragment of the text, Northern in language, and in what little of it there is, it agrees most closely with the Northern text in MS 1. The former is an early, authoritative collection of many of Rolle's writings, in which the fragment occurs minus the ascription to Rolle. Besides perhaps furnishing the source for MS 1's ascription to Rolle, MS 3's early date and authoritative status also tend to corroborate the choice of MS 1 as the base. The table of manuscript affiliations, below, approximates the relationships among the extant witnesses.

MS 4, from Herefordshire, supplies a version of the text misleadingly classified as an abridgement by the few bibliographers who have at least correctly identified it as in part an adaptation of the *Benjamin major*. Their classification of this version is certainly descriptive of its length, since it is considerably shorter than the two long texts in MSS 1 and 2, reducing, for example, the entire middle section on the role of grace in contemplation and the temptation to pride and slothfulness to a single sentence (ll. 119–124) and otherwise producing a kind of medieval Reader's Digest condensed version of the meditation. But 'abridgement' does not account for the minute additions to the text in the form of the repeated phrase, "My sone," found only in MS 4's text, additions which both specify the intended recipient's gender and, by using the diminutive "my sone," establish that intended recipient in relation to the meditation's author: "But, my son, þoue þu haue grete trauell & meditacion. . ."; "For my sone, what tyme þat a soule is fully rauysshed in desyre of a þynge. . ."; "My sone, to þynges I fynde þat oure lady hadde in hirre soule. . ."; "And, my sone, þerfore kepe þu well þes to. . . ." The repetition of this address within the meditation rounds out the sense of a personal letter to a disciple, suggested in the first place by the first-person address found in both versions of the text (and indeed a convention of meditative literature), and in the second place by the content of the meditation, which seems geared to a disciple somewhat lower on the ladder to perfect contemplation than his teacher (as I will explain in a moment). One could also reasonably argue that the address to "my sone" imitates the same mode of address in the biblical book of Proverbs, the starting place for medieval writings on the ascent to Wisdom or contemplation. Previously this MS has attracted attention because it contains Chaucer's *Tale of Melibee*, another work in that tradition.

My characterization of the disciple for whom the meditation was perhaps originally written as occupying a rung lower on the ladder to contemplation than his spiritual advisor deserves comment and raises another interesting point about the meditation. As Hope Allen noted, another Middle English work for contemplatives begins almost identically: "A greet clerk þat men clepyn Richard of Seinte Victore, in a book þat he makiþ of þe studie of wisdom, witnessiþ & seith . . . ." This treatise turns out to be an abridged Middle English paraphrase translation of Richard of St Victor's *Benjamin minor*, a translation that is generally thought to have been written by the author of *The Cloud of Unknowing*, which teaches the so-called *via negativa*, or 'negative way' to contemplation through meditation unsustained by corporeal images or other mental constructs.[26] However, the present meditation's use of such images suggests that its author was at best only familiar with the *Cloud* writings and that he counseled a disciple somewhat further down on the ladder to contemplation, on which image-based meditation was regarded as the first, indispensable step. As even *The Cloud* recognizes: "what man or womman þat weniþ to come to contemplacion wiþoutyn many soche swete meditacions of þeire owne wrechidnes, þe Passion, þe kyndenes & þe grete goodnes & þe worþiness of God comyng before, sekirly he schal erre & faile of his purpos".[27]

Finally, as to whether this disciple was "man or womman" only conjectures are possible given the meditation's obscure origin. However, it is perhaps worth noting that of the four manuscripts which contain the meditation presented here, three without doubt were owned and read by men. MS 1 is a Carthusian manuscript, but there were no Carthusian nunneries in England as there were on the continent. MS 2 is an especially interesting case with respect to the gender of its reader. All the treatises in MS 2 which in their commonly received versions were gender-specific have been carefully revised for reading by the male owner of this MS, probably a West Midlands religious, perhaps with connections to the Brigittines of Syon Abbey (Middlesex), since it contains two texts connected with that foundation.[28] For example, in MS 2's text of a Revelation to St Bridget concerning the active and contemplative lives (*Revelations* VI, 65), reference to the Saint and to the context of her vision have been suppressed, unlike in all other extant copies of this text, which clearly attribute the revelation *as revelation* to her.[29] In the same MS's copy of *The Chastising of God's Children*, a Middle English compendium on temptation written for cloistered women, still visible, at f. 1r, is the scribe's erasure where "religious sister" has been corrected to read "religious frend." MS 4 of course has the repeated address to "My sone," which can hardly been taken other than as indicating a male readership. Thus for a meditation subject prescribed by Aelred of Rievaulx to women readers ('This shuld be a maydens meditacion') the *état actuel* of the extant witnesses shows a curious distribution.

26 Ed. Hodgson, *The Cloud of Unknowing*, pp. 129–45.
27 *Ibid.*, p. 15; cf. p. 17, where such meditations are attached to "þe hier party of actiue liif & þe lower party of contemplatiue liif."
28 In addition to the excerpt from St Bridget's *Revelations* mentioned next (though this text is hardly the sole provenance of the English Brigittines), MS 2 (Pepys 2125) also contains the "Four Requests of Our Lady to Her Son," a short prose devotion on the sorrows of the Virgin "made for . . . Quene Isabell of Fraunce," otherwise found only in Cambridge University Library, MS Ff. 6. 33, ff. 33v–37, written for Syon by the Sheen Carthusian William Darker.
29 The text is also found in MSS Cambridge University Library Ii.6.40, Arundel 197, and Bodley 423; for descriptions, see Ayto and Barratt, *Aelred of Rievaulx's De Institutione*, pp. xix–xxix.

*Note on editorial procedure*

In editing the texts, manuscript word-separation is retained, modern punctuation is supplied, and only proper names are capitalized. Paragraph divisions are editorial. The textual notes record substantive variants, orthographical variants, substitutions of common synonyms and cognates (e.g. *clepen/calles, are/ben, lere/teche*), additions and omissions of articles, varying uses of conjunctions *and, but,* etc., and simple transpositions of words, are ignored in MS 2 where these do not affect the sense. All variants in MS 3 are noticed.

*Manuscript affiliations*

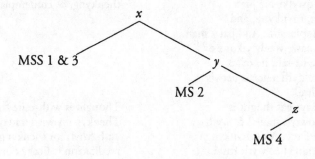

I wish to thank Thomas Bestul, Robert Haller, and Paul Olson for reading early drafts of this introduction. I owe a special debt of gratitude to Louis A. Haselmayer for his gracious, unfailing generosity in supporting my research; and to Valerie Lagorio and Anne Clark Bartlett for providing the occasion to publish my edition. All research into the manuscripts on which this study is based was conducted using microfilm.

[MS 1 – TRINITY COLLEGE
CAMBRIDGE, 0.8.26]

[MS 4 – BL SLOANE 1009]

Off thre wyrkynges in mannes
saule. Richard Hermyte.

De contemplacione.

A grett clerke þat men
calles Richard of Saynt
5  Victoures settes in a boke þat
he made of contemplacyon thre
wyrkynges of crystyn mannes
saule, qwylke are þise:
thoght, thynkyng, and
10  contemplacyon. And þat a man
may knawe verely ylkone of
þise be itt-self, he telles
qwhate dyfference is betwix
þem thre.
15  He says þat thoght is
wyth-owtyn trauell & wyth-
owtyn frute. And thynkyng is
wyth trauell & wyth frute.
Þow schall wytt þat thynkyng &
20  meditacyon is bothe one. And
also contemplacyon is wyth-
owtyn trauell & wyth grett
frute. And he þat desyres
gretely to com tyll
25  contemplacyon, me thynke þat
hym nedes gretly to gyue his
intente vn-to þe wyrkyng of
his saule, and namly to þise
thre. For here I trowe be þe
30  redyest & þe next way þat any

[a] grete clerke, Richard
of Seynt Victores, seyeþ in a
boke of contemplacion þat ther
be þre worchynges of euery
cristen soule: thought,
thenkyng, & contemplacion.

Thought is with-oute fruyt.
Thenkyng is with trauayle and
with fruyt, for thenkyng &
meditacion is bothe oon.
[a]Contemplacion is with-owte
trauayle & with fruyt, and þat
is grete fruyt.

And if þu desyrest to knowe
contemplacion, þu shalt know
it by þes þre þynges.

---

ᵃ *Lower case c at beginning of MS paragraph.*

1 title] *om.* MSS 2–3  8 qwylke are þis] þat er þere MS 3; and þat ben þese thre MS 2  11
verely] witerly MS 3  11–12 ylkone of þise be itt-self] ilkane by þaim-self MS 3; hem MS 2
14 thre] Thought *add.* MS 2  15 þat thoght] *om.* MS 2  19 þow schall wytt þat] for MS 2
20–21 And also] also *om.* MS 3  20–21 wyth-owtyn] grete *add.* MS 3  22 &] but MS 3
22 grett] *om.* MS 2  23 frute] and þat gret fruyt *add.* MS 2  23 he] þou MS 3  23 he . . .
desyres] þu . . . desirest MS 2  25–25 þat hym] þat (*om.* MS 2) þe MSS 2–3  26 gretly] *end*
MS 3  26 his] þin MS 2  28 his] þy MS 2  29 For here] Therfore MS 2  29 trowe] þat here
*add.* MS 2

man may lere an-othyr. And
forthy, þat þow may þe
   redilyer knawe howe þow schall
vse þise wyrkynges, I schall
35  tell þe, as gode sendes grace
to me (þoff I be vnworthy),
how þow may prophett in þem,
vsande þem ordynately as þai
are sett here ylkone eftyr
40  othyr.
   Fyrst I say þat thoght is
wyth-owtyn trauell & wyth-
owtyn frute; & þat schall þow
well see & knawe be þe pruffe
45  & þe fowll custum / f. 74r þat is in
ylke a vayne saule. Þow sees
welle in þi saule þat þe thare
nowght aresse þe to thynke
vanyte, for it wyll cum in-to
50  þi thoght all vnsowght. Þen
thynke me þat he sayde wele
þat sayde thowght is wyth-
owtyn trauell & wyth-owtyn
frute. And þerfor, for þe
55  luff of god, suffyr noght þi
saule & þi lyffe to be loste
in þis vayn custum, bot leue
þis maner of wyrkyng of þi
saule þat is wyth-owtyn frute,
60  [and passe ouer to þat oþer
þat is with fruyt,] noght
lettyng for þi trauell. For I
schall say þe, ay þe oftere
þat þow trauelles þer-in, þe
65  lyghter þow schall thynke itt;
and þat schall be for grete
abundance of grace & of
swetnesse þat þow schall feill
yf þow wyll vs itt as I lere

Ffyrst y say þat þou3te
is withoute trauayle & fruyt.
And this shalte þu se[b] by þe
preue and þe fowle costome þat
is in euery ydel soule.
Þu seest well in þi soule þat
hit nedyþ nou3te to stere þe
to thenke vanyte, ffor it will
comm to thy thought all
vnsought. Þen þynketh me þat
he seide well þat þou3t is
withoute trauayle and withoute
fruyte. And therfor suffre
no3te þi soule in þy life to
be lost in þis veyn costome,
but lese this worchyng in thy
sowle þat is withoute fruyt,
and passe ouer to þat other
þat is with fruyt, lettyng for
no trauayle.

Ffor þe ofter þat þu
travaylest þerin, þe li3ter
hit shall thenke þe.
& þat shall be for grete a-
boundance of swettenes þat
thou shalle fele if þu wilte
vse hit.

---

b  knowe *crossed out, followed by* se.

---

**36** þoff I be vnworthy] *om.* MS 2  **39–40** ylkone eftyr othyr] by rowe MS 2  **42** wyth-owtyn]
*om.* MS 2  **44** & knawe] *om.* MS 2  **46** ylke a] euery ydel MS 2  **47–48** thare nowght aresse]
nediþ nat to styre MS 2  **51** sayde] *om.* MS 2  **53** &] in MS 2  **60** and pass ouer to þat oþer
þat is wiþ fruyt] *om.* MS 1; *supplied from* MS 2  **63** ay] euer MS 2  **64** þow] þe MS 2  **67** of
grace &] *om.* MS 2  **68** þow] þe MS 2  **69** lere] shal telle MS 2

70 þe.

The tothyr wyrkyng is
wyth trauell & wyth frute, &
it is calde thynkyng or
meditacyon. Bot thynkyng is
75 propyr Inglysch þer-of; for
meditacyon is noon Inglysch,
bot it is a worde feyned lyke
to Lattyn. Thynkyng is, as I
sayde before, wyth trauell &
80 wyth frute; & þat is on þis
wyse: Qwhen þow inforces þe to
thynke of any thynge wyth all
þi myght – as of þe Passyon of
Ihesu Criste, or of þine awne
85 wrechednesse, or of þe ioyses
of owre blyssed lady, or of
the ioy of awngels – bot þow
may not ȝitt cum þer-to tyll
itt be lernede þe fro abowue.
90 Many maners of thynkynges þer
are; I may noght tell all.
Bot I trowe yf þow wyll
trauell in þem, þow schall
fynd mekyll frute in þem. / f. 74v
95      And in tyme to cum, þow
schall fynde swylke frutfull
swetnes in itt þe qwhylke no
tonge may tell. And þen
schall þi trauell be takyne
100 fro þe, & so schall þow cum to
the threde wyrkyng þat is
calde contemplacyon. Ffor
contemplacyon is, as I before
sayde, wyth-owtyn trauell bot
105 wyth mekyll frute. Bot þoffe
it be wyth-owtyn trauell, no
man thynke to cum þer-to wyth-

That other worchyng þat is
thenkyng is with travayle &
fruyt, & þat is cleped þenkyng
or meditacion. But þenkyng is
þe propre Englyssh.

Þenkyng with trauayle & fruyt
is when þu enforcest þe to
thenke on eny thyng with all
thy myghte, as of the Passyon
of Criste or of þyn owyn
wrecchydnesse or of the ioyes
of / f. 26r holy seyntes.

And if þu wylte trauayle in
succh thouȝtes, þu shalte
fynde grete fruyte in hem;
for hit shall be fruyt of
succh swettenes þat no thyng
may tell hit.
And then shall thy trauayle be
take fro the, & þen shall þu
comme to the iijde worchyng
þat is cleped contemplacion.

Contemplacion is with-
owte trauayle but with grete
fruyt. Þowe hit be withoute
trauayle, yet no man may
thenke to come therto with-
owte trauayle.

---

71 The] that MS 2   71 wyrkyng] þat is thenkyng *add.* MS 2   73 it] þat MS 2   77 it is] *om.*
MS 2   78 Thynkyng] y sey *add.* MS 2   78–79 as I sayde before] *om.* MS 2   80–81 on þis
wyse] *om.* MS 2   83 of] on MS 2   84 Ihesu] *om.* MS 2   87 ioy] ioyes MS 2   87 bot] þat *add.*
MS 2   88 ȝitt] *om.* MS 2   90 maners] maner MS 2   90 thynkynges] thynges MS 2   91 are]
þat *add.* MS 2   91 tell] þe *add.* MS 2   95 tyme] þat is *add.* MS 2   96–97 swylke frutfull
swetnes in itt þe] much fruyt of swetnesse MS 2   107 man] may *add.* MS 2

owtyn grett trauell. Bot qwho-
so wyll trauell besily in
110    thynkyng of frutefull thynges,
I trowe þat gode of his
gudenesse wyll lyghtyn his
saule wyth sum of his gracyus
gyftes, þat all þe trauell þat
115    euyr was in þis lyffe, a man
walde thynke itt in comparyson
of þat inwarde reste bot a
chyldes play.
    Bot þow schall wytte
120    well, þoff all þow haue grett
trauell in meditacyon (or
thynkyng), þat þis swete gyfte
of þe grace of godd is noght
geuyn to þe þerfore bot of þe
125    free gyfte of godde, qwhen &
howe he wyll do, and take it
away as hym-selfe lyste. And
þerfore, þoff all þow haue
grett trauell, & yf þow be
130    visytt any seldem tyme wyth þe
souereyn swetenesse, gyffe
þerfore grett louyng to godde.
And wytt þow wele, þe more ioy
þat þow feles, þe more arte
135    þow behaldyn to trauell in
prayer & thynkyng & louyng to
god day & nyght. Fforþi me
thynke þe awght / f. 75r to drede
þe ryght mekyll takande swylke
140    gyftes of godde, knawande þi
febylnes so mekyll þat yf þow
hade all þe gostely [mennys
my3t] in erthe, þow myght 3ytt
thanke hym of on poynte of þat

But, my son, þoue þu haue
grete trauell in meditacion or
thenkyng, þat þis swete 3ifte
of grace is no3te yevyn to þe
þerfore but of the fre 3efte
of god.

---

**108** grett] *om.* MS 2   **108** trauell] hym *add.* MS 2   **109** in] *om.* MS 2   **110** of] on MS 2
**113–114** gracyus gyftes] 3iftes of grace MS 2   **114** þat] þow MS 2   **114** all] *om.* MS 2   **123**
þe grace of] *om.* MS 2   **124** þe] grete and *add.* MS 2   **126** howe] þat *add.* MS 2   **126** do] to
þe *add.* MS 2   **128** all] *om.* MS 2   **130** any seldem tyme] oþerwhile MS 2   **130** þe] þis MS 2
**131–132** gyffe þerfore grett louyng to godde] þank hyliche god þerof MS 2   **133** wele] þat
*add.* MS 2   **135** behaldyn] holde MS 2   **136** thynkyng & louyng to] in worshepyng MS 2
**138** awght] so *corrected above the line* MS 2   **139** ryght] iful MS 2   **140** gyfts of godde] 3ift of
grace and MS 2   **142–143** mennys my3t] men syght MS 1; *supp.* MS 2   **143** myght] nat *add.*
MS 2   **144** hym] fully *add.* MS 2   **144** of] *om.* MS 2

145  he has done to þe of þi
     makynge, þoff all þow hade
     neuer receyued gostely
     swetenesse in þis lyff.
     Neverþelesse, ȝytt is owre
150  lorde gode so curtesse þat he
     askes no more of man þan he
     may? Bott who is he þat
     fayles noght, ȝitt in þat he
     may? Sekyrly, noon as I trowe
155  lyuande in erthe bot he be
     more specyally chosyn. And
     forþi, qwhere owre frelte
     fayles, it is to aske helpe of
     owre blissed lady saynt Mary &
160  all þe holy company of heuen,
     wyth a meke louyng to þe grett
     mercy of owre lorde Ihesu
     Criste.
         And yf þe thynk þat þow
165  arte nooght vysytte wyth þat
     swetnes of his gyfte, or yf þe
     thynke þat oþer men are cumme
     þer-to in schorter tyme þan
     þow, or wyth lesse trauell,
170  þen I wyll answere þe & say
     þat þow arte noght as þai are,
     meke & besyly trauelande, bot
     þow arte prowde & slawe. For
     warne þow wer prowde, þow
175  walde noght thynke þat þow
     trauelde more þan þai. And
     warne þow ware slawe, þow
     walde not thynke þi tyme
     lengare þan oþer mense. And
180  forþi, inforce þe in all þat
     þow may thrugh grace to be
     meke / f. 75v and wele lastande in

145 to] for MS 2   146–148 þoff all you hade neuer receyued . . . in þis lyff] *om.* MS 2   151
askes] ne askeþ MS 2   152 he] or what is he *add.* MS 2   153 ȝitt] *om.* MS 2   153 þat] þat
*add.* MS 2   155 bot] if *add.* MS 2   157 frelte] myȝt MS 2   159 blysed] *om.* MS 2   159 &]
of *add.* MS 2   160 holy company] fair felawshipe MS 2   161 louyng] thankyng MS 2
161–162 þe grett mercy of] *om.* MS 2   164 yf] hit so be þat *add.* MS 2   166 his] godes MS 2
167 are] *om.* MS 2   174 warne] if MS 2   174 wer] nat *add.* MS 2   175–176 þat þow
traueled . . . not thynke] *om.* MS 2   180 in] *om.* MS 2

prayer, & thynkyng of gode day
& nyght. And ordayne þi
185  lyvyng wyth discrecyon, þat
euyr more grace may be haldyn
vppe & all þi nature may be
noryscht to þat ende þat þow
desyres.
190  And yf so be þat þow
trauell besyly & haue
ouercumme þe steryng of pride
& sleuth before-sayde, thorow
þe grace of god, and yf þow
195  haue noght 3itt þis hegh
swetnes of god, þen lyghtly
þin enmy wyll make a
suggestyon vn-to þe & say þat
þow trauels in vayne, sayande
200  þus in þi thoght: "Qwhere-to
besyes þow þe so faste for to
trauell aboute swylke hegh
thynges? Wenes þow to cum
þer-to þat hase synned so
205  mekyll?" And so wyll he bryng
to þi mynde all þi synnes, so
þat he wyll eythyr gare þe
cece of þi trauell, or els he
wyll brynge þe in-to dyspare
210  of swylke swetnesse. Bot all
þise schall þow putt vndyr
fute yf þow haue grace to pray
faste & meke þe to consell.
And wytt þow well, yf þow haue
215  itt not here, it is kepyde for
þe full plentevusly in an-oþer
place, qwhere þe wyll lyke it
mekyll bettyr.
And yf þow wyll vse þe in
220  thynkyng, I wyll tell þe a
maner of thynkyng, qwylke / f. 76r

And if þu wylte vse the in
þenkyng, Y will shewe the a
maner of thenkyng þe which is

---

183 of] in MS 2  185 lyvyng] so *add.* MS 2  187 &] þat *add.* MS 2  187 all þi nature] kynde
MS 2  190 yf] hit MS 2  192 þe] þis MS 2  194 yf] *om.* MS 2  195 3itt] *om.* MS 2
198–199 vnto þe . . . in vayne] *om.* MS 2  199 sayande] to þe þus: þu trauailest in veyn,
puttyng þis MS 2  200 þus] *om.* MS 2  202 swylke] so MS 2  205–207 wyll he . . . eythyr
gare] otherwhile make MS 2  208 els] if he may *add.* MS 2  211 þise] þat MS 2  213 consell]
*om.* MS 2  214 And] But MS 2  214 well] þat *add.* MS 2  215 is] wul be MS 2  215 for]
*om.* MS 2  218 mekyll] *om.* MS 2  221–223 qwylke þow has prayed me of before tyme. And

þow hase prayed me of before
tyme. And it is bothe
thynkynge & prayer, & it is of
225 þe ioyes of owre blyssed lady
saynt Mary, and howe þow
schall thynke qwhen þow sayes
þi fifty *Aues.*
Fyrst þow schall ymagyn
230 in þi saule a fayre chawmbyr.
& in þat chawmbyr þow schall
see sitting at a wyndowe,
redande on a boke, owre lady
saynte Mary. And þow schall
235 sett þi selfe in sum cornere
of þis chawmbyr, besyly
behaldand hyre qwhere sche
syttes, and namely þe
cowntenance & þe manere of
240 havyng of hire blissyd body.
Behalde howe deuotely sche
syttes, & hyre boke lyande on
a deske before hyre, & sche
aparty stowpande towarde hire
245 boke & redinde pryualy wyth-
owtyn schewyng of voyce. And
I schall tell þe qwhat þow
schall thynke þat sche redys.
Þow schall thynke þat sche
250 redys wordes of prophecy, howe
it was sayde of Ysai þe
prophete þat *a maydyn schowlde*
*bere a chylde, þe qwhylke*
*schulde saue all man kynde.*
255 And on þat sche ymagyned,
desiryng þat it myght be in
hyre dayes þat sche myght ones
see hyre blessyde lorde þat
sche hade seruede in þe

boþe prayer and thenkyng. And
it is of the ioyes of oure
lady & howe þu shalte thenke
when þu seyest þine ave mary
or ellys owere lady sawter.

[f]yrst þu shalte se by
ymagynacion deuowtly þe blessed
virgyn & mayden Mary,

howe deuotely she sitteth, &
hire boke affore hirre, þeron
redyng priuely withowte
shewyng of voyce.

And there she radde wordys of
the prophesy of Ysaye, that a
mayden shulde conceyve & bere
a childe þe which shulde
save[c] al mankynde. And she
desyred in hirre thought þat
she my3t se þat blessed lorde
þat she had serued in temple
in forme of man.

---

[c]  save *followed by* haue, *cancelled and subpuncted.*

it] *om.* MS 2   228 fifty] *om.* MS 2   234 schall] þen *add.* MS 2   236 þis] þat MS 2   239 of]
hir *add.* MS 2   242 boke] bifore hire *add.* MS 2   243 before hyre] *om.* MS 2   244 hire] þe
MS 2   247 I schall tell þe] *om.* MS 2   248 redys] radde; y shal telle þe þat *add.* MS 2   250
redys] radde MS 2   250 prophecy] of ysaye *add.* MS 2   250–252 howe . . . prophete] *om.* MS
2   255 on þat sche] how MS 2   258 hyre] oure MS 2

260 tempyll in schappe of owre
kynde.
  And besyly behalde vn- / f. 76v
to hyre, & þow schall see hyre
in þis ymagynacyon in hyr
265 saule sitt vppe-ryght in hyr
body, leuande lokyng on hyr
boke & lokande vppe to heuen.
Behalde þen besily þat
blissyde lufely vysage of þat
270 lady, howe deuoute sche is,
hire swette mowthe close, &
hire een closyd, & þer-wythe
no brethe passand oute of hire
mouth ne noyse. And behalde
275 þer-wyth howe pale sche is, &
no blode ne rude in hir
vysage; and þis þe skill qwhy.
For sekyrly qwate tyme þat a
mans saule is full rauyschyde
280 in desyre of any thyng, þen
all þe blode of hym is gedyrde
in tyll a place of hym þer þe
saule moste regnes, & þat is
in þe harte. For þowe schall
285 wele witt þat þe saule is
regnande hole in all þe partes
of þe body, bot qwat tyme itt
is all hole sett on a thyng
synglerly, þen itt is gedirde
290 holy in itt-selfe in-to þat
place qwhylke itt is moste
regnand in, & þat is þe harte.
And so leues itt þe body for
þat tyme as itt wer dede,
295 sauand a lityll hete &
warmenesse leues in þe lymmes
& in [þe vtter] partyes of þe

And with this she cast vp
herre eyen into hevyn, closed
paale,

& no blode nor rode in hirre
visage was seen.
For my sone, what tyme þat a
soule is fully rauysshed in
desyre of a þynge, þere alle
þe blode of hym is gadered
into oo place þer as the soule
moste regneth, and þat is in
the hert. For þu shalte
vnderstonde þat the soule[d] is
regnyng hool in all the
parties of the body, but what
tyme þat it is all holy sette
in a þynge synglerly, þene it
is gadered holy in hit-self
into þat place þat it is most
regnyng yn, and þat is in the
hert. And the body lyueth in
that tyme as it semed dede,
savyng a litell hete &
warmenysse þat leuyþe in the

---

d  soule *followed by cancelled* mos.

---

265 sitt] sittyng MS 2   265–266 in hyr body] *om.* MS 2   266 on hyr] of þe MS 2   267 vppe]
in *add.* MS 2   269 lufely] swete *add.* MS 2   269 þat] oure MS 2   270 sche] hit MS 2   273
oute] neyþer *add.* MS 2   273 hire] *om.* MS 2   274–275 behalde þer-wyth] se MS   278 for]
*om.* MS 2   278 a] oo MS 2   284 in] *om.* MS 2   287 tyme] þat *add.* MS 2   288 on] in MS 2
292 is] in *add.* MS 2   293 leues itt] lyueþ MS 2   293 for] in MS 2   294 wer] semed MS 2
297 þe vtter] othyr MS 1; *supp.* MS 2

body. And wytt þow wele þat
all eftyr a mans desyre is of
300  mekylnesse & worthynes of þat
/ f. 77r thynge qwhilke he desires,
þer-eftyr is his ioy more or
lesse qwheþer þat itt be. Bot
wyte þow wele þat no man is
305  receyued to swilke ioy bot
only þai þat are chosyn þer-
to, and also þai þat haue
besily disposide þar lyfe many
day before in prayer & in
310  meditacyon of goddes luffe &
owre lady saynt Mary.
    And wytt þow wele, þise
is bot a bodely ymagynacyon
þat I haue 3itt sayde of þe
315  hauyng of owre blyssyde lady
in hyre holy body. Butt nowe
I wyll tell þe, as gode & owre
lady gyffes me grace for to
schewe vn-to þe for þi
320  prophete, yf þow wyll do þer-
eftyr, & othyr mens also þat
redis þis tretice,
qwhatekyn[d] a considracyon
þow schall haue gostely in þi
325  saule off hyr preuy wyrkynge
in hire saule; and howe sche
disposede hire for to conceyue
þe grace of godde in hire
saul. And þerfore I conseylle
330  þe fore to dispose þe in þi
saule in gostely wyrkynge, yf
þow desyre tyll haue þe grace
of godde wonande in þe. And
wytte þow wele, wyth-owtyne

lymes & in þe other partys of
the body.

But / f. 26v treuly, þen is none
rauysshed to come to succh
ioye but þo þat haue bysely in
her life dispendet here dayes
in deuote prayers and
meditacion. Þey be chosen of
god þerto.

---

299 all eftyr] as MS 2    300&] of *add*. MS 2    302 þer] *om*. MS 2    302 eftyr] þat *add*. MS 2
303 qwheþer þat itt be] *om*. MS 2    304–305 no man is receyued to] non comeþ to be
rauysshed MS 2    306 only] *om*. MS 2    307 also] *om*. MS 2    308 disposide] dispendid MS 2
309 in] *om*. MS 2    310 goddes] þis loue MS 2    310 luffe] of god *add*. MS 2    312 wele] þat
*add*. MS 2    314 haue] seyd þe *add*. MS 2    314 sayde] *om*. MS 2    315 owre blyssyde lady in]
*om*. MS 2    318 me] *om*. MS 2    319 vn-to þe for] þe to MS 2    320–321 yf þow wyll do þer-
eftyr] *om*. MS 2    322 tretice] book MS 2    323 -kynd a] maner MS 2    326–329 and howe
sche disposede hir . . . in hir saule] *om*. MS 2    329 -fore] after MS 2    330 þe for to] þat þu
MS 2    330 in] and MS 2    334 wele] þat *add*. MS 2

335 þis manere of disposycyon
schalle neuyr man taste in hym-
selfe verely þe swetnes of
contemplacyon & of Cristes
luffe. And þerfore / f. 77v herkyn
340 besily, for þis itt is.

Two thynges I fynde þat
owre [lady] hade in hire saule.
Oon was þe heghest of desyre,
& þe tothyr was þe grownde of
345 meknesse. And þise two hade
sche neuyre verely ore þe
tyme þat sche conceyued
Cryste. For sekirly as it is
impossible tyll any man to
350 fele in hym-selfe þe
swetenesse of contemplacyon &
of goddes luffe wythowtyn þis,
so it is impossible a man þat
hase þis to be wyth-owtyn
355 suthfaste felyng of goddis
luffe & of contemplacyon. And
me thynke þat þise two are
well ioyned to-gydder,
mekenesse & desyre, ffor yf þai
360 wer sundyrde, bothe wer þai
vices. Ffor desyre wyth-owtyn
meknes brynges man in-to
presumcyon, and meknesse wyth-
owtyn desyre brynges man in-to
365 despaire. And qwhen þai are
knytte to-gydder, þai [make] a
wele disposid saule.

My sone, to þynges I
fynde þat oure lady hadde in
hirre soule. The furst was þe
highte of desyre, þe seconde
þe groundeᵉ of mekenys. Ffor
thes to she hadde euer boþe
affore þe concepcion of Crist
& after. Ffor withoute þes to
hit is vnpossible to eny man
to com to contemplacion or to
the loue of god. Ffor treuly
þey be well knytte to-gaderes,
mekenys & desyre, for if þey
were departyd a-sondre, þen
were they bothe vices. Ffor
in desyre withoute mekenys
hangeth presumpcion. And
mekeness withoute desyre
bryngeþ despeyre. And when
þey beth boþe to-gader, þen
þey make a wele disposed
soule.

And, my sone, þerfore
kepe þu well þes to, & treuly
þu shalt haue þine desyre, and
the kyngdom of hevyn to þe

---

ᵉ grande *followed by* and the, *cancelled and subpuncted*; of *inserted above the line.*

335 disposycyon] þer *add.* MS 2  336 man] non MS 2  337 selfe verely] *om.* MS 2  337
swetnes] veryliche *add.* MS 2  339 herkyn] herto *add.* MS 2  342  lady] *om.* MS 1; *supp.* MS
2  343 heghest] heyghte MS 2  344 & þe tothyr] þat oþer MS 2  346 neuyre] euere MS 2
348 Cryste] and euerafter MS 2  349 tyll] *om.* MS 2  350 þe] eny MS 2  352 þis] þo two
MS 2  354 þis] þo two MS 2  355 of] *om.* MS 2  357–358 me . . . ioyned] wonder wel be
þey cowpled MS 2  360 sundyrde] partyd and a sondre þan MS 2  361 Ffor] in *add.* MS 2
362 brynges man in-to] hangiþ MS 2  364 man in-to] *om.* MS 2  365–366 are knytte] be
MS 2  366 to-gydder] þan *add.* MS 2  366 make] *om.* MS 1; *supp.* MS 2

And howe þat þise two wer
in owre lady saule nowe wyll I
370 telle þe. Wele I wote þat fro
þe tyme þat sche had redde how
owre lorde god schulde take
man kynde & be borne of a
maydyn, sodanly sche fell in-
375 to swylke a desyre of owre
lorde þat sche ymagyned of þat
prophecy þus in hyr saule,
sayande / f. 78r þise wordes in hyre
mynde: "A lorde god, yf it wer
380 þi worthy wyll þat þis thyng
myght be in my tyme." & þus
sche sayde wyth-in hyr saule:
"Qwat ioy! Qwatt conforth!
Qwatt blysse! Qwatt welth!
385 Qwatt myrth! Qwatt mede myght
any saule haue more þan to see
& serue þat blyssede lorde
beande in owre kynde, so þat
bothe myght be gladdid, owre
390 body in þe seruyce & in þe
syght of his body & owre saule
in þe lufe & in þe fervoure of
his godhede." And þus for
gretnes of desyre, sche sayde
395 efte sones in hir saule þise
wordes of grett desyre: "A
lorde, yf itt be þi worthy
wyll þat I myght be þe
handmaydyn of þat maydyn þat
400 schall bere þat chylde." And
lo, here, þe heght of hire
desire, and þat here is þe
grownde of mekness, may þow
wele see. Ffor sche wyste wele

rewarde. To the which place
he bryng vs, *qui viuit &
regnat deus per omnia secula
seculorum.*
Amen.

---

368–369 howe þat . . . saule] *om.* MS 2   370 þe] þat MS 2   371 redde] in þat book *add.* MS
2   372 god] *om.* MS 2   374 maydyn] she ymagyned of þat prophecie þus in hir sowle and
*add.* MS 2   376 lorde] sey3yng þus in hir sowle *add.* MS 2   376–379 þat sche . . . hyre
mynde] *om.* MS 2   379 A] good *add.* MS 2   379 god] *om.* MS 2   380 worthy] swete MS 2
387 blyssede] louely MS 2   387 lorde] so *add.* MS 2   388 þat] owr bodie my3t be gladid
boþe in þat seruise and in þe si3t of his body] *add.* MS 2   389–391 bothe . . . body] *om.* MS 2
392 & in þe fervoure] of owre sauyour and MS 2   395–396 þis wordes] þat word MS 2   397
worthy] *om.* MS 2   401 hire] *om.* MS 2

405 þat sche was a maydyn, & ȝitt
helde sche hire selfe so
febyll & so vnworthy þat sche
desyred noght to be þe same
maydyn, bot wyth a grett lufe

410 & dred sche prayed to be þe
handmaydyn of þat maydyn. And
witt þow well þat sche thoght
hire selfe ȝitt unworthy þer-
to. Bott lawere myght sche

415 noght be mekyde, / f.78v haldand
þe heght of desyre. And hegher
myght sche noght desyre,
haldande þe grownde of
mekenesse.

420    And tyll hyre sodanly
beynge in þis disposicyon
apperyde þe awngell Gabriel,
in a body knelande sydelynges
by hyre, sayande þise wordes:

425 *Aue gracia plena. Dominus*
*tecum.*
   *Deo gracias.*

---

405–407 sche was . . . vnworthy þat] such a maiden held she so feeble MS 2   416 heght]
heights MS 2   416 of] hir *add.* MS 2   420 tyll hyre] as MS 2   421 beynge] *om.* MS 2   424
þise wordes] þat word MS 2   425–427 *plena . . . gracias*] And if þu wult haue lenger meditacion of þe cuntenaunce þat was bitwixt þe angel and hire, y rede þat þu lerne hit at seynt luke
in his gospell *Missus est angelus gabriel*

# ST BIRGITTA'S *REVELATIONES* REDUCED TO A BOOK OF PIOUS INSTRUCTION[1]

## JAMES HOGG

### 1. *Liber Revelationum coelestium S^tae Birgittae de regno Sueciae*

ALFONSO PECHA bore the ultimate responsibility for the presentation of the first seven books of St. Birgitta's *Revelationes*. Many of the visions contained therein had been experienced in a state of ecstasy, often accompanied by corporal and auditory manifestations. The Saint had not been spared the dilemma "cognoscendi bonum vel malum spiritum" (*Rev.* I,4; III,10; IV,78). Our Lord and the Blessed Virgin reassured her by instructing her to submit all such manifestations to the judgment of her confessors (*Rev.* I,52; IV,78). Soon Magister Matthias, her spiritual director, had such confidence in their divine origin that he asked Birgitta to consult Our Lord on specific points for his commentary on the *Apocalypse* (*Rev.* VI,89). The revelations impressed themselves on Birgitta's memory so graphically that she had no difficulty in retaining all the details until she could relate them to her secretary, the Cistercian monk Peter of Alvastra, who then produced the Latin version (cf. *Rev. Extravagantes* 48), though thereafter she could only recollect the general drift of the individual visions.[2]

There seems to be no logical order in the *Revelationes* and partial repetitions are frequent. They remain, however, the most significant spiritual document emanating from medieval Sweden.[3] The corpus of Brigittine material that was brought

---

[1] All quotations from *Sunte Birgitten Openbaringe* (abbreviated *SBO*) are taken from James Hogg, "Sunte Birgitten openbaringe" in *Spiritualität Heute und Gestern* 8, *Analecta Cartusiana* 35:8 (1989), 4–265. There is a study of St. Birgitta's life based on the early documents in the introductory volume, *Spiritualität Heute und Gestern* 7, *Analecta Cartusiana* 35:7 (1990), 101–213, here 103–39 (abbreviated Hogg).

[2] As Birgitta's Latin improved, she checked the Latin transcripts: cf. Isak Collijn (ed.), *Acta et Processus Canonizacionis Beate Birgitte, Efter Cod. A 14 Holm, Cod. Ottob. Lat. 90, Cod. Harl. 612 med inledning, Personoch Ortsregister, Samlingar utgivna av Svenska fornskriftsällkapet*, Ser. 2, Latinska Skrifter 1, Uppsala 1924–31, 484–85. Peter of Alvastra produced the Latin versions, but it seems that Alfonso Pecha made final adjustments, presumably of a stylistic nature – cf. *Revelationes Extravagantes* 48 end and 49; cf. also *Revelationes* VII, 31.

[3] Alfonso Pecha also drew up the *Coeleste viridarium*, – an anthology of the *Revelationes* concerning the lives of Jesus and Mary that was translated into Swedish by Jons Budde, a Brigittine monk of Nådendal.

back to Vadstena in 1380 was treasured and revered until the Latin edition of the *Revelationes* was finally printed at Lubeck in 1492.

Alfonso Pecha had, however, presented a first official text for the canonization process in 1377, which had consisted of seven books, the *Sermo Angelicus*, and four prayers. In 1380 he prepared a new version, adding 14 chapters containing the "Tractatus ad Pontifices", which had probably been omitted previously because of its overt criticism of ecclesiastics. Furthermore, Peter of Alvastra inserted 13 chapters into book VI and declarations were furnished for all the other books, a life of Birgitta being adjoined to the whole. The recension made in 1391, the year of Birgitta's canonization, offered book VIII, "Liber caelestis imperatoris ad reges revelatus divinitus b$^{tae}$ Birgittae de regno Sueciae", consisting of 61 chapters, and adjoined chapters 132–44 to book IV under the title "Tractatus ad sacerdotes et ad summos pontifices".

The 1492 edition remained until recent years the basic text of all subsequent complete or partial editions of the *Revelationes*. Here the eight books appear, together with the *Revelationes extravagantes*, collected by Peter of Alvastra, offering much advice to the Vadstena community. Two books were furnished with an individual title: book V: Liber Quaestionum and book VIII: Liber celestis imperatoris ad reges. The prologue preceding book I was due to Magister Matthias, that to book VIII to Alfonso Pecha. Between book VIII and the *Revelationes Extravagantes* the *Regula Sancti Salvatoris dato divinitus ab ore Jesu Christi devotae Sponsae suae b$^{tae}$ Birgittae de regno Sueciae* in the version approved by the Pope and his Curia was provided, together with the *Sermo Angelicus de excellentia Beatae Mariae Virginis, quam ipse Angelus dictavit b$^{tae}$ Birgittae*, drawn up in Latin by Peter of Skänninge, divided into 21 chapters for liturgical use, dealing with Christian history from the Creation to the Glorification and Coronation of the Virgin, three lessons being assigned to each day of the week, and four prayers, *Orationes aliquot S$^{tae}$ Birgittae divinitus revelatae*, two addressed to Jesus and two to Mary, the whole being preceded by a prologue of unknown authorship. Each book of the *Revelationes* has first a summarium and all except books V and VII have "declarationes" and "additiones" taken from notes found among Birgitta's papers after her death and inserted at relevant points by Alfonso Pecha, though they seem to have been compiled by Peter of Alvastra.

Three sections show a more logical organisation than the rest: book VIII *Ad Reges;* the conclusion of book IV *Tractatus ad sacerdotes et ad Summos Pontifices;* and book V *Liber Quaestionum,* a vision dealing with sin, involving a haughty monk and the divine judge.[4] It is not even possible to allocate specific books either to certain periods or places, but, by and large, books I, II, and V are more closely associated with Sweden and can be assigned to the period 1344–49, that is to say from the death of Birgitta's husband until her departure from her home country. Book III concentrates on revelations concerning the clergy, but such items are also

---

[4] On the origin of this section of the *Revelationes* cf. Collijn, *Acta et Processus*, 86.

found in other books. Book IV offers revelations received in Italy; book VII deals with her pilgrimage to the Holy Land; and book VIII, *Liber coelestis imperatoris ad Reges*, contains revelations concerning political matters, particularly touching monarchs and princes. Book VI is a hold-all, drawing together items from all periods of her life, whilst the *Extravagantes*, taken from Birgitta's notes, provides clarifications of obscure points in revelations contained in the preceding books. Books I–IV show a more marked contemplation of Jesus, the Blessed Virgin, Heaven, Hell, and Purgatory.

The *Revelationes* were soon copied and translated into most European languages.[5] A Polish version is recorded in 1392 and another in Bohemia in the same year, whilst surviving early printed editions include the Middle Low German of ca. 1478, ca. 1485, and 1496; the Middle High German of 1481 and 1482 (extracts only),[6] and the complete version of 1502; the Dutch of 1491 and 1502; the Italian of 1518 and 1670; the English of 1530 and 1531; the French of 1622 (extracts) and the full version of 1624; and the Spanish of 1676.

The *Revelationes* were examined at the Council of Constance (1414–18) and again at the Council of Basel (1431–49), but they were always found to be basically conform to the Catholic Faith[7]. Pope Gregory XI had judged the *Revelationes* favourably[8] and Boniface IX had had them scrutinized during the canonization process and recognised their authenticity in his bull "Ab origine mundi", § 39, promulgated on 7 October 1391.[9] Owing to the Great Schism, the antipope John XXIII also approved them at the Council of Constance on 2 February 1415.

---

5   For details cf. G. E. Klemming, *Heliga Birgittas Uppenbarelser, efter gamla handskrifter*, SFSS 14, Stockholm 1857–84, V, 181.
6   Ulrich Montag, *Das Werk der heiligen Birgitta von Schweden in oberdeutscher Überlieferung*, *Münchener Texte und Untersuchungen zur deutschen Literatur des Mittelalters* 18, Munich 1968, 97–100, comments on a fairly complete German translation of the *Revelationes* made at Gnadenburg near Nuremberg by the Brigittine monk Nicholas Koch around 1470, of which a copy was made in Maihingen by Thomas Ritter of Hall (manuscript extant). A second translation was corrected in Maihingen in 1502 and actually printed. Montag, 41–92 (with an addition on p. 337), gives details of all relevant manuscripts containing authentic works or substantial extracts therefrom by St Birgitta. He dealt previously (20–25) with compilations that merely cite passages.
7   Several defences of the *Revelationes* were written to demonstrate not only their authenticity, but also their full accordance with the writings of the Fathers of the Church, learned theologians, and also with the Holy Scriptures. The most important of these were those of the Dominican John of Turrecremata (Torquemada), Master of the Sacred Palace and later Cardinal, and of the Benedictine Cardinal Adam Easton, entitled *Defensorium Sanctae Birgittae*, compiled 1385–88. Turrecremata's *Defensiones quorundam articulorum rubrorum revelationum S. Birgittae* refuted point by point the numerous items in the *Revelationes* that were objected to with considerable acrimony at the Council of Basel (cf. *Acta Sanctorum* Octobris IV, Brussels 1780, 409–12). His *Defensiones* are printed in Joannes Dominicus Mansi, *Sacrorum conciliorum nova et amplissima collectio* XXX, Venice 1792, 697–814. For the debate at the Council of Constance cf. Hefele – Leclercq VII, 184ff.
8   Cf. *Acta Sanctorum*, Octobris IV, 406–08.
9   Printed in *Bull. Rom.* IV, Turin 1859, 621.

Martin V, after initial hesitations, gave them his blessing once more at Florence on 1 July 1419 in his bull "Excellentium principum", though the learned John Gerson remained sceptical. The Council of Basel did indeed reject the aspirations of those who wished to place the *Revelationes* on the same level of authority as the Gospels and asserted that many passages needed explanation and clarification. Benedict XIV also declared in his famous *De Servorum Dei Beatificatione et Beatorum Canonizatione* (1734–38), III, 53, that such revelations did not enjoy "assensum fidei catholicae, sed tantum fidei humanae, iuxta regulas prudentiae, juxta quas praedictae revelationes sunt probabiles et pie credibiles".[10]

The edition commissioned by Pope Paul V, prepared by Gonsalvo Durante, later Bishop of Montefeltro, issued at Rome in 1606, offered notes that formed a theological commentary on the individual revelations. It also included part of Turrecremata's "Defensiones" and an apostolic letter of approbation, "Cum sicut accepimus", issued by Paul V on 24 July 1606. A reprint of 1628 contained a substantial "Tractatus de Revelationibus Sanctae Birgittae", demonstrating the Saint's submission to the Church on all points of doctrine and her general agreement with accepted authorities on issues not regulated by dogmatic pronouncements and her overall concordance with the tenets of thomistic theology. This did not prevent later scholars from associating her thought with the Cistercian, Franciscan, and Augustinian schools! The 1628 edition was reprinted in Munich in 1680 with detailed indices prepared by the Brigittine Simon Hörmann of Altomünster in Bavaria.

The leitmotiv of the *Revelationes* is the omnipotence of God, Sovereign of the universe, who exercises justice tempered with mercy: "Nunquam facio iustitiam sine misericordia" (*Rev.* I,7, 12).[11] Particularly striking is Birgitta's devotion to the humanity of Christ and to the Blessed Virgin, whereby the Compassion of Our Lady enjoys great prominence.[12] She also urged the neglected cult of St Joseph and that of the angels, particularly the guardian angels (*Rev.* VI,59; I,9 respectively), though without furnishing material for the Opus angelorum.[13]

Her whole life was centred on God: "O Deus noster, gaudium nostrum, et omne bonum . . . O Deus gaudium nostrum est de Te, et in Te, nec indigimus alio" (*Rev.* III,3 towards the end). To be Christ's bride she had to renounce her own self totally: "Venisti praesentare mihi vas cordis tui, vacuum a te, et a voluntate propria: ideo Ego implebo te delectatione et gloria mea, laetitia mea erit tua, et gloria tua nunquam finietur a me." *(Rev.* III,3 at the end) Nevertheless, she maintained close

---

[10] Cf. *ibid.*, II, 32, 11. St Peter Canisius praised them highly in *De Maria Virgine* I, 7.

[11] Cf. *Revelationes* II,12; III, 28 for His "Justice" concerning the damned, where her statements coincide with those of St Thomas Aquinas and St Catherine of Siena.

[12] She asserts the Immaculate Conception several times – *Revelationes* VI,49: Ego concepta fui sine peccato originali. Cf. I, 9; VI, 59; *Sermo Angelicus* 10.

[13] Various partial editions were in circulation, beginning with Alfonso Pecha's *Coeleste viridarium*; others included an extract from the fourth book, *Onus mundi*, Rome 1485, *Opusculum Vitae et Passionis Christi eiusque Genetricis Mariae*, Antwerp 1498, and *Thesaurus animae fidelis*, Cologne 1517.

ties with her surviving children up to her death. Birgitta recognised in any case that absolute perfection reigned only in heaven: "Perfecta vero est charitas, quando nihil dulcescit homini sicut Deus. Haec in praesenti inchoatur, sed in caelo consumatur." (*Rev.* III,28 towards the end)


## 2. *Sunte Birgitten Openbaringe*, Lubeck 1496

The Middle Low German version of St Birgitta's *Revelationes* must have been prepared between 1492, the year of the publication of the Latin text in Lubeck, and 1496, the year in which the German version was actually printed. It was almost certainly compiled in the Lubeck area and very probably in Marienwold, a Brigittine monastery founded in 1412 by Brigittines from Marienthal (Reval) in the village of Bälau near Mölln. The house played an important rôle in Brigittine history in the Middle Ages as it lay on the direct route from the continental monasteries to the mother house in Vadstena.

That *Sunte Birgitten Openbaringe* was closely connected with Marienwold is demonstrated by the relation of a series of miracles in book III, – the compiler declares that over 600 miracles had in fact occured at Marienwold (*SBO*: 163–65). Two miracles are given in some detail: the cure of a crippled child and that of Hans Kerckhoff, also an invalid, who, after his cure worked by the intercession of St Birgitta, not only entered the community of Marienwold, but also produced a number of copies of the *Revelationes* (*SBO*: 164–65). The Mohnkopf (Poppy-Head) publishers in Lubeck must have found its conglomeration of "legenda" and spiritual guide more suited to a wider audience than previous extracts from the *Revelationes*, even when these were translated into the vernacular.

Thirteen copies of the 1496 incunabula *Sunte Birgitten Openbaringe* seem to exist, – a fourteenth has been missing from the Benedictine Abbey Library of Göttweig in Lower Austria since the Second World War.[14] The thirteen are conserved in Staatsbibliothek, Preußischer Kulturbesitz, Berlin; Staats- u. Universitätsbibliothek Göttingen; Staats- u. Universitätsbibliothek Hamburg; Staats- u. Universitätsbibliothek Cologne; Royal Library Copenhagen; Stadtbibliothek Luneburg; Stadtbibliothek Oldenburg; Bibliothèque Nationale, Paris; Royal Library Stockholm; University Library Uppsala; Fürstliche Bibliothek Werningerode; and Herzog August Bibliothek Wolfenbüttel.

The edition is listed under no. 4395 in the *Gesamtkatalog der Wiegendrucke*, Leipzig 1925ff., and in C. Borchling and B. Claussen, *Niederdeutsche Bibliographie: Gesamtverzeichnis der niederdeutschen Drucke bis zum Jahre 1800*, 2 vols., Neumünster 1931–36, no. 267.

Quarto in format, it has 214 leaves numbered II–CCIII, but XV and XVI appear twice in the numbering, whilst XXXIX was omitted. There are 29 lines to the page. No catchwords were employed, but the gatherings are marked a–z. The

---

[14] Full details in Hogg, 140–48.

type is typical German black-letter of the period. It has been identified by Isak Collijn as probably that of the Lubeck printer Steffen Arndes as utilised for his Bible.[15] The initial letters are sometimes black on a white background or white on a black ground. Those of medium size certainly resemble closely typefaces used by Steffen Arndes.

Eleven woodcuts illustrate the text, five representing St Birgitta.[16]

The content of *Sunte Birgitten Openbaringe* is: p. 5 – "Dat register desses boekes"; p. 13 – "Eyne vorrede"; pp. 16–17 – three prayers in Middle Low German to the Bl. Virgin, St Birgitta, and her daughter, St Katherine, followed by two prayers in Latin addressed to St Birgitta; p. 17 – Text of Book I; p.58 – Text of Book II; p. 107 – Text of Book III; p. 165 – Text of Book IV; p. 232 – Text of Book V.

The five books can be summarised as follows:

Book I (Biography of St Birgitta). pp. 14–15 – introductory matter; pp. 16–17 – prayers in Middle Low German; pp. 18–19 (chapter 1) – summary of the contents of the Latin *Revelationes*; pp. 20–23 (chapters 2–4) – Birgitta's parents, her birth, the death of her mother; pp. 23–25 (chapters 5–9) – Miracles, visions and temptations during Birgitta's childhood; pp. 25–36 (chapters 10–14) – Birgitta's marriage, the birth of her children, depiction of her holy life, pilgrimage to Spain, premonition of her future visions; pp. 36–45 (chapters 15–17) – First revelations. Tentative explanation by the Middle Low German compiler of the nature and modality of the revelations and their significance for mankind. Brief extracts from the revelations; pp. 45–54 (chapters 18–25) – Birgitta lives in close proximity to the Cistercian Abbey of Alvastra. The prior of the monastery, Peter, is ordered by God to record the *Revelationes* in writing. Miracles in connection with Birgitta demonstrate the divine origin of her revelations. Her special graces; pp. 54–56 (chapters 26–28) – Death of Birgitta's husband. Birgitta's ascetical life thereafter.

Book II (drawn from *Revelationes*, Books I and IV). pp. 56–58 – Introduction, underlining that the whole of humanity is addressed in the *Revelationes*, from which only a selection will be presented; pp. 58–65 (chapters 1–4) – Christ speaks of His incarnation, true faith, and describes the nature and duties of a bride, His love for humanity, and His obligations as judge; pp. 65–67 (chapter 5) – Christ discourses of the good and the wicked, characterizing both classes; pp. 67–76 (chapters 6–11) – The Blessed Virgin characterizes the Bride; God's admonitions to lead a Christian life; enumeration of the sins; pp.76–81 (chapters 12–15) – God speaks of His attributes, depicts those of a bride; the Blessed Virgin talks about good and evil, and Christ of His justice and mercy as regards the good and the wicked; pp. 81–91 (chapters 16–19) – Birgitta's vision of all the Saints and Angels; Christ speaks of the first human beings, good and unhappy marriages, the state of

15 "Lübecker Frühdrucke in der Stadtbibliothek zu Lübeck", *Zeitschrift des Vereins für Geschichte und Altertumskunde* 9: 1, Lubeck 1908, 312.
16 Details in Hogg, 148–50.

the clergy. The Blessed Virgin depicts her sufferings. Christ gives Birgitta rules for the conduct of her life. Dialogue between God and the Devil concerning Birgitta; pp. 91–105 (chapters 20–27) – An angel pleads for Birgitta in God's presence. Christ elucidates the nature of mercy. Our Lady stresses Christ's prolonged sufferings on account of the contemporary sins of mankind. Christ remonstrates with all classes of society. All the Saints and Angels praise God. God underlines the mildness of His laws. The Blessed Virgin intercedes for the souls in purgatory and for those still living in the world; pp. 105–07 (chapter 28) – The Middle Low German compiler stresses the authenticity of the *Revelationes*, basing his arguments on the apology of John of Turrecremata at the Council of Basel.

Book III (taken from *Revelationes*, Books IV, VI, VII, and the *Regula Salvatoris*). pp. 107–09 (chapter 1) – Birgitta describes her vision of the Blessed Trinity and the Saints in heaven; pp. 109–11 (chapter 2) – Report on the insults to which Birgitta was subject on the part of the Swedish nobility during her journey to the Swedish King; pp. 111–19 (chapters 3–7 first part) Christ speaks about the counsellors of a king and gives advice for kings, queens, and princes; pp. 119–20 (chapter 7 second part) – The Middle Low German compiler speaks about books and the art of printing; pp. 120–21 (chapter 8) – Account of the virtues and patience of Birgitta; pp. 121–23 (chapters 9–10) – Christ speaks about Birgitta's new Order and its rules. Birgitta relates how she received the revelations; pp. 123–29 (chapters 11–15) – Account of the foundation of the monastery. Christ decrees various details concerning the new Order; pp. 129–33 (chapters 16–18) – Account of the miracles in Birgitta's lifetime that took place in close connection with her person; pp. 133–38 (chapters 19–22) – Birgitta's journey to Rome and her life in the eternal city; pp. 138–43 (chapters 23–25) – Miracles in Rome. Katherine's life in Rome. Minor pilgrimages; pp. 143–56 (chapters 26–28) – Journey to Jerusalem. Vision of the Nativity of Christ and the Crucifixion; pp. 156–65 (chapter 29) – Birgitta's return to Rome. Her death. Translation of her mortal remains. Miracles.

Book IV (taken from *Revelationes*, Books II, VI, and VII) pp. 165–87. (chapters 1–4) Apparition of her deceased husband, who recounts his sins to his wife. The Blessed Virgin speaks to Birgitta about the soul of her deceased brother, who is in purgatory. Birgitta witnesses the tribunal judging her deceased son. God, the Devil, and angels dispute over the possession of his soul. Birgitta sees the salvation of another soul before a similar tribunal. In a dialogue between God and the Devil every sin committed is recorded; pp. 187–205 (chapters 5–6) – Three damned souls appear to Birgitta, who report about the sins they committed and the punishment that has been meted out to them. Christ's elucidates the relation between the human body and the soul and God enumerates the sins of a damned soul; pp. 205–29 (chapters 7–11) – Our Lady stresses to Birgitta that good works should be undertaken for the benefit of the dead. Christ speaks of good and wicked priests, – a monk, a bishop, and a cardinal appear to her. Christ teaches Birgitta contempt for all earthly things. Christ announces impending punishment for all classes on account of their sins, particularly pride. The Blessed Virgin depicts the same sins and the insult to God committed thereby. She nevertheless indicates the possibility of pardon; pp. 229–32 (chapter 12) – Our Lady consoles Birgitta, who has to propagate God's laws, but is, as a result, scorned by the world and subjected to mockery. She instructs her in the practice of good works.

Book V (Biography of Birgitta's daughter, Katherine). pp. 232–33 – The Middle Low German compiler explains in an introduction why he recounts the life of St Katherine and the nature of her sanctity; pp. 233–48 (chapters 1–6) – Childhood, marriage, and ascetical life of Katherine. Dreams, visions, miracles. Her life in Rome. Her penances, temptations, and pilgrimages; pp. 248–55 (chapters 7–10) – Revelation concerning the soul of her deceased brother Karl. Her voluntary poverty and penitential way of life. Our Lady praises Katherine to Brigitta. Katherine's rôle in the translation of her mother's mortal remains and in Birgitta's canonization; pp. 255–65 (chapters 11–14) – Miracles. Katherine gives advice to mankind and offers consolation. Miracles after her death.

Though the Latin *Revelationes* can only have appealed to a learned reading public, and the various vernacular versions were intended for a limited, but growing lay audience of the pious, extracts were incorporated into many works, particularly those offering counsel on the Christian life, but also along with selections from the Gospels and sermons, and in florilegia. Birgitta was referred to in two Middle Low German prayer books that Ghotan published in Lubeck in 1484 and 1485. She was classified as an authority along with the evangelists, prophets, and approved teachers of Catholic doctrine.[17]

Extracts from the *Revelationes* appear in a totally different Middle Low German version in *Plenaria* of 1448 and 1492 published by the Mohnkopf publishers.[18] In a 1488 *Plenarium* of the same publishing house a passage attributed to St Birgitta is not authentic. A devotional guide printed by Steffen Arndes in Lubeck in 1495 under the title *Dat bok der medelydinghe Marien*, reissued by the same printer in 1498, presents a direct reference to St Birgitta on pp. 90–90a.

Many of the details of Birgitta's depiction of the Passion can also be found in late medieval paintings. Artists of the period delighted in realistic portrayals of nails and the crown of thorns. Andreas Lindblom[19] indicates a number of depictions of the crucifixion that correspond to the details contained in the *Revelationes*, but much of Birgitta's account is traditional, and caution as regards her influence on the arts is called for. The Saint herself appears frequently in paintings and woodcuts, but on the whole she is portrayed in a didactic attitude rather than a mystical one.

---

[17] Cf. Hogg, 153.
[18] Cf. Hogg, 154 for details.

## 3. Sources of *Sunte Birgitten Openbaringe*

The Middle Low German must depend very largely on the *Revelationes*, magnificently printed in Lubeck in 1492. That the compiler worked from a manuscript seems unlikely. He almost certainly drew on two earlier Middle Low German compilations, which also offered abbreviated and selective versions of the *Revelationes*, though the first only survives in fragmentary form and thus can scarcely be compared with the 1496 edition. Unfortunately, neither can be dated precisely.

Under no. 28 of their *Niederdeutsche Bibliographie* C. Borchling and B. Claussen indicate the first of these compilations and date it before 1478. It is also listed in the *Gesamtkatalog der Wiegendrucke* under no. 4393. Only 22 leaves are extant. Twice two of the single leaves present a continuous text. Otherwise the texts are isolated. The volume must have been a small folio in format. The pages lack catchwords and signatures. 19 leaves have 33 lines, 2 32, 1 badly damaged on the margins and with holes affecting the text 34 lines. This damaged leaf presents a meditative prayer in verse on the sufferings of Christ, terminating with hommage to the Holy Trinity. It does not seem to belong to the *Revelationes* at all. Borchling and Claussen maintain that these 9 double leaves and 4 single ones were proofs prepared by Lukas Brandis in Lubeck, a view accepted by Collijn[20] and Gustav Kohfeldt.[21] The sheets are printed on one side of the paper only, which indeed suggests proofs. Kohfeldt noted that 7 of the sheets were used as end-papers in books printed in Lubeck, which were owned by the Lubeck ecclesiastic Conrad Stenhop. Kohfeldt demonstrates that a number of proofs prepared by Lukas Brandis appear in books from Stenhop's library and maintains that the sheets must have been glued into the volumes as soon as they were acquired by Stenhop, as the pages from the Brigittine volume bear notes from Stenhop himself that clearly date from the period of the acquisition of the volumes.[22]

---

[19] *Den Heliga Birgitta I Bildverk, Skulptur och Maleri från Sveriges Medeltid*, Stockholm 1917, 51ff.

[20] "Lübecker Frühdrucke in der Stadtbibliothek zu Lübeck".

[21] "Zur nd. Birgittinerliteratur", *Beiträge zur Geschichte d. ältest. lüb. u. rostockschen Buchdrucks, Beiträge zur Geschichte der Stadt Rostock* 4, Rostock 1907.

[22] Gustav E. Klemming, *Bibliographie der Birgittenliteratur, Kongl. bibliotekets Samlinger* 6, Stockholm 1883, held, however, that the sheets originated in Rostock. Hildegard Dinges, " 'Sunte Birgitten Openbaringe': Neuausgabe des mittelniederdeutschen Fruhdrucks von 1496", Diss, Münster 1952, 2 vols., I, XXI (cited hereafter as Dinges) sums up: "Dafür spricht nach seiner Meinung die benutzte Druckertype, die identisch ist mit derjenigen, die die Rostocker Michaelisbrüder beim Druck des Bernhardus Clarevallensis benutzten." The matter is not quite so clear as Klemming thought. He explained the fact that the same typefaces were employed by Bartholomeus Ghotan in Lubeck by asserting that Ghotan on his amalgamation with Lukas Brandis had sold his type to the firm in Rostock, but Collijn, "Lübecker Frühdrucke in der Stadtbibliothek zu Lübeck", 296, cites the opinion of H. O. Lange, *Les plus anciens imprimeurs à Peraise 1471–1482*, who identified the printer as Lukas Brandis and dated the sheets before 1478: "Eines von ihnen hat nämlich einen Holzschnitt, der auch in anderen Brandis-Drucken vorkommt, z. B. in De nye Ee (1478), obwohl der

Collijn held that the sheets came from a work that was never completed, – a view shared by Wilhelm Pieth[23] and Gustav Klemming, but rejected by Kohfeldt, who from the evidence of sheets from various sections of the *Revelationes* argued that the print-off must have been terminated.[24]

Hildegard Dinges, after painstaking researches, established that the range of extracts was indeed considerable.[25] Even she, however, was unable to identify all the passages in the Latin *Revelationes*. The work was probably not a complete rendering of the Latin text, as surviving fragments do not follow the order of the Latin. E.g., an extract from Book V is followed by one from Book II. After Book VI,57 Book VII,2 appears immediately. A certain amount of illustrative material drawn from the Old Testament, not in the *Revelationes*, has also been inserted.[26] Only one passage in the fragments corresponds to the 1496 *Sunte Birgitten Openbaringe:* leaf IIb with *SBO* p. 79, 1. 32 – p. 80, 1. 19, correspond to *Revelationes* I, 22. The superiority of the 1496 version as regards literary quality and fidelity to the Latin original is striking.

The second Middle Low German version of the *Revelationes*, printed by Bartholomeus Ghotan, is also undated, but the *Gesamtkatalog der Wiegendrucke* places it around 1485 (no. 4394). Gustav Klemming is more cautious, suggesting a date between 1484 and 1494. The volume is octavo in format and contains 128 unnumbered leaves, which has led to some confusion in descriptions of the volume, as the pagination indicated by Borchling and Claussen in the *Niederdeutsche Bibliographie* does not correspond to that in the *Gesamtkatalog der Wiegendrucke*. Copies are extant in the Staatsbibliothek Hamburg (presumably used by Borchling and Claussen), the Royal Library Copenhagen, the Germanisches National-almuseum Nuremberg, the Bodleian Library Oxford, the Stadtbibliothek Rostock, the Royal Library Stockholm, and the University Library Uppsala. The Hamburg and Stockholm copies contain a supplement of prayers from 121$^v$ onwards, but the Stockholm volume is defective, lacking leaves 9, 11, 18, 123–28. The Hamburg copy reveals the following content: 1a Hijr hevet sik an dat Register desses yeghenwardighen bokes . . . The table of contents continues up to 6a. The leaves 6–9 are blank, except for 9a, which presents a wood-cut of St Birgitta. The text of the

---

Stock zu demselben hier gewisse Defekte aufweist und demnach später angewendet worden ist."

[23] "Lübeck als Pionier der Buchdruckerkunst", in Fritz Endres (ed.),*Geschichte der freien Hansestadt Lübeck*, Lubeck 1926.

[24] It is disconcerting that Klemming only actually gives details of two of the sheets, *Revelationes* IV, 74 and I, 17, though in the latter case the text itself falsely indicates chapter 9!

[25] "Teile aus folgenden Kapiteln sind mit Sicherheit behandelt: Buch I, Kap. 17 (nd. Bl. I), 22 (nd. Bl. IIIb, IIb); Buch II, Kap. 1 (nd. Bl. IIIa), 6 (nd. Bl. Va); Buch IV, Kap. 74 (nd. Bl. VIa, VIIa, VIIb, VIII); Buch V, 4. Frage (nd. Bl. IIIa); 12. Frage (nd. Bl. XIb = Anfang d. Kap. u. Xb = Fortsetzung; dazwischen scheint eine Seite zu fehlen); Kap. 58, ein Satz (nd. Bl. XIa); Buch VII, Kap. 2 (nd. Bl. Xa); Buch VIII, Kap. 34 (bzw. Hinweis auf Buch IV, 74), Kap. 42 (nd. Bl. Va)."(Dinges I, XXII)

[26] For details cf. Dinges I, XXII–XXIII.

version of the *Revelationes* begins on 10a: Dar steit in deme VIII boke der openbaringe . . . continuing apparently up to 119a. 119b and 120 are blank. 120a begins:
Hijr na volghen schone nutte bede alle daghe to lezende . . . , concluding on 127b.
128 is blank. There are regularly 18 lines to the page and the collation is $1^8$ $a^8$
$b^8$–$o^8$ $p^8$.

This work probably did not exercise much influence on *Sunte Birgitten Openbaringe*. It is a meditative, prayerful compilation, aiming at edification and making no
pretension to offering anything like a full translation. On 2a the compiler declares:

> Got de here an synen utherkornen vrunden wunderlike werke ghedan hefft,
> unde heilsamighe lere den yennen de ene leff hebben gheopenbaret hefft. De
> hefft ock syner othmodighen denerynnen sunte Birgitten menninghe vor-
> borghenheit gheopenbaret (beide an ghesichte unde ok an worden) to troste
> synen utherkornen unde to beteringe der sundere. Der hijr etlike in dudesch
> ghemaket sint. uppe dat zodane vorborghenheit nicht vorhalen bleve.

He thus uses isolated passages from diverse parts of the *Revelationes* to introduce
various prayers that were either uttered by St Birgitta or revealed to her for the
benefit of humanity.[27] Additions are made, wherever they seem to be called for:

> Dyt vorschrevene bed gans nutte bed. unde wol dat mit ynnicheit unde mit
> rechter andacht lest. sunder twivel den wert de hillighe geist sokende unde
> wert ene trostende vormiddelst syner gnade. (35a)

As the compilation proceeds, the relationship to the *Revelationes* becomes more and
more tenuous. 53–74 are largely devoted to a narration of the Passion drawn from
Jordan of Quedlinburg,[28] the text being interspersed with prayers. There is an
introductory observation on 52b:

> Hijr volghet to der metten tijt. unde. dusse artikele unde bede synt ghenomen
> uth der passien de dar ghesettet hefft de grote mester iordanus unde is gans
> nutte unde guth.

At 74b an account of the Passion by Christ himself as revealed to St Birgitta
commences:

> Desse passien openbarde christus sulven sunte birgitten wo he sprak mit synen
> iungeren in dem avent etende.

A number of asides addressed to St Birgitta reinforce the impression that the Saint
witnessed the scene in a vision:

[27] See particularly 28–48.
[28] Cf. Walter Baier, *Untersuchungen zu den Passionsbetrachtungen in der Vita Christi des Ludolf
von Sachsen, Analecta Cartusiana* 44:2 (1977), 309–25.

Birgitta myne leve bruth ik apenbare dy van worden to worden myne pine. de ik hebbe gheladen in deme gharden. Desse wort de ik di hebbe apenbaret (unde noch apenbaren will) de geve ik dy alze einen durbaren schat. de scholtu samende schriven alze ik dy secht hebbe unde noch seggen wil. (78b)

Birgitta vragede unseme heren weren erer ok vele do du grepen wordest. Ja sprak unse here . . . (83a)

Birgitta sprak. O du almechtighe got wat dyne pyne to caiphas hus. He antwarde . . . (87a)

Myne leve birgitta du schalt dat weeten dat malchus de eerste was de my sloch . . . (89b)

Ik claghe dy myn leve birgitta dat unsprekeliken vele mynschen verdomet werden. de nicht overdenken (edder betrachten) myn lident. (116b)

On 119a the text concludes:

Desse othmodighe passien apenbarde unse here christus ihesus sulven sunte Birgitten umme eres bedes willen.

This tract on the Passion does not seem to be based either on the *Revelationes* or on ancient Swedish manuscripts. Carl Jungmark, who studied the text closely,[29] concluded that it was compiled from a variety of sources, but mainly from the Scriptures. He holds that it certainly originated from the German-speaking area, – "ein auf niederdeutschem Boden entstandenes, selbständiges Werk von einem niederdeutschem Verfasser". Jungmark demonstrated that with the passing of the years later manuscripts containing it showed increasing stylistic affinities with the *Revelationes,* but no close relationship to *Sunte Birgitten Openbaringe.* The very fact that Christ speaks in his own person in this compilation, whilst in *Sunte Birgitten Openbaringe* the Saint relates what she herself had witnessed in her visions, separates the two works radically. Rarely can any affinity be observed in passages that are not directly based on the Latin text of the *Revelationes,* though the direct translations correspond fairly closely.[30] Only eight passages appear in both works and the phraseology varies from the almost identical to a vague resemblance of sense. Only 184 lines in all are affected.[31]

It seems certain that the compiler of *Sunte Birgitten Openbaringe* was acquainted with the work of his predecessor, as the verbal parallels in seven cases would be difficult to account for otherwise. Nevertheless, the compiler of *Sunte Birgitten Openbaringe* clearly also consulted the Latin text of 1492, for in Book I, chapter 7, the Latin text runs:

---

[29] *Eine pseudo-birgittische Christuspassion,* Diss., Göteborg 1916.
[30] Dinges I XXXI. Details are given in Hogg, 163.
[31] The parallel passages are printed in Hogg, 163–67.

Ut sic speres de misericordia dei quoniam non negligas iusticiam eius. Et sic cogita iusticiam eius et iudicium, ut non obliviscaris misericordiam. Quia nec iusticiam aliquam facit sine misericordia nec misericordiam sine iusticia.

This is rendered more faithfully in the 1496 version, as the earlier text omitted "gherichte" and employed "envorgheten" twice, although the Latin had "negligere" and "oblivisci". Dinges proposes that both versions in fact relied on a Middle Low German manuscript, offering parts of the *Revelationes*, that does not seem to be extant:

> Wahrscheinlich ist es jedoch, daß die wörtliche Übereinstimmung auf der Tatsache beruht, daß der Bearbeitung von 1485 und der von 1496 eine gemeinsame niederdeutsche handschriftliche Vorlage vorausging, die stellenweise von beiden übernommen wurde und die ihrerseits auf einer lateinischen Handschrift der "Revelationes" fußt.[32]

This process of revision and amplification of earlier translations seems to have been common in Brigittine circles, as, for example, with the numerous publications of the English Brigittine monk Richard Whytford, writing slightly later.[33] Dinges notes that this process of revising and adjusting earlier versions was intensively practised "bei den Werken des Mohnkopfverlages . . . , so bei den Plenaren, dem 'Narrenschyp', 'Reinke de Voss', Schachbuch, 'Henseyly' und 'Dodendantz'."[34]

## 4. The *Revelationes Sanctae Birgittae* and *Sunte Birgitten Openbaringe*

The title of the Middle Low German publication is a precise translation of that of the Latin work printed at Lubeck in 1492 by Bartolomäus Ghotan in commission at the expense of the Brigittine community of Vadstena. The *Diarium Vadstenense* records under 27 September 1491:

> In die ss. Cosme et Damiani transibant fratres Petrus Ingemari sacerdos et Gerardus laicus versus Lübeck ad faciendum imprimi libros celestes Revelationum s. Birgitte. Et post annum evolutum, impressis et perfectis cotingentis voluminibus in papyro et sedecim duntaxat in pergameno, redierunt in monasterium suum anno Dni MCDLXXXXII circa festum s. Katharine virginis et martyris.[35]

Ghotan appears to have been on friendly terms with Vadstena, as some years earlier

---

[32] I, XXXVIII.

[33] Cf. James Hogg *Richard Whytford's The Pype or Tonne of the Lyfe of Perfection, with an Introductory Study of Whytford's Works, Salzburg Studies in English Literature, Elizabethan & Renaissance Studies* 89, 6 vols., 1979–89.

[34] I, XXXVIII.

[35] Printed in *Gesammelte Nachrichten über einst bestandene Klöster vom Orden der hl. Birgitta*, no editor or place of publication named, 1888, 42. The Feast of St Katherine was celebrated on 25 November.

he had helped the Brigittine monastery to establish its own printing press. The two members of the Vadstena community who came to Lubeck to supervise the publication of the *Revelationes* were conveniently housed in the Brigittine monastery of Marienwold.

It seems certain that the 1496 compiler used this printed edition, as it is the first that is known to have included the *Liber Extravagantes*. Furthermore, it gathered together such material as had come to light since the magnificent manuscript of the *Revelationes* was prepared in 1391. The *Gesamtkatalog der Wiegendrucke* under no. 4390 records, however, an earlier printed edition, produced before January 1478/79 and reprinted within a year at St Jacobus de Ripoli, Florence. A Brigittine monastery existed at Pian di Ripoli at this period.

Hypothetically, the pedigree of the 1496 Middle Low German could be:

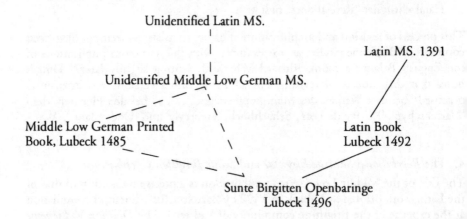

Unidentified Latin MS.

Latin MS. 1391

Unidentified Middle Low German MS.

Middle Low German Printed
Book, Lubeck 1485

Latin Book
Lubeck 1492

Sunte Birgitten Openbaringe
Lubeck 1496

There is, however, a basic difference of concept to be observed between the Latin and the Middle Low German publications. The Latin edition of 1492 was large folio (2°) in format and consisted of 422 leaves, containing *Revelationes*: liber primus – liber septimus. Epistola solitarii ad Reges Domini Alphonsi (the so-called Prologus Alphonsi). Octavus Liber Celestis Imperatoris ad Reges. Regula Salvatoris. Sermo Angelicus. De Virginis Excellentia. Oratio prima – quarta. Revelationes Extravagantes. Vita abbreviata Sanctae Birgittae, to which Miracula were appended. Hymnus ad Beatam Birgittam. Prefatory material by John of Turrecremata and Matthias of Sweden. The Middle Low German publication of 1496 was quarto in format and had 204 leaves, with 29 lines to the page, divided into five books. Taking the Latin text as the norm, the following differences can be observed: Book I – 25 chapters translated, 35 omitted; Book II – 1 chapter translated, 29 omitted; Book III – omitted totally; Book IV – 3 chapters translated, one of which was summarised, 142 chapters omitted; Book V – omitted totally; Book VI – 13 chapters translated, but 7 of them shortened considerably, 109 chapters omitted; Book VII – 18 chapters translated, 12 of which were abbreviated, 13 omitted; Book VIII – 11 chapters translated, all in abbreviated form, 69 omitted; Extravagantes – 2 chapters summarised, 114 omitted; Regula Salvatoris Prologue – 2 chapters translated, 1 omitted; Text – 4 chapters translated, 27 omitted.

On several occasions the compiler of the 1496 version explains the reasons for his selective approach or at least indicates that he is making substantial omissions. Thus he declares:

> . . . so werden hyr ghesettet etlike capittele. ghenomen uth dem boeke der openbaringe sunte Birgitten dat dar heet uppe latyn Revelatio sancte Birgitte.
> *(SBO*: 18)

He adds:

> Unde alle desse openbaringe scholde men de setten in eyn boek. dat worde eyn sere groet boek. wente de sulven openbaringe dar synt in deme latine negen boeke. *(SBO*:18)

In his introduction to Book II he is more expansive:

> Merke ock dat in dyt boek wert gheseth nicht alle openbarynge. met etlyke so hyr vor in deme ersten boeke is ghesecht. wente scholde men hyr in setten alle de boeke der openbarynge. so worde dyt eyn groet boek bykant alze eyne byblye. unde worde velen mynschen vordretlick al ut to lesen. unde to duor in deme kope. alzus is umme desser sake willen genomen ut alle den hilgen boeken ichteswes unde is mit vlite to hope sammelt unde gheset in dyt yeghenwordyghe boek. umme salicheyt wyllen aller guden mynschen. de hyr inne lesen efte lesen horen. *(SBO*: 57)

The proportions of the Latin edition and the Middle Low German compilation are entirely different. The *Revelationes*, including the *Extravagantes*, run to 9 books, whilst the *Vita abbreviata* occupies 4 pages. The first book of *Sunte Birgitten Openbaringe* is entirely composed of biographical material and the *legenda*; half of the third book and a slight section of the fourth are orientated in the same direction; whilst the fifth book contains the life of St Katherine, St Birgitta's daughter. It is noteworthy that for these sections the compiler drew on other Latin sources, besides what was available in the *Revelationes*. Already in his introduction to the first book he explained his method:

> Eyn gud boem drecht gerne gude vrucht. secht de here in deme hylghen ewangelio Mathei VII. [Mt. 7. 17] desse worde moghen wol gesproken werden van der eddelen hilgen vrowen sunte Birgitten. wente se is eyn seer gud boem gewest. unde is noch in deme wingarden der hilgen kerken unde heft gode dem heren gebracht gude vrucht eres hilgen levendes. erer lere. unde erer hilgen kindere. wente so alse desse boem gud was. unde gud is unde blift. so is ok de vrucht gud. sunderliken de hilge maget Katherina. Van welkere twen hilgen. alze van sunte Birgitten unde erer hilgen dochter Katherinen hir na in dessem boeke meyst wert gesecht, wente se sint gelik den eddelen perlen de

men weinich vindet mankt velen anderen unnutten stenen. Alsus sint se van
gode dem heren sunderliken gevunden mankt velen anderen unmutten stenen.
dat is. manckt velen anderen unnutten minschen. Unde desse sulven twey
eddelen perlen alze Birgitta unde ere dochter Katherinen. heft god de hemmel-
sche keyser mede ghelacht in den schat unde mankt de kleynoede syner
behegelicheyt. dat is. mankt de anderen groten hylghen. welkere hilgen wol
mogen geheten werden duorbare kleynoede des hemmelschen keysers.

(*SBO*: 13–14)

Nevertheless, the Middle Low German version does offer a good picture of the
contents of the original Latin text. The compiler's description of the *Revelationes*
volume shows that he was in full command of his material. He sums up the first
seven books, leaving apart the fifth, and demonstrates their thematic union, even if
the emphasis varies. Thus in each of them one finds God's warning to all classes,
the threat of impending punishment, God's lamentation over the iniquities of
humanity, etc. Significant for his control over the whole *Revelationes* is that already
on p. 19 he indicates St Birgitta's mission and rôle as mediator, which is first stated
in chapter 45 of Book VI in the Latin text.

The 1496 compilation shows a progressive liberty as regards the utilisation of the
1492 *Revelationes* text. Throughout he offers precise and adequate chapter headings
and indications of the contents of the various books, though these may have been
furnished when the version as a whole was otherwise terminated. In his second
book he only selected from Book I of the Latin *Revelationes*, and, although he
abbreviates, the chapters correspond to those in the Latin original. Only in his
concluding chapter does he incorporate material taken from elsewhere.[36] Thereafter
the method changes considerably in Books 3 and 4 of the Middle Low German
compilation. Selections from the Latin are taken wherever appropriate material is
to be found, with an almost total disregard for the ordering of the Latin text. Even
within passages taken from the Latin, the sequence of the sentences is often
modified, and in the biographical sections chronological indications are introduced, presumably in the interest of greater clarity.

The Middle Low German Book 3 draws on the Latin *Revelationes* VIII,
1,2,3,4,5 (2nd half),6; IV,48; VII,12,13; Regula Salvatoris Prologue 2,3 (2nd
half); 1,29,30,31; *Revelationes* VI,100; IV,137; VII,1,6,9,13,17,14,21,22,23,
24,15,26,31.

Book 4 utilises Latin Liber extravagantes 56; VI,95; VII,13 Part B; VI, 39,40;
Declaratio following VI,39; VI,52,66, 10 (Declaratio);21 (beginning); 20 (last
section of Part C); VII,20; VI,35 (+ Declaratio); VI,70,27; VII,27,30 (beginning);
VII,30 (second half); VII,57; VI,47 (1st half); VI,46 (3rd section); II,16 (2nd
half).

---

36 For a detailed analysis cf. Dinges I, XLVI.

## 5. Saint Birgitta's Biography in *Sunte Birgitten Openbaringe*

Whilst most Latin editions and many of those in the vernacular contented themselves with the *Vita abbreviata* of St Birgitta, the Middle Low German version of 1496 drew extensively on various sources for the life of the Saint and that of her daughter St Katherine. In fact, almost half the entire work is devoted to biographical elements, if one includes the miraculous material so dear to the hearts of medieval hagiographers. In all the 28 chapters of the first book and in 16 chapters of the third book (II, VII, VIII, XI, XVI, XVII, XVIII, XIX, XX, XXI, XXII, XXIII, XXIV, XXV, XXVI, and XXIX) biographical material can be found, of which the source cannot be traced either to the *Vita abbreviata* or the *Revelationes* themselves in the majority of cases, though a number of passages are translated from the *Liber Extravagantes* (III, XV, XLVII, XLVIII, LIII, LV, LX, LXI, LXIII, LXXII, XCII, XCVIII, CIII, CVII, and CVIII). The Middle Low German compiler does not, however, indicate the chapters from which he extracted his material; nor does he follow the order of the chapters in the *Liber Extravagantes* for the selection which he incorporates into Book I, chapters X, XII, XIII, XIV, XV, XIX, XX, XXVIII; and Book III, chapters XVI, XX, XXII, and XXIV. The tracing of sources can, on occasion, be a hazardous undertaking, as some of the material found in the *Liber Extravagantes* is also present in the life of the Saint compiled by her confessors, Petrus Olavi of Alvastra and Magister Petrus Olavi of Skänninge, drawn together as early as 1373 and presented to the commission for Birgitta's canonization that was convened in Rome in 1378. The earliest extant MS. dates from 1378. This work was first printed from a manuscript in the Royal Library Stockholm by C. Annerstedt.[37] It is also listed by G. E. Klemming.[38] All subsequent biographies drew heavily on this compilation, and the Middle Low German writer was clearly considerably influenced by it in organising his own book. Yet another source certainly used for *Sunte Birgitten Openbaringe* can be indicated: the *Acta* of the canonization process, which contain numerous accounts of miracles.[39] This material is assembled in 3 manuscripts that are still extant: MS. A. 14 of the Royal Library Stockholm (from Vadstena); MS. Ottobonianus lat. 90 of the Vatican Library; and British Library London Harley MS. 612 (from Syon Abbey).[40] Presumably similar compilations were available in most Brigittine monasteries.

Another source was the *legenda* compiled by Birger Gregorsson, a contemporary of St Birgitta, who was Archbishop of Uppsala (+ 1383).[41] Again this work seems to have circulated widely in the Brigittine Order, as manuscript copies of it are

---

[37] In *Scriptores Rerum Svecicarum Medii Aevi* III, 2 (1871), 188–206.
[38] *Heliga Birgittas Uppenbarelser* V, 244.
[39] Cf. Collijn, *Acta et Processus canonizacionis Beate Birgitte* I.
[40] *Ibid.*, ivff.
[41] First printed in *Acta Sanctorum*, Octobris IV, 485–95. This edition has been replaced by that of Isak Collijn, *Birgerus Gregorii, Legenda Sancte Birgitte (Efter Cod. Und. Perg. 21 och*

known from the following houses: Marienbaum near Kleve, dating ca. 1445; Vadstena (first half of the 15th century); and Maria-Maihingen (late 15th century). His *legenda* was selective and he added some new material, adapting the whole for pious reading by interlarding numerous passages from the Bible and exhortations to prayer. There is, however, no evidence that the Middle Low German compiler used either the late fourteenth century Swedish account of St Birgitta's life,[42] which presumably originated at Vadstena, or the *Vita Metrica S. Birgittae.*[43]

The Middle Low German writer is much freer in his use of sources than his Dutch contemporary in the *Opusculum vita et passionis Christi*, printed by Gerard Leeu at Antwerp in 1491,[44] where St Birgitta's life is traced step by step, followed by an account of her canonization and extracts from the Papal Bull.

To his credit, the Middle Low German compiler did not allow himself to be immersed in the flood of miracles and wonders, but selects those which serve his purpose, declaring in Book III, chapter XVI:

> Van welkeren wunderwerken men wol mochte setten eyn heel boek, men uppe dat der yo ichteswelke mede werden ghesath in dyt boek, so volgen hyr etlyke ock welke gesychte. (*SBO*: 129)

Furthermore, he follows Archbishop Berger of Uppsala in omitting the names of the persons involved in miraculous happenings and also fails to localise them, though such details were readily available in the Latin sources. He thus endows them with a certain universality.[45]

A host of minor additions were rendered necessary by the compiler's personal arrangement of the narrative, but there are also a few major insertions. In Book III, chapter 11, after referring to St Birgitta's foundations, there is a fairly detailed description of a Brigittine monastery and the habits worn by members of the community (*SBO*: 123–25). He devoted Book I, chapters XVI and XVII to furnishing an explanation of why the *Revelationes* were actually accorded to St Birgitta and their value for his contemporaries. In chapter XVII he comments on a passage in the *Revelationes*, where rewards are promised and punishment threatened. This obviously had special significance for the compiler, for he reinforces the text with quotations from the Scriptures and ecclesiastical writers.[46]

It is possible that the compiler knew Jacobus de Voragine's *Legenda aurea*, of which there were both Middle High and Middle Low German versions,[47] and

---

Holm. A. 7), *Samlingar utgivna af Svenska Fornskrift-Sällskapet*, Ser. 2, Latinska Skrifter 4, Uppsala 1946.

[42] Cf. G. E. Klemming, *Heliga Birgittas Uppenbarelser* V,247.

[43] *Meddelanden frå det lit. – historiska Seminariet i Lund*, Lund 1892, I.

[44] Cf. *Gesamtkatalog der Wiegendrucke* no. 4398.

[45] Dinges describes his method in detail: I, LII–LIII.

[46] Cf. Collijn, *Acta et Processus Canonizacionis Beate Birgitte*, 81, 484, 485, 619, – the last three items involve the testimony of eye-witnesses.

[47] Cf. C. Borchling & B. Claussen, *Niederdeutsche Bibliographie*, no. 34: Jac. de Voragine,

Antonius Florentinus's *Summa historialis seu Chronicorum*,[48] but if he did they do not seem to have influenced his text, even though some editions were printed by Steffen Arndes in Lubeck. Thus the *Passional* published in 1488, 1492 and 1499 gave the *legenda* of St Birgitta on pp. LXVII–LXXa, but the text is strictly biographical and chronological. On pp. LXVIa and LXVIIIrb the reader is referred to the *Revelationes* for further information. The compiler of the *Passional* concludes his account with a number of miracles that he is careful to localise. The *Passional* also offers parallels in the Scriptures and in other *legendae*, such as that of St Augustine and St Monica, that are not present in *Sunte Birgitten Openbaringe*. Though the wording and order of presentation is on occasion very similar, the texts translated from the Latin are seldom rendered identically, so a common author seems most unlikely.

## 6. The Life of St Katherine

Book V is devoted to St Katherine, whose life was closely intertwined with that of her mother, with whom she lived in Rome, supervising the transport of her mortal remains to Vadstena after her decease. The source is not indicated, but appears to be the Brigittine monk Ulfo Birgersson's *Vita Catherinae*, compiled in Vadstena 1423–26: Incipit vita sive legenda cum mirakulis domine katherine sancte memorie file sancte Birgitte de regno Suecie, – words that appear in *Sunte Birgitten Openbaringe*. This was first printed in 1483.[49] The Middle Low German compiler employs his wonted technique with omissions, summaries, minor and major additions. Thus whilst the Latin source details 50 miracles after Katherine's death, indicating both the place and date, only two of them are incorporated into *Sunte Birgitten Openbaringe*. One passage, retailing how Katherine saved a hunted deer, is, however, considerably longer (*SBO*: 263–65), and at the end the Middle Low German compiler adds several miracles that are not related in the Latin: how lights appeared near Katherine's body after her death, the help given to a woman of Naples plagued by the Devil, and how a pilgrim became a Brigittine monk through Katherine's intervention.

The Middle Low German compiler may well have consulted a Dutch publication that contained a *Vita Catherinae*. Published in 1491 by Gerard Leeu at Antwerp, the *Opusculum vitae et passionis Christi* contains extracts from the *Revelationes*, as well as the *legenda* of St Birgitta. On p. 140 a new tract commences: Hier beghint dat leven der edelre weerdigher vrouwen katerina van watsteyn, die een

---

Legenda Aurea, ndt. L. Brandis 1478; no. 86: Jac. de Voragine *Legenda Aurea*, ndt. *Dat Duytsche Passional*, Cologne, Ludwig v. Renchen 1485; no. 118: Jac. de Voragine, *Passional*, Magdeburg, Simon Koch 1487; no. 131: Jac. de Voragine, *Passional*, Lubeck, Steffen Arndes 1488; no. 202: Jac. de Voragine, *Passional*, Lubeck, Steffen Arndes 1492; no. 314: Jac. de Voragine, *Passional*, Steffen Arndes 1499.

48 Published in Nuremberg in 1484 and the following years.
49 Cf. G. E. Klemming, *Bibliographie der Birgittenliteratur*, 257.

dochter was der overheyligher vrouwen sinte birgitta. The *Vita* consists of 18 chapters with the incipit: Wi broeder Peeter prioer des cloesters alvastra, licenciaet in beyden rechten. . . . The text is considerably longer than that of Ulfo Birgersson. The *Opusculum* is duly listed by G. E. Klemming.[50]

A further important compilation on the life of St Katherine appeared in Stockholm in 1487 as the first book printed in Sweden, though the printer was Bartholomäus Ghotan of Lubeck, who resided in Stockholm from October 1486 until September 1487. Only two complete copies – today in the Royal Libraries of Stockholm and Brussels – are known. Though drawn in part from Ulfo Birgersson, it also used material collected by Bishop Henrick Tidemansson of Linköping (1467–74) for the canonization process of Katherine.[51]

The relationship between the Latin, the Dutch, and the Middle Low German texts for the *Vita Catherinae* is complex. In many passages all three agree basically.[52] It seems, however, probable that the Middle Low German writer used the Latin text of the *Opusculum vitae et passionis Christi eiusque Genitricis Mariae*, printed by Leeu at Antwerp in 1489 and reissued in Southern Germany in 1491[53] rather than the Dutch version; otherwise one would have expected closer identity in the actual choice of words.[54]

## 7. The Prayers

Only one of the prayers that precede the *Revelationes* was taken over by the Middle Low German compiler – O Birgitta mater bona. The first prayer, which is accompanied by a wood-cut showing the Blessed Virgin radiating sunbeams, is presented as bearing an indulgence of Pope Sixtus IV (1471–84). It appears in a further work from the Mohnkopf publishers: the *Speygel der Leyen*, a catechetical work containing prayers that was also issued in 1496. There it is placed at the end of the book (p. XLVIII) in a commentary on the Ave Maria, accompanied by the same wood-cut. The indulgence is also noted in similar terms. Further prayers in *Sunte Birgitten Openbaringe* were probably inspired by the Brigittine office. The source of the prayer to St Katherine has not been identified.

## 8. The Aims of the Middle Low German Compiler

Obviously, the Middle Low German compiler did not aim at producing a faithful translation of the *Revelationes*. His adaptation was governed by different principles and his public was clearly wider, as the audience for vernacular literature was

---

50 *Heliga Birgittas Uppenbarelser* V, 228ff.
51 Cf. Andreas Lindblom, *Birgitta Utställningen* (Beskrivande förtekning över utställda föremål. Redigerad af J. Collijn och A. Lindblom, Uppsala 1918.
52 Cf. Dinges I, LXII–LXIV.
53 Cf. G. E. Klemming, *Heliga Birgittas Uppenbarelser* V, 205.
54 For a number of minor disagreements among the three texts cf. Hogg, 179.

growing. However, if the omissions he made from the Latin text were surely his own, the additions were only partially so.

These additions stem mainly from the Bible (e.g. *SBO*: 120, 151), particularly the psalms (e.g. *SBO*: 109). He also drew on ecclesiastical writers (*SBO*: 218), prophets (*SBO*: 64), including Sibylla, a virgin endowed with the gift of seeing (*SBO*: 45), and contemporary authors, whom he called "lerer" (*SBO*: 227–28). He wishes to stress the unending struggle against sin, – sin that infiltrates whole strata of society, and, as ever present, calling down the wrath of God on sinners. As an efficacious antidote he proposes leading a Christian life, practising good works, and prayer. Man himself can be a king, if only he follows God's commandments, for the psalmist declared:

> Ock mach wol eyn islick mynsche heten eyn konninck synes sulves de syck wol regeret, alze de hylge david secht in deme CI salmen. In conveniendo populos in unum et reges ut serviant domino. Hyr menet de profete mede alle de dar synt konninge over der erdeschen licham. unde dwyngen den under der ee godes. Desse noemet he konnige.  (*SBO*: 109)

St Jerome is cited for his condemnation of those in orders, who do not live up to their calling, and the priesthood as a whole is urged by the Middle Low German compiler to offer an example of Christian living, thereby exemplifying their preaching. He roundly condemns the pursuit of worldly rewards on the part of the clergy:

> Unde de sulven provene synt nicht ghemaket umme dat. dat se scholen werden beseten in homode. efte in velen andern sunden. yd sy quatzerye. efte iennige andere suntlike stucke. de ene behorde to straffende. unde se den ungelereden sympelen scholen vor ghaen in ghuder lere in deme worde. men alder meyst in guden exempelen der guden werke. alze de hilghen gheystliken vaders ene hebben vorgheghaen. Se hethen gheystlik darumme dat se de gheystlyken werke scholen vullenbryngen.  (*SBO*: 217)

St Jerome is directly alluded to as an authority on this point (*SBO*: 217–18). He returns to the same topic in Book IV, Chapter 10 (*SBO*: 225).

Humility is the hallmark of the Christian life:

> Hyr up antwordet eyn lerer alzus. Isset dattu nemandes begherest. unde dy doch tzyrest alze eyn aff god. so en bystu nicht seker dath dyn vleghe effte utherlyke tzyrynge andere de dy seen nicht en reytze tho quader lust. efte ander quade dancken unde vulbort. Vorware ein minsche en is neen engel. wes he uthe dessen in sunde valt. in slapende efte wakende. in dancken efte vulbord. desser sunde bistu de wortel. unde bist der mede delaftich. spricckt de sulve lerer. De homod herschoppet in mannyghen unde doch wyllen se schynen unde heten othmodich. is dath nicht glytzerye. komen hyr ock wol uth vromede sunde etc. Nycht en wert vorboden dath men syck schal holden slicht efte sympelyken. Men vorware vaken unde vele unde in mannigen landen unde steden wert vorboden. dat men syk nicht schal holden alto

uterliken mit klederen. mit utliende so vor ghesecht is. so men oldinges de
duvelschen afgoede unde ok de lodder boven efte boesinnen plach ut to
vylende. wente de sulve unhoevescheyt wert nu geheten hoeveschyt leider.
Unde vorwar sprikt de sulve lerer. dar en is neyn hylghe in deme hemmele de
dyt den wertlyken sunders hefft na ghelaten. edder de dat en hefft gheleret
edder de sodane instrumente hefft ghebruket. dar andere mede tho sunden syn
gekomen. in erer lesten belevynge. dath is so vele ghesecht. Dat vyllichte wol
hylghen by gode syn. de sodanes hebben ghebruket. men dorch den wech synt
se neneleyewys ghekomen tho gode. men durch ruwe umme de sunde. unde
warafftygem otmode. Eya sprickt de sulve lerer. wo dwelen se dede einen
anderen wech menen to vyndendeme hemmele. wen alze en de here Cristus
unde Maria hebben vor gheghaen unde dat in alleme otmode. (*SPO*: 227–28)

Book IV, chapter 11, presents the Blessed Virgin speaking to Birgitta about the
three most widespread capital sins, – pride (superbia), offences against chastity, and
avarice (avaritia), – targets of all the sermon literature of the period. Alms should
only be given from what had been licitly gained:

> Dat andere dar se gode mede soenen moeghen is dyt. dat dar almissen werden
> ghegheven myt vrolicheyt des herten. van wol ghewunneme gude.
>                                    (*SBO*: 228–29; cf. also Book I, chapter 11, p. 75)

Similar passages are to be found in the *Speygel der Leyen* (Lubeck 1496) p. LXIb
and *Reincke de Voss* (Lubeck 1498) p. LXVII.

The Middle Low German compiler goes on to prophesy severe punishment for
sin and that seven terrible plagues would be inflicted on mankind, from which
neither the princes nor the ecclesiastics would be spared. He cites as authorities the
learned Hugwicius,[55] Sibylla, and a holy virgin who enjoyed prophetical gifts,[56] –
maybe Hildegard of Bingen. Sibylla had predicted terrible famines for the year
1400 on account of the sins of pride that pervaded the whole of society (*SBO*: 45).

The pest was regarded as the worst of these plagues because of the enormous
mortality rate it inflicted. The author rejects a natural explanation of its ravages
(*SBO*: 43). He then proceeds to discuss the problem that God often grants the
wicked long life, whilst the good die young (*SBO*: 43). God has promulgated His
commandments and all who fail to observe them will be punished (*SBO*: 43–44).
God, however, is not only the stern judge. His mercy implies that He wishes us to
achieve eternal life. Therefore true penitence, prayer, the practice of the Christian
virtues, alms-giving, and intercession for souls in purgatory not only yield profit in
this life, but also in that of eternity (*SBO*: 44). He stresses particularly the efficacity
of human intervention for the souls suffering in purgatory (*SBO*: 209).

A passive avoidance of sin, penitence, prayer and good works are still not
sufficient for salvation. The true Christian must immerse himself in the sufferings

---

55 Probably the decretalist Hugo of Pisa, who taught at Pisa and Bologna 1178–90, dying in
  1210 as Bishop of Ferrara. He compiled a commentary on Gratian.
56 Cf. Hogg, 183, fn. 79.

of Christ and the compassion of Our Lady, as he explains in Book I, chapter 17, where he summarizes the Latin text (*SBO*: 87–88). St Birgitta is herself held up as a shining example of the practice of the virtues, particularly in Book IV, chapter 1:

> Birgitta de hilghe vrouwe se vorloesede in desseme levende mannigen mit ereme ghebede uthe den sunden. ock myth eren guden exempel. Se hadde vullenkomen an syk de leve godes. unde ock de leve des even minschen. Se bath nicht allene vor syk efte vor de levendighen minschen in desseme levende. Men ock vor de vorstorvene. Wente myt ereme ghebede unde hylgen werken loesede se ock vele sele uthe deme vegevuer . . . (*SBO*: 165)

The Middle Low German compiler stresses again and again that the *Revelationes* were not intended for St Birgitta alone, but were addressed to all mankind. Obviously thereby he wished to underline the universal applicability of their message. Not all the Latin text was, however, of equal relevance for the middle class audience to whom the German version was directed. A century later, the political situation had changed. Thus St Birgitta's monitions to the Holy Roman Emperor, to the Kings of Cyprus and Jerusalem, her counsel how the war between England and France should be terminated, including St Denis's intervention for France in a vision, were all omitted, together with St Birgitta's advice to the mighty on the selection of wives and counsellors.

St Birgitta was outspoken in her exposure of the shortcomings at the Papal Court and criticized ecclesiastics for their unedifying way of life in no uncertain terms. After the tension in England with the Wycliffites and in the southern areas of the Holy Roman Empire with Hus her words at the end of the fifteenth century might have aroused scandal among those who were not able to see them in their historical perspective. Thus virtually all the negative references to popes and the ecclesiastical hierarchy were omitted. Only one substantial passage remains and even that is much shorter than in the Latin (*SBO*: 97–98).

Given the audience for the Middle Low German version, it is not surprising that Book V of the *Revelationes*, dealing with difficult theological questions, was omitted entirely and the passage in Book VIII of the *Revelationes* that seeks to explain the nature of the Holy Trinity is given in much abbreviated form with the explanation: . . . dat velen sympelen mynschen alto behende ist. hyrumme wert dat hyr vorkortet . . . (*SBO*: 108)

Apart from the general tendency to summarize, the Middle Low German author seems to have left out some passages in the Latin text because he found them unseemly. Thus in describing Christ's birth in Bethlehem (*SBO*: 148) he omits from *Revelationes*, Book VII, chapter 21:

> Et statim venter virginis qui ante partum tumidissimus erat, retraxit se, et videbatur tunc corpus eius mirabilis pulchritudinis et delicatum.

and:

> . . . nisi quam venter eius tumidus retraxit se ad priorem statum in quo erat antequam puerum conciperet.

whilst

... tunc igitur virgo mater eis ostendit naturam et sexum masculinum infantis

is rendered:

... unde do se dat seghen ... (*SBO*: 150)

A passage in *Revelationes*, Book VII, chapter 27, seems to have been too much for the Middle Low German compiler:

> Ideo facitis sicut meretrices diligentes voluptatem et delectationes carnis non autem prolem. Cum enim sentiunt infantem vivum in utero suo, statim procurant abortivum herbis et aliis rebus, ne careant carnali voluptate et continua delectatione pessima ut sic semper vacent luxurie et fetide commixtione carnali. Sic facitis et vos.

The German version reads merely: O gy sunders mine viende. (*SBO*: 224) This tendency is seen again in Book IV, chapter 4 of *Sunte Birgitten Openbaringe*, where a 15 page translation of the judgment of a male soul before God in the presence of Satan is offered. All the evil deeds of the accused are faithfully listed, except one:

> Secunda columna erat quod nimis procax erat in verbis. Inducebat enim non solum uxorem suam in maiorem ardorem libidinis ymo etiam alias ad audiendum et cogitandum scurrilia multociens per verba sua attraxit.
>
> (*Revelationes*, Book VI, chapter 29)

The Middle Low German writer makes his only abbreviation at this point, merely observing:

> De andere syde is dat he alto kleppesch was unhoeveschen unde sundighen to sprekende. (*SBO*: 178)

Stylistically, the Middle Low German writer scarcely shows himself to be an author of real significance, but he produced a competent version of a difficult text, adapting it skilfully for a new, more popular audience. He thus made a significant contribution to the ever increasing vernacular devotional literature of his time. Much of the work is presented in simple narrative form, but parts are conceived as a dialogue between Christ and the soul, whilst some reflections are also in direct speech. Indirect speech is only employed for the opinions of authorities who are cited and – very occasionally – for the relation of actual words within reported speech. The prayers are, by their very nature, more formal and stylised, but do not bear comparison with the polish of humanistic examples. His general competence should not be underestimated; on p. 215 of *Sunte Birgitten Openbaringe* he even corrects the Latin text. His powers of paraphrasing and condensing sometimes lend his version greater clarity than is to be found in the original Latin. In Book III, chapter 11 the German compiler compresses the essential of 27 chapters of the Latin *Revelationes* concerning the *Regula Salvatoris* and St Birgitta's intervention with the Pope to secure its approbation into a single chapter, presumably because it was of less relevance for the new audience (*SBO*: 123–25) Some stylistic blemishes remain, but these are often due to too slavish an imitation of the Latin original.[57]

## 9. *Sunte Birgitten Openbaringe* as devotional literature

In the Middle Low German version St Birgitta's *Revelationes* was thus transformed into a work of edification, designed to stimulate its readers to the practice of Christian virtue. Its mystical content, which is so psychologically convincing in the original Latin, was toned down to make the book more palatable to an audience that faced different problems to those with which the Saint was confronted 1346–73, when she experienced her visions. Canonised in 1391, her cult had spread widely, even if it was particularly prominent in her homeland, Sweden, and throughout the Baltic region.[58]

The late thirteenth and fourteenth century had been an epoch of great mystical writing, with Suso, Mechtild of Magdeburg, Tauler, and Eckhart in Germany, Richard Rolle, Walter Hilton, and the unidentified author of *The Cloud of Unknowing* and its related treatises in England, Beatrix of Nazareth, Hadewijch, Ruusbroec, and Gerard Groote in the Low Countries, and Margarete Porete with her ill-fated *Mirror of Simple Souls* in France, to name only the most conspicuous representatives.[59] Such writing declined sharply as the fifteenth century progressed. Thus when the Mohnkopf publishing house at Lubeck presented *Sunte Birgitten Openbaringe*, the work had been adapted to suit an audience that showed little interest in mystical writings as such, – the works of Suso and Tauler were first printed in the sixteenth century. Much more popular were translations from the Bible, particularly from the Gospels, Biblical commentaries, collections of psalms, *Legendae* of the saints that sometimes approached biographical accounts, narrations of the Passion, relations of miracles, books of devotions, and prayer books furnishing texts for all occasions. Narratives of the sufferings of Christ and the compassion of the Blessed Virgin were numerous, as were treatises in the *Ars moriendi* tradition. A further genre was constituted by the *Mirror (Speculum)* literature, offering counsels for the practice of virtues and monitions for the avoidance of sin. Catechisms and dogmatic works appealed to a more limited audience.

Thus the visionary *Revelationes* became a treatise on leading the Christian life,

---

[57] For details cf. Hogg, 188.

[58] For her cult in England, for example, cf. F. R. Johnston, "The English Cult of St Bridget of Sweden", *Analecta Bollandiana* 103 (1985), 75–93.

[59] For a perceptive survey of Vision literature cf. Peter Dinzelbacher, *Vision und Visionsliteratur im Mittelalter, Monographien zur Geschichte des Mittelalters* 23, Stuttgart 1981. For the general background cf. Peter Dinzelbacher & R. Bauer (eds.), *Religiöse Frauenbewegungen und mystische Frömmigkeit im Mittelalter*, Cologne 1988; Peter Dinzelbacher (ed.), *Mittelalterliche Visionsliteratur. Eine Anthologie (Texte zur Forschung)*, Darmstadt 1987; Peter Dinzelbacher, *Revelationes*, Turnhout 1988.

whereby St Birgitta was held up as an example, offering advice and warnings to her readers. Her prophecies fell on fruitful ground, as the foretelling of the future – and particularly of the end of the world, with the return of Christ in glory, – was a topic that exercised a distinct fascination throughout the medieval period. The Middle Low German compiler was well aware of the true nature of St Birgitta's *Revelationes*, and thus he is careful to explain her visions. He even devotes the concluding chapter of Book II to a fairly detailed resumé of John of Turrecremata's defence of their authenticity at the Council of Basel (1431–49) (*SBO*: 105–06).

In Book I, chapter 15, after mentioning the first of the Saint's visions, he outlines the various categories of visions and explains how they come about, indicating the Latin terminology which is used to describe them. Before discussing these categories, he comments on visions in general:

> Aver desse openbaringe enheft se nicht ghehad slapende in droemen, men wakende in ereme ghebede. unde doch nicht alle tyd. Aver wanner dat er god wat wolde openbaren, so opende he ere geystliken synne, dat se mochte seen unde horen geystlike dynge. unde sloet up ere vornuft. dat neyn boesegeyst don enkan. unde goet in ere vornunft eyn overnaturlik licht, dat dar twyerley werkynge in er hadde. (*SBO*: 37)

The first category is the "Revelatio imaginaria", which, despite its suspicious label, actually implies that St. Birgitta was carried off to heaven and that she describes what she saw and heard there:

> To deme ersten so gaf yd er de kraft. dat se syck in erer sele mochte vorheven boven syk. alzo dat se mochte seen de dinck. de dar synt boven de nature. wente se sach god unde de engele. unde ok de boesengeyste. aver se sach se in formen unde staltenisse desser lifiiken dynge. unde desse wyse alze geystliken to seende is ghenoemet in dem latin visio vel revelacio ymaginaria. unde in desser wyse heft se ghehat de openbaringe der ersten dryer boke. (*SBO*: 38)

The second category is the "Revelatio intellectualis", whereby he envisages rather prophecies and monitions concerning future conduct, where no actual vision is involved:

> Aver dat middel des verden boekes heft se ghehad in eyner anderen wyse. de dar ghenoemet is in dem latino visio vel revelatio intellectualis. unde de wise schuot. wanner dat god einen minschen wat openbaret in eyner over natuorliken wise ane alle formen unde liknisse desser lyfliken efte tytliken dinge . . .
> (*SBO*: 38)

The third category is the "Revelatio sensibilis", involving the appearance of spirits, particularly of the dead, to persons living on earth:

> Aver dat leste boek dat dar ghenoemet is de engelsche rede. dat wart er geopenbaret na eyner anderen wise. de dar ghenoemet is in deme latino visio vel revalacio sensibilis. unde de schuot in den utwendighen synnen, alze

wanner de geyste to syk nemen lyflike staltnisse van der lucht. unde openbaren syk den minschen in sodanen staltnissen. alzo dat se de mynschen mogen horen unde seen myt erem lyfiyken ogen. unde in der wyse wart sunte Birgitten dat boek gheopenbart . . . (*SBO*: 38)

The Middle Low German compiler rates the "Revelatio intellectualis" as more important than the "Revelatio imaginaria", whilst the "Revelatio sensibilis" is a poor third:

De erste wyse der openbaringe is hoeger unde eddeler wente desse drydde wyse. Aver de andere wyse is hoeger. unde eddeler und gheyt boven de anderen byde. unde werte ock ghenoe in den hilghen schryft de drydde hemmel. dar sunte Pawel was in gherucket.[60] (*SBO*: 38)

On several occasions he stresses the efficacity of the revelations for inciting the faithful to lead a more perfect Christian life:

. . . dat is myt den hylghen openbaringen dar he den minschen inne lovet syne barmherticheit. Isset dat se laten van den sunden. unde beteren ere levent na uthwysynge der schrift. unde desse hilghen openbaringe. Aver isset dat se dessen bref vorsmaen und nicht entfangen. so wyl ick god dat an en wreken. also dath se scholen spreken. we uns dat wy iw gheboren worden. Unde darumme so synt desse openbaringe ghescheen. (*SBO*: 40)

. . . wanner dath se denne in groten droffenissen staen unde begheren trost van gode. so wert yd god alzo voegende. dat en denne desse openbarynge to der hand komen unde lesen dar inne. unde in deme lesende wert god de here grote gnade in se getende. dat se myt groten vrouden werden sprekende. wol mi dat ick desse vorghegangen droffenisse ye hebbe gheleden. Ghebenediet sy god. dat he dat alzo ghevoeget heft, dat desse hilghen openbaringe to my ghekomen syn. Alzo keren se denne ere herte to gode. unde bydden vor de gennen. van der weghene en de openbaringe in der hand synt ghekomen.
(*SBO*: 49; cf. 57, 103)

He rejects the assertion that there are already enough works, from which the faithful may learn the path to salvation, insisting that God's wrath over the sins of mankind has grown more intense in recent decades, as man's wickedness has reached new heights. The indignation of God, the Blessed Virgin, and the Saints is graphically depicted (*SBO*: 38). The Middle Low German writer insists that every Christian should accept the revelations that were made to St Birgitta as if they had been made to himself, for they signify the road to eternal life:

[60] The reference is to 2 Cor. 12, 1–2: Must I go on boasting, though there is nothing to be gained by it? But I will move on to the visions and revelations I have had from the Lord. I know a man in Christ who, fourteen years ago, was caught up – whether still in body or out of body, I know not; God knows – right into the third heaven.

Hyrumme so merken alle mynschen de dar lesen in den openbaringen. dat god de almechtighe here nicht allenen umme erer salicheit wyllen er so vele heft gheopenbaret. men en erer personen so menet he alle mynschen. Darumme so neme dat eyn yowelck alzo to syck. alze eft dat to eme van gode worde ghesproken. (*SBO*: 57)

Thus, though the compiler was anxious to produce an edifying guide to Christian living, he remained fully conscious that St Birgitta's book was visionary, a manifestation of the mysticism that flourished in her day, and he reached a compromise whereby he selected the didactic elements and inserted them into the frame of the Saint's life. The biographical section thereby assumed the proportion of half the total work, thus placing it partially in the genre of the *legenda*. The visions, in which God the Father, Christ, the Blessed Virgin, Angels, and Saints speak, are distributed over Books II, III, and IV, those in Book III being mainly concerned with political questions, exhortations to practise a higher level of morality, and matters concerning the foundation of the Brigittine Order. There is no real break in the transition to Book V, dealing with the life of St Katherine, as St Katherine was with her mother both in Rome and in the Holy Land. Book V concludes with Birgitta's canonization soon after her daughter's death, and so the work is brought to a satisfying conclusion both as regards contents and artistic symmetry.

Typical of the later medieval period is St Birgitta's intense interest in the minutest details of the Passion, of which she delivers an account in the first person. The Middle Low German compiler, who shares her fascination, comments before presenting her text in translation that her relation in no way contradicts the facts found in the Gospels but supplements them. Thus St Birgitta sees how the cross lay before Christ was nailed onto it and how his arms were bound before the nails were driven into his hands.

Also typical of the time is the interest in the appearance of the souls of the dead, one coming from hell and another from purgatory to report on their respective fates. The macabre state of their bodies is described with hideous realism.

The publications of the Mohnkopf publishing house at the end of the fifteenth century were distinguished by a certain traditionalism and conformism to the hierarchical Church establishment, which allowed only moderate criticism of abuses; but all their books display a desire to educate the literate classes in the Christian virtues, – an attribute which is even apparent in non-religious works, such as *Narrenschyp* and *Reinke de Voss*.

In Book III, chapter 7, following a passage on the duties of queens, the importance and utility of printing as a means of disseminating religious knowledge is stressed. The Middle Low German compiler declares that God allowed the discovery to be made to aid man on the road to salvation. Those living in the German-speaking lands should be particularly proud that this art was discovered in their homeland; but with this discovery came the obligation to acquire and read religious books. In the time of St Anthony no books were available for the general public, so less could be demanded of his contemporaries. Those living in the modern world will have no excuse! (*SBO*: 118–20) Similar thoughts about printing appear in the Middle Low German version of Sebastian Brant's *Dat Narrenschyp*, LXV, 51–52, issued by Mohnkopf in 1497.[61]

The special devotion that the compiler shows to the Blessed Virgin might suggest that he was a Brigittine monk or closely associated with the local Brigittine monastery, for the Brigittines had a great devotion to Our Lady. The efficacity of the Blessed Virgin's intercession is stressed again and again:

> Men dat ghebet Marien quam er meyst to huolpe alze in deme sulven boke steyt in deme XXI capittel, dar Maria alzus sprack. . . . (*SBO*: 209)

> Darumme so heft god umme der bede wyllen syner werden moder der iunck-frowen Marien . . . desse hylghen vrowen sunte Birgitten uthgekoren. unde heft se ghesant alze eynen sendeboden myt synen breven in de werlde . . .
> (*SBO*: 40)

Our Lady frequently appears in scenes of judgment in *Sunte Birgitten Openbaringe*, where she intercedes for souls on account of their devotion to her. Such manifestations must, however, be seen in the context of the mariology of the later Middle Ages. Clearly, St Birgitta had been markedly influenced by her contact with Benedictines, Cistercians, and Dominicans in Sweden, particularly with the Cistercians through her close contact with the Cistercian Abbey of Alvastra and its prior Peter, but Franciscan spirituality also came to play an important rôle during the long years she spent in Italy.[62]

---

[61] For further parallels in other Mohnkopf publications with *SBO* cf. Dinges I, XCIX–C.

[62] Cf. Tore Nyberg, "Bemerkungen zum benediktinischen und zisterziensischen Einfluss auf die Satzungen des Birgittinordens", *Revue bénédictine* 83 (1973), 351–82. Ulrich Montag, *Das Werk der heiligen Birgitta von Schweden in oberdeutschen Überlieferung*, 94, states that besides the Brigittines themselves Dominican nuns were mainly responsible for the diffusion of the *Revelationes*.

# AFTERWORD
## VALERIE'S GIFT

We met for the first time one evening in a Biergarten in Austria, near the monastery at Stift Lilienfeldt. I had just arrived from Hong Kong after a long flight and train ride and was still trying to adjust from tropical heat to Austrian chill, from Chinese to German. Suddenly I realized that I had no idea what Valerie looked like. And then I saw her: holding court as usual, Valerie was lifting a glass of Riesling in my direction. Without batting a famous eyelash, she greeted me in Mandarin Chinese. In retrospect I cannot imagine it happening any other way.

Mother Julian of Norwich is my spiritual mother, and Valerie Lagorio (better known to many as "Auntie Val") is my spiritual God-mother. I heard of Valerie not long after I heard of Julian, while living in Scotland twenty years ago. It is hard to believe it now, but at that time Julian was not on anybody's calendar of saints. Most theologians had never heard of her and the *Revelations* was not required reading anywhere. Even pious Christians who knew the mystics hardly knew Julian, even in England. The fact that she is known today is largely Valerie's fault, as I learned at that meeting in the Biergarten near Vienna.

In the seventies I was a student at New College, the University of Edinburgh. One of the lecturers, Canon Roland Walls, was an ascetic who had founded the Community of the Transfiguration near Edinburgh. His lectures were half-meditation, half shared prayer, reflecting the contemplative lifestyle of the community. In that context he would move freely from the Desert Fathers to Dorothy Day, from St Gregory of Nyssa to Saddhu Sundar Singh or the Christian-Hindu dialogues of his friend Dom Bede Griffiths. Then, before leaving us in order to work with the street people who congregated at his skete, Roland would quote from Julian's *Revelations* and lead us into prayer, often using Julian's own words.

In the beginning whenever Father Roland mentioned Julian, students would nudge each other and whisper, "Who's he talking about?" Some thought we were hearing about Julian the Apostate – the only Julian we knew of in the library – but if so, the prayers didn't make sense. Finally someone raised a hand and asked directly. I will never forget that before Roland could answer, an American student volunteered, "I know who Julian is. He's the one who taught that sin doesn't exist!"

I came to know Mother Julian more personally in 1974 when Roland produced a hazelnut in class and gave it to me. The hazelnut came from the six-hundred years' celebration of Julian's *Revelations*, held in Norwich in May. Father Roland had attended without saying much, and on his return I complained that I missed this chance to learn about another obscure mystic. In reply he gave me the hazelnut and a stack of publications from the centenary. In time I began to study the *Revelations*, not as a curious text but for personal spiritual growth under Roland's direction. I still have it – the hazelnut, I mean – and I still wonder what role Julian herself played in changing my life that spring.

Two years later I was weighing topics for a dissertation, and Roland suggested writing about Julian's theology. After all, I was Lutheran and Lutherans are supposed to be systematic. I can still see him take his pipe out of his mouth and jab it in the air. "Write a systematic approach to Julian's theology," he said. "There, now, nobody's done *that!*" And he was right – nobody had.

Valerie, meantime, was urging graduate students to write about Julian from the standpoint of English literature. I learned about Valerie during a trip to Leeds that spring. I had gone to see Sister Anna Maria Reynolds, who produced her own critical edition of the *Revelations* as a PhD thesis in 1956. She gave me Valerie's name, along with that of Valerie's friend Sister Ritamary Bradley, and let me photocopy the most recent edition of *Fourteenth Century English Mystics Newsletter* (now *Mystics Quarterly*), a single sheet mimeographed on front and back. At the time it struck me as odd that some Americans were actually sending out a newsletter about Julian of Norwich, but I wrote to Valerie anyway.

Valerie's life, like mine, had been claimed by Mother Julian. I think that Julian spoke to us, not because she wanted to be popularly recognized in our time – publicity distresses her greatly insofar as a saint can experience distress in the presence of God – but because she wanted to communicate her message of divine love to spiritual seekers in our century. The seventies was the ideal time: there was growing spiritual confusion all over the world, so that people needed to hear about God's compassion; and there was growing interest in women in literature, including women mystics. Julian knew that Valerie would do anything she could to make the vision known.

For me, the big concern was to show that Julian was a serious theologian. Almost every published reference to her presented her either as a platonic mystic who skirted heresy, or as a sweet visionary without a real thought in her head. So the first task was to establish her orthodoxy and to show that she had a true systematic theology. Valerie encouraged me in that and urged me to the conclusion that Julian was the greatest English mystic of all time and one of the greatest theologians of the West.

Unexpectedly, Julian also began to emerge as a unique bridge between western spirituality and the mystical theology of the Orthodox Church. This insight was prompted by the arrangement of classes at New College at the time. First, Father Roland, from whom we learned most about Julian, was living an eremitical life modeled on Athonite monasticism. Therefore, whatever he said about Julian was already colored by Orthodox tradition. But each week after we heard from Father Walls, we would also hear from a Greek Orthodox theologian, John Zizioulas (now Bishop John). The juxtaposition made it easy to see Julian in light of Orthodox tradition, and suddenly her development of Orthodox themes (the Trinity, Being and economy, transfiguration, sin as non-being, and so on) seemed obvious.

I found I was unable to focus on Julian in a purely academic way. For one thing, Roland warned against it, saying that it would hurt Julian to think she was being dissected by graduate students who did not apprehend the reality of divine love. For another, Julian was capturing my soul, prodding me to let go of long-held prejudices in order to accept the sheer grace of God. What started as an academic pursuit became a personal struggle.

I spent a short time with my family at the All Hallows guest house in Norwich next to Julian's own cell; and then some weeks enclosed in the monastery at Ditchingham. I had the sense that Julian was speaking to me. I rejected the idea, then gave in to it and finally (heresy for a Lutheran!) asked for her help in fishing out the important points of the *Revelations* and discerning some kind of order through the chapters. Suddenly things fell into place. Julian showed me passages of scripture which she knew, and laughed at the notion that she was quoting male theologians she had never heard of. She comforted me. She prompted me to read the ancient mystics of the Church.

Although a sense of order did emerge for me, Julian warned that her writing was something like that of St Maximus the Confessor's *Centuries on Love*. The *Revelations* was a jumble to the uninitiated, but not to people who are thirsty for consolation. The true spiritual seeker, she said, would figure everything out; the rest would get it all wrong, not taking her whole work together, and they would someday accuse her of teaching things she didn't teach, or worse, praise her for the same errors.

The results of those early meditations on Julian were far too many for a single publication, but there was no more time for academic pursuits. I had to begin parish ministry as a Lutheran vicar, and writing did not fit into that scheme. The dissertation was sent away and forgotten. Valerie, meantime, was trying to arrange for its publication – a project which she pursued everywhere she went, in America and England and Austria. She wrote to me about it wherever I was, in country Lutheran parishes and inner-city slums and eventually in the remote New Territories of Hong Kong.

In the years since then I have spoken about Julian from time to time and have written a little more. But no academic work has equalled the experience of sharing Julian's visions with seekers in distress who want to know about the love of God. I have introduced Julian to Christians, Tibetan Buddhists, Hindus, and followers of New Age; to agnostics and cultists and fundamentalists. In these encounters my friends do not discover a universal mystic who says what they already thought, but a holy Christian apologist who moves them into new ways of thinking.

One of these was a doctor from Germany whom I met while riding a bus through the night to Lhasa, Tibet. She told me about her conversion to Buddhism and explained that for her, Christianity was only a set of impossible rules which an angry God invented in order to throw us into hell. As we bounced along under the full moon, Tibetan monks snoring nearby, I groped for a way to answer and finally settled on Julian's explanation of God's humility and love: the *perichoresis* of the Trinity and the self-emptiness within God. I told her about Julian's vision of the cross, and how the incarnation and crucifixion demonstrated the true compassion of our Creator. I related Julian's vision of the great Lord who spoke to the peasant as an equal. At length my new friend said, with tears streaming down her face, "Why haven't I heard that before?" I didn't know.

Today, I have heard graduate students lament that Julian has been "done" too many times, and perhaps in a way it is true. Dissertations continue to analyze how many literary devices Julian used for this and for that, but these explorations of Julian are not to the point. The real question is whether we will allow Julian to speak to the spiritual explorations of our time.

In recent months a best-selling book in America tells about being "embraced by the light." It is not a very theological book, but it reflects our culture and an important interest among our people in what happens when we die. Julian has much to say about this, of course. I have no doubt that she had an experience very much like the one in the book. To say so in university circles is academic suicide, but I believe that very simply, Julian died and then recovered. She entered into profound silence for thirty years because of that experience, and she could hardly put what she saw into words. But when she did write about it, she did not conclude from her after-death experience that we are all reincarnated or that we are all automatically saved by the "light" whatever we may call it, or that there is no hell or judgment or accountability. Rather, Julian had a dramatic affirmation of ancient Christian doctrine: that in the crucified Jesus there is grace enough for a world in despair, for Christ our Mother keeps us at every moment in a surpassing love which no human being can understand.

It is time to look carefully at this Julian. There is room for graduate students to explore every corner of mysticism here – from the mystery of the Eucharist to the nature of hell, from the interaction of beyond-being with space-time to chaos theory and the meaning of "spirit" in culture and Christian orthodoxy. Above all Julian wants, I think, for us to understand true joy, which is so far above our culture's cynicism and scholasticism as to be almost outside our vocabulary. She urges us to seek the Holy Spirit to lift us out of fear and paganism and superficiality.

Valerie's special gift is that she has worked hard to introduce students and friends, young, healthy, or dying, to Julian's joy. No one who knows "Auntie Val" will forget the sheer freedom which Valerie has brought into our lives. And the trust is, this freedom and joy and exhuberance is that of a true mystic. Whatever accolades we may want to bestow upon her, these will be nothing compared to the voices of those to whom Valerie brought a knowledge of divine love. Someday these will say to Valerie, "You are the reason I have heard of this before!"

*Brant Pelphrey*

# Tabula Gratulatoria

Anne Clark Bartlett & Mark D. Johnston
Thomas H. Bestul
Michael W. Blastic
Florence S. Boos
Ritamary Bradley
Carolyn B. Brafford
Sarah Bromberg
Caroline Walker Bynum
Joan Cadden
David Chamberlain
Paul Chandler
Sister Christine, SLG Press
Renate Craine
Lloyd W. Crawford
Rev. Prof. John E. Crean Jr
Julie Crosby
Sr Phyllis Cusack
Mary Beth Davis
Heath Dillard
Ed Folsom
Joan Isobel Friedman
Kate Galea
Abbot David Geraets
Joan Gibson
Dr M. Patrick Graham
David Hamilton & Rebecca Clouse
Sr Kym Harris
Marian E. Harris
Norman D. Hinton
Nanda Hopenwasser
Vivian Kay Hudson
Ann M. Hutchinson
Catherine Innes-Parker
Elaine Kalmar
Robert E. Kelley & Dixie Saylor
Sr Gertrude Kelly
Cynthia M. King

Jerome Kroll
Felicia Lavallee
Juris Lidaka
Mary M. McLaughlin
Michael Martin
E. Ann Matter
Peter Meister
Barbara Newman
The Rev. Virginia Noel
D.C. Nugent
Marthiel O'Larey
Paul Olson
Mrs Doreen Price
Dr Patricia Ann Quattrin
Janine Rogers
Robert Schottner
Joy Schroeder
Tom Sherrard
Walter P. Simons
Anne Stanton
Helen Clare Taylor
Margaret Susan Thompson
Marianne Trevorrow
Willem G. Ubink
Dr Rosalynn Voaden
Sr Mary David Walgenbach
Bonnie Wheeler
Ulrike Wiethaus
Jon Wilcox

Alcuin Library
The Order of Julian of Norwich
A.P. Mahoney Library
St Placid Priory
St Scholastica Monastery
Ambrose Swasey Library
The United Library

235